AN

INTERNATIONAL

ECONOMY

AN INTERNATIONAL ECONOMY

PROBLEMS AND PROSPECTS

by

GUNNAR MYRDAL

FORMERLY LARS HIERTA PROFESSOR IN
POLITICAL ECONOMY AND PUBLIC FINANCE AT STOCKHOLM UNIVERSITY

HARPER & BROTHERS PUBLISHERS

NEW YORK

CONTENTS

Trends. The Economics of Large-Scale Net Emigration. A Free
International Labor Market. National Bondage for the Common
Man.

Capital Flow in Europe and to the New Continents. Enclave-Build-
ing in the Backward Continents. The Period Between the World
Wars. After the Second World War. The Capital Flow to Under-
developed Countries. Underdeveloped Countries from the Wall
Street Point of View. In Western Europe. Governments in the
Lending Business. The Practical Problem. The Present Situation.

A Hesitant Beginning. Sharing Between the Rich. United Nations'
Proposals for Aid to Underdeveloped Countries. Reasons for Inter-
nationalizing International Aid. The Necessity of a Fairer Distribution of the Burden. The Awkward Fact of the United States'
Bigness. The Problem Will Stay with Us. Relation to Internal Inequalities in Underdeveloped Countries. Aid as Insurance Against
Revolutions.

An Independent Variable. Migration, Capital Movements, and
Trade. Effects of the Armament Expenditure. Other Economic
Effects. Effects on Our Culture. A Political Effect. The Soviet Con-
cept of International Integration.

Inequality. The Liquidation of Colonialism. The Impact of Color.
A World in Revolution. The Attempts to Achieve Democracy. Economic Development: the Demand for a Short Cut. Are We Exporting a Revolution?

Defining the Problem. The Need for Rapid Social Reforms. The
View of Cultural Anthropologists. Some Main Assumptions. Social
Cleavages. The Class Structure. Land Reform. Not Without Strug-
gle. Education and Health. Population Pressure. The Economics
of Population Growth. Population Policy. The Need for Large-
Scale Fresh Research. The Role of the State. The Problem of Ad-
ministration. Balancing the Economic Development Program. The
Stage Set for a Great Human Drama. The Capacity to Absorb
Foreign Capital. Access to Knowledge. The Role of Technical
Assistance.

An Intellectual Suspicion. *Unbalanced Economies:* The Role of
High Exports in Economic Development. *The Terms of Trade:*
Long-Term Price Trends. The General Level of Export Prices and
the Question of International Distribution. The Political Issue.
Instability of Markets and Stabilization Policies: Widely Fluctuat-

PREFACE

This book is devoted to an examination of the present state of international economic relations within the non-Soviet world. The problem of the political split between the East and West and the possibilities for future development—either towards a third world war or towards one form or another of more or less peaceful "co-existence"—deserves a study of its own which is not attempted here. One of the chapters, however, deals with the economic effects of the cold war on the non-Soviet world. Otherwise, I am not treating the political problems related to the East-West conflict.

The book grew out of a paper I contributed for a conference on "National Policy for Economic Welfare at Home and Abroad," held by Columbia University at the end of May of 1954 as part of the celebration of the university's Bicentennial. The special topic assigned to me by the conference committee was: "Toward a More Closely Integrated Free-World Economy." The volume containing the proceedings of the conference includes an earlier version of the introductory and concluding chapters of this book—Chapters I to IV, XIV, and the Appendix; a draft of Chapters V to XIII was also distributed to the participants of the conference. Needless to say, my participation in the Columbia conference was entirely in my individual capacity as a social scientist and this book has no direct relation to my functions in the service of the United Nations.

Integration is, of course, an ideal, not a realized fact. Defined as a set of value premises it affords a fixed viewpoint from which social reality can be studied. In this way it determines what things we are looking for and what questions we ask.

The ideal is also a living force in our society and it is, therefore, part of the social reality we are studying. If this were not so, the specific direction of a study determined by the value premises would lack relevance and significance. The ideal works through people's valuations, their political attitudes. Whether we can hope for a gradual attainment of the ideal, and with what speed and to what degree, depends in great measure upon how strongly entrenched the ideal becomes in this sphere of human valuations.

Our discussion will have to devote considerable importance to people's valuations. I take lightly the criticism that my approach is that of a philosophical idealist; I consider it realistic to seek to account in a methodologically satisfactory fashion for all the facts. People's strivings are, indeed, among the most important social facts and they largely determine the course of history. To shy away from the volitional elements when analyzing a social issue and to deal with it in a purely "factual" manner is just as unrealistic as to study the life and behavior of an individual without regard to the fact that he has a conscience. At bottom international economic integration is, like all other economic and social issues, a moral problem.

This does not, however, justify any license in ascertaining and analyzing the social facts; on the contrary, it represents the one and only way to objectivity in social research. "Things look different, depending upon where you stand"; defining the value premises fixes the viewpoint. Biases can creep into research precisely because the value premises are not made explicit. Only when the valuations are exposed can biases be eliminated. But the viewpoint is still arbitrary until the value premises are tested by the criteria of relevance and significance to the society in which we live. I would much appreciate it if my readers would do me the favor of looking through the condensed methodological note in the Appendix, where I refer to the deeper logical justification for this approach.

The definition of economic integration in terms of value premises thus brings the direction of our analysis under logical control. The explicit value premises will also make it possible to evaluate situations and events and even to formulate policies that are rational in terms of these premises and the facts as ascertained from their viewpoint. The main purpose of this book is, however, to find out where we are heading by studying actual trends and the degree to which they can be expected to be changed by means of policy.

The spreading use of the general social science concept of "integration" in relation to some of the old and familiar problems of economic analysis implies a conscious need for a broader vista than that of economic science. By a more comprehensive approach of this kind human interests and valuations are brought to the foreground to a far greater extent than by the type of partial study to which economists traditionally confine themselves. In this book the problems will be allowed to determine the scope of the discussion, without regard to the limitations of traditionally assigned fields and specific methods of a particular discipline. Admittedly, the task then becomes more difficult; the very difficulty may warrant a greater degree of indulgence for shortcomings. The open treatment of opinions and prejudices is another reason why this book makes greater demands for tolerance on the part of the reader.

The wider scope of the study and my wish nevertheless to present a readable volume have naturally resulted in an exposition wherein details have had to be dealt with in a summary fashion and the interest focused entirely on broad perspectives and essential interrelations. Attempting to sketch the contours of an exceedingly complicated part of reality may not be without value, as I have the feeling that in our discussion of international integration we tend to lose sight of the forest through too much attention to the individual trees. The book has scientific pretensions in the sense that I have tried to state my premises explicitly, get the facts straight, and think things through stringently. But I am aware that at best it can only be considered as an outline of the really comprehensive study of the problem of international integration that we still need. The amplification of this outline would require not only a much more systematic bringing together of the results of social research in many fields, but also the undertaking of much new research.

To remind the reader and the author of the deeper methodological problems connected with the choice and use of a value premise, the value-loaded term "integration" is in this book systematically referred to as an ideal, and its vagueness noted. For the same reason I have often taken the precaution of using the first person in expressing judgments, particularly when it can be expected that they are not altogether in line with conclusions which everybody else might draw from the facts presented.

In preparing this book I have been most fortunate in the great number of friends and colleagues who have read various drafts of the text; their critical observations have in almost all cases led me to make amendments and additions. I owe a very special debt of gratitude to Charles Kindleberger and Hal B. Lary who, in the anguish and intellectual bewilderment of the three weeks before Christmas 1953, when I faced the necessity of quickly producing my first draft, generously shared with me their thoughts on the subject matter. Reading over the final text, I find that I have capitalized greatly on this first aid of theirs and in some cases even retained their formulations. Sydney Fairmont has assisted me when working through the large amount of material for the book and preparing the text for print. Hal B. Lary and Paul Streeten read through the final manuscript and made a great number of suggestions for improvement of the argument and the form of its presentation.

Geneva   Gunnar Myrdal
January 1955

AN

INTERNATIONAL

ECONOMY

CHAPTER I

International Economic Disintegration

A BROAD VISTA

The disintegration of the world today, compared with the world of 1913, is partly—but not entirely—more apparent than real. The more closely integrated world community before the First World War was a partial one, excluding in the main peoples of color, colonial lands, and backward countries in general.

International migration, capital movements, and trade functioned on the whole rather effectively within the small group of advanced countries and between them and tiny enclaves cut out of the submerged world about it. The "world" of 1913 was, like Athens in the days of Pericles, in many respects a model civilization—if one forgets the fact that it excluded from its benefits the larger part of mankind. Any new international system ensuring stability, broadly shared progress, and a commonly felt confidence in the future must be attained on different terms, since the peoples who were then excluded are unwilling to resume their earlier passive role.

Social science regularly lags behind events, and there is still a tendency to discuss the world economic problem from the narrow point of view of the small minority of mankind in the nationally integrated and prosperous countries, and to do so in terms all too exclusively of their trade and payments problems. This was perhaps an adequate approach in the nineteenth century, but it is now illusory and totally inadequate. By far the most important symptom of the failure of international integration is the fact that so many countries, with such large populations, are relatively so poor. The trend is actually towards greater world inequality.

It is, in fact, the richer countries that are advancing while the poorer ones, with the large populations, are stagnating or progressing much more slowly. This has been the case for several generations. In the richer

1

countries we are conscious of being part of an economic civilization that has given us, and promises to continue giving us, rapidly rising economic standards; but for mankind as a whole there has actually been no progress at all.

As Mr. H. W. Singer has rightly pointed out, world real income per capita, and with it the standard of living of the average human being, is probably lower now than twenty-five years ago, and perhaps lower than in 1900, because the nations that have rapidly raised their economic standards have been a shrinking proportion of the total world population.[1] Singer adds a comment that should be pondered carefully: "Marxist analysis, in which rising standards of living for given groups and sections are somehow held to be compatible with general deterioration and impoverishment, is much truer for the international scene than it is for the domestic."

In a sense, the awakening of large, barely subsistence-level sectors of the world, previously ignored, and the general trend towards their political and economic independence, imply an enlargement of the international economy, which in itself is a step towards closer economic integration. But the resulting entry onto the sphere of attention of enormous—and steadily increasing—economic differences, which may take centuries to overcome, signifies a glaring lack of international integration, and dramatically enlarges the scope of our problem, precisely because of the extension of the international economy.

Labor migration has ceased to function as a factor of integration even between the advanced countries and offers no prospect of playing any important role in integrating the underdeveloped countries into the world economy. The international capital market has shrunk and, with the breaking down of the colonial structure, it can even less be depended upon to provide the underdeveloped countries with capital for development. International aid has, within limits, effectively come to the rescue of floundering national economies in the old partial world of advanced countries, but it has barely begun to face the bigger task of integrating the world as a whole.

Trade has limits as a substitute for factor movements in effecting integration, even in a partial world. In any case, no liberalization of international trade can be expected *by itself* to change radically this situation of open international disintegration or this trend towards an increasingly widening gap in levels of production and consumption and of living standards. *By itself* "freer trade" would even tend to perpetuate stagnation in the underdeveloped regions.

Migration, capital movements, international aid, and trade are **not** the primary means of achieving this closer integration. In a real sense they are the products of integration, not the cause. They can help, but they cannot be relied upon to do the job. The major task is first to force economic development in the underdeveloped countries to the point where a more unified world system can be solidly built.

In the poor and backward countries this task will have to take the form of measures to start the process towards national integration; for the main weakness of these countries is undoubtedly that even nationally they are badly integrated. A number of steps must certainly be taken which—to put it mildly—in the short term are not calculated to promote closer international integration. Yet without national integration the present enormous differences in standards and rates of development will be maintained and even increased.

These countries need national integration—and, if possible, regional cooperation—also in order to win bargaining power, a very necessary condition for the achievement of some political balance in the world. It would be a poor international integration of a democratic world that left so little bargaining power in the hands of the great majority of its peoples.

The practical problem is to find a *modus vivendi* which promises steady progress towards international integration. A short-term solution in more absolute terms is out of the question.

Meanwhile, and mainly for independent reasons, the advanced countries themselves have not yet found a new and viable international balance among their national economies. In the world setting this is the smaller and simpler, practical problem, but much the greater part of current international discussion is presently devoted to it. As an element in the greater complex of world problems, the international integration of the advanced countries is not unimportant, particularly because a solution would create a climate where we could tackle with more zeal and vigor the much bigger task of promoting the development of the underdeveloped countries.

Unfortunately, there are no valid reasons to expect an early solution even of this simpler problem. There is one thing, however, that we do know about any new system of better international relations among the advanced countries which may eventuate: it will bear little resemblance to the old, pre-1914 system with its gold standard, free labor and capital movements, and multilateral trade.

Over this whole complex of world economic problems there looms ominously the political split between the Soviet and the non-Soviet power blocks. The division of the world into two hostile camps—with some countries in various degrees of neutrality—represents the biggest single element of acute international disintegration. This problem as such falls outside the scope of this book, which is entirely focused on the limited problem of international economic relations in the non-Soviet world. Yet it has direct and indirect effects upon the economy of every single country. It would be unrealistic to discuss the development of economic relations in the non-Soviet world if these effects were not taken into account.

THE IMPOSSIBILITY OF A DEMOCRATIC WORLD GOVERNMENT

Those are the problems that should be studied under the value premise of closer international economic integration. In recent decades a few countries have come a long way towards *internal* economic integration. As I demonstrate in Chapter III, national economic integration has increasingly been a process of social organization, in the course of which social and economic barriers were abolished and greater equality of opportunity realized. In this process a complex system of interference with the functioning of the price mechanism has played an important role. The principle of sharing risks and of equalizing income and wealth has been applied ever more effectively. The whole process has been proceeding upon the basis of attitudes of national belongingness and solidarity; this basis has continuously been strengthened as a result of the integration process itself and the participation by the citizens in the political responsibility for its direction.

When international integration is held as an ideal, the corresponding political image, carried to its logical perfection, is a world state under a world government, directed by a democratic process in which, directly or indirectly, all people participate. Such a world government would have good reason to instigate policies which, viewed from the *status ex ante* position, discriminated in favor of the great majority of backward peoples.

Like governments in all well-integrated national states, the democratic world government would establish impediments to free mobility when that was believed to be appropriate to reaching greater equality of opportunity, but more often it would take measures for encouraging mobility when it was hampered. In any case, it would rarely find it desirable to organize impediments to mobility along geographical lines. It would, like national governments, regularly sight its discriminatory interventions more directly upon their objectives.

To national governments, national frontiers represent limits of political authority and responsibility, and barriers to international trade or movements of persons and capital over the boundaries have always been an important instrument of national economic policy. But from the point of view of the ideal of international integration, these barriers are poor substitutes for the more rational and more positive policies a world government would adopt in order to discriminate between the interests of different localities and industries in favor of the general interest.

The primary reasons why a democratic world government in our era is not conceivable are, of course, social and psychological. In the world at large, or even in such a large and diversified part of the world as the non-Soviet group, the valuations are too varied. More specifically, there does not exist that human solidarity which in the national state is a result of the historical process towards integration and which induces individuals and social groups to accept rules and regulations that are not to their own immediate advantage.

The international solidarity in a war alliance can, as historical experience shows, be solid and strong, but it is not lasting and does not furnish a stable basis for continued close cooperation under less pressing circumstances. Any careful study of the present situation demonstrates that the East-West tension has barely produced a precarious modicum of international solidarity in the non-Soviet world, and particularly so outside the narrow field of military preparedness. This is, for obvious reasons, especially true in relations between rich and poor nations.

INTERGOVERNMENTAL COOPERATION

The way to reach the modest degree of international cooperation towards closer economic integration which is at all possible in our age is by means of bilateral or multilateral agreements between separate and sovereign states. The goal is always to approach a unified policy through these agreements, implying an intergovernmental coordination of national policies and their application within each country for agreed precise purposes, so that they are directed toward a common goal. This is still a far cry from the ideal of democratic world government, since such agreements establish rights and obligations only for the governments of states, and not directly for the individual citizens.

During the Second World War, when thinking and planning were free and courageous and when illusions had unhampered play, a great effort was made to build up for times of peace a structure of international organizations that would effectively coordinate national economic policies on a world scale. As a huge intellectual war memorial the libraries have catalogued and placed on the proper shelves an outburst of literature, culminating in the year following the war, in which the hopes of what these organizations would accomplish were given architectural elevation and the likeness of realism. To recall these hopes now is awkward but, I believe, necessary for any attempt to give a critical perspective to popular beliefs today, which in 1965 may well be equally illusory.

We should, at the same time, face the fact that, on the whole, these organizations have not been permitted to function effectively, and that even on limited issues practical results have been difficult to achieve. Professor Jacob Viner's dictum five years ago, that "despite . . . the elaborate planning and negotiation and the impressive array of agencies, charters and noble pronouncements, the world is without effective formal international economic organization today"[2] is even more true now.

GATT, the remnant of the International Trade Organization, has nevertheless been an important forum for discussion of commercial policy between certain governments—as the International Monetary Fund has of financial policy—and has also had an immediate and practical, though limited, significance in keeping tariffs under certain international control. Efforts are now under way to strengthen both GATT and the Fund and to enlarge somewhat their scope of activity.

Of all the new organizations, the International Bank for Reconstruction and Development—of which more in Chapter VIII—has probably come nearest to realizing the original intentions of its founders, though its operations have been on a relatively small scale.

The Food and Agriculture Organization has a mandate to tackle the problems not only of more productive methods in agriculture and greater prosperity among farmers, but also of higher nutritional standards through international action for the disposal of surpluses; however, suggestions and discussions concerning these wider issues have not so far been transformed into practical solutions. Meanwhile, like the other United Nations specialized agencies, the FAO is successfully carrying on an important technical assistance activity, though again on a relatively very small scale.

The Economic and Social Council and the General Assembly of the United Nations have been primarily discussion forums and propaganda platforms. This is by itself a reasonably important function in the present world situation, though it is far from the main purposes accorded them by the Charter of both initiating and coordinating international action on a broad scale in the economic and social field. Important issues —such as the struggle against colonialism or the need for economic development in underprivileged countries—are kept alive; governments and the general public are continuously compelled to worry about them and to take positions. Studies are requested and carried out and proposals blueprinted; there is a gradual pressure to take certain preliminary steps towards tackling some of the major international problems by concerted action.

Thus, after President Truman's encouraging initiative, the United Nations sponsored the significant experiment of international technical assistance. It is not impossible that, under the pressure kept up by the poorer countries, some practical beginnings on a modest scale may soon also be made towards creating international institutions for distributing capital aid for economic development in underdeveloped countries and for giving international credits other than, and beyond, those the International Bank is permitted by its mandate to handle.

Neither have the regional efforts as yet borne much fruit. The three Economic Commissions—For Europe, for Asia and the Far East, and for Latin America—have pioneered in sponsoring intensive economic research of value to each government individually and have also made modest beginnings towards regional cooperation in a great number of practical, technical fields; but in the prevailing political climate their attempts to tackle the major economic issues have mostly been frustrated. The work on West-European economic integration is reviewed in Chapter V; the results till now have largely been a failure, though at least the present author is not prepared to join the defeatists.

In the other regions of the non-Soviet world there is even less cohesion than in Europe. The underdeveloped countries have joined their forces in making demands upon the rest of the world in the course of general encounters in the various organs of the United Nations and other discussion forums, but their readiness for actual economic cooperation among themselves, which is put to the test in the relations between neighboring countries in the regional organizations, is feeble or altogether nonexistent. Not only the former colonies, but also the other underdeveloped countries, demonstrate a psychological and political fixation in relation to one or several "metropolitan" countries—to which they react positively or negatively—and their economic relations tend to be under the same spell.

Thus there is still very little economic cooperation among countries in Asia. The regional approach to economic questions on the part of the governments in Latin America is also almost entirely lacking when it comes to its practical application. The Arab League, which fought for the partial exemption of a customs union from the principle of nondiscrimination in the ITO charter, is itself making no progress in establishing effective economic cooperation. The only type of economic cooperation between the Arab states which has borne some practical result is the negative one of keeping up the boycott against Israel. Africa is still mainly a chessboard of colonial dependencies of West-European countries which do not cooperate more effectively in Africa than in their own continent.

Against this background, the British Commonwealth stands out as a nongeographical grouping of independent nations with a common history, joined together by a considerable social sense of solidarity and in many instances by political allegiance to the symbol of the Crown. In spite of many centrifugal forces, tensions, and internal conflicts it remains a reality which is asymmetric, vague, and shifting but nevertheless of considerable practical importance. A relatively high level of labor and capital mobility has been continuously preserved, mainly between Britain and the Dominions with European populations, and has been facilitated by close ties of trade; these political and trading relations have also served as the foundation for the sterling area, which is the remnant of the old gold standard system, directed by the Bank of England. The Colombo Plan is another outgrowth of the solidarity of the British Commonwealth, even if the circle of participating countries has now been enlarged; it represents a hesitant beginning on a diminutive scale of accepting a common responsibility for economic development in Asia.

What must be recognized as a relative failure till now of practically all attempts at organized international cooperation should be thought over carefully, not with a view to discouraging new attempts, but rather to guiding them more wisely. There are compelling reasons to keep pressing on to international economic cooperation whenever there is a chance to accomplish something, even on a modest scale; and in this book I propose to spell out those reasons.

CHAPTER II

The Viewpoint

The foregoing pages gave a vista of the range of problems to be tackled. This chapter contains a number of assertions that I am afraid will not be self-evident to every reader; they are inferences from the analysis contained in later chapters. Before proceeding further with the argument, however, it is necessary for me to clarify my main concepts and to indicate briefly the dependence of my analysis on value premises. The interested reader is referred to the Appendix for a somewhat fuller treatment of the value problem. Those who are allergic to this type of methodological clarification are advised to turn instead to the beginning of the next chapter where the actual argument is taken up again.

From Social Statics to Social Dynamics

The term "economic integration" is one of the expressions that emerged after the Second World War as new popular banners in the political discussion of international questions. "Economic development of underdeveloped countries" is another species of the same genus, actually closely related to the first. Their appearance as banners in debate reflects a changed world situation to which our scientific exertions have to be adjusted. The new terms symbolize interests, ideals, aspirations, and visions, which on the international scene are new, at least in their present political significance.

Literally, "integration" means nothing more than that parts are brought together into a whole. Until the Second World War the term was used almost exclusively in the social sciences by sociologists and cultural anthropologists. They were still working under a stronger static bias than the economists, and the term, having then as now a positive value connotation, was usually employed by them to characterize stable social relations within a stationary community: most typically an

9

isolated primitive community in Malthusian population balance with fixed mores and an established division of functions and responsibilities. When exogenous influences caused changes in the social relations within such a community, these changes—which at least in the shorter run could be considered as detrimental disturbances to its functioning norms —were characterized as "disintegration," with a meaning similar to the other statically conceived sociological concepts with a negative value connotation: "disequilibrium," "disorganization," "maladjustment," and "crisis."

This static concept of "integration" and its employment to characterize isolated and stagnant primitive communities corresponded—with a time lag not unusual in the development of social science—to the international political situation as it existed before the First World War. Broadly speaking, this situation was that, with the exception, on the one hand, of the partial world of advanced and industrially progressive countries in Europe and those countries in the New World that were being populated mainly by people of European origin and, on the other hand, of colonial enclaves cut out to serve the interests of the advanced countries, mankind in general stagnated passively at extremely low levels of technical culture and standards of living.

Within, as well as between, the advanced and progressive countries there was lively intercourse, and continuous and far-reaching mutual adjustments constantly took place. For them the term "integration," if it had been used, would have implied a dynamic process instead of static balance. But in this period there was no realistic basis for posing the question whether the far larger submerged part of mankind could be effectively integrated with the partial world of advanced and progressive countries, or even for putting forward the idea that, within this orbit of backward civilizations, any integration made sense other than that which took place within isolated and stagnant local communities.

This political situation has now changed and so our concepts acquire a new meaning. World development, in response to which the new term "integration" has also become popular and politically significant, has its very essence in a violent and radical breaking down of cultural isolation and in the rising tide of demands from the formerly passive and silent masses in the backward regions for greater equality of economic opportunity and fuller participation in our modern civilization. The term "integration" is now employed in a sense almost contrary to the old one: as signifying a goal of social change instead of static balance and, more specifically, of the internal and mutual adjustment of national communities rapidly brought into much closer interdependence.

The sociological problem at which I hinted now receives a new, dynamic, and practical setting: how to direct, by a planned policy, economic development and all other social changes, so that institutions, patterns, and mores are adjusted to avoid cultural impoverishment and social chasms. Integration becomes a norm for national and international intervention in the process of social change. I return to this problem in Chapter XII.

The general acceptance of the dynamic term "the underdeveloped countries" signifies by itself this big transformation of the world political scene. The expression commonly used until recently was the static term "the backward regions."

THE IDEAL OF ECONOMIC INTEGRATION

"Economic integration" is the realization of the old Western ideal of equality of opportunity. The essential element of this ideal, as we commonly understand it when it is related to social relations within one country, is the loosening of social rigidities which prevent individuals from choosing freely the conditions of their work and life. The economy is not integrated unless all avenues are open to everybody and the remunerations paid for productive services are equal, regardless of racial, social, and cultural differences.

The things that have to change in a social process directed towards the realization of this ideal are mainly those that customarily, by means of broad structures of formal abstractions, are kept outside economic analysis. In that sense, economic integration is at bottom not only, and perhaps not even mainly, an economic problem, but also a problem of political science, sociology, and social psychology. The gradual achievement of equality of opportunity assumes the emergence of a community with ever freer social mobility, based on a fuller realization of the norms of equality and liberty. In this community there must be a growing social cohesion and practical solidarity. The members must increasingly come to feel that they belong together and have common interests and responsibilities, and they must acquire a willingness to obey rules that apply to the entire community and to share in the cost of common expenditures decided upon by political process. This political process must assure an ever wider participation on the part of all citizens. In fact, as we proceed, it will become evident that economic integration is a complex phenomenon that cannot be properly studied without looking at the full range of social change.

It will be assumed—and this assumption will be shown to be realistic —that conditions of general economic progress are necessary for giving a greater degree of realization to the ideal of equality of opportunity; at the same time it is understood that equalizing opportunity is a condition for sustained economic progress.

For over a century it has been part of Western democratic thinking that redistributional reforms, evening out large and frozen differences in incomes and wealth between regions and social classes, are needed in order to give reality to attempts to establish equality of opportunity. Because wealth may be transmitted by inheritance and because large elements of monopoly and windfalls exist in our economy—causes of inequalities unrelated to different innate abilities—redistributional reforms are assumed to be needed to create a real equality of opportunity.

In the Appendix I refer to the fact that these ideals are not only rooted in Western democratic thinking generally but are basic to the classical economic doctrine. I am, therefore, in line with the traditions of political economy when in this study I define economic integration in terms of these broad valuations, centered around the ideal of equality of opportunity.

That economic integration in this sense—international as well as national—is desirable, is the specific value premise of the present study.

Reality is always studied from the viewpoint of the ideal. The practical problem is how—by what policy changes—reality can be made to approach the ideal. It is recognized that reality is very far from the ideal. In this situation a move towards the ideal is assumed to be desirable, while a move away from the ideal is undesirable.

The primary task of scientific enquiry is, however, to ascertain the actual trends: whether, and to what extent, they imply a process of closer economic integration or whether the world economy is continuously disintegrating. The causes of the trend need to be studied and specified in the different fields of international relations. Closely connected with this is the other factual question of the degree of probability that integration policies will actually be pursued, the effects they would have, and, consequently, whether and to what extent the trends are likely to be changed into a process of greater integration.

A few of the industrially most advanced countries have succeeded in recent decades in attaining a relatively high degree of internal economic integration. In order to render our concept of economic integration more concrete, it is important to study the actual processes of social change in these advanced countries, where integration is in fact being gradually achieved; the next chapter is devoted to this task of giving empirical substance to our value premise. It may be useful, however, at this point to anticipate a few of its main conclusions.

We shall find that in the advanced countries where economic integration has gone furthest, it has been the outcome of fundamental changes in all social relations; these changes have generally implied a fuller realization of the Western ideals I referred to. Economic progress has been woven into this process of social change by being both cause and effect; redistributional reforms have gradually been given more and more importance as the national communities became richer. Looking backwards, the achievement of the high level of economic integration in these countries appears as the result of interactions within a dynamic social process of cumulative causation. This process has continuously been furnished with new momentum by economic progress—which, however, itself has been conditioned and spurred by the other changes—and by the norms and ideals constantly operating through people's valuations, the fuller realization of which has, at the same time, gradually strengthened them as social forces.

As a goal-directed process—i.e., from the point of view of attaining an ideal—the higher economic integration stands out as an achievement of social organization, resulting from an effective political technique by which people could voluntarily organize their living together through the development of policies appropriate to seeing this ideal realized! During the progress towards economic integration this political technique has everywhere been perfected, assuring an ever fuller active participation of all citizens in directing the course of development in the national communities; and this change by itself is an important element in the cumulative social process.

Only to a minor extent, however, have the specific policies been directly aimed at allowing market forces free play. As a matter of fact, many of the policies required for reaching higher economic integration have cut right across market forces. This is the reason why economic integration cannot be realistically defined in terms of the classical free market economy and why we have had to reach underneath this theoretical concept to the common heritage of much more general ideals in Western society. If we do not find the ideal or methods of a free market economy to be characteristic of an integrated economy, but rather the opposite, we do nonetheless find a gradually fuller realization of those basic ideals.

"International economic integration" is the realization of the same ideal of equality of opportunity in the relations between peoples of different nations. This may seem far-fetched but is, in fact, what we must mean, if we consider the matter. If we hesitate to express it so clearly, it is only because we are further away from the goal and because we of the richer countries are not yet prepared to accept in practice, even in a small measure, the consequences of the ideal of international integration.

This book will be devoted to analyzing this situation and its causes. My thesis is that the lack of advance in international integration is due to three main factors. There is, first, still little social cohesion and solidarity across national boundaries, and they are just as much a prerequisite of international as of national integration. Second, the technique of international political settlement is primitive and scarcely effective. Finally, the processes of national integration in the several countries and the perfection in each country of the national political machinery for its advancement tend, in the present stage of world development, to lower people's international allegiances. This results in increased international disintegration.

The Vagueness of the Ideal

This definition of "economic integration" and, consequently, the specific value premise for our study, is vague. But this vagueness is not caused by careless or faulty logic. It is in the nature of things. It corresponds to the fact that within a wide area different people think of different policies when they express their allegiance to that ideal, depending on differences both in their basic moral and political valuations and in their beliefs about reality—in particular, about the feasibility of changing reality by means of policy. They mean different things not primarily because their mental processes are different, but because they have different beliefs and interests, aspirations and ideals.

No rational purpose is served by disguising these differences. Rather, it is by itself a scientific task to lay them bare; their analysis forms, indeed, an important part of the scientific problem. The value premise then becomes, instead of a fixed point, a field of coexistent and partly conflicting valuations, concerning how far opportunities should be equalized and by what methods, what sacrifices could reasonably be expected, to what extent redistributional policies should be adopted, and so on. Even when there is a substantial agreement about the goal of integration, this is so far off, and there are always such a large number of alternative policies, that for these reasons alone there is room for wide disagreement about the way to reach it.

Any international discussion of problems of international integration —as, indeed, any national discussion—demonstrates the disparity of valuations; they are not entirely, and not even mainly, the result of ignorance or wrong thinking. That the ideal "economic integration" can nonetheless be generally accepted as a concept that has logical content, and that it does not become unmanageably vague, is an indication of the relative homogeneity of the basic valuations in our Western heritage of ideals. As a matter of fact, these ideals are now rapidly spreading to the underdeveloped countries and their "awakening" consists to a large extent in the spreading to them of this particular system of Western ideals.

Other Value-Loaded Concepts

The concept "the underdeveloped countries" is also value-loaded, implying that the development of those countries is assumed to be desirable. Many discussions, even in recent literature, about the correct meaning of this term reveal lack of clarity on the important methodological point at which I hinted in the Preface and which is somewhat more fully developed in the Appendix: that in the social sciences our main concepts are value-loaded by logical necessity and have to be defined in relation to value premises.

Indeed, little vagueness attaches to this concept. "Underdeveloped countries" means to all of us the relatively poor and backward countries, where people are beginning to feel an urge for development and for less inequality with the advanced countries. This definition of the concept does not, of course, imply either that they will succeed or that they have the economic, social, and political conditions necessary for success. These things form part of the problem to be studied but do not determine the definition of the concept.

Another value-loaded concept is "the free world." It reflects a deeply rooted ideal in our Western civilization. We assume of the international integration at which we aim that the component national parts are democracies; and we believe in a general way that political democracy is a favorable condition for strivings towards a higher degree of international, as well as national, integration.

As an ideal, a free world is as distant from reality as an integrated world. The countries in the Soviet orbit are far from being free, according to our standards of democracy, though in their official, as well as in both scientific and journalistic usage, the term "the democratic world" is systematically employed to characterize their part of the globe in contradistinction to the non-Soviet world.[1] In the non-Soviet world all shades of democracy and oligarchy are represented, from old stable democracies with civil liberties firmly entrenched in people's mores, to the outright military dictatorships. The short-term trend, at least, does not seem to be in the direction of greater freedom and democracy.

There are thus individual countries in the non-Soviet world that we can meaningfully speak of as political democracies, as there are national communities that are integrated. Just as we can hardly speak of any large group of countries as being the internationally integrated world, so the expression "the free world" can scientifically be used only to express the direction of a development that we desire, but not an actual state of affairs and, unfortunately, not even an actual trend.

That the attainment and preservation of a democratic form of government is desirable is a general value premise of this study.

THE THEORETICAL FRAME

The theoretical frame of the analysis will be the social mechanism of cumulative causation which I believe has a wide if not universal application.[2] It is often popularly referred to as the "vicious circle," but it should be borne in mind that it works upwards as well as downwards. The underlying fact is the existence of such an interdependence between all the factors in a social system that any change in any one of the factors will cause changes in the other factors; these secondary changes are generally of a nature to support the initial change; through a process of interactions, where change in one factor continuously will be supported by reactions of the other factors, the whole system will have been given a momentum to move in the direction of the primary change, though much further.

In condensed form the general line of the argument is presented in the fifth and the last sections of the concluding Chapter XIV, and some readers may wish to read those pages before proceeding further. Generally speaking, while the all-important disparity between the industrially advanced and the underdeveloped countries is constantly borne in mind, the analysis starts out from the problems of the advanced countries and only gradually takes in the problems of the underdeveloped countries. In the later chapters the analysis is focused on the problems of the underdeveloped countries, but the role of the advanced countries is not lost sight of. For the most part the international relations of the underdeveloped countries are with the advanced countries, and this fact is of primary importance even in the study of the internal problems of underdeveloped countries and the problem of their mutual relations. Also, comparisons with the advanced countries can contribute to an understanding of their own problems which we should not ignore.

CHAPTER III

National Integration

COMMON CHARACTERISTICS

The countries in the Western world that today come nearest to the ideal of economic integration, in national terms, are those in Northwestern Europe and North America, with the addition of Australia and New Zealand. In all these countries their relatively complete integration is a rather new attainment; none was anywhere near social and economic integration a hundred years ago, and the difference the last fifty years has made is enormous.

All of the old European countries in this group have had, for centuries, a tradition of political independence. Some of them were split and later united, they were often involved in wars with each other, political boundaries were moved, provinces had to shift allegiance, and some countries experienced periods of outside political control. But they were never submerged in anything like the type of political dependency pressed upon backward peoples under the colonial system. National independence was to everybody the normal and right thing and even when it was not fully achieved it was a force determining everybody's political outlook. This was, of course, true of the United States, Canada, Australia, and New Zealand even while they were still colonies; the tradition of political independence was an important part of their cultural inheritance and, indeed, a political force in their development to separate statehood.

These countries are now all stable democracies. Long before the establishment of formal political democracy with universal suffrage, their peoples—or, in the New World, those peoples from whom they stemmed and whose culture they had taken with them—had for centuries been living in states where the relations between citizens and between them and the community were regulated by law in a firm and nonarbitrary pattern. They have enjoyed relatively "orderly government"

17

as a matter of course—albeit with occasional interruptions, which have been due to war and occupation more often than to revolution. An inherited hierarchical system of law courts, civil administration, and public service, gradually adjusted to changing circumstances in a pragmatic fashion, gave the institutional basis for this rule of law.

They have all had a century or more of almost general literacy. Again relatively speaking, their cultures have always had a strong streak of rationalism and even of materialism. Most of the nationally highly integrated and economically advanced countries also happen to be Protestant or predominantly so; no country with a large Protestant share in the population belongs to the backward group of countries or even to the middle group placed below the very progressive one. The Protestant religion, in its Lutheran and still more in its Calvinist branches, retained comparatively little place for grace and indulgence and advanced a hard morality of efforts and deeds; it prompted a social spirit of individual responsibility and personal emulation, if not competition, and therefore gave a moral value to the individual's social and economic advance.

These countries are all located in the temperate zone. Many are well endowed with natural resources and are, relatively speaking, sparsely populated, or were so when their economic development began to gather speed. Others have had natural advantages—or procured them, in such forms as colonies—or have by other means acquired an early momentum to economic progress.

The industrial revolution came early in these countries, and in all of them several generations have passed by since then. Political and social conditions, and, in Northwest Europe, the huge labor reserves in the rural areas, which could be tapped to man the growing industries, enabled profits and capital accumulation to be maintained at a high level during the era of early industrialization, while the real income of the masses rose less rapidly; in the new settlements overseas immigration played a role parallel to the internal migration to urban areas in Europe. The redistributional policies, which in the last two generations have formed such an essential element in the national integration process, did not take effect until national productivity had attained a much higher level than in the preindustrial stage.

As each of these countries approached the early industrialization era, the international capital market stood wide open to them, providing foreign capital at very low rates of interest. Migration was free between these countries and large-scale movements of labor assured continuous population adjustment to the development opportunities.

All of them are now highly industrialized and are continuously increasing their degree of industrialization. Even in those countries where agriculture plays a large role in the economy, it employs directly only a small fraction of the working population, tending to drop below 20 per cent as agriculture itself becomes industrialized. While the agricultural population has been decreasing, agricultural production has generally been increasing.

After the Second World War these countries enjoyed on the whole continuous full employment, which has sustained rapid economic progress. Because recurrent periods of mass unemployment, with their very serious social and economic effects, have been regarded as the Achilles' heel of industrial society, its absence for a number of years—for which governments in all these countries take the credit—and the political determination to banish large-scale unemployment for ever are generally felt to be the crowning achievements of national integration.

Moreover, full employment and the rising levels of income have created the additional space for settlement of interest conflicts within which further big strides toward equality of opportunity have been possible. The "depressed areas" are disappearing; in Great Britain the term has even disappeared from the language and, significantly, been replaced by "development areas." Standards of living are relatively high. The common expectation in these countries is that the future holds in store still higher levels of production and consumption.

Sweden is typical, or even "overtypical," of the countries moving rapidly to an ever higher level of national integration. Unlike most other countries in the group, it maintained industrial progress during the Great Depression of the thirties, managed to stay out of both world wars, and its terms of trade have developed favorably. Economic and social conditions have changed so radically in the short span of years covered by the author's personal experiences that there now exists an almost completely different society from that of his youth, with totally different problems.

Levels of real income and standards of living have doubled; abject group poverty has virtually been abolished. Only a small—and ever-shrinking—minority of older workers has any personal recollection of serious unemployment. The rigid class structure is also a thing of the past; an efficient ready-made clothing industry has provided all with good quality clothes, taking away a class distinction of earlier days; no social groups are undernourished; housing standards are rising and the housing shortage is largely due to the fact that the building industry cannot possibly keep pace with this rapid rise in demand; every citizen is provided with a minimum protection against all major economic risks in life. All avenues in life are open to the newborn. And, meanwhile, there has never been a better time for business.

The national community is, of course, by no means perfect. Yet, for example, a list of social reforms presented as recently as the middle of the thirties and aimed at providing a firmer basis for the family economy[1]

—commonly regarded at that time as revolutionary and utopian, if not dangerously socialistic—had fifteen years later, and in spite of the war and other international disturbances, been almost fully realized. Even more important, these reforms have been carried out with the consent of all the parliamentary political parties.

Ideologically, these rapid economic and social changes are taking the wind out of the sails of the social reformers, whose demands are being met almost as an incidental by-product of the rising levels of productivity and income. Society as a whole has accepted their ideals and put them into effect. As a result, discussion of domestic problems has undoubtedly lost something of its perspective and tends to show signs of triviality and even pettiness in comparison with the heroic times when the great reforms were first put forward as proposals and vigorously championed —when trade unions were built up, universal suffrage won, and social security schemes propounded.

The disorientation and confusion in regard to a political program for the future on the part of the Labor parties in Northwestern Europe, Australia, and New Zealand, and of the "Liberals" in North America are, of course, in many ways, directly and indirectly related to the impact of the cold war, as I suggest in Chapter XIV. But more generally, and also more fundamentally, the disorientation of the reformers springs from the fact that so many of their proposed reforms have become realities so effortlessly. They must also feel disturbed by the fact that the resulting large and broadly shared moral, spiritual, and cultural growth which they firmly expected has been either slow to materialize or altogether absent.

THE HANDICAPS OF UNDERDEVELOPED COUNTRIES

Together these progressive and highly integrated nations constitute some 12 to 15 per cent of the non-Soviet world's population; their importance and power is, however, much greater, as they produce almost three fourths of the total income of the non-Soviet world. The rest of the non-Soviet world is poor, mostly very poor, and to various degrees rather badly integrated nationally.

In enumerating the common characteristics of the advanced countries, I imply that their coexistence is not merely accidental. An explanation of their recent economic growth and national integration would have to give the factors mentioned their due weight. It must be remembered, though, that the development took place in one particular epoch of world history and under very special political and cultural circumstances. The correlations between these factors should not be exalted to the status of immutable laws of social development.

Indeed, to infer that they spell out permanent conditions that are necessary for economic progress and national integration would be to imply continued stagnation for the greater part of mankind. This would be the part that was kept under colonial rule for generations and to whom political and economic independence is not an established norm; the part that did not inherit a society based for centuries on the rule of law and that never had an effective democratic form of government; the part whose religious and cultural traditions are less rationalistic and less stimulating to enterprise, competition, and individual advance; where the climate is not that of the temperate zone; where, as a result of prolonged stagnation, there is now a less favorable relation between population and resources; and where none of the other prerequisites for an easy start of industrial growth are present.

These common characteristics point to some of the special and great difficulties facing the underdeveloped countries in their strivings for economic development. The view that underdeveloped countries can develop by a process of change fairly parallel to that followed by the now advanced countries is superficial and false and corresponds to the bias of easy opportunism in research to which I refer in Chapter XIV. All their problems are in many fundamental ways different and, as I show in Chapters XI to XIII, the practical policy followed will also have to be different.

From one point of view the differences imply the existence of vicious circles which can only be broken by large-scale state planning and state intervention. The state played a more important role in the early development of the developed countries than is often conceded. And it was from the beginning a much more efficient state than the underdeveloped countries today have at their disposal. As is now generally recognized, the countries that have been lagging behind, and where continued stagnation has built up and fortified tremendous impediments to development, will have to use much more radical measures of state policy.

A Complex Process of Social Change

In the course of reaching their present high standards of living and sustaining their economic progress an important common trait in all these advanced countries has been the gradual elimination of inherited obstacles to the individual's social mobility. The class structure and other social rigidities have gradually been dissolved into looser and more flexible social forms, the avenues of social and economic advancement have been broadened and made accessible to ever deeper social strata, and opportunities have been progressively equalized for both social groups and individuals.

In the development of these countries, this has been the essential element of integration. But this particular set of social changes can hardly be said to have been the operative cause of progress and definitely not the exclusive one. They were usually not primary causes but rather the outcome of a manifold development.

If any individual factors were to be singled out as of basic causal significance for this development, I would attach particular importance to certain ideological and cultural forces, among them the early attainment of general literacy, the established respect for the rule of law and the implicit idea of equality before the law, and, not least, the ethical value attached to work, individual emulation and personal responsibility, and social and economic advance. This code of ethics has undoubtedly from the beginning owed much to the rationalistic religious and moral teaching prevalent in those countries, and to the general impact of this teaching upon social mores, even in regard to individuals who did not accept it; this applies even in later periods, when society became secularized, while the moral heritage, even if considerably weakened, was retained.

When once the industrialization process had begun, the process itself tended to loosen fixed social patterns. As Professor Wilbert E. Moore observed: "It is characteristic of industrialism, or of modern economic activity in general, that it is constantly subversive of established ways, even its own, and entails a constant emphasis on change and improvement."[2] In the old countries, the building of the railroads, a part of the early phase of industrialization, dealt veritable mental shocks to the population in one isolated farming community after another. The exploitation of the forests for lumber and of the mines for ore had the similar effect of partially reproducing in the old countries small samples of the frontier community of the New World. Its history can be studied, for instance, in the court records of those times. The urbanization of the population, following the establishment of industrial centers, broke down family and social ties and enforced a process of mobility which was not only geographical but also economic and social.

The railroads, the telephone network, and other means of communication, together with the improvement of the schools, all represented powerful forces for altering the social stratification and the mores of the local communities. An effective labor market, larger than the local one, began to function; and retail trade carried an even richer variety of commodities produced in all parts of the country. New ideas began to flow and popular movements were given their send-off: in favor of teetotalism, trade unionism, universal suffrage, freer conditions for religious worship, equal rights and opportunities for women, etc. Each had its stamp of the new era of freedom and social rationality.

The complex social processes that I am here sketching have had a cumulative character. There are reasons to stress particularly the role of economic progress itself as a driving force. The abolition of social and economic barriers and the gradual realization of greater equality of opportunity, which is the essence of the high degree of integration gradually being accomplished in these countries, have themselves been partly the effect of economic progress and rising living standards. It is a common experience that when a country tends to become economically static it also loses in flexibility and internal social and economic mobility.

Many French critics make this point about their own country, which has today a level of production not much higher than a quarter of a century ago and at the same time is almost strangled by social and economic rigidities. The problem with which the former French Prime Minister, M. Pierre Mendès-France, was heroically grappling is the complex one of both initiating a rapid economic progress and breaking down the barriers to internal adjustment.[3]

The task is at bottom that of changing the community attitudes and behavior patterns of 45 million Frenchmen, which have been partly shaped under the influence of economic stagnation. At the same time, these attitudes and patterns have been mutually enforcing each other and together preventing economic progress. If, by some miracle or exceptionally good luck in the movement of the terms of trade and other exogenous economic determinants, the French economy were to experience a real spurt of progress, it would be easier to initiate all the other changes necessary to sustain that progress. National integration would develop almost incidentally to economic growth.

To take another example, if the South of the United States remained comparatively stagnant after the American Civil War and two decades ago could still rightly be characterized by Franklin D. Roosevelt as "America's problem number one," the cause was not that there were formal barriers to mobility. The hillbillies, for instance, had been free to move up north. Their American citizenship and their knowledge of the English language would have given them an immense competitive advantage over the poor European immigrants who swarmed into the labor market in the northern states. Nevertheless, they stayed in their destitution. Freedom to move is not all that matters; its exercise depends on cultural, social, and economic factors. Southern stagnation was not overcome until the era of the extended and accelerated economic progress initiated in America by the Second World War.

Now, after fifteen years of uninterrupted economic progress and a rising demand for labor—and also, it is true, of significant ideological changes, as well as the rise in educational standards and some key decisions of the Supreme Court—national integration of the European immigrant groups has almost reached its completion and the final integration of the Negroes in the labor market is within sight, if that sight can reach some few decades ahead.

The increased freedom for the individual to move around in these countries has thus not been attained as a result simply of breaking down earlier barriers. A condition as well as a result has been the sustained economic progress, making it easier for people to give up established privileges and relinquish the support of barriers keeping others out.

A Process of Social Organization

Even apart from the question of causation, the increased opportunities for social mobility have, by and large, not been brought about by the outlawing of social impediments, but rather by social reorganization. New rules and new institutions have been created, gradually taking over the functions of the old ones; this reorganization has, however, been directed toward the goal, felt by the people as an increasingly practical ideal, of broadening and equalizing opportunities for the individual.

In this process legislation was important from the beginning and has become increasingly so, as a means of laying down conditions for the individual's competition and cooperation within society. In earlier times, and particularly in the historical stage of economic liberalism, legislation often served the purpose of abolishing restrictive mores or institutional structures and of enforcing competition. This is still a main function of legislation in all these countries: but legislation has, increasingly, become instead a means of organizing competition and cooperation in a special way, which was felt to be in the common interest.

Trade unions and other professional and industrial associations have at the same time become ever stronger; they are organized in a national frame and are acquiring a quasi-public significance in all our countries. Some businesses have become big and powerful in their markets; small businesses and farmers have cooperated to organize their markets.

The economic life of the individual in the integrated countries is thus, indeed, very much "regulated." That these countries have nevertheless gone so far towards equality of opportunity and a greater social and economic mobility is due to the fact that the regulations have been framed in a political setting where this ideal has been an important norm.

More generally, it should be stressed that these countries have not reached their present status simply through a policy of nonintervention. All of them—and I can here include also all other modern states that are laboring to reach a higher level of national integration—have achieved their political unity by the gradual unfolding of a comprehensive system of economic and social measures, aimed at influencing, redirecting, and speeding up their economic development.

In these countries the existence of a poor and stagnant region has given rise to policies aimed at stimulating the growth of its production and the raising of its living standards, or at inducing emigration to other regions. Such considerations have always in some degree influenced the planning of railways and other communications, the disposal of the rights to exploitation of the natural resources, legislation on commercial banking, and, of course, tariff policy (how wisely, is for the moment outside our purview). These policies have regularly been "discriminating" in the sense that they implied the favoring of some industries, some social groups, and some geographic areas at the expense of others. A purely liberal—i.e., nondiscriminatory and "impartial"—national community has never existed and is almost a contradiction in terms. Much remaining localized stagnation—nonfulfillment of the ideal of economic integration and nonrealization of equality of opportunity—has been due to the fact that the curative discriminatory measures had not been taken at all or not been taken early enough.

The "Organizational Economy"

In all advanced countries the secular trend has for a long time been away from a free market economy governed by the interplay of market forces, and towards an ever greater volume of interventions by governments and organized social groups.[4] These interventions change the basic conditions for the "markets" and the operation of the "price system." It is a paradox that only a well-integrated community can abide by the rules of economic competition; but that an integrated community will modify the rules if changes in prices impose too drastic a decline in the income of any one sector, or require too sudden shifts in resources or, more generally, if the community favors a course of economic development other than the one that would result from the free play of the market forces.

We can, of course, still speak about the "markets" and the "price system" in these countries. Individuals earn wages and receive payments in money and they buy goods and services with their incomes in "markets." But the "markets" and the "price system" are regulated and conditioned by the actions of the community and of organized interest groups; we are far from our old theoretical model of the self-governing free market economy.

Thus the labor market is under the control not only of public laws and regulations but also of collective bargaining between employers and employees. In our countries today there is a commonly recognized "due process" for collective bargaining in the labor market just as there is for legislation. Constitutional issues aside, legislation and collective bargaining between organized interest groups are fundamentally similar forms of socially sanctioned, regular settlements of interest conflicts. Indeed, the prototype of the institution for collective bargaining is the parliament.

The complex Austrian system of official chambers for industry, com-

merce, agriculture, and labor—with provincial branches but united at
the national level—is, in fact, only a comprehensive frame for collective
bargaining. The Australian and New Zealand systems of arbitration in
the labor market, the Swedish system for annual establishment of farm
prices by agreement between representatives of all interested parties, and
many other institutional forms for regulating prices and incomes fall in
this same category of organized group bargaining, determining the
"market." The assembly of the elected representatives of the people, together with its executive instrument, the government, exert a supervisory
power over this ever growing multitude of organs for voluntary collective
settlements of interest conflicts. In principle, these organs all function
subject to the permission of the state, sometimes at its instigation, and
often under rules laid down by legislation.

In all these countries it has been deemed desirable to attempt to curb
by various means the possibilities of monopolistic exploitation which big
business has because it is big and which small businesses acquire as they
become organized. The result has nowhere been anything like complete.
In all our countries we are approaching a situation where everybody is,
or attempts to be, a monopolist in regard to what he sells; as consumers
we are usually much weaker. As producers we are specialized, but as
consumers our demand spreads out and touches directly only the retail
market. A tightly knit small national community like Switzerland is
perhaps—though it is hidden behind a different type of rationalizing
ideology—the best example of an advanced development of this all-
round supply monopoly, operated by everybody against everybody, where
everybody is strong as a producer, distributor, and worker but weak as a
consumer.

Commenting upon the situation in the United States, Professor Calvin
B. Hoover has coined the term the "organizational economy," which he
defines in the following manner: "Competition, possessing tremendous
survival value, always present somewhere and present almost everywhere
in some degree, *cum* oligopoly and anyhow price leadership, often incomplete and/or intermittent, together with collective bargaining, in which
economic power, always liable to become political, conceivably may countervail just enough but just as likely may countervail too little or too
much, perhaps followed by governmental intervention and/or control."[5]
He makes excuses for the verbal monstrosity but maintains that it may
be more descriptive of our actual economic system than a shorter name.
He adds his valuation that this system has served society well in terms
both of goods produced and of liberties preserved.

Since a free market is unattainable—and is, in fact, not desired, as
the political process reveals—but since there are obvious dangers of in-
fringement upon the public interest, the state is everywhere pushed into

economic settlements, sometimes curbing by legal means the more apparent examples of exploitation by loosening up the system here and there and enforcing competition, sometimes by making it compulsory for firms to make public their restrictive business practices, sometimes by actually entering into the settlements on behalf of the public interest.

To counterbalance organized producers, consumers in many of our countries have built up organs that can give effective influence to their dispersed buying power; as Professor John K. Galbraith rightly observes, in the United States "the chain stores preempted the gains of countervailing power first."[6] In a country like Sweden the consumers' cooperative movement has for decades been able not only to compete on the retail market, but also to represent forcefully the consumers' interests in all sorts of collective bargaining with the various producers' groups. And it has acquired the capital and management resources necessary to apply the sanction of competition as a producer.

More generally, the community has asserted itself by giving positive support through legislation and administration to the weaker members of society, so that they can organize themselves more solidly. In the United States, as Galbraith points out, "the support of countervailing power has become in the last two decades perhaps the major peace-time function of the federal government"; this is even more true of the other industrially advanced countries.[7]

In all our countries we have had to accept the fact that to an increasingly large extent prices are no longer "objective" phenomena—in the sense that they are a simple function of free market competition—but are manipulated and directed and are, indeed, results of "political" group actions.

THE WELFARE STATE

As one of the important means of equalizing opportunities for individuals and of stamping out impediments to social mobility, all these integrated countries have gradually found it appropriate to take vigorous measures to even out differences in incomes and wealth. This line of policy has been advocated by the liberal economists for about a hundred years,[8] but only since the beginning of this century has the principle of redistribution taken on a political importance. Without exception, all the advanced countries now have effective systems of taxes on income, capital, and inheritance which are strongly progressive and tend to prevent or limit the continued passive existence of private fortunes for several generations.

In all these countries the public purse has, at the same time or even earlier, increasingly taken on the responsibility of paying for public health services and of defraying the cost of many other social necessities. Equal and free access by all citizens to primary and higher education, paid out of public funds, is an ideal that has gradually been given reality; the principle was, in fact, inscribed in the constitutions of many of the states of the United States. Complex and very expensive systems of social security have gradually been built up against all sorts of income and expenditure risks.

Taxation, the provision of free essential services, and in general the social security system represents the immediate policy measures applied in accordance with the redistributional ideal; but the same ideal determines to a greater or lesser extent all public policy in the economic field. In a period of rapid and continued industrialization, when the agricultural population was shrinking almost continuously and when unhampered market forces would have provided the farming population with much lower incomes than those engaged in other pursuits, agricultural policy in most of these countries has brought about an income redistribution in the interest of the agricultural population. Usually this has been accomplished by means of some price parity arrangement.

Similarly, other low income groups are protected by the economic policy. After the Second World War even the English and European coal miner, for so long the least favored of skilled laborers, finally saw his status raised largely as a result of the reorganization of the coal industry, carried out as a public policy.

All the industrially advanced and progressive countries have in fact for some time been moving rapidly along the road to the "welfare state." Changes in political power, and even rather violent shifts in general political development, seem only ripples on the surface of these powerful historical trends. People are not prepared to consider a country well integrated if there are large and frozen differences between rich and poor regions and social classes, and still less if the gaps in wealth and welfare are widening.

The ideological motivation and the political spirit of this development in the advanced countries is concisely formulated by a distant observer, Dr. Humayan Kabir:

The basis of the welfare state is recognition of the dignity of the individual. It is because each individual is recognized as uniquely valuable that the state seeks to interfere with the normal functions of society to assure him certain inherent and inalienable rights. It is significant that the concept of the welfare state emerged only as a further development of the concept of democracy. Democracy was at first only a political concept and sought to regard all individuals as equal in the eye of the law. For purposes of political decisions, it laid down that each one must count as one and no one as more than one. It was however soon discovered that this equality would remain illusory unless backed by equality in other fields. This led, on the one hand, to restrictions on the individual's right to exploit others, as seen in labour and social legislation. On the other hand, it made the state provide on an increasing scale the welfare services which equalize opportunity for all citizens.[9]

THE SOLIDARITY BASIS

The development towards an integrated state; the growth of the complex public, quasi-public, and private institutions by which this development takes its form; and the effecting of the economic and fiscal policies that such a state employs and that interfere very greatly with the individual's disposal of his own person and his property, must all have a firm psychological foundation. The citizens of the country must have such a strong feeling of belonging to the nation that they are prepared to bear their share of common sacrifices when these are decided upon by due political process.

The feeling of a national community of interests and aspirations, the common willingness to make sacrifices for purposes other than immediate economic return, and the development of institutions and rules appropriate to these ends are the historical results of living for a long time closely together under a united policy and of actively participating in the determination of that policy. Should this psychological basis weaken, the state would disintegrate. But in the process towards economic integration, and in conditions of continuous economic growth, it is apt to become ever firmer.

National solidarity is heavily tested by the highly redistributional tax systems in these countries. The unstable social basis for national integration in countries like France, Italy, or Greece is reflected in their inability to stamp out large-scale tax evasion and to give effect to progressive direct taxation. The fact that the United States, on the contrary, in spite of its peculiar centrifugal forces, succeeded during the last generation in giving effect to its increasingly progressive direct taxation, is a confirmation of the fact that the psychological basis of solidarity was becoming firm and that the country was successfully reaching national social integration.

The gradual conditioning of the citizens to pay taxes, even when they constitute a heavy burden, is not the only test of national solidarity. If strikes, instead of being rarely used safety valves, socially sanctioned and institutionally controlled in an organized process of collective bargaining, develop, as in France and Italy, into recurring and seemingly aimless mass demonstrations of general dissatisfaction on the part of all the lower income groups—workers, farmers, clerks, teachers, and government officials—then we are confronted with the open reappearance of the "class struggle."

There are also conflicting interests in the nationally integrated countries. But the different interests evolve within the specialized institutional forms developed for this purpose—the legislative and all other machinery for collective bargaining—and they manage to merge into continuously changing *modi vivendi*. The participating groups feel the institutions to be "theirs," they think about the entire organized community in terms of "we," whereas the striking masses in France and Italy are dissatisfied with the "system" and do not identify themselves with the social forms for settlement of conflicting interests. Rather, they look on organized society as if it were outside their control by normal means—it is in the possession of "the others," who do them wrong.

The term "class struggle" should not be taken too literally, however. For it is indicative of the real situation of faltering social integration in these countries that the spirit of the strikers is not fundamentally dissimilar to that of the doctors, the lawyers, and the small industrialists, agriculturalists, and shopkeepers when they individually cheat the state on taxes or when they join hands for collective defense actions of an extra-legal kind. In all these cases the common trait is a lack of personal identification, solidarity, and loyalty to the community, which is caused by a widely disseminated feeling that they are being mistreated and that their ambitions are frustrated. Basically, all this is very much a symptom of economic stagnation.

The most significant differences between those countries where the "price system" is accepted and those where it is openly challenged by group actions outside the established and sanctioned social forms is, of course, that the former countries have been progressing economically and the others have not. Undoubtedly, part of the explanation why the former countries are progressing is that there the "class struggle" has been successfully held in leash and, in the ideal case, tamed by being harnessed to collective bargaining, where all interest groups act upon the agreed assumption that a settlement shall be reached and that it shall be respected. But equally important is the recognition that it is economic progress itself that provides room for expansion of legitimate group interests and permits the element of mutual generosity, which is the condition for successful collective bargaining—successful in the sense that a settlement is reached and that the parties to it feel that they are, for the time being, satisfied or, at least, acquiescent.

The necessity of reaching collective agreement is continuously exercising pressure on the limits of possible expansion. The postwar tendency to inflation in the northwestern countries of Europe is undoubtedly in part because the interest groups in these countries could only resolve their collective bargaining on wages and farmers' prices by overstepping the limits of expansion and thus causing a modicum, and sometimes more than a modicum, of wage and price inflation.

Variations Around a General Trend

This summary analysis of the process of economic integration in the advanced countries attempts to take into account what happened there, in the specific institutional and ideological setting and under the influence of the contemporary forces. It is a valuation only to the extent that national integration, the total result of many elements—of varying degrees of popularity—is a commonly accepted ideal which was in a large measure realized.

Such was the process in the existing integrated national communities. As a general and therefore vague characterization of the trend of social and economic relations in those countries, the term "economic integration" makes sense: the essential idea it emphasizes is the relatively wide range and equality of opportunity those countries have gradually succeeded in offering the individual under conditions of steady economic progress. Countries that have not come this far may likewise and in a manner that makes sense characterize their effective national goals as "closer economic integration."

But the concept is vague: in every country individuals, social classes, and political parties have ideas on how to move towards a more integrated state that have differed and do differ. Most people see shortcomings in their national community and in its laws.

Nevertheless, viewed from a distance, the differing political attitudes to the community as it is functioning and constantly developing dwindle to ripples on the surface of the fundamental similarities, to variations built around a main theme. From this distance the common features in our national communities can be abstracted and fitted into a coherent image. This fact testifies to the general community of ideals in our Western civilization and to the fact that, when these ideals can be fulfilled under exceptionally favorable conditions and with ever widening political participation, they tend to result in a type of nationally integrated community, whose contours can be ascertained.

CHAPTER IV

National versus International Integration

THE GROWTH OF ECONOMIC NATIONALISM

Prior to the First World War, and in the partial world which was the center of attention in that period, there was little apparent conflict between the two lines of development: towards national and towards international integration.

The rapid economic growth in all the countries in this partial world was both a condition and an effect, actually an essential phase, of their development towards national integration, as was pointed out in the preceding chapter. To a considerable extent, this economic growth was made possible only because of the relatively unhampered movement of labor, capital, goods, and services between these countries; these movements signified a high level of, and a continuous development towards, international economic integration. International trade was increasing, not only absolutely but—unlike towards the end of the nineteenth century—also in comparison with total production; rather high—and in some cases rising—tariff walls could not stop but only slow down this development. And the trend of international capital movements and labor migration also pointed upwards, at least in absolute terms.

Beginning with the First World War, however, when an uninterrupted sequence of international political and economic crises gradually removed even the expectancy of a return to normalcy, a discord between the two lines of integration became increasingly visible. Gradually, all these countries built up an armory of national policies to defend their economic welfare and stability from the adverse influences of outside events.

In the course of this development—and more definitely after the onset of the Great Depression—all international movements were securely curtailed by national policies. Movements of labor over national boundaries were restricted to localized and tiny streams, and the international capital

32

market ceased to function after the financial crisis of 1931. At about the same time international trade became tied up in national regulations that in their general effects were restrictive and discriminatory, exchange rates became nationally managed prices, often unrelated to market values, and general convertibility was finally abandoned. The Second World War saw a new upsurge of national regulations and the postwar years were so filled by international crises, partly due to structural maladjustments, that a return to anything like the pre-1914 situation was impossible.

It is tempting to consider this trend towards international economic disintegration as simply the result of "bad" national policies. That would be an overoptimistic view; for a corollary would be that the development could be turned back equally simply by a reversal of these policies, thus instigating a return to free entrance and exit of labor and capital and to free trade. But in the sequence of emergencies we have passed through the individual states had for the most part no alternative to taking these measures.

Furthermore, there are deeper causes for these national policies. They have become so entrenched and so solidly supported by all political parties because they represent in many ways essential elements in the welfare state of mutual solidarity and economic stability, the growth of which I sketched in the last chapter. The succession of international crises during the past forty years has had such lasting effects on national policies simply because these crises have been pushing in the direction of national economic consolidation—a trend that, however, had its own independent causes which were merely strengthened by the repeated economic crises and the emergency policies adopted to meet them.[1] Particularly in the field of trade, the later development toward autarky had, in fact, its forebodings in the rise of protectionism from the eighties and nineties onwards.

By this I do not imply the existence of logical elements of conflict between the ideals of national and international integration. I am more convinced than ever that, on the contrary, national economic progress and integration can only reach the highest possible levels in a well-integrated world. But in the severely disintegrated world in which we actually live, there is an obvious lack of institutional balance that works forcefully against international solutions that would satisfy people's cravings for economic progress, equality, and security.

National political machinery is strong and effective and has a firm basis in people's attitudes of allegiance and solidarity; this machinery is getting stronger and its psychological basis firmer every year. It is used in the service of interests that are felt to be commonly shared within the nation. Machinery for international cooperation is, by contrast, weak and ineffective, and it lacks a solid basis in people's valuations and expectations. Even without any real inherent conflict between the two goals, this tremendous and steadily increasing preponderance of national political machinery has deflected—and, if a radical change of the trend is not induced, will continue to deflect—the development of practical policy towards economic nationalism.

Under these circumstances, internationalism tends more and more to be relegated to abstract utopianism. There is in the world of today so little possibility of giving reality to such strivings that they appear unrealistic and impractical; they are dreams and theories, while economic nationalism is realistic and practical. The only effective counterforce I can think of would be the knowledge, if it could be widely spread, of the very great gains that would accrue to all countries from every step, however modest, towards international cooperation; and the great dangers inherent in the present development.

NATIONAL INTEREST CONSOLIDATION

Meanwhile, the national integration processes are proceeding in all the advanced countries to ever higher levels and, generally speaking, national integration is apt to hamper international integration by directing the individual's interests ever more exclusively to the national state.

Undoubtedly, there exists an emotional basis for this. A state boundary, almost independently of its origin and location, satisfies directly an urge, felt by most people, to be set apart from other people. The studied mutual uncooperativeness which, for instance, the English and the Scots would have been able to develop, had they been divided by a state boundary invested with the awe of some centuries' existence, can easily be imagined. Psychologists might find the explanation of this strange negative attitude in those elements of frustration in our education and in all our daily lives that seek an outlet in aggression. To draw distinctions is always a temptation; it is generally easier to divide than to unite. But as the modern national welfare state develops, existing emotional nationalism will be forcefully strengthened by motives which are, indeed, rational to the individual.

One result of national integration is that decisions of the national legislatures and operations of all other public and quasi-public institutions and of organized interest groups, functioning within the national framework, come to have a greater and greater bearing upon the life and welfare of every citizen. Even individual professional careers become predetermined according to closed systems of merit and seniority, built up as national standards and defended by national organizations. Neither the doctor nor the teacher, nor the postman, the policeman, nor the building worker, can leave the nationally paved road without economic loss, often amounting to total exclusion from his means of livelihood. The national boundary thus takes on increasing practical importance for everyone. Undoubtedly this tends by itself progressively to lessen the experience, and weaken the feeling, of international solidarity.

The modern welfare state is also not inexpensive; even people in the lower and middle income brackets carry comparatively heavy burdens of taxes, insurance premiums, and membership fees. It is natural that they are bent upon getting the maximum benefits for themselves out of the national welfare state which they very intensely feel has been built for them and is being paid for by them. We can witness in all advanced countries how people's interests become more and more focused upon salary scales and other material rewards—a very remarkable effect of the higher levels of income and of the intensified democratic participation in determining the course of economic process.

Organizations become increasingly directed towards winning material advances for their members; when the advances are procured, these are felt to have been earned by group solidarity. As they all operate within the national framework, this whole trend tends to turn people's interests inwards, towards the situations and problems at home, and to spread a defensive ideology of national group protectionism. In these relatively rich countries and in the mental climate of the protective welfare state, international issues other than those related to national defense become embarrassing. For, at least in the short view, which is also the common man's view, international interests, if they aspire to the more than platonic, would imply willingness to carry sacrifices for others, who are outside the comprehensive national security system the citizens have provided for themselves by their mutual solidarity and are paying for out of their own earnings.

Cultural differences between populations on different sides of state boundaries, which were originally minor, are steadily accentuated as interests are focused on national issues and increasingly institutionalized within the state framework. The improved schools and the press have a similar influence, as have the radio and television. It is also unwise to assume that, under these circumstances, technical developments in transport and other means of communication, which are now forcibly bringing even distant peoples into more frequent contact with each other, automatically create a basis for greater international solidarity. Popular awareness of cultural dissimilarities and conflicts of interests may, at least in the short run, have strong effects in the opposite direction.

By the mere fact of its existence and its functioning the modern welfare state is thus continuously strengthening its own psychological foundation in people's valuations and expectations. I have on another occasion called this effect of the national integration process the "miracle of the sovereign state," and illustrated it by the development in Scandinavia. In that corner of the world the division into a number of small and separate states is no more than an accident of history, without any foundation in racial, religious, economic, cultural or—until very recently, as the schools improved—important language differences. The conscious political strivings on a more abstract level have, moreover, for a long time been directed towards fostering solidarity among the Scandinavian peoples. It is, indeed, something that cannot be left unexplained why a farmer in the southern tip of Sweden feels an allegiance to far-off Stockholm in the north, rather than to neighboring Copenhagen across the Sund, and does so with increasingly important consequences for his entire political outlook and his concepts of rights and obligations, interests and aspirations.

This important problem of the social and psychological consolidation of the national welfare state and of its influence in weakening internationalist attitudes has not been given the intensive scientific study its crucial importance justifies.

THE FALTERING STRENGTH OF INTERNATIONALISM

It is interesting to note how in this development popular movements which fifty years ago were imbued with internationalism have now become narrowly nationalistic. This is true of the Socialist Labor movement. An operative cause of this defection to nationalism was the severe disillusionment brought about by the First World War, when the Second International split wide open and its members joined the national camps, whereas the plan—and, with many, the hopeful expectation— had been that the workers' noncooperation would stop the war. The more important and permanent cause, however, was the fact that the Labor parties in many countries became a power in internal politics and thereby responsible for the active pursuit of national policies.

Labor was often the main architect of, and always a driving force towards, the modern welfare state, the nationalistic features of which I discuss in this chapter. The international ideals were long preserved in verbal formulas. Slogans, flags, and songs expressing allegiance to these ideals were a revered heritage from the pioneers of the movement, though gradually fading out as new generations succeeded the old ones. Meanwhile, practical work absorbed more and more of the party member's energy and was focused on the national and local issues where concrete results could be reaped. Per Albin Hanson, the late Swedish Socialist leader and Premier in a government which has now been directed by the Labor Party for more than twenty years, found an entirely adequate expression for Labor's aspiration in the new age when he described it as that of making the country "the people's home" (*folkhemmet*).

It is indicative of this trend that in the many countries where the Labor parties have come to power and been confronted with the task of forming cabinets, they have always had an abundance of competent candidates for their ministers of social and economic affairs but have usually had great difficulty in manning the post of foreign minister. In the last British Labour Government Bevin and Morrison had to be drafted for the job of Secretary of Foreign Affairs from lifelong political pursuits of very different interests. Foreign policy was no longer a central issue for the Labor parties.

Another indication is that there has been so little practical cooperation between the national Labor parties since they acquired political influence. Labor economists have usually carried out their practical studies under more narrow national premises than their colleagues to the right. And labor ministers have taken what amounts almost to pride in showing their senior civil servants that they could be just as nationalistic as the members of any Conservative government—in fact considerably more so—and that they had no inclination to let Labor "comradeship" soften their hearts. I am, of course, thinking of Great Britain in particular but the phenomenon is more common. The history of the Labor movement in several countries might well have been different if more of the internationalistic spirit of bygone times had been preserved.

Many other popular strivings besides the political Labor movement before the First World War and even somewhat later had strong international allegiances. All the movements for liberty, equality, and welfare for the masses—the movements for universal suffrage, for women's equal rights and opportunities, against alcoholism, for consumers' cooperation, for trade unionism, etc.—that later, in the progress towards national integration, saw their ideals gradually realized, started off as internationally inspired efforts. The pre-1914 movement for peace and international arbitration belonged to this same group.

Various professional groups kept close international contacts, particularly in Europe, which was at that time a much larger part of the world. National integration was then only in its beginning and class differences were often rather sharp; in the upper classes the social distance from foreign aristocracy was often shorter than from the lower classes at home; greater equality and closer ties within the nations, when they were achieved, have undoubtedly been won at the cost of losing some of the earlier international social integration on the upper-class level. Even in the crafts, however, there had been, before the First World War, close international ties, supported both by the movements referred to above and by free migration of labor.

A study of a half-century's contents of professional journals and journals of organizations for various political, cultural and social causes, from the point of view of the kind and degree of interest they showed in people and events in other countries, would be an excellent topic for a doctoral thesis in international social psychology. Such a study would reveal, I believe, the strong inward turn of sympathies. Some time ago I had occasion to glance through some such publications from various countries for the years 1914 to 1918, and I was struck by their reserved friendliness—indeed, guarded solidarity—towards persons, organizations, and accomplishments in enemy countries; I found even appreciative obituaries. This caused me to reflect how much less civilized in this particular respect of international understanding the world has become in the course of little more than one generation—in spite of all our tourist travel and the increased volume of other secondary contacts resulting from rapidly improved means of communication, and in spite of the growing number of international conferences of all kinds.

THE TREND TO NATIONAL AUTARKY

Apart from the effects of national integration on the all-important factor of psychological identification and solidarity, the modern integrated welfare state is likely to enlarge vastly the scope of public or quasi-public responsibility for the economic development of the country. The limits within which the state can freely dispose and organize in accordance with directives emanating from the national political process are fixed by its territorial boundaries. The state is in a position to control capital exports; usually there are reasons to preserve capital within the country in order to push ahead with national economic development. The state is also in the position to keep out foreign labor; it will find the means to discourage immigration if it is commonly felt to be harmful or even if this is demanded by powerful pressure groups that take advantage of public apathy.

To all economic planning—whether done by the state, by organized interest groups, or by private enterprise—investment in the country itself, internal production and consumption, and internal supply and demand are factors which are more or less calculable and which can even be influenced in accordance with national, group, or individual interests. The international markets, on the other hand, are independent variables, that is, they represent an economic risk that purely national planning cannot control.

National economies simply have to adjust themselves as best they can to external market conditions. Among these exogenous and nationally uncontrollable conditions to be found in the international markets are not only ordinary business fluctuations but also the interventions of other governments in their own economy and, in particular, in their imports and exports. When the economies and the policies of other countries follow the same course, these outside interferences can, as seen from the viewpoint of every single government, be expected to multiply and grow in magnitude, thus increasing the general riskiness of foreign markets.

While foreign markets, determined by the actions of other governments and groups, thus increasingly involve economic risks, one of the surest and simplest means of stabilizing the conditions for production and employment at home consists in regulating imports. Such public controls usually have the political advantage—at least immediately—of shifting the effects of adverse developments on to the foreigner, while helping domestic industries or leaving them undisturbed.

For four decades this secular trend towards national autarky has been spurred on in each of the highly integrated countries by the risk, or actual fact, of war and involuntary isolation, and also, of course, in most of these countries for most of the time, by foreign exchange considerations. More recently the cold war and the dollar shortage have again intensified these drives towards autarky.

In this way international disintegration feeds national autarky, which in turn tends to further intensify international disintegration. The process is cumulative; and every new policy step along the autarkic line is followed by a redirection of national investment of capital and employment of labor to fill the protected space created; the new situation is thus consolidated by vested interests.

"World trade is directed by a monstrously complex network of trade and payments arrangements which has minimized the role of market forces in determining what nations will produce and what they will sell to one another"—this is the conclusion Dr. Raymond F. Mikesell reaches from his comprehensive study of present trade and payments relations.[2]

THE ROLE OF THE LARGE COUNTRIES

The decisive and leading role in this development towards national autarky played by the great industrial powers has usually not been sufficiently stressed. One of the interesting parts of Professor Ingvar Svennilson's recently published investigation of European economy between the two world wars is the analysis he devotes to this problem.[3]

Svennilson finds it a striking feature of the development of world trade since the First World War that the manufacturing industries of the United States, Great Britain, Germany, and France have become national autarkic units:

The Soviet Union completes, in an excellent way, this picture of a world economy where a few countries, which together dominate world industrial output, provide markets for each other's industrial output only to a very small extent. . . . The five largest industrial countries in the world have almost completely isolated their industrial systems from each other. In this respect, the division of the world into a number of isolated economic blocks is almost a reality. Work on a unified world market is useless if these large countries are not prepared to open up their frontiers to imports of manufactured products.[4] . . . It is to the economic relations between these large countries that the world disintegration can most properly be applied. The smaller industrial countries, on the other hand, are not only highly dependent on the supply of industrial goods from the larger countries but also maintain a comparatively intensive trade between themselves.[5]

Because of its position as the main creditor country in the world, the extreme protectionism of the United States, effected by high tariffs and many other devices, is of importance in this context. In the United States there are, of course, local and special interests behind every protective measure. The collusion of these interests and the appeal to nationalist sentiments have ensured their application, and it has proved impossible for successive administrations, though all with good intentions, to do anything substantial about it. Professor Jacob Viner, who recently has again surveyed the situation, reaches the conclusion that "the duties of our tariff which have survived the trade agreements negotiations probably account for almost all of the restrictive effect on imports of the tariff as it was before 1934";[6] the other devices of national protectionism have been still better preserved and even strengthened.

The United States, with a gross national product now exceeding 350 billion dollars a year, proud of the great resilience of its economy, accustomed by now to absorbing one violent shock to its economy after another, prepared for a continuous economic growth of truly startling dimensions,[7] and having since Cordell Hull's time assumed the leadership in a virtual world crusade to break down the barriers to international trade, does not see its way to permit the few hundred million—or, at most, a few billion—dollars a year of additional imports of various commodities that would follow a lowering of its own trade barriers. The content of the Randall Report,[8] the discussion around it, and the reception by the United States Congress of its rather timid suggestions, have made it clear that the whole movement towards trade liberalization in America—urged by a unanimous world, dramatically and movingly staged by American administrations of both political parties in repeated prologues, and widely publicized as the main American contribution to international economic integration—is in great danger of becoming an anticlimax with worldwide repercussions on all our strivings towards internationalism.

After the election of 1954, it seems that the main proposals of the

Randall Commission may be carried through. In the present discouraging development even such a small step would be of tremendous importance—particularly if it is being stressed that it is only a small step in the right direction and if the work is immediately taken up for a courageous continuation. The problem of trade liberalization in the United States and other countries in similar positions will be discussed in more technical terms in the concluding sections of Chapter XIII.

Undoubtedly, Svennilson is right in pointing out that the big countries played the leading role in the development towards world disintegration in the field of trade; undoubtedly, also, the United States has been in a particularly strategic position in this context, both because of the height of its trade barriers and because of its size and its dominant position as the main creditor country. But in this general climate, the smaller countries are following the same course, even if they have not yet moved so far towards effective autarky.

The above analysis has been focused on the industrially advanced countries; it is, however, also fully relevant to the underdeveloped countries. They are now emerging from the lethargy of foreign political and economic domination and internal stagnation, and are attempting, against heavy odds, to press on with their economic development; but they do not adopt the relatively liberal policies in their foreign economic relations that were followed by the developed countries in their early stages of development. Indeed, they cannot do so, as the world environment into which they have to fit themselves is no longer what it was for those other countries in the nineteenth century.

They are, therefore, bound to equip themselves with the nationalistic economic policies that were forged by the advanced countries after 1914. As a matter of fact, they are compelled to give these policies an even more radical shape, as their national development needs are so much more urgent and as all their margins are narrower and their resources scantier; this question will be discussed further in Chapter XIII, dealing with the commercial policy of underdeveloped countries.

In their struggle for national independence and economic development strong forces of nationalism are released which give emotional force to these policies. Even in this respect the underdeveloped countries are not out of tune with what has been happening in recent decades in the advanced countries.

THE DETERIORATION OF INTERNATIONAL LAW

This play of forces has resulted in the gradual paralysis of the inherited quasi-automatic system of national adjustments to the exigencies of international trade. On a deeper level of policy attitudes, the norms and mores of a previously more integrated—partial—world economy which, as always, derived their social reality from being unquestioned and obeyed, were permanently destroyed as they were repeatedly disobeyed. An example of these fallen idols is the whole complex of functionally purposive behavior patterns and taboos upholding the gold standard.

Related to this has been the gradual deterioration of international law as we knew it prior to the First World War. The closely knit international community of economically progressive countries, which I have referred to as the partial world of the period before 1914, had seen the development of an ever-more-diversified body of commonly respected rules for correct behavior in public and private international relations. These rules had their origin partly in regular intergovernmental treaties and conventions, but they also grew out of a gradually established common law practice. Increasingly they were reflected in domestic laws and their administration and execution; as a matter of fact these national streams of legislation and precedents were a main source of international law. All this was then systematized—and so strengthened and made still more specific—into a consolidated doctrine of international jurisprudence, which also drew on the ancient inheritance of a *jus gentium*.

The true nature of this international law as it existed in the era before 1914 and, particularly, the crucial question of its sanctions, was widely disputed; but meanwhile it functioned with considerable efficiency and resulted in a high degree of security in international business. Obligations stretching over national boundaries were honored, and the foreigner's rights were respected. We may recall that before the First World War alien property rights were protected even during war and even when the property owner belonged to an enemy state.

Under the pressure of the sequence of wars and international crises and the growth of the new nationalism since 1914, this situation has changed fundamentally. The precedents in interstate relations set during this period, beginning with the German invasion of neutral Belgium in spite of solemn written commitments, have everywhere and continuously been breaches of the agreed rules. By a mutual process of competition in ruthlessly exploiting strategic interests, the whole body of international law governing the conduct of warfare—built upon the distinction between the soldier and the civilian and incorporated in the Hague and Geneva Conventions—is thus in almost complete ruin, as we all know too well. Conventional war has changed to total war, bound by no limitations other than those imposed by military expediency; with the enormous destructive power of the new, unconventional weapons there seems to be no way back.

Even in the economic and financial sphere the rule of international law has been severely weakened. As the volume of state interference has increased the very concept of property has gradually changed in all countries. The now accepted practice that belligerent states can do as they please with enemy property—which is only an application of the new doctrine of total war—has naturally dealt a severe blow to the basic principle of the old international law that foreign property is inviolable. A principle is, so to speak, indivisible and must be universally applicable; failure to apply it in one field tends to undermine its general validity.

For a time—and particularly in countries under economic and political domination—this principle of the inviolability of foreign property frequently resulted in preferential treatment of the foreigner. It was, for example, often accepted, or still is accepted, that foreigners have a right to compensation for nationalization measures, even when such an obligation is not recognized for citizens.

In the modern state nationalization is, however, only one among a large number of state interferences with property rights, many of these implying financial burdens on the property owner. With the present increase of state activity in the economic field, it becomes practically and politically impossible to preserve a sanctuary for foreign property. In fact, the old principle was related to quite a different kind of state and in the new state now coming into being it loses its original meaning. The effect is, however, a lowered degree of security throughout the whole field of international business.

The evolution of international law in the economic and financial field, like that of all other law, is, of course, only one element in the totality of changes in the national economies and their interrelations, and it is hardly one of the basic elements. A reconstruction of international law aimed at recreating a measure of security in international business will naturally and to a large extent have to be in the nature of an adjustment to new circumstances.

It will, in fact, concern the same problems and meet the same difficulties as generally do the efforts to coordinate national economic policies, about which I have some comments later in this chapter. As a matter of fact, the reconstruction of international law is part and parcel of this more general problem; law has no independent existence outside its social context. Law must be operational; it can be established neither by pronouncements, nor by majority votes in international organizations, nor by writing constitutions for "superstates" which have as yet no basis in international solidarity.

For the time being, what we have seen is the breakdown of international law as inherited from the nineteenth century, without its replacement by a body of rules better adjusted to the rapidly changing world and, therefore, accepted as part of social reality with standards that are actually being applied. The present state of legal anarchy is a significant element in the process of international economic disintegration which we are here studying. It hardly needs mentioning that in this sphere, too, it has been the bigger of the industrially advanced countries that have taken the lead in gradually destroying a functioning international system, while for natural reasons the smaller ones in this group have had a greater interest in attempting to preserve and uphold the crumbling international law.

INTERNATIONAL DISINTEGRATION FROM A NATIONAL POINT OF VIEW

Ordinary citizens in our advanced countries are usually only mildly disturbed when confronted with this grim diagnosis of the world's economic disintegration; they are naturally more concerned with problems nearer home. Paradoxically, on this closer national scene there has meanwhile been progress and integration.

In spite of world wars and depressions, we have seen in each of our advanced countries a tremendous rise in productivity, security of employment, and standards of living, and also greater equality of opportunity for the individual citizens and a general equalization of incomes and wealth. In the last forty years, with all their international turmoils, these countries have witnessed a more rapid national integration than ever before in history. The ordinary citizen is apt to believe—and very largely with good reason—that the national policies by which this has been brought about are good, even if they are exactly those which are here pictured as the causes of international disintegration.

I believe we may completely misinterpret the whole problem of how the development to international disintegration may be reversed if we do not try to go deeper in our understanding of the purposes of the national policies we are bound to criticize when we apply the value premise of international integration. These policies are, indeed, mostly —by no means always—motivated by good reasons, and nationally they have on the whole been successful.

If we want to avoid their resulting in increasing international disintegration, our duty is to propose such adjustments to them as will be favorable to international integration, while at the same time taking care to protect equally well or even better the national interests that they serve. That this should theoretically be possible is implied in the faith I have expressed, that national economic progress and integration can only reach the highest possible levels in a well-integrated world.

We might first observe that the interest in stable markets—which also implies stable employment and continuous high utilization of plant and machinery, as well as of the distribution apparatus—is naturally a very legitimate one. If we wish to prevent this interest from expressing itself in national policies implying discrimination against foreign markets, we must find the means of giving increased stability to the international economy. This special reason for a nationalistic economic policy is bound to become ever more urgent; for the importance to individual enterprises and to the national economies of stable markets—and hence the economic disadvantage of unstable markets—has been steadily increasing, and will continue to do so, as modern industry progresses towards a higher level of mechanization and capital intensity.

More particularly, full employment is a legitimate national interest, not only socially but also economically. Full employment largely explains why investment and production have been held on such very high and generally rising levels after the Second World War in most industrial countries and why productivity has been making such strides. At the high level of capital costs, typical of modern industry, enormous productivity gains follow from a high and stable level of employment. A high level of output permits higher savings, investment risks are at the same time reduced, and the more capital-intensive methods, resulting from the higher savings and investments, induce a further rise in total output.

The experience of the Great Depression and the popular appeal of the type of thinking we have become accustomed to associate with the name of Keynes have been epoch-making in our countries. No well-integrated nation will now hesitate to assert its control over exports, imports, and foreign exchange, if it is a question of maintaining the level of employment. Once more, to avert national discrimination against foreign trade and restrictive controls of foreign payments, invoked to defend full employment in the individual countries, we must organize the whole world economy by concerted international action in such a way that depressing effects on national welfare from events outside a country's national boundaries are less likely to arise.

The conflict between the aims and policies of the national welfare state and the ideal of international integration becomes intense when we consider the redistributional aspects of national economic policy. All the advanced countries have embarked in recent decades upon a comprehensive complex of fiscal and social policies aimed at a fairer sharing between their citizens of the exigencies of economic fortune; but this ever more intensified solidarity stops at the national boundary.

However, the main reason why these national welfare systems tend to disintegrate the world economy is that, as I pointed out in Chapter III, the redistributional intentions are not limited to a direct transfer of income via the collectors of taxes and insurance contributions, but invade the whole field of national economic policy, changing the basic conditions for the operation of the price system.

Workers in the United States have a long-standing tradition of regarding protective tariffs over practically the whole industrial field as a justifiable defense of their own living standards—which they know are high—since they prevent the products of cheap foreign labor from intruding upon the American market. The fact that this argument has logical flaws, and yet, in spite of all the orthodox teachings of the theory of comparative costs by generations of professors of economics, is nevertheless so tenaciously upheld, demonstrates how solidarity is limited to the nation. Nationalism is stronger than reason.

When the redistributional policies come to be applied in the broader field of economics, this is usually, however, not the result of an intellectual mistake but, in the given setting of international relations, quite a rational approach. In almost all the advanced countries farmers have needed state assistance to preserve their living standards on more or less the same level as other social groups and, following the principle of solidarity, the nonagricultural majority of citizens has everywhere been prepared to accept very far-reaching modifications of the price system in order to ensure some degree of "price parity" for farm production.

Such agricultural price policies have everywhere become important cornerstones in the construction of the modern welfare state, but it has never seriously occurred to any influential and politically responsible group in any country that this expression of solidarity should expand beyond the state boundary. Instead, the international market has been freely used as a dumping ground, hurting particularly those exporting countries that have narrow margins and have to count their foreign exchange carefully.

In this connection it is interesting and illustrative to compare, on the one hand, the universal acceptance by a national political majority of the obligation to support economically the farming minority at home—almost as if it were self-evident—and, on the other hand, the cold-hearted disinclination in the industrial countries to do anything at all in order to stabilize the prices of raw materials and staple agricultural commodities of the underdeveloped and very poor countries, whose whole economic and political existence is continuously in jeopardy because of their unstable export markets. We are faced here, not only with an unwillingness to accept a real redistribution of incomes, like the one that has been accepted within their own countries, but also with a reluctance even to consider schemes that would merely stabilize the markets over a period of years, without any international redistribution.

Agricultural policy is only one example, but an outstanding one, because of the large number of beneficiaries and the large aggregate amount of income redistribution involved. The same principle of national solidarity and almost total disregard of the interests of the foreigner operates over the whole field of economic policy. Everywhere there is demonstrated a readiness to improve the economic basis of national production; at bottom, a social equality and welfare interest is often the driving force. This is true of the coal policy in Britain, of the regulation of the fishing industry in Norway, and of wine production in France, to mention only a few examples.

The fixing of differential tariffs by the publicly owned and publicly managed railroads offers a flexible means in most countries of reallocating the relative advantage of national industries—and of discriminating against the foreigner. The same often goes for other means of communication, like ports and airlines. The whole body of regulations in the shipping industry follows the same pattern; a Norwegian is apt to point out that the high subsidies paid to the American shipping industry and the protection given it by other means in the postwar period may have cost the Norwegian economy more than all it received in the way of Marshall aid. As the state and local authorities handle ever larger budgets and so become increasingly important as buyers in many markets, their orders for goods and services are, by law or custom, directed so as to encourage so far as possible domestic industry. In all cases the purely national interest is emphasized and the principle of national solidarity followed.

Measures against restrictive business practices are a good illustration of the nationalistic direction of economic policy. While most governments have introduced legislation against internal cartels, in order to protect the consumers from exploitation, few responsible politicians would be prepared to extend this kindly interest to the protection of the foreign buyer, and in the international markets cartels have so far been given free play. In most parliaments it would, indeed, be looked upon as a strange and almost subversive thought if somebody were to suggest that sometimes the foreigner's interests in paying less for exports from the country than he is at present obliged to might need protection. Directed towards the outside, monopolistic exploitation becomes a patriotic virtue.

To except the international cartels from control is, incidentally, often a mistake from a national point of view. In many cases the international cartels are in reality collusions of industries in different countries, agreeing to leave each other undisturbed by competition from taking what the traffic will bear in their established markets. The powerful Scandinavian pulp and paper cartel has many purposes, but one is to permit the paper industry to charge higher prices at home; for decades stationery, produced from Scandinavian raw materials and often exported in the form of paper, could be bought cheaper in London than in Stockholm.

Apart from this and other self-deceptions—and economic policy is, relatively speaking, less influenced by ignorance and emotional irrationality than foreign policy in general[9]—the nationalistic economic policies of the modern welfare state are rationally suited to their purposes: to create more stable markets and to bring about a redistribution of incomes within the nation. The greater capital intensity of modern industry tends continuously to magnify the first interest. The progressing national integration is partly a result of the pursuit of the second interest, but is at the same time continuously strengthening its driving force.

This process, by which national integration induces international disintegration, is thus cumulative. International disintegration in its turn implies that foreign markets become even more unstable, which again strengthens the rational urge to concentrate on the home market and give it better protection, for the sake of internal stability. Progressive international disintegration makes it likewise ever more difficult to visualize clearly, and to urge effectively, a policy of international, instead of national, solidarity.

The international payments problem is discussed in Chaper VI. It has naturally taken its present aggravated form as a result of the international crises, with their major disturbances of the trading and payments positions. A deeper and more permanent cause, however, is the unwillingness of the national welfare states to accept the infringements on their policies of economic stability and economic equality that an automatic trade and payments system would imply if it were to bring about changes in the national economies corresponding to changes in international economic relations. The whole complex of national policies, to which I have referred above, introduces rigidities—from an international point of view—that limit the possibilities of adjustments to ensure balance of payments equilibrium without short-term controls over international trade and payments.

To restore convertibility and eliminate trade discriminations that are caused by payments difficulties and that do not, per se, represent national interests, would seem to be a first step in preventing further international disintegration. The problem is, however, whether even this very modest goal can be reached in a world where the more basic national interventions have gone so far and are backed by such strong national interests.

INTERNATIONALIZATION OF NATIONAL POLICIES

This general world conflict between national and international integration obviously cannot be resolved in the interest of the latter ideal simply by preaching internationalism and denouncing nationalism. No advanced country is prepared to give up, or even to risk slightly, the fruits of national integration, which remains a supreme value to its citizens. And the goal for underdeveloped countries must be to start their own processes towards national integration; their success in doing so is also a first precondition for their incorporation in a better integrated world. To deprive nations of their right to organize their own affairs and, in particular, to control and steer their internal economic development, is out of the question.

It is wrong to believe that the volume of national interventions that could be abolished in a process of simple "international economic disarmament" is large. It is true that some of them stem from misunderstandings of reality; even more of them have been instigated by special interest groups without ever having been intellectually tested by having their consequences thoroughly explained to and understood by the people. It is my view, for instance, that the strict control over international migration, which is discussed in Chaper VII, largely belongs to this category of measures, which it was possible to push through only because of ignorance, apathy, or nationalistic emotionalism among the general public, as does also the high protectionism of the United States, whose economy stands for various reasons in a special position.

More generally, we should note that some smaller and highly developed national welfare states, such as the Scandinavian ones, have traditionally followed a much less autarkic economic policy than the bigger ones and have nevertheless succeeded in reaching an exceptionally high level of national economic integration and in maintaining a rate of economic progress and a standard of living as high as or higher than the bigger, more autarkic countries. This should serve as an indication that there is room for reconsidering many of the present national economic policies.

We should only be deceiving ourselves, however, if we did not recognize the fact that in most cases there are valid national reasons for these policies. In many cases there exists also an interrelationship between different types of national policies which makes it difficult or impossible to abolish even those that are not strongly backed by national interests for their own sake. Most industrially advanced countries may sincerely want to abolish, if they could, those trade and payments regulations that are directly caused by payments difficulties. However, the lack of international balance revealed by the payments difficulties is itself the result not only of the changes caused by wars and the like, but also of the trend to national integration and the national policies, inherent in this trend, aimed at stability and equality. These policies the governments are not in a position to renounce. They have mostly very important national purposes, even if their total effects—direct and indirect—are disastrous for international integration.

"The fact is that we have moved far from a world in which complete international specialization of labor is possible. Some of the rigidities . . . are here to stay. . . . This means that completely free trade is not feasible." Behind this statement of a commonly accepted negative fact, which I have chosen to cite from the recent Randall Report,[10] is the more important and positive fact stressed in Chapter III, that national integration, though it has its essence in equalization of opportunity for people in all social groups and geographical areas, has not been achieved simply by the abolition of barriers within the country, but rather by a process of social organization.

If, therefore, we realize that it is a misdirected and, in any event, hopeless attempt to try to reach international integration unless it be as a concomitant and, indeed, as a further development of national integration, we have to draw the further conclusion that international integration in this age has similarly to imply more than a breaking down of national barriers; it has to attempt reunification and harmonization of the national policies of cooperating states.[11]

The task for international integration becomes, then, a matter of coordination. International labor and capital movements or freer trade cannot be expected to re-emerge simply as a result of agreements to undo national policies. On both sides of every boundary practically all "markets" are now highly organized by the state and by interest groups. What is needed is *an internationalization of these national policy structures themselves, preserving the essential values they represent to the several nations.*

If governments came together intent upon a more ambitious cooperation of this kind, some of the present policies would clearly be seen to be misdirected and irrational. In many other cases it would become apparent that national protective measures served interests which, even when not unimportant viewed unilaterally, are minor compared with the major common gains that could be realized by mutual agreement to abstain from them. This is all in the realm of what I called "international economic disarmament."

There are, though, other policies—for example, agricultural protection or other intentional support of industries as part of a national development program—that are indispensable from the national point of view. If, however, these policies were worked out on the basis of international solidarity, they could be framed so as not to lead to a competition between the countries to shift their burdens onto each other.

A primary object of cooperation would naturally be to create stable international markets and, in particular, to guarantee a stable world trend of business and production. To the extent that stability was achieved, a great number of existing national policies would prove unnecessary and, in the first instance, the quantitative trade and payments restrictions, unpopular with all governments, could be abolished.

In this new type of international relations, founded upon a widening of economic solidarity, freer movement of labor and capital would play a natural role, as also would, in some measure, the sharing of burdens for common objectives, and even the giving of economic aid.

As was the case in the advanced nation-states, which offer a prototype for our model of international economic integration, this whole process would need the impetus and momentum of economic progress. Only in an expanding world economy will there exist the conditions for mutual generosity without which the integration process would not get far.

The whole movement towards international integration along these lines will have to be argued in positive terms of the wider community of interests and aspirations, not the negative ones of wanting to break up the defenses of national integration. Indeed, the stepping stone will have to be the recognition of the great accomplishment that national integration really is in a few advanced countries. The goal has to be one of transforming this national integration into a more inclusive international solidarity. It must meet the request of actually strengthening the values of national integration—and it will have to be realized that a great hindrance to international integration is the fact that so many countries are still badly integrated nationally.

This is a technically much more difficult task than the old internationalists, who saw the problem only in terms of tearing down barriers, have ever grasped. Yet this task of coordinating national policies is the one we are actually attempting to grapple with in the international organizations when, on occasion, we succeed in proceeding one step beyond the delivery by delegates of propaganda speeches and the voting of pious resolutions. Even though our attempts so far are feeble and the results small and insecure, this is the task and there is no way around it.

THE NEED FOR INTERNATIONAL SOLIDARITY

Too often, when the internationalist denounces nationalistic economic policies, he finds himself in the company of the reactionaries, who in all our countries are waging a rearguard battle against the developing welfare state. And so he becomes allied with—and, with him, unfortunately, his ideal of international integration—historical forces which in the long run are bound to lose out.

There is to my mind no doubt—and I shall develop this thought in the next chapter—that, basically, the reason why efforts towards international integration in Western Europe have achieved so little is that the deeper questions have not been faced honestly and courageously. It was assumed that international integration could be attained without the basis of solidarity that national integration required, and without accepting the consequences of such widened solidarity. Under these circumstances the common man in Europe remained cold and suspicious. He felt that this was perhaps a new way of raising obstacles to national welfare policies.

There is no retreat from the welfare state, and its further growth is intimately bound up with further progress in national integration. The events of the last two years in America under a Republican regime, where the main social advances made under the Democratic New Deal and in the entire field of economic policy have been preserved or extended,[12] and similar features of Conservative rule in Britain, Australia, and New Zealand after an era of Labor governments, seem amply to illustrate this point. The biggest break we can expect in the trend towards the welfare state is the flatness of an individual step in a staircase.

A social trend is never an entirely straight line but moves by fits and starts. In addition to a natural tendency for a certain slowing down after a prolonged and rapid upward movement, we have had in recent years the complicated reactions to the cold war and the heavy burden of defense expenditure. These changing historical circumstances, and the counterbalancing main trend towards the welfare state, firmly backed by the interests and valuations of a democracy, have such an overwhelming preponderance that the fluctuations of political parties and personalities in power are almost without influence, if we take the broad and long view. As a matter of fact, the break in the upward movement has not been very much larger in the United States and Britain than in those Scandinavian countries which have been continuously governed by the Labor parties, as a matter of tradition.

From an international point of view, national economic policy is not to blame for seeking stability and equalization. Its failing is that it restricts solidarity to the individual nations. We have to attempt to build a better integrated world upon states that are all, and for the most excellent reasons, continuously seeking better integration nationally. To face this issue clearly is the first requirement when attempting to tackle the problem of international integration.

I have criticized traditional internationalism—that seeks a short cut to international integration by the simple and wholesale abolition of national economic policies—as not only reactionary but also as ineffective, since it goes against an immutable historical trend, determined by people's interests and valuations in a democracy. I do not pretend that my proposed substitution—a policy of international coordination of national policies based upon a widened international solidarity—is an easy road. All the succeeding chapters demonstrate the almost insurmountable difficulties that have to be overcome; the present trend undoubtedly points in the direction of continued and increased international disintegration. I do, however, believe that while the other solution is not practical—and, in addition, would harm values that are dear to us and destroy accomplishments that are the pride of our generation—this one is, at least, a sensible goal, however difficult to reach, and one that good and well-informed people would wish to strive for.

ATTITUDES AND INSTITUTIONS

To meet this challenge, the moralist will urge a stricter adherence by people in their actual behavior to their expressed valuations on the more general plane, where those valuations are freer from group and national prejudices and other narrow, immediate interests; sometimes he will also urge a change of those valuations. The modern educator—following the usage of the psychologist—prefers to speak about attitudes while meaning much the same thing; he stresses that to build up a better world community people must first be trained to become more loyal world citizens. The reformer-politician attempts to lead people towards a gradual change in attitudes and tries to stabilize, and sometimes to cause, such changes by creating the *fait accompli* of political action.

The social scientist has no quarrel to pick with the moralist, the educator, or the politician, whose different approaches to reform are determined by the fact that they are moving on different levels of social activity and, consequently, view social interrelations under different perspectives. His own contribution to the discussion about how to reform society is to stress the institutional factor: admitting the undoubted truth that the gradual realization of a world community will need people with changed attitudes, it is also true that it is most difficult to change attitudes, except by conditioning people through their life and work within the framework of a changed society.

The social scientist is then exposing the real difficulty that all reformers meet. Every induced social change has to follow the pattern of lifting oneself by one's own bootstraps: society with its forms and norms has to be altered *pari passu* with the people, and its advance should, if possible, be a little ahead of the people. Since, under democracy, society can only be altered with the consent of the people, this explains why it is most often a slow process. That, nonetheless, reform is possible is explained by the fact, first, that people's attitudes are not homogeneous but composed of very diversified and partly conflicting valuations and, second, that in their activity in the formal organs for democratic decisions individuals can be induced to allow their more general valuations to dominate; these valuations are closer to basic ideals and, consequently, more liberal and generous than the diversified valuations determining behavior in everyday life.[13]

This relationship between attitudes and social institutions is not, however, exclusively an obstacle to the reformer. It also provides a measure of assurance, since the implication is that every time a step is taken in the right direction by inducing an alteration of society, this will tend to condition the people living in that society to uphold the change and will make them readier to take a further step.

In the international field reforms are much more difficult than in the national one. To be really effective, the efforts to make a radical change in nations' attitudes to each other and to educate all nations for international solidarity would assume an existing world community, a functioning system of norms, policies, and patterns of behavior within the framework of which people could experience their participation in the developing wider solidarity. We always learn best by doing.

It is the strength of the national state that it is actually functioning. As I have stressed, the national machinery, based upon—and constantly developing further—the national solidarity, is strong and becomes ever stronger. The international machinery is, in contrast, weak and still without any appreciable basis in people's allegiance; it is constantly being weakened because of the very fact that the national machinery of the modern welfare state is strengthened.

We have to start from where we are. Those hesitant approaches to a world community so far made belong to the realm of institutions represented by the various weak international organizations and of bilateral and multilateral negotiations and agreements between sovereign governments within or outside these organizations. The existing formal organs for intergovernmental cooperation in the economic field—however weak they are for the time being and however meager the practical results of their work—do nevertheless constitute our only existing institutional basis for efforts to build up practical international solidarity. They were created when there were hopes for very much greater and more immediate practical achievements; the fact that they still survive even under circumstances where they have become rather ineffective can be explained only by the existence of certain general internationalist attitudes, which in their turn depend for their survival in the less favorable conditions of today upon the continued existence of these institutions.[14]

When, inside or outside these organizations, an intergovernmental agreement is reached, even on a minor issue, this usually has an additional and cumulative effect of strengthening the basis for the internationalist attitudes and thereby making further agreements more possible. This relation between attitudes and institutions, even if not spelled out in this way, is sensed by all international and national officials who are engaged in the drudgery of the intergovernmental organizations and in intergovernmental negotiations. It gives significance and meaning to labor on the details of all the technical issues into which the efforts towards international understanding and cooperation branch out as soon as they are directed towards reaching practical results. From this point of view of their cumulative effects upon attitudes and, therefore, possibilities for further advance, even small institutional accomplishments become potentially important.

The vision should be preserved, the broad goals marked out; but the road goes over laborious mountains of small and big obstacles to intergovernmental agreements which, when traversed, move us only a fraction of an inch forward. On the present level of low institutional efficiency and faltering popular allegiance, the movement is of necessity slow, but if enough good people keep on plodding—not giving up even in periods like the present one, when practical goals that ten years ago seemed in their reach are constantly appearing more unattainable—and remain prepared to cash in on every favorable change of the circumstances, momentum may gradually be gathered that will then give speed to progress.

That this will happen is by no means certain; an objective forecast at the present time could not give it a high probability coefficient. But if it happens, the change of attitudes will not come as a sudden dramatic conversion of nations to internationalism but will, as always, be in the nature of a gradual maturing of the effects of countless efforts, spread over years and decades.

It is thus not inconceivable that, under favorable conditions and in the course of time, the common experience of a growing volume of intergovernmental agreements, aimed at synchronizing and coordinating national policies, and of the beneficial results to all nations of such agreements, may tend to strengthen the basis of international solidarity and thus make possible an ever greater volume of agreements. The process would be cumulative and self-perpetuating, as are all social processes, whether they go upwards or downwards.

The crux of the problem is, however, that to start the international system moving upwards towards cooperation and integration instead of downwards, as in recent years, would itself require fundamental changes of popular attitudes. By some means the growing nationalism would have to be counteracted. As it is rooted in all present policy trends and as support from an existing international community is weak, this great educational process has to be pursued against great odds.

It is not possible to feel optimistic. The process of national integration makes the need for international integration ever greater but, at the same time, increases tremendously the difficulties of accomplishing it. This is one of the main contradictions implicit in practically all our present economic policies in all our countries.

CHAPTER V

Note on West-European
Economic Integration

The problem to be dealt with here is a limited one, as it concerns only a regional group of countries which have for so long had such close relations that for centuries it has even been suggested seriously that they should unite politically.

Apart from the recent attempt to unite Western Europe, the last time European unity was actually planned in practical terms, and even partially realized by political action—in a fashion—was during Nazi Germany's drive for what was then called "the new Europe." Nobody since has analyzed the rather detailed programing for regional economic integration which was encompassed in the German stratagem under Hitler.

Postwar plans for the political unification of Western Europe will not be touched upon here, nor their motivation as policy measures in the East–West conflict. The present analysis is technical and confined to the ambitious movement for the economic integration of Western Europe. The international importance of this region lends a special interest to the question; its discussion affords, in addition, an opportunity for carrying out a case study with a bearing on the general theme of this book.[1]

THE RECORD

Indeed, the relative failure of the strivings during recent years towards West European economic integration makes a somber record that deserves the most careful examination of its deeper causes; we should not be allowed to forget it too comfortably. To find out why this dramatically staged policy did not meet with greater success should be of particularly serious concern to the internationalist who has his heart in the matter.

56

Goals were proclaimed in general but specific terms, basic agreements were signed by the governments and ratified by the parliaments, institutional forms were created in abundance, beginnings were made on a large scale towards coordinated over-all economic planning for the region. More specific plans for decisive practical steps towards economic integration in Western Europe were drawn up and from time to time generously acclaimed and sometimes even formally adopted by the governments.

The creation of a European customs union was one of those plans, and an agency was set up in 1947. The agency still exists, now doing useful though humble work on the unification of customs nomenclatures.

Parallel to this comprehensive plan, the idea of a number of smaller customs unions was launched, each embracing two or three neighboring countries. Negotiations followed—among the Scandinavian countries, between France and Italy, and Greece and Turkey—and in the case of the Franco-Italian customs union a treaty was signed by the foreign ministers. But at the end of it all there were no practical results to be shown, and these attempts are no longer actively pursued. The Benelux union, founded during the war, has not reached the goals it had set itself; but, against this background, it still stands out as a relative success, and efforts towards further development are being pursued. Likewise, in Scandinavia a redefinition of the problem in terms of partial, more specific, and practical tasks of economic cooperation is under way and may perhaps in due course achieve some results.

At a somewhat later stage the international coordination of investments was acclaimed as a main solution of the problem of economic integration. This attempted an attack on a somewhat deeper level. The need to reconstruct and expand the physical bases for industry in Europe after the decay caused by the Great Depression and the destruction of the Second World War presented a great opportunity, even if it is one we hope will never recur. Furthermore, the extraordinary American aid to Western Europe furnished large quantities of capital from outside; this should have made coordination of investments much easier, apart from the fact that a reasonable coordination was a natural condition for American aid. Intensive investigations and negotiations involving industries as well as governments were actually carried out. But again there were scarcely any practical results, and these attempts have since been largely abandoned.

Instead, the emphasis was for a time laid on trade liberalization. In the years immediately after the war the European countries had had to open up channels for the flow of trade by means of bilateral trade and payments agreements. The quantitative regulations of foreign trade, which were implied in this first drive to get trade going again, were repellent to all West-European countries and were nowhere absorbed into national long-term policies. At that early time it was confidently expected in all these countries that they were passing through a transitory phase towards freer, multilateral, and nondiscriminatory trade.

The practical problem of freeing intra-European trade from bilateralism and quantitative restrictions was now tackled with determination, and substantial American capital aid was allocated with the special purpose of giving momentum to this policy. Without doubt the trade liberalization program of the Organization for European Economic Cooperation contributed effectively to the revival of intra-European trade. With its European Payments Union arrangements, it still stands out as one of the more solid achievements in the efforts towards Western European integration.

The severe setback in 1951 demonstrated, however, its rather frail foundation. Further, and for several reasons, the "liberalization percentages," by which progress was popularly measured, implied a large overstatement of the true degree of trade liberalization reached. It turned out to be particularly difficult to make real progress with the abolition of quantitative restrictions on agricultural products. In many cases liberalization from quantitative restrictions has been accompanied by increases in tariffs.

Taking an over-all view of the present situation, trade liberalization in Western Europe has not reached the normalization of trade relations which was confidently hoped for in all these countries immediately after the war, when bilateral agreements and quantitative restrictions had to be relied upon as a transitory means of opening up trade. Neither should it be overlooked that the whole program rests upon a systematic and general discrimination against the United States and the dollar area.

The apparent limitations to the freeing of trade through liberalization led to the search for other methods. "Integration by sector" became for a time the new practical goal. The one important step that has so far been taken is the European Coal and Steel Community. Its experiences up to date illustrate the peculiar difficulties of coordinating one sector of different national economies while leaving the other sectors, as well as the national monetary and social policies generally, uncoordinated. If the Community has, so far, been weathering these difficulties and actually been able to take certain steps towards creating a more unified market in coal and steel for member countries, it is largely because these commodities, in spite of their basic importance, nevertheless represent only a comparatively small part of total production and trade, and also because nothing has been changed very much. Attempts to apply the sector approach to other economic fields that, like coal and steel, are apt to fall outside the scope of trade liberalization—for example, agriculture and transport—have met with little success.

In this situation a mood of general skepticism has been spreading. It is hardly broken by a courageous continuation of the attempts, which have been going on all the time, to seek, simultaneously, a solution of the economic problems while creating new political forms and writing constitutions for new political entities embracing all Western Europe or a part of it. For reasons which will presently be touched upon, these attempts are not likely to succeed.

THE SUPERFICIALITY OF APPROACH

This sketch of goals and accomplishments in West European economic integration should be read against the background of what were in many ways unusually favorable conditions for unification that existed in this part of the world after the war.

The countries concerned—even the South-European countries—are all fairly advanced, industrially and culturally, when compared with the world average. Literacy is high, and all these nations have for centuries lived in very close contact with each other. Internal trade in Europe, unlike every other region, has always been a very important part of its total international trade. Until the First World War there was in Europe an almost free market for capital, and to a large extent these countries constituted a common labor market. In ideals and aspirations they show, with all their differences, a great similarity.

After the war, most of these countries had big reconstruction problems to tackle and all of them embarked upon ambitious development plans. The large-scale American aid they received, together with the prevailing circumstances, enabled them to carry out their policy of extraordinarily high investment in a general climate of boom and expansion. All this should have increased both the opportunities and the practical possibilities for the economic cooperation to which they had pledged themselves. The Americans, in fact, and with increasing emphasis, made economic integration an assumption and a condition for further aid. To the intrinsic good reasons for integration was therefore added powerful outside political pressure.

In spite of all this we have now to admit relative failure in terms of the goals declared and the government commitments undertaken. One major explanation is the superficiality of concentrating the efforts mainly on trade and payments and evading the more fundamental problems of the factors of production. This approach is easily understandable, as trade and payments have been for all governments the most pressing day-to-day problems, while international integration is typically a long-term proposition.

To some extent I assume we are also all, to a greater or lesser degree, influenced by the classical theory of international trade, which by assuming international immobility of factors of production laid all the responsibility for international adjustments on trade and nevertheless came out with a beautiful equilibrium. It presupposed, however, fluid internal markets, including the labor market, instantaneous adjustments —and consequently automatic and continuous full employment—and a lot of other things.

In any event, when European and American mentors in their plea for the "single market" pointed to the example of the United States, they regularly forgot to mention that there is free and unhampered passage over the state boundaries in the United States not only for commodities, but also for labor and capital, and that under modern conditions the one thing is very much a condition of the other. Also, it was seldom pointed out that industries in the United States grew up and expanded in a unified market; the conversion of existing industries to a new pattern is much more difficult. It cannot be done simply by freeing trade if all the other rigidities are left undisturbed.

From an economic point of view, the advantage to be reaped from a closer economic integration is higher productivity. Freer competition within a larger market would squeeze out less productive enterprises while permitting the more efficient ones to expand. This in its turn would lead to a more rational division of labor, in which each country could specialize in the lines of production in which it had the greatest comparative advantage. This reallocation of factors and resources would also bring with it the benefits of large-scale production.

To this general trend of thought one reservation should be made and one corollary stated. The reservation is that a larger home market is not the only factor in productivity and perhaps sometimes not even the most important one. Among the countries of Western Europe that have reached relatively high levels of productivity—and which are therefore, on the whole, economically progressive and enjoy high living standards —the smallest countries are well represented: Sweden and Switzerland, who succeeded in staying out of both world wars, are general examples; for high productivity in industrialized agriculture we have Denmark and Holland; in shipping, Norway; in forestry and timber, Finland; and in fishing, Iceland; to those can be added Belgium and Luxembourg for the steel industry.

It is typical and in line with our general argument that all these smaller countries seek the international market for selling the goods in the production of which they are particularly efficient and which they succeed in producing on a large scale. The examples mentioned are all export industries. In the last chapter I pointed to the general tendency of the smaller countries to be less autarkic than the large ones. Yet they face the international market, with all its restrictions, on equal terms with the bigger countries—actually on considerably less than equal terms, as they cannot exercise the pressure of size and, with the exception of Belgium and, to a lesser extent, Holland, have no dependencies where they can discriminate in favor of their own products.

On the other hand, one may ask whether the home markets of the larger countries in Western Europe—each with 40 to 50 million people, not to mention the populations of the dependencies they have succeeded in incorporating in their home markets—are really too small to permit their industries to enjoy the benefits of competition and large-scale production or whether there are not other causes for these deficiencies.

We are not attempting to deny the very great importance of the larger home market, or the probable increase in this importance because of the progressive intensity of capital in modern production. We only wish to remind ourselves that the failure to attain higher productivity in West-European countries in general is obviously not due only to the limited size of their markets.[2]

The corollary is this: the reallocation of production between countries, which is the very means by which the larger market leads to a gain in productivity, presupposes a mobility of capital and labor resources within the larger area and, furthermore, the scrapping of many less efficient plants and, *in toto,* a large volume of new investment.

As we know, however, the international capital market in Europe remained frozen as it was inherited from the frustrated thirties,[3] and no attempts whatsoever were made to unfreeze it, not even during the period of the big influx of American capital aid, when the task would have been relatively easier. Similarly, no serious and large-scale attempts were made to re-establish a European labor market.[4]

Under these circumstances, the efforts towards West-European economic integration were bound to meet with frustration. The Norwegians, for example, who after the war had concentrated their investments on reconstructing their merchant marine, were not prepared to join in a Scandinavian customs union in which their own less efficient manufacturing industry would have been outstripped by the more efficient Swedish and Danish ones. The Norwegians are only three million people living in closely knit national solidarity, and they would not want to see their industrial workers thrown into unemployment; nor would they want to find them migrating to Sweden, even if the Swedes, who are themselves barely more than seven million, received them as brethren—by no means a certainty, if they came suddenly and in large numbers.

I have already pointed out that if the European Coal and Steel Community has been able to take certain steps in order to free the markets of coal and steel as between its six member countries, this is largely due to the fact that, in spite of the basic importance of these two commodities, they nevertheless do not amount to a very large part of total production and trade. It must be added, however, that the two countries in the group which show significant cost disparities, namely Italy and Belguim, are still protected and that, more generally, heavy transport costs provide a measure of national protection to compensate against whatever cost differences do exist. In addition, both industries have strong traditions of cartelization which the Community has been careful not to break down in any violent way. As usual, such tendencies do not support dynamic forces for change but are rather in the nature of collusions for protecting a *status quo* on the principle of "live and let live." All in all, not much has happened to the basic structure of these industries. And it is fairly safe to predict that if ever the actions of the Community should really threaten a wide-scale reallocation of productive resources in the coal and steel industry as between the individual countries, this would immediately call forth tremendous political pressures to which the Community would have to give way or else disintegrate altogether. In other words, the Community lives and thrives only because it is so relatively inconsequential.

The fact is that each country in Western Europe is a welfare state and looks upon its own industry, its own population, its natural resources, and the nationally available capital for investment as a completely separate collection of economic resources to be utilized for the benefit of its own citizens. Even taking due account of this economic nationalism, it should still have been possible, one would have thought, in this new era of West-European integration, to coordinate at least such investments as were intended to create capacity for the production of new commodities or the exploitation of new industrial processes.

For these new industries Western Europe could have become a unified market like the United States. In new and rapidly expanding lines of production no established interests could justifiably have demanded protection. Avoidance of a wasteful spreading out of investments and of grants of special protection to new industries should in particular have been possible during the large-scale influx of capital aid from America. It is true that such new industries are particularly desirable for all countries because of their dynamic impact on the rest of the economy; but in a region that really had taken to heart the ideal of economic integration it should have been possible to reach an agreement on a fair distribution between countries of these industries which allowed their concentration and their economical localization. It is sad to have to report that even this was not achieved. In fact, American aid was used by the receiving countries to raise their national production while consolidating still further the autarkic structure of West-European industry.

Where labor does not move and capital resources are scarce and confined within national boundaries, the international reallocation of industry, which is the condition for gains in productivity through economic integration, is narrowly restricted. By itself international trade cannot accomplish this result and, further, it will not be permitted to do so; for all our countries in Western Europe are definitely committed to full employment and to defending the standard of living of their citizens. *Trade liberalization will therefore inevitably be stopped precisely at the point where it would lead to the progress of productivity through international changes in the location of industry.* This is the real limitation of an economic integration that is mainly focused on trade and payments.

Even in the little Benelux union, where it is at present possible to import Dutch agricultural products into Belgium in greater quantities and at lower prices than the Belgian farmers are asking for their own produce, these cheap imports are hampered, because it matters more to the Belgian politicians that their farmers are Belgians and voters, while the Dutch are foreigners, than that prices in Belgium are higher. This counts for very much more than the ideal of Benelux, not to speak of West-European integration.

No country in Western Europe is today prepared to accept a significant increase in unemployment or even a serious scaling down of living standards in one industry as the price of economic integration with other countries, even its closest neighbors. As a matter of fact, many West-European countries—and, for natural reasons, particularly those that are economically least progressive—have been neither able nor willing to enforce a high level even of internal competition and of large-scale factor movements within their own borders. They did not feel in a strong enough position to permit the liquidation of their own inefficient industries; this, of course, constitutes an extra obstacle to international integration.

Even if we should have to accept as unchangeable facts of life the immobility of labor and capital in Western Europe—which I am not prepared to do—and the serious implications for economic integration and trade liberalization, it is nevertheless discouraging that during years of public speaking and writing on the "single market," these deeper issues have been systematically avoided. Practically, this means ignoring the basic issues of economic integration; and it also means treating the surface issue, that of trade, in a superficial way. Such an approach is bound to lead to disillusionment.

The Issue of Economic Equality

Another issue that was also avoided is that of economic equality. If in the United States—which, unlike the small Western European states, embraces half a continent—the national integration process is rapidly accelerating, the significance of this fact is primarily that in a climate of expansion that country increasingly offers equal opportunities to all its citizens, without regard to national origin, race, or religion. In Europe this is not so and, as between the national states, nothing whatsoever has been done to approach this ideal.

The issue was—until very recently—never seriously raised in all the negotiations and propaganda. The fundamental inequality is, of course, between the underdeveloped rural South and the industrialized North. In the South there lives one half of the region's total agricultural population, but it produces barely one quarter of the total volume of agricultural produce.

Trade by itself is no solution to *this* problem, and the trade liberalization which has actually taken place has even tended to perpetuate, if not widen, this inequality. West-European trade liberalization if unaccompanied by any concerted development policy, may in the end come to stand out as a repetition, on the wider European scene, of the hampering of industrial growth in southern Italy begun by the unification of that country almost a hundred years ago.[5]

Equality of opportunity is also a question of the labor market. In the industrialized Northwest-European countries unemployment has almost been abolished and in many of these countries there has been for a long time overfull employment with an acute scarcity of labor. Meanwhile unemployment, open and disguised, has been increasing so very much in Southern Europe that for the region as a whole the unemployment level has until recently not been very much lower than in the blighted thirties.[6]

Equality of opportunity also concerns the disposal of capital. In a Europe which was really moving towards integration, the southern countries should have had at their disposal some of the capital which the richer countries of the region kept for themselves. To step up Greek gross capital formation by 50 per cent would take only 0.25 per cent of the total resources used for investment in Western Europe, or 3 per cent of gross investment in Sweden, which has about the same population as Greece. The explanation of why capital has not been moving to the less-developed countries in the region is not only the richer countries' control over capital export but primarily that investments there are considered poor risks. But economic integration in a region, as in an individual country, assumes making sacrifices in the common interest.

Now it must, of course, be realized that the basis of solidarity and belongingness among people in this group of nations of Western Europe is for the time being not firm enough to permit them to think in terms of a common development, to shoulder an effective attack on the problem of inequality, and to allow an unfreezing of the labor and capital markets.

The practical question is then what can be done to strengthen this psychological and ideological basis.

I for one would definitely not want, in this crucial period of European history, to belong to the defeatists. Political leaders have always to some extent to accept prevailing attitudes. But the mark of great times has always been that the leaders have themselves reshaped the attitudes of their peoples and so changed the conditions for practical policy. I believe that our West-European nations have hitherto unexploited reserves of generosity and common sense—*if* the issues are squarely brought home to the peoples.

LACK OF POPULAR SUPPORT

Somehow, the appeals that can move nations have not been found. Official speeches and governmental and parliamentary publications have played up to the utmost the meager achievements and have profusely endorsed bigger things for the future; this has, indeed, been the etiquette when making the stereotyped acknowledgements of American generosity. In addition to this, organized propaganda for economic integration in Western Europe has had big funds placed at its disposal—to a great extent paid, directly or indirectly, by American subsidies—and it has filled space in the newspapers, sponsored studies, issued booklets, and distributed posters; it has financed journeys and conferences and run exhibitions.

"Movements" have been started, but they have been confined largely to a small fraction of ideologists and to specialized politicians and government officials. They have never reached out to the peoples, and the courage has been lacking to attempt to change their attitudes on the material matters that are at stake. The propaganda has been kept on a most general plane and never faced the awkward practical issues. In fact, the deeper problems I have raised above have almost never been discussed.

The basic commitments to economic integration were, in the first instance, made by the West-European governments to the United States as a sort of counterpart to American aid and only incidentally to each other. Moreover, the big plans and the splashy appeals were usually aimed not at Western Europe but at the American public and the American Congress. This—from the point of view of popular effects in Western Europe—was a deviation from the straight line and was bound to be of fateful significance. There was continuously during these years some decision to be taken by the American Congress that could be influenced one way or another, and this was the most important concern of the moment.

The programing was a programing for receiving American aid. This concern spread even to the economists, who were tempted to feel a higher responsibility, a higher loyalty, than the simple one of relentless truth-seeking and unhesitating frankness in making public their findings. Such intentions had their effect on what was actually proposed. The proposals were often explained—privately and sometimes publicly—as necessary means of stirring up American public opinion and winning approval for the various aid appeals. It is difficult to believe that realistic European economic statesmen could have been moved in 1947 to start work on a European customs union if it had not been so motivated. The plan worked wonders in America but produced no results in Europe.

In this period I used to warn my European friends that they issued bills of exchange to the American nation which would subsequently have to be met by cash or bankruptcy. I was mistaken. The plans and the commitments were conveniently removed from the headlines and left in oblivion when little came out of them. The explanation is that the American administration, and all good Americans who wanted to keep their nation aiding Western Europe, had the identical interest of influencing and molding the American public and the American Congress. But I should add that the Americans, being farther from the European scene and looking on our matters from the viewpoint of their larger entity, were, understandably, more conditioned in advance to believe in the feasibility of plans for integration and to do so wholeheartedly and honestly.

For a long time France was particularly prominent as the origin of inspired suggestions for economic integration. French patriots felt convinced that the only way to solve France's intractable internal problems was to create a wider unity within which more general solutions would impose solutions to the French problems. Admittedly, the hold of this argument over a wide circle of French intellectuals is largely explained by the glorious tradition in France of meeting with open enthusiasm great, general, and generous ideas. Nonetheless the question is whether that particular idea was not escapism. Given the limited ability of French economic interests to merge their identities within their own country, it seems hardly likely that they would agree to integration in a wider social and economic unit.

I am old-fashioned enough to believe, for instance, that a reasonable degree of internal monetary stability in individual countries is a condition for the success of a larger union. It can also be put negatively: the failure to enforce internal financial stability is as fatal to effective international cooperation as it is to national planning. In watching over the years so many French attempts—and similar attempts in other countries—to forget their own worries at home by indulging in bold schemes for West-European integration, I have often been reminded of a famous literary quarrel in Sweden a little more than a hundred years ago, stemming from a review which had stated: "Admittedly, every single poem is weak, but the collection may be a success." This represents an excess of faith in integration.

One consequence of the implicit address to far-off America of so much of the planning for economic integration in Western Europe during these years, and of the origins of so much of it in national escapism, was, of course, that it became largely irrelevant to actual conditions in our part of the world and to the practical possibilities that existed here. It did not grow, as successful political solutions usually do, from our established practices and from worries about the actual economic and social organization of our society, but descended as a body of strange and abstract ideas from another world. The ideas were discussed in that context by some intellectuals, but they neither reached down to the peoples, nor induced them to change their basic attitudes to each other; in particular they did little to encourage a readiness to accept the consequences of solidarity and to share each other's burdens. This turned out to be the weakness of the schemes when they faced political reality.

This particular weakness on the psychological level—the attempt to inaugurate international cooperation without bothering to establish a basis of solidarity—cannot, of course, be solved by political artifices and legal constitutions of superstates, least of all in a democratic milieu like that of Western Europe. The situation can certainly not be compared with the national situations that preceded the German *Zollverein* and *Reich* or the unification of Italy, whether for Western Europe as a whole or for "little Europe." The idea of overcoming practical difficulties by trying something much bolder and even more difficult is, like all exaggerated gallantry, attractive but unrewarding.

Some Lessons

And so our integration problem is still unsolved. I mentioned in the beginning of this chapter the spread of a certain weary skepticism, which is a not unnatural result of the experiences of recent years. But such skepticism springs from a weak mind's reaction to adversity. In history failure is never final, if it is not accepted as such in advance.

But we should certainly try to learn something from our experiences. They suggest that the institutional setting in Western Europe requires a very empirical approach to the practical problems of economic integration. We have to find specific solutions to specific problems. We should learn above all that economic integration in Western Europe cannot be accomplished by the "big solutions" of recent years, by spelling out catchwords into political edicts.

There is another danger in using big words in the way in which we have for some time become accustomed. The habit of measuring everything in terms of whether or not it "solves the problem of Europe" has caused us to underestimate the importance of a large amount of practical, detailed work continuously carried out in many intergovernmental and nongovernmental organizations. Unnoticed by the big publicity machines, modest results have been reached in a large number of technical projects which, measured by any historical standards, have meant some real progress towards a closer integration of Europe, though in limited fields.

On that technical level much is accomplished every year and every month: little by little it can help to turn the tide from increased autarky towards internationalism. Much more could be accomplished if some of the energy released by the collapse of now frustrated plans could be made available for these practical tasks. There is a chance, to take one important example, for the Coal and Steel Community, if it survives effectively, to do a real and much-needed job on this technical level, and not simply to be the catalyst for schemes of a European superstate.

We shall have to recognize also that, as always, social changes must proceed simultaneously with, and indeed be a little ahead of, economic changes, and also that fundamental changes in a society are a time-consuming process. The practical task we are faced with is actually nothing less than changing people's attitudes. Therefore, we will have to turn not to America, but to the peoples of Europe and speak in terms of their worries and hopes, their ideals and their interests. In the last resort it is they who will decide—as, in fact, they have done up till now—how far and how fast West-European integration will be allowed to go.

IRRITATIONS BETWEEN WESTERN EUROPE AND THE UNITED STATES

It should be clear from the analysis above that I lay the main responsibility for the failure of the strivings towards West-European economic integration on the European politicians.

In my view, the Americans are much less to be blamed. If the American people and the American Congress had grossly superficial ideas about what West-European integration really implied, its particular difficulties, and the rational means to overcome them, and if under these circumstances they often pressed for the wrong policies and opposed the right ones, this is not to be wondered at. It should have been up to the Europeans to furnish the deeper and more realistic insights into their own problems, instead of trying, as they often did, to adjust their thinking to what the Americans expected. The Americans can also be criticized for having forgotten that whatever good reasons there are for

West-European economic integration apply also to the wider Atlantic community and should have had consequences for their own economic policies which, except for the aid, remained ultranationalistic. But the United States is a much bigger and stronger entity and can easily afford much more economic autarky, without great costs for itself.

For a time the United States provided considerable capital assistance, which was intended not only to tide Western Europe over the acute postwar emergencies, but also to facilitate a determined move towards economic integration. Instead, Western Europe used it exclusively for national consolidation, contrary to American advice.

The American advice was actually in the beginning given in considerate terms. The standing instruction from the United States Government to their officials in Western Europe was not to impose themselves but leave to the West-European governments the responsibility for working out the plans and reaching the settlements; their function should be to give their backing to every positive and constructive effort and to explore the possibilities for the United States to give its material support. During the initial years of the European Recovery Program it was, indeed, a very remarkable group of competent and devoted Americans from many walks of life who felt the challenge of this task. I used to say, and I see no reason now to withdraw it, that among the best Europeans were some of the American officials who had come to understand our situation thoroughly and to identify themselves with our values and aspirations.

As a matter of fact, it was mainly at a later stage that a tendency developed on the American side to interfere in the economic policies of West-European countries somewhat more actively and not always wisely. This tendency should, however, be easily understandable in the light of the lack of progress made with West-European integration. By that time economic aid was being increasingly replaced by military aid, with a consequent additional strain on West-European countries' own budgets; the interest in rearmament in Western Europe spread beyond Europe and even farther than did interest in its economic recovery. The political basis for this tendency to adjustment of American diplomatic methods was therefore weak and nothing very much came out of it.

I have already commented on how the interest in securing American financial aid distorted West-European planning for economic integration. From the beginning it was also easy to foresee the complicated and unfortunate psychological results of that aid. Unilateral handouts of large sums from one nation to a number of other independent nations imply a most unusual relationship between the donor nation and the recipients which, without much more human solidarity than exists now, was bound to end in a certain amount of mutual irritation. It is, indeed, indicative that the two countries that could abstain from civilian as well as military American aid, Sweden and Switzerland, are probably also the ones where there is now least anti-American feeling among the public.

On the European side, the frustration of the widely publicized integration goals gave a further spur to just that type of displaced aggression that we have witnessed and that vaguely and irrationally puts the blame for what went wrong on the Americans instead of on ourselves. On the American side, the same frustration tended to encourage those primitive nationalistic forces that have always felt that the West-European governments should be told in no uncertain terms what they should, or should not, do. Had it not gone so deeply against American political philosphy, the increasing coldness of popular response in Europe might have tempted the Americans to court even greater dangers in making arrangements with sometimes shaky and unrepresentative West-European governments without paying much attention to public opinion in those countries.

Psychologically and politically, the idea that Western Europe could be integrated under "American leadership"—with the stimulation of carefully apportioned American gifts, determined after compromise decisions in the standing committees of the United States Congress and provided with ingenious riders to sanction more specific guidance—is, of course, preposterous. For combating the spreading irrational anti-Americanism in Europe, it is important to emphasize that it is nothing else, and can be nothing else, than a red herring. It could, of course, never work for any length of time as long as Western European countries are democracies that carefully watch their own politicians.

In a democracy, effective initiative must spring from the home ground. There are, indeed, narrow limits to the amount of direction that independent nations, even the poorest, are prepared to accept from a foreign government, however tactful—and the limits are even more confined when, as is true of most of Western Europe, the nations are not really so destitute.

In these circumstances, the recent gradual withdrawal by the United States from participation in European economic affairs has been a natural development. The ending of both American aid and American political pressure is becoming the mutually accepted basis for economic relations between the United States and Western Europe. At the same time the West-Europeans feel increasingly free to urge, in the opposite direction, that the United States should undertake a really substantial trade liberalization at home, if that were politically feasible—which, however, as I have pointed out in the last chapter, does not seem to be the case.

In the meantime, we in Western Europe have an urgent duty to carry out the type of simple psychoanalysis necessary to dispel the complex of displaced aggression that has been turned against the Americans. We should recognize that we have only ourselves to blame for our failures in economic integration. We should also drop the illusion that international integration can serve as a substitute for reforms at home and understand that it can only be built on sound financial and other policies in the several countries. We should, further, appreciate the necessity of going deeper in our analysis of what economic integration really requires of us. Above all, we should begin to lay the basis more firmly in all our countries by developing greater international social solidarity, without which all efforts towards economic integration will come to naught.

An Optimistic Conclusion

I am well aware that this is an optimistic view, as I do not consider failure as final.

It should also be some consolation to remember the reservation made above that international economic integration is not the only, and perhaps often not the most important, factor in productivity. As I pointed out, the large-scale Marshall aid did not contribute towards the economic integration of Western Europe; but it promoted very effectively the national integration of the separate states in Western Europe. This capital influx from America, together with Western Europe's own exertions and the favorable business climate in the postwar era, accompanied by an appreciable inflationary pressure, enabled almost all of those countries to maintain a high level of investment and employment and to raise production substantially.

National expansion is a condition for renewed and strengthened efforts toward international integration. Even if our strivings for West-European integration were directed less superficially and in the more practical manner proposed here, they would have little chance of real success in the absence of a general milieu of expanding production and rising living standards. Economic stagnation, or even a low rate of expansion, would inevitably imply a new spur to the autarkic tendencies that have been at work for several decades.

CHAPTER VI

International Payments

A Lost Social Automatism

The gold standard before 1914 was essentially a sterling standard—tied to gold—managed by the Bank of England, which acted as a sort of trustee for all the members of the gold standard club. It was never a completely universal system and its history reveals many limitations and temporary setbacks; but to the considerable extent to which it did function it was founded upon two types of economic facts.

To the one type belonged, first, Britain's dominating position both in world trade and in the international capital market, the relatively large share in the national product of its foreign trade and lending and, more generally, its fairly consistent liberal commercial and financial policies. Second, there was the multilateral pattern of international trade, which in part was a result of this international monetary system and of the influence of Britain's commercial and financial policies and which, in spite of the large and rapid changes of economic relations in the highly dynamic period before the First World War, was continuously maintained.

In this first type of economic fact we find an explanation for the absence of a general sterling shortage in this period comparable to the dollar shortage which preceded and followed the Second World War. Stated another way, the present dollar problem is largely due to the fact that the economy of the United States is not like that of Britain in the nineteenth century and that the United States does not follow today the commercial and financial policies that Britain then did. However, not only is America now unlike Britain then. The whole world position has changed.

To the second type of economic fact belong aspects of the political and psychological climate, resulting in the readiness of all the participating countries—with Britain as leader—to obey the implicit rules of the system. A high degree of automatism was required for its proper functioning.

Through the working of the monetary mechanism in the several countries, primary changes in the international payments situation were to be transformed into secondary changes in production, employment, prices, wages, consumption, trade, and capital movements. In this way international payments equilibrium at the prevailing rates of exchange, as fixed in relation to gold, would be preserved. This implied for a large part the absence of "monetary policy" in the adhering countries and assumed, in particular, that central banking was kept outside national "politics."

Like all social automatisms, the automatism of the gold standard was in the last analysis founded on certain commonly observed and unquestioned reaction patterns on the part of the institutions and social groups actively involved in the operation of the mechanism—in this case primarily the central bankers—and certain equally unquestioned inhibitions on the part of governments and parliaments. It is precisely for this reason that the gold standard, as we once knew it, can never be restored. There are irreversible processes in the field of social relations; and social automatisms, when once their spell is broken, can rarely be revived. Functioning adequate patterns of behavior and taboos, invested with common respect for "soundness," are the result of historical development. They represent a sort of social innocence which, once lost, never returns.

Since the development of the national economic policies described in Chapter III, which were pushed for four decades by international crises of various kinds, no country is any longer prepared to permit its internal business situation to be determined by automatic reflexes to developments outside its boundaries. All countries are committed to preserve stable markets and "full employment." This implies, among other things —and contrary to the rules of the gold standard—the pursuit of a consistent national monetary policy. No country is in a position to pay the price for equilibrium in its foreign exchange relations that an automatic international monetary system of the gold standard type would require.

This would not exclude, however, agreements between governments, aimed at reaching a maximum degree of exchange stability by means of an international synchronization of these national monetary policies. Since, according to both theory and experience, changes in the business climate tend broadly to go in the same direction in all countries, rational monetary policies would also be fairly similar, and a synchronization would be more feasible.

Individual countries are, however, differently affected by changes in the general business climate; some disturbances have also specific causes as, for instance, crop failure or changes in the relative supply and demand situation of a nationally important commodity. The synchronization of national monetary policies would, therefore, have to be supplemented by a system of agreed measures for tiding over exchange transferences. In case of more lasting changes in the relative payments position of different countries rules for orderly and agreed changes in the exchange rates would also have to be given a place.

Such agreements would thus not imply the abolition of national monetary and financial policies, which is out of the question, but rather their coordination on an intergovernmental level. The creation of the International Monetary Fund was a bold venture and was intended to accomplish such a deliberate international integration of national monetary policies. It was to be an agency for intergovernmental determination of exchange rates and at the same time for performing certain functions of a central bank of the central banks. Its courses of action were to follow rules decided upon by the consensus of national governments. Until now it has only been operating on a token basis, but there is no reason why it should not gradually take on its intended role, if payments relations reach greater stability.

QUANTITATIVE CONTROLS

In the years since the war all sorts of national restrictions on international trade and payments have been necessary in order to preserve short-term exchange equilibrium and, in face of the common dollar shortage, these controls have generally been discriminatory. The important point is that, on the whole, this particular kind of intervention in the operation of the price mechanism has not been primarily motivated by broad purposes of national planning but has had a myopic focus on foreign exchange difficulties.

State regulation in this sphere has had the character of things the governments were compelled to do rather than of things they chose to do. To the administrations, the business world, and the general public this entire system of trade and exchange restrictions has proved cumbersome and irrational. It creates unearned profits, by conferring special advantages on those receiving import or foreign exchange permits, and thus lends itself to corruption and lowers the moral standards of business. It has unintended, haphazard and, therefore, undesirable effects on production and trade.

As they never formed part of a comprehensive and rational commercial policy, the measures taken were largely *ad hoc* and provisional. In no country was an attempt made to construct a rational system of discriminatory trade and exchange restrictions, designed to be a permanent part of its economic policy. The present regulations are the historical product of improvisations and continuous adjustments, conceived in the half-heartedness which stemmed from the conviction that they were all bad anyhow and would sooner or later go.

In all the industrially advanced countries the dominant theory has been that freedom from this type of trade and payments restrictions was the goal to be attained as soon as possible. Meanwhile, however, valiant and partly successful efforts to reach international agreement on lowering tariffs and preserving the principle of nondiscrimination have forced governments to rely even more than they otherwise might on less desirable quantitative controls over trade and payments.

Governments experiencing balance of payments difficulties after the war were similarly compelled to take a number of anti-inflationary measures. These internal controls were, in the first instance, largely direct controls over prices and distribution and bore the same character of policies forced upon the governments by temporary circumstances rather than chosen by them as rational instruments for reaching positive policy goals, and so they had unwanted and irrational effects on the national economies.

As a matter of fact, the necessity of combating internal inflation by direct controls has probably been more responsible than anything else for the damage done to the idea of national economic planning in the postwar years: it diverted planning efforts into a kind of spread-out guerrilla warfare against the symptoms of inflation, absorbed the available administrative manpower, monopolized public attention, and, in the end, diminished popular support for economic planning, which was blamed for a multitude of petty interferences with the individual's economic freedom. One lesson from these postwar years is that internal monetary balance attained by the general means of banking and fiscal policies is even more a necessary condition for national economic planning than it is for a policy of *laissez faire.* I might be permitted to add that I was an anti-inflationist at that time, too.

The common experience of the irrationality and the undesirability from a purely national point of view of the quantitative controls over trade and payments and, likewise, of direct anti-inflationary controls, forms the political basis for the strivings to reach an international system of payments which could dispense with them. In the absence of the social automatism of the gold standard, which cannot be restored, elements of quasi-automatism will have to be deliberately introduced and voluntarily adhered to by governments and recognized as policies that are rational from the national point of view.

Hopes of Reaching Convertibility

In the last three years international payments relations seem to have been approaching something like an equilibrium. The improvement in Western Europe's balance of payments, as reflected in the rise in gold and dollar holdings, has, however, a fortuitous base.

It was, in the beginning, partly due to a combination of circumstances. On the one hand, there was the high and generally rising business activity in the United States, accompanied by a lively import demand. On the other hand, there was a considerable slackening in the tempo of economic development in most West-European countries, with consequent effects on their import demands. A higher level of agricultural production contributed to the saving of imports from America, as did a rising trend of imports of "dollar goods" from other regions, not least from the colonies and dependencies of some of the West-European countries. The more recent recession in the United States did not have serious repercussions on European exchange reserves, partly because the general level of domestic and import prices in the United States remained fairly stable. The economies of many European countries had meanwhile resumed a rising trend of production; the import demands from non-dollar areas have been on a high level, compensating for the decrease in exports to the United States.[1]

There have been none of the speculative capital flights from West-European countries which so aggravated the exchange situation in 1949. The main explanation for this difference is, of course, the fact that this time the West-European currencies showed strength, and nothing succeeds like success. This strength was based not only on the factors in the trade field already hinted at but also on some other developments. For one thing the widely publicized prospect of early convertibility tended by itself to turn speculation into support; the governments, therefore, had an interest in nurturing this expectancy and did so continuously.[2] Furthermore, just as a strong motive for capital flight from Western Europe in earlier years had undoubtedly been the fear of war, so the spreading feeling in Europe that the risk of an imminent war was diminishing probably also played its role.[3] Whether this continuing improvement in the political climate is of any permanence is difficult to judge.

The precariousness of the improved balance of payments becomes, however, even more evident when we account for two basic facts in the situation. One is that the United States is continuously making available considerable sums of dollars outside the normal course of business. As direct aid from the United States has declined, there has been an increase in American military expenditure abroad. There are no certain signs that as a result of changes in the basic political situation, in the strategic plans for a possible war, or in military technique this expenditure will decrease substantially in the near future, but it would, of course, be hazardous to count on American military aid on this massive scale as a permanent feature of America's financial relations with the outside world.

The second fact is that, even after the not inconsiderable relaxation in West-European countries of trade and payments restrictions, there remains a hard core of limitations on purchases from the dollar area. The whole trade liberalization scheme under the aegis of the European Payments Union implies a mutual protection of markets and concerted discrimination against dollar goods, as does also the organization of the sterling area.

Taking into account both of these facts, Professor Donald McDougall recently stated in an analysis of the dollar problem that "there is still a real underlying gap of, shall we say, 'a good many billions of dollars.' The gap is certainly much smaller than it was seven or eight years ago. But it is still uncomfortably large and it would be a grave mistake to think that it could be at all easily closed by devaluation or deflation or in any other way, without risking other serious difficulties."[4]

A factor strengthening Western Europe's payments position during these last several years has been the favorable development of its terms of trade; but this change has correspondingly weakened the payments position of the underdeveloped raw-material–exporting countries. The international payments problem has, however, always been dealt with as a reserve of the industrially advanced and nationally integrated countries, and it is they who will decide the convertibility issue among themselves. The rest of the world will have to remain fairly passive and adjust itself in one way or another to the solutions that are adopted. I revert to the special problems of the underdeveloped countries in Chapter XIII.

The More Basic Problem

I have already pointed to the important political fact that all governments would like—and for good reasons—to be in a position to dispense with quantitative controls over international trade and payments. The recent improvement of the balance of payments for West-European countries has therefore caused government officials in most of their capitals to come out in favor of an early return to convertibility; there was no risk in doing so, as this expectancy could only strengthen their currencies. Against the background of our summary analysis of the situation above, however, we should not be surprised that the time considered appropriate for the big change to convertibility is continuously being put off. Nor will it be astonishing should convertibility, if and when it is restored, still be subject to a number of qualifications.

In most countries, for instance, control over capital movements can scarcely be abolished, and this will necessitate controls and restrictions also over commercial payments.[5] Further, currency convertibility will not necessarily bring freer trade; on the contrary, even stricter controls on trade may be needed to defend it, at least for a time. Theoretically there is no inherent contradiction in a policy of introducing currency convertibility without removing any of the discriminatory trade restrictions against dollar goods, and it would undoubtedly have some useful effects. Politically, however, there is a consensus that convertibility should be accompanied by trade liberalization; this will also tend to put off still further the day when it can be achieved.

The favorable development in recent years, which has enabled many industrially advanced countries outside the dollar area considerably to liberalize their imports from the United States as well as from other countries within the dollar area, while at the same time strengthening their exchange reserves, has been, as I pointed out, the outcome of a singularly happy constellation of short-term changes. Even in the short run the further course of events is by no means sure to be a continuation of progress towards freer trade and eventual convertibility. Without making any prediction I would simply point out that the recovery from the recent recession in the United States, which seems now well under way, and its possible development into a real business boom, may well strengthen the inflationary forces which are visible in North-Western Europe, as well as in Australia and New Zealand. This, in its turn, could easily weaken the exchange positions of these countries, particularly if import demands from the under-developed countries slackened. In the end, these countries would then be compelled to reverse their recent policy of trade liberalization, and the prospect of early convertibility would again disappear for the time into the distant horizon.

The bigger problem involved is whether such changes in the world trading system are now taking place, and whether they are of a sufficiently permanent nature to restore a more reliable multilateral payments equilibrium and to wipe out for good the dollar gap.

In the longer run, the degree to which West-European countries will be able to adhere to an international system of freer payments with a minimum of discriminatory trade restrictions will depend upon how far their exports can compete in America and the rest of the world and how far they can diminish their dependence on dollar imports by increasing their trade with other areas and their domestic production in certain lines.

The unlikelihood, referred to in Chapter IV, of the United States substantially lowering its protective import barriers certainly darkens the prospects of a really large increase in West-European countries' exports to the dollar world.

The political East–West split and the shrinkage of trade with the Soviet orbit, which will be discussed in Chapter X, has from this point of view been a costly blocking of one important trade avenue. Meanwhile, United States exports to other "third" countries—backed by rapidly rising productivity levels and by short- and medium-term credit facilities and many other advantages—represent a formidable competition to European exporters. In this situation a large part of the solution will have to be sought in increased self-sufficiency of West-European countries. A decrease in dollar imports of food and raw materials— Western Europe still imports from the dollar area some 30 per cent of the cereals consumed and 40 per cent of cotton—and a substitution of domestically manufactured goods for imported ones will be important policy goals.

Another of the heavy odds against the restoration of a reliable international payments system is the decline of the international capital market and the small chances of its effective resuscitation, a problem upon which I comment further in Chapter VIII. I think it no exaggeration to say that no economist of the earlier generation would have given any chance whatsoever to an international payments system— without discriminatory interferences in trade—under presently prevailing and foreseeable conditions for long-term capital movements.

He would, however, have felt even more apprehensive about the speculative short-term capital market. Since the beginning of the thirties, short-term capital movements have almost completely abandoned their old role of contributing towards equilibrium and stability. As Professor Arthur J. Bloomfield points out, "both speculative and flight movements in the post-war period have been predominantly of the disequilibrating variety in that they have characteristically accentuated rather than moderated balance-of-payments disequilibrium."[6] It is true, as I mentioned, that during the recent recession in America speculative capital movements did not play havoc with the European exchange reserves as they did in 1949, but this single experience does not permit the conclusion that we are back in the good old days.

Since 1931, and still more since 1914, speculative international capital movements have changed their character: capital is now not so much moving to cash in on marginal gains as to avoid the risk of heavy losses. The political insecurity prevailing in many parts of the world after the second World War, the fear of inflation and of other inimical domestic developments, and the high rates of direct taxation in all advanced countries have provided incentives to capital flight in an undesirable direction. None of these new causes seems to be of a passing nature; as long as the capital floating between countries is largely moving under the influence of these new incentives, it is difficult to rely on the short-term capital market as a force working towards stability.

The prevention of capital flight and speculative capital movements in undesirable directions is, indeed, a primary reason for exchange control, although it has gradually been used for many other purposes as well. Professor Richard B. Bissel, Jr.—who, from his association with the European Recovery Program has recent experience of the problem —has stressed that "even the most efficient exchange controls in the world can only slow down and cannot halt the flow of capital across the exchanges when the incentives for selling one currency and buying another are strong enough."[7] But even if the control is not perfect, few countries are prepared to open the sluices wide. To keep them closed to capital flight and to speculative movements adverse to the official aims, but open to capital movements in the interest of stability, and to keep up and increase the flow of this latter type of capital movement will, however, be a most difficult achievement.

Certainly, the peculiar character and strength of the new distorting motives behind capital movements greatly enhance the need for reserves when countries are trying to revert to a freer system of payments. But for that very reason it is doubtful whether any practicable increase in reserves would be able to cure this illness of the capital market. It is assumed, of course, that the reserves were really utilized exclusively for stabilization purposes and were not turned simply into additional aid rapidly exhausted to cover a passing period's dollar shortage.

The almost total suppression of the international migration of labor, upon which I comment in Chapter VII, and the virtual certainty that we shall not see a great change in the near future, must also have effects in counteracting any development towards international economic stabilization, even if it is somewhat more difficult to judge how comparatively important this factor is for trade and payments equilibrium. Though he never developed his thoughts in writing, I remember very well that Gustav Cassel looked upon the inauguration of United States immigration bars after the First World War as a most sinister cause of long-term world disequilibrium.[8]

It should, perhaps, be added that the experience of 1949 demonstrated that a large and sudden devaluation of the currency in welfare states of the West-European type is neither a wholesome nor an efficient means of curing a structural disequilibrium in trade and payments. Moreover, if it is not a part of a whole complex of other policy measures, it tends to have only temporary effects and can, in no event, be repeated often. This does not, of course, mean that adjustments of unrealistic exchange rates, or even the institution of flexible exchange rates, might not be useful as part of a wider effort towards currency convertibility.

INTERNATIONAL MEASURES FOR BUSINESS STABILIZATION

Apart from the question of structural and long-term adjustments, business fluctuations are, of course, a crucial difficulty to be faced by any scheme for freeing payments and trade. In the present world an international monetary system needs a prepared set of agreed measures to counteract general business fluctuations by concerted action and, in particular, to prevent the spread and deepening of depressions. If it is not equipped in this way, steps to convertibility and trade liberalization will only be taken with mental reservations.

The highly industrialized countries, which are the main participants in the discussions and decisions on the convertibility issue, have enjoyed an unusually long perod of full employment. The basis of the protracted postwar boom is again composed of rather fortuitous elements: among them rearmament and, in Western Europe, large-scale American assistance and—more recently—heavy orders for so-called "off-shore procurement" and other military expenditures. In these circumstances, the responsibility of all our governments to preserve full employment has naturally tended to lose prominence in the public eye; but any new threat of mass unemployment would see this issue move again into the foreground. Meanwhile, the organization of the labor market, the perfection of social security and, indeed, practically all economic policies in the welfare state, have made the internal cost and price structure ever less adjustable to outside changes.

Professor Robert Triffin, commenting upon the continuation and even acceleration which he expects of the recent progress toward currency transferability and trade liberalization, is cautious to characterize such goals as "fair weather objectives which can only be pressed forward in an environment of high economic activity and employment,"[9] and adds: "In times of depression, each nation will almost inevitably resort again to trade restrictions and currency inconvertibility in an effort to insulate its own economy from external deflationary pressures. These policies cannot be successful in the end, as each country's actions tend to aggravate the difficulties of others, widening and deepening the contractionist tendencies at work. National anti-depression policies of this character have always proved in the past one of the main factors in the spread and aggravation of international recessions.[10] This spiral can be broken only by collective arrangements giving operational meaning to the interdependence of the various countries' policies."

Laying the foundations for effective international cooperation to preserve full employment in the world at large was the dream of economic planners during the war. Their ideas, after many compromises, were embodied in the Bretton Woods Agreement. In the years immediately following the war many economists urged that the system of international organizations should be perfected by an agency for international business stabilization.

In 1946, for instance, Professor Jacob Viner—arguing that, while general pledges had gone too far, sober and carefully thought-out planning had not gone far enough—proposed the creation of an International Employment Stabilization Fund.[11] Similar proposals, though with greater stress on mechanical formulas, were made by the United Nations experts in *National and International Measures for Full Employment*,[12] and again, in forms more realistically adjusted to the unfavorable political climate, by the group of experts who later restudied the problem.[13]

It should be clear that—secular trends apart—this problem of international cooperation to stabilize business and employment conditions is the underlying and significant issue when a new international monetary system is discussed. The course of gradual relaxation of payments and trade restrictions upon which we have now entered does not by itself inaugurate a new era of stability. It does not prevent business fluctuations, nor does it mitigate the impact of such fluctuations on production, incomes, and employment in different countries. A real depression would bring back the need for all the present, and a number of additional, quantitative controls. The highly integrated countries have so firmly established such internal aims and policies that this retreat to strict national controls over trade and payments would have the appearance of a necessity.

Today we are far from the attainment of this kind of organized international economic cooperation; it says much for the present political situation that the recent Randall Report hardly mentions it. The deeper reason for this gradual collapse of an idea which not long ago had almost unanimous support is, of course, that in the non-Soviet world of today the United States is, economically and financially, of such crucial and predominant importance.

Developments in the United States are recognized as largely influencing changes in the business climate in all other countries, while the reverse does not apply, since the rest of the world is not such a large and single economic unit and since the United States economy is also much more self-contained. The financial burden implied in an international scheme for mitigating business cycles would also fall mainly on the United States. The whole purpose would be the creation of an international mechanism which, in case of a serious American depression, would distribute dollars in a semi-automatic way to the outside world to make up for the fall in exports to the United States.

It is quite understandable that, when it comes to the practical task of implementing such a scheme, the Americans cannot feel very enthusiastic, since the idea is that they should underwrite an obligation to provide dollars to the world if their efforts to stabilize their own economy are unsuccessful. The fact that the recent moderate recession in the United States did not have more disturbing effects on the world economy will strengthen this reluctance.

At the same time, it should be equally understandable that the outside world will continue to feel apprehensive. It would indeed be contrary to all tradition for the United States, without a prearranged and agreed obligation to do so, to react to a real business depression at home by making more dollar funds available abroad. This political fact naturally implies a serious defect from the point of view of international economic cooperation. In all countries it becomes important to be prepared to cope with the effects at home of an international depression, and the policies drawn up inevitably take on a nationalistic character. Naturally, trade and payments restrictions figure prominently in this armory of national policies.

I see no reason, however, why these restrictions should be preserved only because they might be needed later. With the experience we have behind us, we are fully capable of restoring them, if and when we should need to do so. It is true that if a convertibility experiment should fail, some time—and exchange reserves—will be lost, tending to throw the international system further off balance. Even a fairly short period of relaxed restrictions would, however, have had favorable and cumulative effects in the contrary direction.

There is also the possibility that meanwhile the political climate might change, making possible concerted international action designed to enable well-integrated countries to adhere to trade liberalization and convertibility with reasonable assurance that it can serve as a permanent national policy. If, nevertheless, the countries are faced with the necessity of resuming a policy of stricter national controls over trade and payments, there is the hope that the controls might then be constructed in a more rational manner than the ones we now have as a heritage from the depression of the thirties, the war, and the postwar dollar shortage.

Degrees of "Financial Soundness" in Western Europe

Western Europe, impoverished in so many respects by the Second World War and faced with tremendous problems of readjusting its foreign trade, yet steadfastly clinging to old aspirations of economic progress, rising standards of living, and social welfare, has been going through a period of great internal financial weakness. I cannot escape the general feeling that—together with the rapid and continuous rise of productivity in the United States, its adherence to protectionistic policies, and many other things already referred to—this has been a basic cause of the dollar shortage.

I have much sympathy for the common feeling that at the bottom of the dollar problem has been the hard fact that we in Western Europe and in other industrialized countries outside the dollar area, as well as the peoples of the underdeveloped countries, have all been trying to maintain and improve standards of living and to invest in economic development at rates that could not be supported by our own productive capacity. For many of the countries of Western Europe this period may now have reached its end. But it is still questionable whether we are really reaching a level of "viability"—to use a term popular in the early Marshall aid era—and whether we are really engaged in restoring a world trade equilibrium.

We are now advising the underdeveloped countries—quite correctly— that they must create capital from savings, directly or indirectly taken away from the low incomes of their poverty-stricken masses, if their development aspirations are not to be frustrated. We are well aware of how desperately difficult it must be for these countries to follow that advice.[14] Clearly, if we were to apply in all honesty the hard value premise of international integration, we would, in addition to giving such sound advice, also reach the conclusion that we should follow the same policies, turning Western Europe as soon as possible into a capital-exporting region.

Large-scale investment to modernize its capital equipment and raise productivity is continuously necessary for Western Europe's own development, in the long run as much as in the short run. The rapid economic development both in the Soviet sphere and in America is likely to provide an additional urgent reason for raising investment in the years to come. The southern part of the region is, furthermore, itself underdeveloped and is not putting to full use its human and natural resources; it needs more capital for development.

From the point of view of international integration, however, West-European countries—which are incomparably richer than the underdeveloped countries—should, in addition to the saving necessary for investment at home and in the region, make available a substantial surplus of capital for export to other regions. This would, indeed, not be irrational from their own point of view, as they would then also be able to compete more successfully with the United States in Latin America and the Far East. By investing in the development of these countries they could hope to lay the basis for a more rapid attainment of a new and stable equilibrium, based on multilateral trade, which would not leave them "in the backwater." At the same time, a significant contribution would thus have been made towards a solution of the international payments problems. A partial restoration of the international capital market might be possible.

There are differences of political climate within Northwestern Europe, but I fear that in most countries the carrying out of such an austere financial policy is beyond the realm of practical possibility. No political party depending upon popular support would stand for policies appropriate to raising savings to the considerable extent required and, at the same time, increasing business incentives so much that full employment would be preserved by the utilization of the higher savings for higher investments at home and abroad. Even with a lower level of savings, many of these countries often have to make some compromise between full employment and monetary stability.

It would not be a matter of relinquishing the welfare state; that is out of the question. The lifting of the horizon to a larger international economic solidarity would require a much greater solidarity at home also, and a stricter budgeting of incomes and resources. I do not believe that for the time being this is practical. I have raised the exacting value premise and drawn the severe conclusion primarily to illustrate again how far we are from a real reconciliation between the ideals of national and of international integration. The highest goal for "financial soundness" even in most countries in richer Northwestern Europe that, for the time being, has any political practicability, is the prevention of such internal inflationary pressures as would, in spite of continued capital autarky, throw their currencies out of exchange balance with the dollar.

My presentation has been focused on Western Europe's problems. Particularly in a situation where very little capital will be forthcoming from either the United States or the other industrially advanced countries,[15] the underdeveloped countries will almost of necessity be in foreign exchange difficulties, if they want to push on with their economic development. To this and related problems I shall return in Chapter XIII.

PAYMENTS ONLY A SMALL PART OF THE PROBLEM

By themselves, international payments are only a small part of the problem of international economic integration. In this chapter we have been dealing merely with symptoms, not with deeper causes, of international disintegration, and I have tried consistently to point this out by cross-references to other chapters.

Current discussion on international economic integration seriously misses the main points on three counts. First, it grossly exaggerates the importance of international economic relations among the small minority of industrially advanced countries, whereas the far greater and politically more important part of the problem concerns the economic development of the underdeveloped countries. Second, far too much of the discussion is devoted to trade, pushing to the background the equally important problems of factor movements, factor proportions, and factor remunerations. The much higher degree of international integration that once existed in this smaller part of the world was made possible to a large extent only because labor and capital moved more freely.

Third, even the trade problem is too often dealt with from the limited viewpoint of the present inconvertibility of currencies and the quantitative trade and payments restrictions caused by payments difficulties. The trend to autarky has for long, however, had deeper causes, as was shown in Chapter IV. They would operate even if countries had no payments difficulties; the United States provides an outstanding example.

Undoubtedly, though, the payments difficulties end by being not merely symptoms but a factor that actually worsens the illness. Continuing for a period of years, they contribute to the instability of international markets and so provide more reasons for a further dose of economic autarky. Even when this was not the primary intention, they also build up new walls of protection—albeit temporary and uncertain—and behind these walls national investments and employment advance in the ordinary way, with the result that often new permanent vested interests in protection grow up. In the cumulative process towards autarky they are thus not only effects but causes. The important political fact that all industrially advanced countries do want convertibility—in some fashion—and removal of those trade and payments restrictions which exist merely because of payments difficulties, should naturally be exploited to the utmost, and as soon as possible, in order not to give further force to this cumulative process.

As to strategy, I would be inclined to agree with Mr. Roy Harrod that we should be prepared to accept the continuation of straight trade discrimination—even, if necessary, a temporary intensification of it—if that is the condition for an early attainment of some measure of currency convertibility; it could not fail to reduce eventually the need for trade discrimination. The following observation by Harrod is logically unobjectionable and relevant: "It is quite possible to have a world currency despite an imbalance in the structure of trade and services; nay more, it is just when there is such an imbalance that a single world money may perform its most useful function. A general freedom of payments must surely ease adjustments and tend to shift trade towards a more balanced pattern."[16] It is, however, a political fact that what people have been led to expect is a return to convertibility concomitant with a substantial relaxation of trade restrictions. And such a change might have to wait for some time.

Meanwhile, I believe we should be ready for a reform of the way in which trade discrimination is applied. If a general dollar shortage, even though not so apparent at the moment, is expected to be a continuing problem, accompanied by continuing discriminatory trade restrictions which themselves are motivated solely by considerations of the foreign exchange balance, one other problem should nevertheless finally be tackled: the simplification and rationalization of the controls. Present trade and payments regulations are, as I pointed out, the result of an un-planned growth of *ad hoc* emergency measures. Their rationalization into a simpler and more purposive system, involving fewer unrelated—and in their effects undesirable—quantitative interferences with the working of the price mechanism, has undoubtedly been prevented in part by the unwillingness of governments to conceive of them as more permanent features of their economic policy.

In this connection it is well to bear in mind that, as Professor John H. Williams has put it: "Non-discrimination under present circumstances may become a weapon throttling international trade: if countries cannot buy from us (*i.e.* the United States) they may not be permitted to buy from each other even though they have the money or the goods to buy with."[17] The European Payments Union, as an instrument for trade liber-alization in Europe, has, therefore, had its basis in a systematic discrimi-nation against the dollar area. The national policy measures by which this discrimination is carried out can, however, undoubtedly be improved greatly.

Instead of quantitative restrictions, a special—and perhaps flexible—*ad valorem* tariff on all American goods could be considered, for example. A wider and more rational grouping of non-dollar countries for mutual trade and payments liberalization could also be discussed. The transition from quantitative restrictions to more generalized trade discrimination can, of course, also be made to some extent by mutual tariff reductions within a preferential system, as was envisaged in the so-called Strasbourg Plan, adopted by the Assembly of the Council of Europe in the fall of 1952, and subsequently strongly endorsed by the recent Westminster Conference.[18]

The introduction of discriminatory tariffs and preferences would, of course, infringe upon the unconditional most-favored-nation clause. The retreat from multilateralism would, however, concern form more than substance—and, on balance, there would actually be more, and not less, multilateralism in such a system. If imports from the dollar area have to be kept back by discriminatory measures, the substitution of general nonquantitative measures for administrative and individual ones would equally be in the interest of the United States. In addition, as Harrod points out, if there is going to be discrimination it is important that it be as universal as possible. "A little all-round discrimination against dollar goods should serve to bring the pattern of trade nearer to ideal equilibrium than would intense discrimination by some countries combined with no discrimination by others."[19]

Such arrangements assume, however, far-reaching international agreements and are probably not possible for the time being. Different countries are in different trading positions. The difficulties of building up a joint scheme for rationalization and simplification, however, should not stand in the way of individual states' making a thorough overhaul of their own quantitative trade restrictions.

There are, then, two possible reforms:—rationalization and simplification of trade discrimination, as long as it is still needed; and the return at an appropriate time to currency convertibility, though probably qualified in certain ways such as with regard to capital transactions. Neither of these is outside practical possibilities. They would have their significance in abolishing some symptomatic but aggravating factors— even though they would not work wonders in overcoming the deeper trend towards international disintegration.

CHAPTER VII

Labor Mobility

THE PRE-1914 ERA

The era that came to an end with the First World War had seen a big migration from Europe to populate the new continents and to form small strongholds of white people in Africa and Asia. This emigration served as an outlet for surplus population in Europe, arising from a higher natural rate of increase from around the beginning of the nineteenth century, when death rates were brought down by the gradual spread of elementary hygiene and birth rates still remained high. During this period emigration from the industrializing Northwestern European countries was actually a movement closely parallel to internal occupational shifts from agriculture to industry and to migration from rural to urban areas.

As the nineteenth century moved to a close, the poorer and less progressive countries in Europe—Southern and Eastern Europe and Russia—also became sources of emigration, particularly to America. On the whole, other regions of the world, the largest and most backward, contributed relatively few migrants to the new continents. One important cause of this was, of course, the color bar, which was operative even before it was written into the laws.

Meanwhile, and to a great extent under the protective wings of the British Empire, there was considerable migration within the non-European peoples' world. Indians settled in all the surrounding countries and in British Africa and other British colonies and there was some movement also to such places as Dutch Guiana and the French West Indies. While the Europeans had moved as free men for many generations, and long after the trade in Negro slaves had also been abolished, this emigration from India was largely made up of "indentured labor" which involved payment of a mortgage-loan on the emigrants' bodies before they were free to move around and settle permanently in their new homelands.

89

In later decades, however, they were followed by small numbers of commercial and professional people.[1] Similarly, the Chinese fortified their positions in Malaya, Indonesia, Burma, Thailand, and other Asian countries. Many of them were traders and craftsmen, and assumed in some ways, though on a much larger scale, the position of the Jews in Central and Eastern Europe.

In Europe, migration was free and streams of migrants flowed between most countries. Eastern Jews settled in London's East End and built up Jewish settlements in many other West-European cities. German and Italian merchants and craftsmen moved in small numbers to many countries. Swedish building workers in Stockholm took work in Christiania when trade was slack at home. Often they stayed on, married, had children, and became Norwegians. Young workers in the skilled crafts often traveled extensively in the old medieval tradition of improving themselves in their trades, or in order to increase their world experience, or just for fun.

THE PERIOD BETWEEN THE WORLD WARS

The First World War demarcates an abrupt end to this great era of relatively free mobility. That vicious instrument for state control of subject citizens, the national passport, which until that time had been associated mainly with movements within and out of Tsarist Russia and Ottoman Turkey, became increasingly a requisite for passing all frontiers.[2] The possession of a passport was necessary for a citizen to get out of a country as well as for a foreigner to get in.

The institution of passports is important as an indication of a totally new regulative and restrictive attitude towards people's movements. There was in old Russia a saying that man consisted of three parts—soul, body, and passport; we might be moving in that direction. As changes in respect to the controls of the individual's international movements, like other fundamental social changes, occur gradually, step by step, and as the steps are synchronized with, and merged into, international and national crises of much greater consequence, the cumulated result in a new social situation, implying a change in civil rights, will hardly be noticed much. Its true import will, anyhow, not be appreciated, often not even by the social scientists who themselves are participants in the society whose forms are changing.

Throughout this new era of restrictions on international mobility the main impediments, however, have been immigration bars. America took the lead by passing the quota legislation of 1921 and 1924, aimed at severely cutting down the total number of immigrants, but above all at closing its doors to those from the backward countries of Southern and

Eastern Europe and elsewhere. The very heavy immigration from these areas during the decades before the First World War had created stresses and strains in many American cities, where the new immigrants settled in relatively isolated clusters. The immediate cause of the new legislation was the powerful upsurge of nationalism in the United States as a result of her participation in the First World War.[3]

European countries followed close behind. They relied less on immigration controls and more on a licensing system for the foreigner's permission to work. Vested interests on the part of trade unions and professional organizations developed speedily, and these vested interests became more vocal as unemployment rose during the Great Depression. This licensing system gradually came very near to prohibiting international movements of labor in Europe. The liberals of that time were happy indeed when they succeeded, as they did, in legislating a hole in the protective wall around national employment in order to accommodate the stream of political refugees from Fascism and Nazism.

In Canada, Australia, New Zealand, and South Africa the tendency between the two world wars was to use licensing rather than statutory quotas. As immigration was still considered per se desirable and as British policy favored emigration to the Dominions, there was no apparent decline after the First World War in the number of immigrants to these countries, except in Canada. True, in the earlier thirties numbers fell considerably, but there was a revival in the latter part of the decade. Both legislation and administration, however, were aimed primarily at restricting immigration to British subjects and West-Europeans.

PRESENT TRENDS

After the Second World War the situation remained on the whole unchanged.

The war left a big refugee problem to settle. In Europe, two countries that were on the losing side, Finland and Western Germany, have on the whole successfully taken care of most of their own refugees, who amounted to about 10 per cent of the total population in the one case and about 20 per cent in the other. Austria also assimilated a large group of German-speaking refugees, adding about 5 per cent to her population. These are great national accomplishments, for which these countries have not generally been given the credit they deserve. In fact, though laboring under difficult circumstances, they succeeded in making out of this abrupt and large increase of their population a positive asset for development and a spur to economic progress.

But besides the Germans and the Finns there remained a great number of refugees in Western Europe who for a large part had to be resettled overseas. A great deal of work has been done to effect this resettlement. Under the auspices of the International Refugee Organization, and including those who were received by West-European countries, altogether a million had been resettled by the end of 1951; very much smaller numbers have since been resettled by the Inter-Governmental Committee for European Migration. Yet out of the one and a half million or so refugees in Western Europe, estimated to come within the mandate of the High Commissioner for Refugees, there still remain at least 350,000 who cannot yet be considered as absorbed within the economy in which they at present live, and whose resettlement overseas is far from assured.

There are refugees of non-European stock, too, such as Arabs from Israel in Jordan and other neighboring countries; they are kept alive and, indeed, are multiplying fruitfully, but even if they were prepared to move, no country outside the region would be prepared to take them. In the region itself there is such a lack of practical cooperation between the various Arab states that, in spite of political pressures from outside and the promises of capital aid, their settlement would have been very difficult to arrange even if Arab irredentism and the fear that the refugees would compromise their right to return had not blocked these efforts. There are Chinese in Hong Kong, who can stay on that overcrowded island but have nowhere else to go if they do not want to return to China. To the nationalist Chinese who have fled to Formosa and with American aid built a bastion of resistance there against the Communist government, the knowledge that there is no country—except China itself, under certain conditions—that would receive them if they had to leave, must be one of the most important gnawings at their morale. Generally speaking, the discussion of migration problems as raised by the existence of refugees has in practice been focused entirely on people of European origin, as it is evidently taken for granted that no country is prepared to receive immigrants of other ancestry.

Overseas emigration from Europe—even including the refugees—has on the whole tended to settle on a low level. Current Italian and Irish migration to the United States is only a fraction of what it was in the thirties. Altogether, the United States has taken one and a half million immigrants in the eight years between the end of the war and mid-1953,[4] Canada nearly a million, Australia three quarters of a million, and Latin American countries probably a further million.

Thus, some four to four and a half million immigrants have entered the main receiving countries in these eight years. These figures include a fair amount of continental migration, especially within the Americas. The rest are almost exclusively Europeans, the preference being for Northwestern Europeans in the United States, Canada, and the Commonwealth countries, and Italians and Spaniards in Latin

America. This whole migration stream over the last ten years can be compared with the total immigration into the United States alone in the decade of the twenties, which was of about the same magnitude and, of course, much lower than in earlier decades.

Intra-European migration is probably adjusting to a lower level than in the period between wars, particularly if we take due account of the relative levels of business and employment in the receiving countries.

Immigration from the poorest regions, with the largest amount of surplus labor, is excluded in almost all receiving countries by statutory or administrative color bars. Overseas emigration from Asia, with the exception of the return of European settlers, has come to a virtual end. When there are no such bars and where political and economic relations have paved the way, there is a steady flow of migrants—of Puerto Ricans to the United States, Algerians to France, and Jamaicans and others to Great Britain; in Britain there is now talk of limiting the free entry of West-Indian labor.

Meanwhile, the new countries recently emerging from colonial domination, together with other countries in Asia, have themselves become increasingly conscious of their surplus labor situation and its significance as a cause of poverty. The violent and tragic exchange of populations between India and Pakistan, at the time of partition, has left large groups of unsettled refugees in both countries, and the pressing problem of their integration into the national communities does not make these countries particularly favorable to an open-door immigration policy, either towards each other or in relation to other countries.

Past migrations have also left serious problems of incomplete social integration, and the consequent tension in many countries in Asia, which has been rising, hardly creates a favorable climate for a liberal migration policy. The Chinese population enclaves in Malaya, Indonesia, and Thailand are cases in point. India is now having difficulties with Ceylon because of large-scale illegal immigration by Indians. My observations during a recent journey in many of these countries have convinced me that national communities in Asia are all going to use their improved administrative controls to check immigration. This area may thus also split up into closed compartments preventing the mobility of persons. It becomes one of the fruits of their recently won independence.[5]

In the Near East the intrusion of a new, vigorous, and largely European state, Israel, has, of course, immensely increased nationalist tensions among the Arabs. In Israel itself the immigration of Near Eastern and African Jews does not proceed without causing internal tension.

So far as intracontinental migration is concerned in Latin America there are either similar problems of national sentiment or else the flow of labor is unaccompanied by a corresponding and adequate flow of capital.

In Africa there is, on the whole, not much shifting of either individuals or tribes over boundary lines; the indenture system is not entirely stamped¹ out, however, and Portuguese territories are rather large-scale suppliers to the South African mines.

The Economics of Large-Scale Net Emigration

The conclusion that emerges from our rapid survey is, broadly, that we are now coming to the logical conclusion of a development which started with the First World War and which implies that the world will henceforth have to strive for international adjustment without any sizeable population movements over the boundaries. The permanent settlement of refugees will continue to be an urgent problem for some considerable time; only for those refugees who are of European stock is there any hope of international migration.

Immigration will still mean much for individual countries, like Australia. Important motives behind the positive attitude to immigration were, at least until recent times, strategic considerations—a queer incidental characterization of our age—and the desire to provide a more reliable basis for the White Australia policy; there is, of course, a continual and uneasy feeling in the native-born Australian of being a very small European population holding the title of occupation to vast uninhabited areas of land which, whether or not very suitable to Europeans, would have great attraction to immigrants from the large and severely overpopulated countries in Asia.

In Australia, the procurement of the capital necessary for an increase in working population will be a major limitation to immigration even from Europe; there as everywhere the international migration that does take place will be highly selective, and the selection will be done by the receiving countries. Colored people will continue to be almost totally excluded everywhere.

From a narrowly economic point of view this closing of the boundaries to mass migration is perhaps not to be very much regretted. As a long-term policy, large-scale emigration is an irrational and very costly means of getting rid of surplus population. The country of emigration bears the cost of feeding and bringing up generations of emigrants, which has the effect of further depressing the already low living standards.⁶ The poverty in West-European rural areas during the era of mass emigration to America and to industrial centers within the country was to a large degree correlated with the abnormal age-structure caused by the continuous depletion of the population of the most productive working age. Poverty would, of course, have been even greater if they had stayed behind only to become superfluous labor. The ultimate cause of poverty

was, quite obviously, a population increase which outstripped production.

To ask the richer countries to open up their boundaries to mass immigration from the poorer countries, which have not solved their population problem, would, indeed, be very questionable international
idealism. If a surplus labor situation persists in a country because economic development does not match the increase of population, that is
a reason to speed up development so far as the natural and other resources of the country permit. If that cannot be done to the point
required for the full and economic employment of the available labor
force, the population increase should be controlled. It is the road to
continued poverty to rely on foreign countries to take their pick of
grown-up workers who, if they do not account for much productive
value in their own country as long as it remains underdeveloped,
nevertheless represent large costs spent in catering for them till they
are ready to emigrate.[7] The population problem in the underdeveloped
countries is further discussed in Chapter XII.[8]

A Free International Labor Market

From a broader point of view this enclosure of the individual within
national boundaries is, however, frankly one of the most reactionary
trends of our time and intrinsically damaging to strivings for international integration. Albert Thomas, head of the International Labor
Office in its early days, felt this in his bones when he vainly took up the
fight against the trend and demanded international action to defend the
free labor market.

More fundamentally, it is a question of liberty, of elbow room for the
common man. The doors are closed at the very time when cheaper
travel makes movement easier and the spread of knowledge opens up
new vistas and horizons. The closing of the boundaries is also one of the
many factors leading to an absurd intensification of national allegiances
which is continuously weakening that basis of international solidarity
upon which international policy has to be built. It tends to lower the
sights and restrict the horizons of individuals and of nations.

From the point of view of our value premise—international integration—the ideal situation would be the following: that by a policy of
national integration each country should succeed in matching its economic development to its population increase, thus eliminating the need
for one-sided and persistent international migration movements;[9] but
that individuals and groups of individuals should have full opportunity
to move over the boundaries and seek employment in foreign countries.

This would mean a free international labor market. It would imply a wider scope for individual aspirations; at the same time it would facilitate economic adjustments to short-term changes and, if need be, the relocalization between countries of particular industries. This, in its turn, would make for greater flexibility in the whole industrial system and create possibilities for freer trade.

It would, of course, be a utopian hope that this dream of the internationalist could be applied to the disintegrated world of today; but it could well be a policy for countries that are fairly well integrated nationally and enjoy standards of living and of culture that do not differ widely. It has been noted in Chapter V that one of the basic shortcomings of the organized efforts for West-European economic integration was the almost total failure to face this issue and to attempt to re-establish the free European labor market that existed before the First World War. While Albert Thomas' initiative was doomed to failure, since he was advocating a free labor market on the very edge of the Great Depression, it could have had some hope of realization for this generation, as the employment conditions were for a long time so much more favorable in Northwestern Europe.

Meanwhile, in the industrially advanced countries the process of economic integration, dominated by exclusively national values and institutions, has created ever stronger ties binding every individual to the nation-state of his birth and early employment. As I pointed out in Chapter IV, the professional careers of almost everybody have been confined within closed national systems. This may have facilitated movement within the national boundaries but has made it much more difficult to leave the country without risking one's livelihood or, at least, one's seniority. The improved economic status and security of employment of the working classes have given even the laborer vested interests at home as a professional.

The national integration process ran parallel to and supported the other impediments to international migration, so that even when legal and administrative restrictions on migration are relaxed or abolished— for example, between the small Scandinavian countries and in the Benelux union—very little cross-boundary movement of labor actually takes place. It is significant, on the other hand, that when the established pattern of migration was not broken by legal or administrative restrictions—as in the case of movements between Britain and Ireland—even political separation did not stop migration.

A recent study of the problem concludes that "it would seem that, in addition to the mere removal of administrative obstacles, more positive incentives are needed to promote the movement, especially of young workers. This conclusion, of course, implies a judgment on the desirability of inter-change between nations which is based on more than purely economic considerations: there is this important difference between the international movements of goods and of labor, that the latter may well be regarded as an end in itself."[10]

NATIONAL BONDAGE FOR THE COMMON MAN

What we conclude from all this is not so much that we should regret the passing of an era which saw a major stream of one-way human traffic—as we have noted, the stream has not altogether dried up. What is to be regretted, rather, is the loss of the freedom for the individual to migrate if he wants to and, consequently, the virtual cessation of those marginal two-way movements of population within the European continent and elsewhere, which could be a real factor making for economic adjustments and for cohesion and international solidarity.

The network of ever quicker and progressively cheaper transport is rapidly drawing the countries of the world closer together. Rich people in all countries and not so rich people in the wealthier countries will be able to travel for pleasure. Students from the poor countries will be received in the advanced countries for a year or two. The very rich will continue to be able to choose where they want to live more permanently. Scholars and experts of world repute will have an international market and considerable freedom to choose where they want to live and work.

But the common people, the workers and the farmers, the ordinary businessmen and professionals who do not happen to be leaders specialized in the international fields, will be tied to their land of birth as firmly as in feudal times the serf was tied to the estate of his lord. He could go sightseeing or visit the market, but he had to return. This national bondage for the common man is a deeply dismaying trait of the world now coming into being. It operates against the development of the feeling of belonging to a world and not merely to a small part of it.

CHAPTER VIII

Mobility of Capital

CAPITAL FLOW IN EUROPE AND TO THE NEW CONTINENTS

International capital movements have closely followed those of labor. During the nineteenth century, and until the First World War, capital from those countries in Western Europe that were already relatively developed flowed in the large amounts needed for the economic development of the continents that Europe was at the same time supplying with labor. British capital financed the building of American and Canadian railroads, and much capital also went into industrial investment, real estate, and agriculture in North America. Australia, New Zealand, South Africa, and Latin American countries also absorbed a relatively large capital influx.

In fact, much the greater part of the capital export from Europe during this era was directed towards those sparsely populated regions in the temperate zones with large natural resources. It contributed to increasing their exports of primary products, thus, in addition, sustaining industrial development in Europe. The largest part of this capital was furnished by acquiring bonds and equities. Capital movements, the migration of labor, and international trade made for a rapidly progressing international integration which, as I pointed out in the introductory section of Chapter IV, in this period and in this part of the world proceeded in harmony with the development towards national integration.

The story was repeated nearer home, though without the inducement of simultaneous large-scale labor immigration. For example, a hundred years ago Sweden was a poor agricultural country with an overcrowded and land-hungry peasant population and some small, old-established industries spread along the forest streams; only 10 per cent of the population lived in the cities. But it could borrow money freely in London, Hamburg, and other financial centers in Western Europe at a rate of interest around and often under 3 per cent.

In all capital-importing countries the state was active as an agent for organizing through its economic policy favorable conditions for economic development and capital import. This was true in the United States, as any serious study of its early economic development reveals. In some countries the state even did the actual borrowing. In Sweden, for instance, no private business had the managerial capacity for such big enterprises as building the railroads, nor the credit standing necessary as a collateral for such large foreign loans as were needed for that purpose. And so the main railroad lines were from the beginning state-owned, and the so-called private lines, which were owned by the municipalities, were also financed largely by the Exchequer.

The state, in addition, guaranteed the bonds, the foreign sale of which provided the quasi-public mortgage banks with foreign capital and canalized this capital in two big streams, to agriculture and to the rapidly growing urban real estate. From the beginning the conditions were present in Sweden for an expansion process along the lines described by Schumpeter. Exploitation of the forests for export of timber was the first mainstay of the progressing industrialization, but very rapidly the process branched out in a diversification of industry, adjusted not only to exports but also to the expanding home market.

A country like Australia followed, *mutatis mutandis,* very much the same model of successful economic development as Sweden, nurtured by the state and sustained by generously supplied cheap credits from the international capital market. By jealously preserving its political and economic independence, Japan succeeded in escaping the colonial destiny of other backward colored nations. Under strict government control it managed to lift its economy out of inherited stagnation and proceeded to industrialize at an extraordinary rate; it was also able to rely on imports of foreign capital, mostly acquired by the sale of government bonds, though capital import did not assume large proportions.

In the new continents, immigration was never more than first an impetus and later a supporting factor in population growth; throughout the nineteenth century the natural increase of population in the United States was larger than the immigration. In the same way, once economic development had acquired its momentum, it was increasingly financed in all these countries by the very high rates of domestic savings, regularly forthcoming out of rising profits.

ENCLAVE-BUILDING IN THE BACKWARD CONTINENTS

A small part of the capital stream also went to the colonial empires in Asia and Africa, continents which, like Europe, are called old continents —the real implication being that the inhabitants were so numerous that even in the rougher conditions of earlier days they could not be exterminated like the aborigines in the new continents, or pushed into native reserves.[1] The Europeans instead established reserves for themselves in these countries, as islands in the ocean of colored people.

The course of events in these other regions took a very different turn. There investments also became to a significant degree economic enclaves. These so-called underdeveloped regions seem to have been little affected in their general economic development by direct foreign capital investments. Even when the enclaves were large, as in mining or the plantation system, they were seldom really integrated into the local economy, but remained attached to the interests of a metropolitan state.

The increased employment opportunities in countries with large enclaves—consistently limited to unskilled labor—were rapidly filled by population increase, usually without raising the average standard of living. Apart from the increased employment opportunities, the population increase was also—and more generally—favorably conditioned by stable and orderly governments, set up by the metropolitan powers, which preserved social peace and prevented internal feuds and wars. The spread of elementary sanitation and public hygiene and other policies under colonial rule which were per se beneficial also played their part.

That is why a country like Indonesia, having now gained independence, finds itself with a population more than three times larger than in 1870, and with a standard of living that has not risen substantially during these three generations. It is equipped with large and in many ways well-organized rubber, copra, tea, and sugar "estates" and tin mines which produce almost entirely for export and employ a part of the labor force; but it has to import almost every single tool for the economic development it is now beginning to plan, literally every nail, and in addition bulky industrial commodities, like cement and coal, of which about half the import price is freight.

The development was not very different when the enclaves were relatively smaller in size and represented by communities of individual settlers, acquiring by various means the right to the good land. Nor did the commercial establishments make any fundamental contribution to an over-all balanced economic development of the backward countries.

That the course of events took this "colonial" character was not mainly due either to the designs of those who provided the capital and built the economic enclaves, or to the intentional policies of their governments. It was much more the natural outcome of the unhampered working of the contemporary market forces. These countries were already heavily populated and offered no possibility of large-scale immigration of labor from Europe. The colonial natives were extremely poor and were not employed very productively; to take them on at low wages for unskilled work was for the enclave-builders simply to exploit the natural resources. To preserve these dependencies as markets for the manufacturing industry at home and not to encourage them to any large-scale industrial diversification on their own was an almost self-evident commercial policy towards a foreign country under political control.

The native populations were, furthermore, not white, and whatever culture they had was not of the European variety. Strict segregation on racial and cultural grounds developed therefore as a matter of course and, as always, hampered or stopped cultural adaptation and growth. The few who were selected for partial Europeanization usually ceased to identify themselves with the poor masses, but also failed to be completely absorbed by the foreign culture. They remained what the sociologists call "marginal men"; usually the half-castes shared this fate.

Colonial government, directed from a metropolitan capital, implied that these peoples had no home government of their own with the power to plan and direct policies in their own interest and aimed at raising the level of the masses. The regular colonial device—variegated considerably by the different metropolitan states—was for the European metropolitan authorities to work with, and strengthen the hold of, the local feudal chiefs and other social classes who had an interest in preserving the political, social, and economic *status quo*.

This was again not a sinister design on the part of the colonizers but simply a manifestation of their obvious interest in the prevailing circumstances. The political expediency of this type of arrangement is now being pressed upon the United States almost by the logic of events. Sympathy for the underdog is here a strong historical tradition, as is anticolonialism; the United States is also the only advanced country with any long-standing tradition that in its policy towards backward peoples maintains that the nation should support and encourage the forces for change. However, now that the United States is increasingly inheriting responsibilities in the underdeveloped regions, it, too, to the great dismay of its enlightened citizens, feels the sinister weight of political expediency which tends to push it into alliance, *nolens volens,* with reactionary personalities and social groups.

As mentioned before, Japan escaped this common destiny of backward colored nations because it preserved its political and economic independence and because its government embarked early upon a vigorous policy of economic development: borrowing the money and procuring the new techniques, investing in public utilities and other external economies, starting new industries, training the workers, creating the conditions for squeezing out the domestic savings, and keeping out foreign influences which would have been inimical to the process of economic development —for example, foreign consumption habits.

The East-European countries failed to develop like the West-European ones and some of them were even affected by foreign investments of the enclave type, which exploited their raw materials and cheap labor on behalf of foreign interests. Latin American countries experienced a development which, on the average, came nearer the truly colonial variety. Nevertheless, some countries in Latin America, or parts of some countries, started before the First World War on a fairly independent, gradual economic development of the progressive type. Others conformed much more to the patterns of colonialism, though with the important difference that the majority of the owners and operators of the economic enclaves among the masses of primitive and illiterate Indians, Negroes, or half-castes of various blends were natives of their own countries, sometimes not even of pure European stock.

In the regular way of business, the plantation economy, once it got started, largely fed itself with investment capital from profits. Not all capital that went from Europe to the backward countries was in the form of direct investments. There was a parallel stream of capital lent to the colonial governments, public or semipublic corporations, or private firms for building the railroads or for investing in other public utilities, and this stream was larger. Even when, as was usually the case, these investments primarily served the needs of the colonial economy, they naturally had a relatively greater importance in increasing the general possibilities for economic development. In most of these countries, however, these new elements of external economies did not suffice as a stimulus and general stagnation continued.

It has been said that the European investors of the nineteenth century have left Americans in the twentieth century saddled with the worst part of the problem. The "easy" investment opportunities—from the outsider's point of view—have been largely exhausted. The empty spaces that could receive immigrants as well as capital and to which most of the capital went are largely filled. In the other areas there are now heavy arrears of social investment to be made up, most of which will not yield immediate return or profits.[2] Even when this is not true in a material sense, it is true in a policy sense. Standards have changed; ruthless exploitation with little thought for the welfare of the peoples of those countries is today becoming less possible. Social investments have become necessary adjuncts to narrowly productive ones. This same development, incidentally, occurred long ago in the advanced countries themselves.

Populations in the backward areas have meanwhile increased tremendously, while they have usually not advanced much in average welfare. They have attained, or are attaining, political independence and are now inaugurating policies of economic development in order to raise the living standards of the masses. They are through with segregation and discrimination and demand a conduct of their economic life in accordance with the interests of their own people.

The great volume of capital export before the First World War, whether to independent and rapidly developing or to colonial and on the whole stagnant economies, occurred during a period of relative peace and stability; part of the basis for this stability was, of course, the tractability of the nonwhite peoples under colonial rule.

The capital movements were closely related to international trade and the confident expectation that its volume would continually grow. Long-term capital movements represented also only one sector of the capital market. In all international trade, short-term and medium-term credit played a most important role. The structure of international finance was indeed founded upon the speculative market in foreign exchange, which gave strength and flexibility to the gold standard in the countries that adhered to it.

The Period between the World Wars

The First World War brought about considerable changes in the pattern of international indebtedness.[3] But after the temporary lapse in the operation of the system during the war and when the losses and liquidations had been consummated, the international capital market was built up again and the gold standard gradually restored. This was one result of the big drive in the early twenties to "normalcy."

We may note in passing that this movement in its time had a much sounder psychological basis—and therefore greater prospects of success—than a similar movement would have had after the Second World War. The Great War was looked upon as a horrible mistake, a once-for-all deviation from the normal course of peace and steady progress. As usual, the expectancy was a powerful cause of its realization. From the fundamental psychological point of view the different expectation after the Second World War, the absence of belief in the reality of continuous normalcy is not only indicative but also a basic cause of the much stronger forces working towards international disintegration.

In the twenties, long-term capital movements on a large scale even started to flow from the United States. America, emerging after the war as a creditor country, opened its banking resources to Weimar Germany. The money was eventually lost to a large extent, and this, coupled with a risky scramble for high-interest earnings in the Balkans and Latin America, had disastrous effects on the willingness of American investors to venture again into foreign lending.

As apparent monetary stability in Europe returned, long-term lending by Britain and France, and to a smaller extent by Belgium, the Netherlands, and Switzerland, was renewed; Sweden also emerged as a creditor country. The chief borrowers were Germany, in Europe, and Argentina, Australia, and Canada, outside Europe. The large underdeveloped regions received much less: the influx of capital into India and China in the period between the world wars was in each case only about the same as, or less than, that into Argentine and Australia, although their population was forty times as great.[4]

The whole structure of this newly restored international capital market broke down with the spread of the Great Depression. As the international commodity markets collapsed, the basis for long-term capital movements disappeared with them and, in its turn, the cessation of the capital flow caused a deepening of the depression. The international short-term capital market finally expired during the financial crisis, culminating in the collapse of the British gold standard on September 21, 1931.

One immediate cause in this chain of developments was that Britain and some other countries had borrowed short and lent long. This is, indeed, a normal banking practice; but speculative capital was no longer out to exploit marginal differences of profit and rates of exchange. Instead, it was fleeing for safety. With the exception of capital flights, there were only very limited movements of capital of any type in any direction during the thirties.

AFTER THE SECOND WORLD WAR

The short-term capital market and the whole international payments mechanism remained disorganized after the Second World War. Because of the close relations between different compartments of the capital market, this was a most unfortunate condition for the resumption of long-term capital movements, which are so important from the point of view of international integration because of their potential contribution to economic development.

Such long-term capital movements as have developed since the Second World War have several unwelcome features. The floating in international capital markets of foreign government bonds, once so important in international financing, has almost ceased. Floating of shares and debentures of business enterprises, and trade in outstanding securities, have likewise become of minor importance. Loans are gradually being repaid and even equity interests in railroads and public utilities are being liquidated. This implies that there is virtually no longer a private long-term capital market in the old sense.

Lending by governments has succeeded but by no means replaced the floating of bonds and equities on the capital market. Such private capital movements as have nevertheless taken place have scarcely been directed in favor of a balanced development of the underdeveloped regions. Rather, they have been an element in widening the gap by assisting first and foremost—directly or indirectly—the further development of countries that were already industrially advanced.

A great deal—three fourths or more—of the private capital invested abroad has been in the form of reinvested profits which, for exchange control or other reasons, have not been repatriated. Further, the total amount of private capital made available is in real terms only about half the annual rate of the twenties (though recently it has been somewhat higher —at a rate probably exceeding two billion dollars a year, compared with the average for all postwar years of about one and a half billion); the rate would be considerably lower still if measured per capita or in relation to total production and income of the lending countries.

Much the greater part of this private capital, as indeed of all foreign capital, has been forthcoming from the United States, which thus assumed the place of Britain as the world's chief long-term capital supplier. United States private capital exports have, in fact, been proceeding at about the same annual rate in real terms as in the twenties. Outside America, much of the movement of capital has been between metropolitan states and their dependencies or associates.[5]

If the annual rate of United States private foreign investment since the war appears to be roughly of the same magnitude in real terms as it was in the twenties, there has, however, been a sharp shift in its composition.[6] Contrary to the tendency in that period, there has been a strong bias in favor of direct investment through either the establishment or the development of United States enterprises abroad. Private lending to foreign governments, municipalities, and corporations and, likewise, the acquisition of foreign equities as a regular investment—methods of lending without becoming involved in industry abroad and without holding a controlling interest—are more and more a thing of the past.

For the most part the funds have, furthermore, gone to hard currency areas, such as Canada, and have eschewed countries with dollar shortages, except where the product could be sold in hard currency markets. Almost three quarters of United States private investment has been of this direct dollar-recovering nature, and most of the remainder was for manufacturing and other investment in Latin America[7] and Western Europe, where it often served as a sort of substitution for international trade, consisting of production units or assembly plants built up on the other side of protective tariff walls or quantitative trade restrictions.

Thus, apart from the preponderance of investments in Canada, private American capital export has gone largely into petroleum, where the borrowing countries have been prepared to make special arrangements as to transfer of production income. On a smaller scale the same is true for the sharply decreasing investments in agriculture, mining, and smelting. Attempts to induce a greater share of total American investment for industry in Western Europe by a transfer guaranty program have made only slow progress.[8]

Canadian postwar private long-term capital export has consisted entirely of direct investment—there has even been some liquidation of portfolios. Most of the fresh postwar capital exports have gone to the United States or the United Kingdom, and very little ouside the American countries and the British Commonwealth. Even so, Canada remains on balance an importer and not an exporter of capital.

In Western Europe the dollar shortage has offered an excuse for, and the consequent exchange regulations have acted as, a bar against any large-scale capital export. The Swiss capital market, encouraged by higher yields than obtainable at home, and financed in part by funds from abroad seeking refuge from unstable currencies and from taxation, has accepted some foreign commitments, carefully selected for security, with little going to the really underdeveloped regions.[9]

More significant capital movements have taken place within the franc and sterling areas, greatly facilitated in the beginning by the large Marshall aid to Western Europe but continued and even increased in later years. Substantial sums have been invested in French overseas territories —about half in North Africa—as part of the Monnet Plan. There has been a sizeable private capital outflow from the United Kingdom to the rest of the sterling area, especially Australia and South Africa; the rest of the Commonwealth and, particularly, the colonial countries, have received only small amounts.[10]

Within Western Europe itself there has been extremely little movement of long-term capital, in spite of the much publicized efforts towards West-European integration and particularly the coordination of investment. In a recent study it has been pointed out that the tendency in Western Europe to capital autarky has its close analogy in the decreasing importance of the capital market within the countries themselves: "The increasing share of governments in international lending is paralleled by an increasing share of public saving within each country, and the tendency to national 'capital autarky' has its analogy in the growing importance of 'self-financing' in industry."[11]

This rapid survey of postwar private capital movements would not be complete without a reference to the very considerable clandestine movements of capital, mainly finding their way ultimately to the United States and Latin America. These capital flights have frequently run into hundreds of millions of dollars a year;[12] they have probably been on a much bigger scale, for instance, than the annual lending of the International Bank. For very natural reasons part of this money comes from the very poorest countries.

The Capital Flow to Underdeveloped Countries

Insofar as there are still vestiges left of an international capital market, they are mainly contained within closed blocks: on the one hand, the United States, Canada, and, to some extent, the other countries of the dollar area; on the other hand, Britain and the industrially advanced Commonwealth countries. "The historical answer to unbalanced trade and productivity has been international investment," observes Professor John H. Williams.[13] As we have already noted in Chapter VI, it is obvious that capital movements in the present world do not fulfill this important function. This is true for the old partial world of industrially advanced countries, and particularly with respect to their relations with the underdeveloped countries.

Altogether, the underdeveloped countries receive extremely little private capital. Direct investments in the exploitation of oil and other natural resources, which make up much the larger part of the foreign investments accounted for in the statistics, are important only for a few of these countries. Since, moreover, such investments often merely establish enclaves which per se contribute little to the general development of the countries —they usually even have a rather low employment effect—they count for little in any realistic analysis of international integration. In fact, only the royalties and taxes, and these only to the extent that they are actually used for the further development of the economy of the country—instead of being squandered on luxuries or whittled away in the form of private hoardings of gold or foreign exchange—can really be considered as a productive capital influx from these sources.[14]

It seems inevitable that in the course of time more and more of the underdeveloped countries will want to nationalize their natural resources and exploit them themselves or, at least, obtain the controlling interest in their exploitation. This, by itself, hardly acts as an inducement to private foreign investment, even in this restricted field, but the profits are usually very high.

To the foreign capital made available to underdeveloped countries should be added short-term and medium-term commercial credit which, however, cannot amount to very much.

There is also a negative item to be included in the calculation; the gradual repayment of earlier government loans and the return home of earlier investments, particularly from countries recently liberated from colonial dependence. This is one of the costs which these countries have to pay for their independence. There is no doubt that Indonesia in colonial times had easier access to a foreign capital supply from Holland than it has now, in spite of the close relations with Dutch business that are still maintained.

On the whole, in many Asian countries the stream homewards of private capital from underdeveloped countries has probably been somewhat larger than new foreign investment, and definitely so if the fleeing capital of their own citizens is added to the calculation. The Latin American countries seem, on the whole, to have fared better, though there are great differences between the various countries.

In this situation most underdeveloped countries would welcome more direct investment, almost all that is now left of long-term international private capital movements; but so far they have been getting very little. They will not, however, accept it without reservations or without insisting on their own conditions. They are jealous of their economic independence, and they want something more than enclaves. Compared with the capital acquired by the sales of bonds in earlier times, direct investments require also higher returns and appear therefore to them a more expensive source of capital.[15] Their greatest need for direct investments is, furthermore, usually in those fields of manufacturing industry which least attract private business.

What the underdeveloped countries need most of all, however, so as to proceed with their development plans, is capital for large-scale investment in public utilities: railroads and highways, electric power stations, irrigation, port facilities, and the like. With the possible exception of electricity, these are not usually profit-making enterprises and they will have to be owned and operated by the state or public authorities. Formerly, investments of this kind in backward countries were often financed by loans raised in international markets, but it is exactly that type of private capital import which is no longer forthcoming. The supply has dried up, but the demand is greater than ever, now that backward countries have embarked upon economic development.

This is, of course, the background to the new pattern, emerging after the Second World War, of straight government loans, again mostly by the United States, and of lending through the International Bank for Reconstruction and Development. Government loans, as distinct from aid, to underdeveloped countries have probably averaged several hundred million dollars a year in the postwar period. The loans to really underdeveloped countries given by the International Bank since the beginning of its existence do not average more than one hundred million dollars a year; the Bank's current rate of lending is somewhat higher, however.

Even in Latin America—which is relatively better provided with these types of loans than any other large parts of the underdeveloped world— the level of investments in public utilities has been much too low after the war compared with the real needs. This is related to the fact that the amounts of these public loans are not a substitute for the earlier private ones. During the years 1950–53 barely 3 per cent of aggregate public investments were financed by loans from the International Bank and the Export-Import Bank, the two main providers of nonprivate capital, while in earlier times two thirds of such investments were the product of bond issues on the international capital market.[16]

UNDERDEVELOPED COUNTRIES FROM THE WALL STREET POINT OF VIEW

As I shall presently discuss more fully, there are such weighty reasons why private investment abroad is to be preferred to government loans that it is easily understood why strong efforts have been made in America to persuade the private investor to step forward and furnish capital for the underdeveloped countries.

One government-sponsored group of experts after another has pressed for more private investment in this direction, and every distinguished speaker, whether representing government or business, has endorsed the plea. But in spite of these exhortations, the American capital market has given forth very little. The recent Randall Report has followed closely in the steps of earlier reports; the practical proposals it puts forward—if acted upon—would probably make little difference in regard to private investment in underdeveloped countries.

This negative attitude of American investors is not difficult to understand. There is first the memory of past losses. Then there is the unfriendly atmosphere of the cold war, which will be referred to in Chapter X, coupled with an intense feeling of the risks of actual war, as well as concern that some of the underdeveloped countries may be unreliable in their allegiance as political allies and also that they may not always be in favor of the systems of economic organization esteemed by the investors.

Viewed from Wall Street, many of these countries are run by governments and administrations that are ineffective, blundering, and corrupt, and their national economies are looked upon as poor and insecure. Purchasing power in their home markets is limited and usually cannot be increased by individual investment projects, but only by a consolidated development program, which is not a field of interest for private business. Further, the need for complementary social investment raises the level of production costs.

Then there is the great uncertainty about the transfer of profits. Even if there were a more or less general return to some kind of convertibility, many underdeveloped countries would not be able to fall into line and, even if they did, the convertibility of their currencies would not be relied upon as very lasting. The risk of nationalization and uncertainty concerning the principles on which compensation would be calculated and made transferable make things even more unattractive to private investors.

Added to all that is the uncertainty of the future taxation policy of these countries.

To cover imponderable losses, the returns to capital often need to be higher than are socially tolerable to the capital-importing countries. Dominating the whole situation is the fact that, as a competing element, the internal American capital market offers prospective investors high and secure returns and, in addition, ready possibilities of speculation for still higher gain. Thus it is natural that private foreign capital flows into America rather than out of it.

As a matter of fact, in spite of all exchange regulations, a considerable stream of foreign capital, even from the underdeveloped countries, is, as I have pointed out, steadily seeking harbor in America. "It is a part of our puzzle," observes Professor John H. Williams, that "while the role we should play in the world is that of a creditor country, the conditions are often more favorable for investment here, not only for Americans but for others."[17]

Against this background it is, indeed, understandable that the American private capital market is not giving forth much to the service of underdeveloped countries, and that what little is invested is kept under close control and is usually bound up with the immediate interests of an American firm.

IN WESTERN EUROPE

In industrially advanced countries that are not in the unique situation of the United States it is natural that a sort of national protective attitude develops in order to preserve capital resources for internal development. In all the countries of Western Europe, even in the progressive northwestern part of the continent, and not least in Britain, the constant concern is that the investment quota may not be high enough to sustain the desired rate of progress. Particularly when American economic aid is ebbing or ending, it becomes an even greater national interest to prevent the free outflow of capital.

As I pointed out in Chapter VI, in West-European countries there does not at present exist the political basis for financial, fiscal, and economic policies that could increase savings substantially enough for these countries once again to be able to export capital freely on a large scale. Besides the investments by Britain, France, and Belgium within their own monetary areas—which, however, have been substantial—the highest goal for "financial soundness" of the countries in this area that can be set with reasonable prospects of being attained is the prevention of such internal inflationary pressures as will, in spite of capital autarky, endanger their exchange balance.

Exchange controls provide a means of carrying out the policy of checking capital outflow, which is so generally accepted that, as I observed in Chapter VI, it is unlikely that these controls would be relaxed, even if advances were made towards convertibility. If this motive has not played a larger role in current discussion, the explanation is that the foreign exchange difficulties—and, more recently, the desirability of building up exchange reserves—have already provided overwhelming reasons for hindering capital export.

These changes in national attitudes and habits with respect to international capital movements are gradually producing far-reaching effects on the very structure of the private banking system. Once more excluding the exceptional situation of the United States, it can be said that international finance had provided much of the strength of any banking system vis-à-vis the state. It represented a sphere of liberty where the system operated outside the state boundaries and carried on independent foreign relations.

In fact, when these relations are nonexistent or closely controlled, the private banking system loses important elements of its *raison d'être* as private business. If, under the influence of a serious dip in the American business curve, Western Europe should again be confronted with the need for stricter national controls over trade and payments, the City of London would be in a situation which, apart from legal and constitutional forms —and the modern integrated state is very accommodating on questions of etiquette—would not materially differ from its being a part of public administration in the national welfare state. It is already far on the way to this status.

I cannot help feeling that the end of private international finance as we once knew it is somewhat of a loss for our civilization. It represented a wealth of established mores, trained talents, experience, and worldwide relations. Redirected to comply with present needs, it could still play an important role. In discussing these matters with my friends in the American Administration and in the banking world I have sometimes pointed to this and suggested a cooperative solution. There are in many European countries banking houses with traditions and proven ability in international finance that are now largely inactive in the international field because they cannot export national capital. In America there is capital enough and everybody is in principle in favor of a policy of larger investments abroad, but there is much more limited experience and talent in international lending. Nothing would be more natural than that resources should be pooled, so that European bankers, accepting the top risks, would be backed by American capital and would again exercise their dormant capacities.

Sir Arthur Salter once had the same idea: "As private investment becomes possible on a greater scale, and over a wider range, the association of United States institutions with British houses which have had long experience of overseas investment might prove very useful. The institutions through which foreign investment was arranged when the flow of capital was westward from the United Kingdom are still available for a flow in the opposite direction; and the traditional skill and know-how developed from nearly a century ago can be utilised, in appropriate association, by those who now inherit the creditor role."[18]

But this idea has been a failure. I have never yet found a responsible American prepared to believe that the dying private international finance in Europe was worth supporting—not even on straight business terms— while all good Americans have been enthusiatic for giving open grants to the European governments who, together with their administrations, have been expanding their field of internal power and responsibility for economic affairs.

GOVERNMENTS IN THE LENDING BUSINESS

My nostalgia for private international finance is partly caused by misgivings over government activity in this field. Governments may manage to handle well enough the policies and routines of internal finance, but in international finance they are not to be relied on to perform the role previously played by private finance.

Private finance was the guardian of certain functionally very useful taboos and magical concepts which are now gone or are going. The main one was that a credit operation was a business transaction. To be sure, politics were often mixed up with international finance, but, generally speaking, not in quite the blatant and unashamed way as when a loan is negotiated between governments and voted on in an elected chamber.

Along with the concept of a loan being a business transaction there was also the idea that it should be paid back. In most cases, the capital was in effect reinvested and stayed on for good, earning steady profits. With few execptions, all foreign debt retirements have been a by-product of war finance; depreciation through inflation and default have also been important in liquidating foreign debts. Great losses were continually made, and their history is fascinating reading. But at the time when a credit contract was concluded, the clear understanding between the two parties was *pacta sunt servanda*.

Without the fixed idea that credit is business, that profitability is important, and that there is a market where economic demand and supply for capital meet, international finance spills over into the indeterminate ocean of power politics, where the crackpots and the demagogues swim with great pleasure. The real danger is, of course, that with the disappearance of the capital market in the old-fashioned sense of the word, really worthwhile investment projects stand to lose their chance of being financed, or else they are modified for political reasons; in many cases they may then lose much of their economic character as self-liquidating investments.

America, with its unstable traditions and sad experiences in international finance, and faced with the necessity of giving funds outright to governments, has involuntarily contributed to killing the idea of international finance as a business proposition by insisting on calling all its reconstruction loans after the war "aid" or "assistance." In their policy statements, as well as in all statistical summaries, Americans have systematically been lumping together open grants, loans that it is not expected will necessarily be paid back according to agreed terms, and straight credits that are meant to be repaid.[19] Charity and business have been inextricably confused.

Moreover, they have insisted that the governments in the receiving countries should show their gratitude for it all and give the widest publicity to both credits and grants as "American aid." There was a philosophy behind it: America was, indeed, all for aid, but was cool towards, and suspicious of, international credit business. On one occasion, at the beginning of the European Recovery Program, the Swedes were caught up in the general dollar shortage, needed some stop-gap dollar credits, and looked upon themselves as fully credit-worthy—a situation not unprecedented in the old gold standard era. They, too, were urged to accept grants, for the sake of equality and as a gesture of cooperation—this, even though they did not want any grants and did not need them.

Naturally, the most prevalent need in those times was for aid in the usual sense of the word. But *some* countries needed only a credit which, in the normal way of international finance, would be paid back. Even more important, *a portion* of *all* countries' reconstruction needs could certainly have been met in this more regular fashion.

A poor and old-fashioned, though highly progressive country like Finland had demonstrated in the interwar period that repayments are possible if accompanied by some tightening of the belt. After the Second World war, incidentally, political considerations excluded Finland from the benefits of American aid; it had, on the contrary, to make reparations payments to the Soviet Union of about the same size as the aid and credit that in other circumstances it could have expected under the European Recovery Program. In addition, it had on its hands the problem of resettling refugees amounting to about 10 per cent of its population. In the end, however, Finland achieved a volume of investments and a rise in production that compares very favorably with the average in Western Europe.

The distinction between aid and credit should have been clearly made and continuously stressed. By insisting instead on systematically throwing everything into the mixed pot of "aid" and "assistance," the Americans have—certainly without intending to do so—inflicted an injury on the socially useful assumption that international finance is business. There is no doubt that a less sentimental and more selfish people would have handled a similar situation differently—with less generosity, probably, but with more respect for established business mores.

THE PRACTICAL PROBLEM

Professor Richard M. Bissel, Jr., has recently directed an appeal to the profession of economists that they should apply some ingenuity to the devising of new instruments and new forms, in the legal and institutional sense, for the international transfer of capital funds: "In the main, what is required, perhaps through public and quasi-public channels, is a flow of capital, handled much more in the form of capital; and I do not believe that the inter-governmental loan by itself is a broad enough, or a flexible enough, device to handle the capital flow of the scope that is needed."[20]

This is a sound suggestion. Having followed the discussion on this problem in the Economic and Social Council and similar intergovernmental forums, I am convinced that, for once, we would not necessarily speak to deaf ears if, after penetrating, critical, but constructive institutional research in the field of international finance, we economists were able to put forward practical proposals. Since every step towards both reviving capital movements between the advanced industrial countries and, more especially, directing some of the capital to the underdeveloped countries would work towards international integration, we would be in line with the great tradition of political economy.

What is needed above all is a restoration in some form of the long-term capital market. It is certain that such a profound but practical study would end up by endorsing the further development of the International Bank for Reconstruction and Development. Like the old private international financial houses, the Bank has succeeded in putting a barrier between its own operations and the type of opportunistic politics that inevitably dominate national governments when entering the international lending business.

The Bank has successfully insisted on direct and indirect profitability and reasonable prospects of repayment, and in so doing has respected the distinction between credits and grants. Distributing what was in the main American money, it has thereby begun to undo part of the damage the American government has unintentionally inflicted during the postwar period on the important old concept that international finance is business rather than charity. This has naturally caused the Bank to be more restrictive in its lending and to distribute the loans in a way other than would have been desirable in view of the development needs in the world. But by its conservative policy it has preserved itself as a sound financial institution and, as it now stands, it is therefore an international asset of no small value.

There are other reasons why its operations so far have been of limited scope and quite disproportionate to the capital needs for development.[21] For one thing, the Bank acquires funds on the private capital market and must be interested in preserving a good credit standing. There is also the point that the Bank may not engage in equity financing and its loans must be underwritten by governments or central banks. Further, the original intention and hope, that the Bank could act as a catalyst and, by guaranteeing certain risks, induce private capital to do the larger part of the job, has not been realized except on a very limited scale.[22] A fourth reason, and the main one, is that so few of the underdeveloped countries have as yet had the time and ability to spell out their development aspirations in terms of well-prepared and well-planned, credit-worthy projects ready for immediate execution.

As an instrument for handling government credit the Bank is so obviously superior to the governments themselves, precisely because it has protected the old decorum of handling credit as business, that it should now be entrusted with the handling of larger sums. It should be given the green light for the extension of its lending to the limit of its available funds and for the worth-while projects that are adequately planned by cooperation between the Bank and the governments of the underdeveloped countries.

Its activities should also be extended to enable it to induce a greater and more regular flow of private capital. To this end, the proposed International Finance Corporation, planned as an affiliate, would undoubtedly have a useful function to fulfil. However little such a corporation can do in the present political and economic climate, and however small the funds at its disposal, even that much would constitute a modest beginning and a first step forward to getting private capital moving to the underdeveloped countries. It is, indeed, discouraging that this sound, modest, and well-prepared project has so far been held up by the unwillingness of the advanced countries—principally the United States— to contribute the basic operating funds; a change of policy has, however, recently been announced by the United States Government and there is now some hope of seeing the project realized.

If the judgment generally stands that national governments are bad international bankers, that does not exclude state institutions being formed to operate under established principles of law that permit a semi-independent management and, above all, prohibit *ad hoc* interference from the government or, still worse, the elected assembly. On the whole the American Export-Import Bank meets these requirements and can easily be reformed so as to meet them even better. The public investment institutions set up in Britain for economic development in the colonial territories are interesting institutional innovations. Also the one or two private investment foundations in the United States—basically nonprofit-making—have certainly their role to play.

One result of a comprehensive, practical, and institutional study of the possibilities of reviving the international capital market would be to demonstrate the need for a large number of different instruments, which could operate side by side. Both the demand for and the supply of capital are very diversified. Thus, the need for medium-term loans for financing specific export deals is a very special credit demand. In this restricted field the national governments, incidentally, have proved to be much more up to the task than they have in long-term lending. This is understandable, insofar as that is the aspect of international banking which comes nearest to internal finance.

The problem is not so much one for America, where business has a high liquidity and can afford to take big risks on its own account or supported by either its normal banking connections or the Export-Import Bank. It is European business that has been losing out in Latin American markets, and also in some parts of Asia, partly because it has not been able to compete with the easy credit terms offered by American exporters. In this field governments and their national banking dependencies can render their own export industries a significant service by supplying capital or underwriting the risk; and more generous grants of medium-term credits in connection with exports would also be of considerable importance to underdeveloped countries. If they added up to a certain volume they could actually serve as a revolving long-term credit devoted to initial investments for economic development.[23]

The granting of such credits is both rational and economically feasible, even on the part of a country that has no capital surplus and is in fact itself out to acquire foreign capital. The Italian equipment industry,[24] for instance, has since the war worked at only a part of its capacity and many of its workers have been unemployed or uneconomically employed in the industry. If the rendering of export credits is a condition of a considerable increase in production and the fuller utilization of workers and existing plants, these credits are in reality financed by the increased production itself. This is a restricted field in which the international finance market can be considerably stimulated. Western Germany and Japan are well ahead in this field in many overseas markets.

It would not be excluded that, as a sort of extension of the practice of export medium-term credits, industrial firms might be prepared to extend their engagements in new industries in the underdeveloped countries to a somewhat longer or even permanent partnership, and might obtain the necessary financial backing for this at home. A recently reported German financial undertaking connected with the export of equipment for a steel plant in India suggests one way in which this might work.

A similar thought is also behind the proposal of the Secretariat of the Economic Commission for Europe, made in its recent study of the economic development of Southern Europe.[25] It is there suggested that there are possibilties of increasing the amount of long-term and medium-term capital forthcoming by enabling underdeveloped countries to issue bonds for purchase in equipment-exporting countries, part of which would be resold to an international lending agency. Armed with the association —though not the guaranty—of the lending agency, the country would then be more easily able to raise the remaining part of the credit in those countries where it could obtain the equipment to its greatest comparative advantage. Private capital could also be forthcoming, directly through purchase of part of the remainder of the bonds, or indirectly through a kind of international financial consortium comprised of the international lending agency and a number of private commercial banks, in countries where balance of payments considerations do not bar such investments.

The underdeveloped countries need to buy technique as well as equipment. In the advanced countries industries are usually intent upon producing products for sale, rather than selling their techniques. There must be more possibilities than are at present realized for industrial firms to undertake the setting up of plants in an underdeveloped country and keep a part-investment in it, either permanently or for a determined period, while at the same time the government guarantees the transfer of profit and, in the latter case, also the general amortization of the investment.

Professor P. N. Rosenstein-Rodan has devised an ingenious technique for this purpose, which he calls a "management contract." The foreign firm contracts to set up and manage—for a limited period—a new plant in the underdeveloped country; the plant is owned from the start by its government, but the foreign firm helps to finance it by granting a fixed interest-bearing loan for the duration of the management contract, say 5–8 years. This would avoid permanent foreign ownership and control, yet yield technical assistance and some outside capital.[26]

It will be a slow and painstaking task to rebuild an international capital market yielding any substantial amounts of capital for economic development in underdeveloped countries. A great number of existing and newly created institutions and instruments need to be utilized. Governments must become involved in many of these efforts, though so far as possible prevented from *ad hoc* interference in actual credit operations. The institutionalized saving, which is increasingly coming to dominate the capital supply in all advanced countries, must in some way or another be drawn into international lending, too. And the underdeveloped countries need in many cases to readjust their attitude to foreign capital investment. As the lack of monetary stability and economic progress is a main deterrent to capital influx, the most general request to them is simply that they should be more successful in their economic development policy. However, this in its turn would be easier if foreign capital were more readily available.

THE PRESENT SITUATION

The main conclusion of this chapter is, however, that for the time being —and taking into account private loans and direct investments, government loans and loans from the International Bank, short- and medium-term export credits, etc.—capital just does not flow to underdeveloped countries in amounts that are in any reasonable proportion to the general development needs of the world. Further, the little flow that there is trickles out in the most haphazard way, usually without any relation to real economic opportunities and real economic needs. There is no longer in existence a competitive international capital market where supply meets demand, but only a broken remnant of a market, where the movements are blocked and perverted.

In this chapter I am not discussing the need either for outright grants or for subsidies in the form of lower rates of interest than the market rate for capital—including payments for the element of risk. Such grants and subsidies are required to enable the execution of social investment projects which neither the International Bank nor any other regular credit organ in the capital market can handle, precisely because the projects do not directly increase the borrowing countries' repayment capacity in the original currency of the loan. These grants and subsidies are, indeed, very different operations, and it is most desirable that they be kept separate.

Rationally, credit on regular business terms should be allowed to perform as large a part as it can of the common task of providing capital to the underdeveloped countries. The funds for aid will always be severely limited, and the need for them would be correspondingly smaller, the more effectively the capital market operates. It is therefore also very much in the interest of the underdeveloped countries that credit on business terms be enlarged to the practical limits, which will in any case be a much smaller amount than the actual needs.

On the other hand, it is equally clear that international aid, devoted to external economies and social investments that are not directly profitable, will increase the number of really credit-worthy projects and so lay a basis for more credits on straight business terms.

CHAPTER IX

International Aid

A Hesitant Beginning

As I have suggested in Chapter III, in the few countries within the non-Soviet world that have succeeded in approaching the ideal of national integration—among them the United States—that goal has not been attained by the unhampered operation of an automatic price mechanism and abstention from discriminating interventions on the part of the state and other collective units in the community. The achievement of national integration has, instead, been a political and social process aimed at organizing, controlling, and changing the conditions for the functioning of the price mechanism. This process has, however, been determined largely by the ideal—a living force in the minds of these nations—of achieving an ever-greater equality of opportunity for all their citizens. One of the most important of state interventions in the nationally integrated economies has been the increasing application of the principle of sharing burdens. The readiness to share displayed by the various groups comprising a nation-state has been an index of the strength of the psychological basis for integration.

From the evolutionary point of view, this process started in the local community. A village in any of our countries a couple of centuries ago expected that a large part of the economic activities of the community would be handled through the "market economy." The functioning of this market economy was closely regulated by mores and by formal established laws and regulations. In addition, however, there were a number of activities where benefits and costs were distributed not by the market mechanism, but in accordance with the principle of sharing.

Benefits were meted out according to certain criteria: on a sort of insurance principle for those requirements which were of a universal character, such as legal and police protection, and protection against, and compensation for, fire; or on the basis of simple needs, such as education and the exigencies of old age, sickness, and poverty. For this part, costs were apportioned on the principle of equity: per worker or per household, per unit of land owned or harvest reaped, etc. The scope of activities under communal financing differed considerably, and in some countries it stretched far into the sphere of production.

One universal trait of the historical process of national integration was that functions were gradually taken over at a higher level of social organization: from the individual household to the local community and from both of these to central state organs. In particular, as the scope of socialized activities increased, the financing, or part of it, was taken over by the state, even if it was left to the local communities to administer them. National defense was made necessary by international disintegration and early became almost exclusively a state responsibility, but much more generally the sharing principle was gradually applied on the national level in an increasing number of fields.

In our time we witness hesitating attempts to extend this principle to the international level. Alliances have always involved some sharing of treasures as well as of blood, and the most common kind of international sharing we have seen has had a very clear national motive: the economizing of blood. Nondefensive international transfers without repayment have been limited to immigrants' remittances, along lines determined by consanguinity, and contributions for the relief of victims of disasters, whose plight can vividly be visualized. The extension of international sharing to economic and social needs after the Second World War and its organization as an interstate responsibility are new things. In the turmoil of today's increasing international disintegration, this is one element working towards integration.

To meet the needs of reconstruction and rehabilitation after the war a unique international organization was set up, UNRRA. It was liquidated in Europe barely two years after the end of the fighting in the area, and in Asia a year later. This was, as we know, one of the crucial steps in the disintegration of the war's Great Alliance. Fiorello La Guardia fought gloriously, but in vain, against what he considered to be great shortsightedness on the part of the government of his country,[1] but only UNICEF survived—a salvaged remnant of a great humanitarian plan. It proved a little easier to preserve international solidarity for the needs of children.

Thereafter—and with the exception of the budgets of the United Nations, the Specialized Agencies, and the Technical Assistance Program, etc., which are quantitatively insignificant—international sharing of the costs of reconstruction and of development has followed a principle different from that of internal sharing in an integrated national community: the determination of the size of benefits and of their distribution has been virtually a matter for unilateral decision by the distributing nation. The form may vary, but that is the essence. It is akin to the charitable contributions by the lord of the manor, rather than to the levying of burdens upon themselves by the free men of the village or the elected representatives of the citizens in the modern integrated state.

It is true that the elected representatives of a contributing country decide upon the award of a gift and impose a corresponding tax burden upon their citizens; but the gift is handed over to the receiving country without any participation in the decision by the government of that country and its citizens, other than to accept and to use it for the general benefit, under certain conditions laid down in agreement with the contributing country's government. Governments have authority only within state boundaries.

It is inevitable that some individuals and regions in the receiving country will be richer than individuals and regions in the contributing country—for example, in the case of the Marshall Plan, some areas of Denmark or even Britain, France, or Italy, compared with certain areas of the United States. The same is true for individuals, even if the receiving country is a much poorer one, such as India. This is a serious psychological and moral difficulty in any intergovernmental scheme for the redistribution of income and wealth. More generally, the difficulty is, however, the lack of a really collective responsibility exercised through a democratic political process which can give reality to the demand that taxation shall be based on representation.

The ultimate reason for this difficulty is, of course, that we are not living, and shall not in our time be living, under a world government which, through due political process, would decide upon a sharing of burdens and bring about a redistribution of incomes and wealth by establishing individual, but impersonal, obligations and rights under the law. While fiscal and other redistributional policies have long been operating within all well-integrated countries, and with considerable equalizing effect on internal economic conditions within their boundaries, economic inequalities between the various nations have been permitted to grow continuously. These inequalities are becoming increasingly explosive as the poorer countries' development aspirations are frustrated while the already advanced countries forge ahead. The very imperfect instruments at our disposal—our weak intergovernmental organizations—are, as will be discussed presently, nonetheless superior to unilateral national philanthropy.

SHARING BETWEEN THE RICH

So far, capital aid, as distinct from loans, to underdeveloped countries from the industrially advanced ones has not been channeled through such organizations. It has, further, been a comparatively tiny stream, and has been distributed to individual countries without any real regard to relative need or economic usefulness.

The United States has been the chief donor, but by far the greater part of its donations, including most of the Marshall aid, has not gone to the underdeveloped regions. From their point of view this aid has in the main been a sharing between the rich and industrially developed countries, leaving the poor and underdeveloped ones not entirely, but largely, in the cold. In the whole postwar period, until December 1953, United States' foreign grants—as distinct from loans—amounted to a net figure of $33.2 billion. Of this, $23.4 billion went to Western Europe, including its dependencies and Greece, Turkey, and Yugoslavia, of which $7.7 billion was military aid,[2] leaving $15.7 billion for strictly economic aid. Asia and the Pacific received in all $7.6 billion, $2.3 being military aid. Of the $5.3 billion nonmilitary aid to this area, $4.9 billion went to Formosa, Japan, the Philippines, and South Korea and rather less than half a billion dollars to other countries of the region. Latin America received virtually no aid.[3]

Marshall aid was of great benefit to the individual West European countries. It helped tide them over a period of serious exchange disequilibrium and enabled them for a number of years to keep their national investment quotas and their rate of industrial development at a high level. Indirectly, their economic advance—and, in particular, their improved exchange position—also benefited countries outside Europe, especially those in the sterling and franc areas and in Latin America.

Furthermore, Marshall aid was in itself a highly significant act of international solidarity by one nation towards a number of other nations. It does not require any comprehensive or deep study of the American motives for this extraordinary aid to say from first-hand observation of the American people that, in the beginning, the main attitude was much more the positive one of sympathy and solidarity, rather than the negative one of fear of Communism.

Willingness to spend out of simple Christian neighborliness has always been a cultural trait of the American people, stemming from their Puritan background and the living conditions in a frontier economy, and preserved by rapid economic progress. If, for instance, America did not institute a modern system of social security until almost the Great Depression, one of the explanations, which should not be forgotten, is that America had, and still has, the world's most generous and best-organized system of local voluntary sharing. It is true that the Americans tried eagerly to convince themselves at the very inauguration of the Marshall Plan that they were acting solely with their own national interest in view, but this was only a further example of the strange suspicion on the part of the American people of their own generous motives, which I once analyzed as a slightly perverted element of their Puritan tradition.

Even though the solidarity shown by the Marshall Plan was one-sided and largely confined to the United States, and even though it embraced only a selected number of nations, with which the Americans are closely related by cultural and blood ties, it nevertheless, and regardless of the underlying motives, demonstrated a concept that goes beyond immediate national interests, and so is important to our problem. If, with all the ups and downs, this feeling of oneness with those abroad could be gradually stimulated in other advanced nations, and especially if it could be translated into feelings of solidarity with the untold hundreds of millions of poor colored people in the backward regions of the world, serious progress could be made towards international integration.

UNITED NATIONS PROPOSALS FOR AID TO UNDERDEVELOPED COUNTRIES

In the foreseeable future, however, the basis of international solidarity will not be firm enough to support, at the best, more than a very modest scheme of international aid to underdeveloped countries. To make a comparison that inevitably comes to mind, it can hardly be more than a tiny fraction of what the advanced countries are prepared to pay for their own defense.

The United Nations experts on economic development calculated that for the underdeveloped countries the capital needed annually from abroad for industry and agriculture alone (that is, excluding complementary social investments), in order to ensure the very modest increase in per capita income of 2 per cent a year, would be around ten billion dollars.[4] This would hardly be 15 per cent of the total burden of expenditure on defense undertaken after due political process by the citizens of the advanced countries.[5]

One may think that this estimate of the capital needs for such a limited development effort is a little on the high side and that, in addition, as I have argued in the last chapter, as large a part as possible of these capital needs should be provided for by ordinary credits rather than aid. But even a tenth of that amount, corresponding to no more than 1 or 2 per cent of real armament costs, would for the time being not be forthcoming from the present inadequate basis of human solidarity.

The United Nations experts quoted above urged most strongly that some mechanism be created for transferring to the underdeveloped countries grants-in-aid, reaching eventually three billion dollars a year. This, according to their calculations, would be less than 1 per cent of the aggregate national incomes of the advanced countries in the non-Soviet world. These nations are not yet prepared to set up the proposed Special United Nations Fund for Economic Development, with the modest initial minimum capital of two hundred and fifty million dollars—less than a tenth of what the experts wanted to become the annual aid and corresponding to only a fraction of 1 per cent of the advanced countries' annual defense burden.

Interestingly enough, the main reason invoked by the major powers for refusing the scheme was their defense burdens. From many points of view this is faulty logic; for even the size of the annual fluctuations of the defense burden is many times larger than the proposed minimum amount of the fund. Bad logic can be realistic psychology, however. The refusal probably corresponds accurately to popular feelings or, anyhow, to feelings in the legislatures, as they respond to the cold war.

REASONS FOR INTERNATIONALIZING INTERNATIONAL AID

Whatever the level of international aid to underdeveloped countries, there are important reasons why we should continue to press for organizing as large a part of it as possible through international agencies with policy-making responsibilities. I shall try to spell out what some of those reasons are.

Only by insulating in this way the ultimate receiver of financial aid from the contributor will it to some extent be possible to remove the political element from this international redistribution of resources, or at least to keep to a minimum elements of demagogy, log-rolling, and pressure politics. It is true that at the present stage of international integration, or rather disintegration, where the solidarity basis is almost nonexistent, it will be difficult to induce the contributing governments to abstain from national glorification, the possibility of manipulations, and the political pressure value that governments who give want to gain in return. For their part, some of the receiving countries that are in a stronger bargaining position to secure unilateral aid from the United States or other advanced countries may occasionally feel that they have good reasons for wishing to by-pass an international agency possessing responsibility for a just and economic distribution of aid.

All in all, and notwithstanding the strain of the cold war and the fact that aid has been mainly unilateral, I believe that there are reasons for astonishment that there have not been more ulterior motives behind the considerations of aid, particularly in the United States. Narrowly conceived national motives have never been exclusively dominant at any time. Further, we should not hide from ourselves the fact that even if the function of distributing aid is handed over to an international agency, it will often be impossible to keep out some of the undesirable sorts of national pressure.

And yet, even if only part of the aid is canalized in this way, and even if an international aid agency displays certain weaknesses in the face of national political pressures, the very establishment of such an agency would be a significant step in the direction of international integration. Many of the successful institutions in our well-integrated national states have had imperfect beginnings.

I am acutely aware that the cold war has caused feelings to harden and that the present trend is rather towards the national and political organization of international aid. Professor Jacob Viner has recently stressed this trend in a rather blunt way.

He first expresses his opinion that "if only strictly economic considerations were involved, such requests [for aid] would have no chance of receiving serious attention on the part of the advanced countries. . . . It is only because strategic considerations are involved that requests of this kind by the underdeveloped countries have any degree of political practicability. The underdeveloped countries are to some extent pawns in the play of power politics."[6]

After some further reasoning—where he also notes that "sympathy for the distress of peoples subject to mass poverty will play a part"—he reaches the following conclusion:

> The only factor which could persuade us to undertake a really large program of economic aid to the underdeveloped countries would be the decision that the friendship and alliance of those countries are strategically, politically, and psychologically valuable to us in the cold war, that economic aid on a large scale can be relied upon to assure such friendship and alliance to us, and that the cost to us of a greatly enlarged program of economic aid would not be an excessive price to pay for these strategic gains.

To Viner's statement, I would add a few remarks which I believe are of importance for a fuller and more rational appreciation of the problem. Viner does not mention the serious possibility of a deterioration of standards when international aid is distributed according to strategic principles and its use is conditioned by political considerations in the receiving as well as in the contributing country. As experience has shown, bringing politics into international aid carries the danger that the moral and economic foundations may crumble.

One obvious danger is that economic aid becomes reserved for the emergency cases, which usually are also the bad cases. Mr. Eugene Staley, who has written a book on the United States policy towards the underdeveloped countries from the explicitly stated viewpoint of how to save them from Communism and draw them into political alliance with the United States in the cold war, formulates in the following way the practical dilemma which meets the strategic aid policy:

> If we do not give vigorous support to governments that are trying to move in progressive, democratic directions when they need it and want it, we are likely

to be forced into the position later of having to back a government that is bad by our standards for the sole reason that it is the only available alternative to a Communist regime. . . . When in order to prevent a Communist seizure we have to back a corrupt or unpopular or foreign-dominated government, we do immense political harm to our world position. . . . In that case, also, the appropriations are likely to go mainly for military measures, with bad political repercussions, much more than might have been required to get better results by forehanded economic aid. . . . How long will it take us to learn that when a progressive reform government happens to be in power in an underdeveloped country we should go all out in aiding it to grapple with its economic and political problems?"[7]

A selection according to political needs is often bound to imply the diversion of aid into the "rat holes," to use an American expression.

The case against the strategic aid policy is well brought out by Mr. Adlai E. Stevenson in his recent book *Call to Greatness*:

A policy based just on anti-Communism and military potency is not in the spirit of this great movement of the twentieth century and will win few hearts. The challenge to us is to identify ourselves with this social and human revolution, to encourage, aid and inspire the aspirations of half of mankind for a better life, to guide these aspirations into paths that lead to freedom. To default would be disaster.[8]

I am not one of those who think that economic aid is a miracle drug and a sure cure for all ailments, and especially when it is allocated and judged here at home not on its value in building stable, democratic societies, but in winning a country, India for example, to our side. . . . We shall have to learn that we cannot buy agreement or effective alliance among the new states of the Middle East and Asia with economic or military aid. All we can do, and in my judgment must do, is to help with the building of free and independent governments whose people will defend them.[9]

The danger is also, as a wise European historian of diplomacy has recently explained, that "when one state is completely dependent on another, it is the former which can call the tune; it can threaten to collapse unless supported and its protector has no answering threat in return."[10]

The underdeveloped countries, on their side, are reluctant, and will be increasingly reluctant, to accept the role assigned to them by the strategic aid policy as "pawns in the play of power politics." Lord John Boyd Orr is aware of this:

It is given not in the interest of the people, but to stop the spread of Communism in the interest of the Western powers. An American has said that 600 million dollars could save India from going Communist. To bring India within the sphere of influence of the United States at a cost of a dollar and a half per head of its population would be a good bargain if it could be carried through. But India, proud of its independence, could not be bought by all the wealth of the United States, and that goes for all the resurgent nations.[11]

Former Ambassador Chester Bowles explains similarly, and from careful and intelligent first-hand observation:

Anyone who knows South Asia also knows that if Point Four aid seems to be in any way tied to our military and alliance system it will be rejected by most of the nations which are in greatest need of help. For their own reasons . . . these countries are determined not to become formally identified with either the American or Soviet side in the cold war, and if our offer of assistance has even the most indirect military overtones, that will be the end of it.[12]

I have already observed that some governments in underdeveloped countries might feel they can obtain more from a unilateral than an international management of aid and so favor that alternative; many of them, however, will not. Even in the former group of countries, there will be a tide of public opinion opposed to this policy of their government, and the end result may well be animosity towards a contributing country, accused of trying to buy for money friendship and strategic alliance in the cold war.

As to how the money should be spent, it is, further, obvious that a poor country will willingly and gratefully take much advice from, and even control by, a properly established international body, working under intergovernmental sanctions, which it will not willingly accept, or— because of public opinion—not be able to accept when prodded by a rich and exuberant world power.

Giving and taking aid is an extremely delicate matter, the psychology of which should be studied with utmost care before a position is taken. This is particularly needed when the giving country is a world power involved in a violent world conflict. In the interest of international harmony and understanding I would, however, warn off any country from giving, or receiving, unilateral aid, except when there are no other means available. If this is the situation and unilateral aid becomes a necessity, I would advise the most circumspect consideration of the political and institutional form in which it is going to be awarded and received. In this connection it should be especially noted that the blunt political practices in Washington and the controversial habits in American public discussion, which are so admirably suited to the needs of domestic politics in a great and consolidated democracy, are not conducive to saving the faces of governments in underdeveloped countries which receive unilateral aid on political conditions.

Finally, in the United States itself, this hard-boiled policy, which is so definitely out of line with the cherished humanitarian traditions of the nation, will not be an inspiring one. I personally doubt very much whether a comprehensive and lasting policy of international aid on a strategic basis will ever have the chance of becoming accepted in the United States. To the minor—and, from the point of view of real economic needs and real effects in promoting economic development, rather haphazard—extent that this policy has been tested out, the results abroad are not very encouraging. The effects at home of unilateral, strategic aid policy will in the longer run almost certainly be disappointment and frustration, compunction and bitterness over the aid-receivers' ingratitude; in the end the result is likely to be a reduction in the amount of aid forthcoming from the United States. I have further comments on this problem in Chapter XIV.

The Necessity of a Fairer Distribution of the Burden

A second important reason for distributing aid through international institutions is that only thereby will it be possible to achieve a semblance of a fair distribution of the burden among the countries that are better off.

So far the burden of aid to independent underdeveloped countries, to the extent that there has been any, has been shouldered almost entirely by the United States and, to a lesser degree, Britain and the economically advanced Commonwealth countries associated with the Colombo Plan. There are really no grounds at all why other countries, such as the Scandinavian group, should not accept a fuller share of responsibility for international aid. Neither is there any justification for certain countries, and in particular the United States, to shoulder such a disproportionately large part of the burden.

All those other countries which now hold back from giving their full share can answer that they need the funds for their own development; but this is hardly a legitimate answer. Almost every farmer or businessman could give the same argument when he has to pay his taxes. In fact, even the United States can point to other useful employment for its taxpayers' money. Though foreigners have been led to forget it, and sometimes Americans too, the United States also has city slums which it wants to rebuild; in many parts of the country the need is felt for more classrooms and more teachers, and it is generally recognized that the teachers are underpaid; many remote areas are pleading for modern medical facilities. And there are many courthouses and Post Office buildings, bridges, and dams that have not been erected because the budget was too tight.

But international aid, like national redistribution, is founded upon the idea that from the viewpoint of common goals and in a spirit of solidarity somebody's money is better used for assisting somebody else; this does not presume that the giver has no other good use for it himself. Furthermore, if fairly apportioned, the share in the total amount of aid to under-developed countries that has any likelihood of being generally accepted in the present circumstances would not be overwhelming to any country. If the industrially advanced countries were prepared, not to lower their standards (which has never been suggested), but to set aside a small share of the expected future continuous rise in their standards, say, a fifth of the normal annual rise in their per capita national incomes, this would amount to a sum several times greater than that presently discussed.

As things are today, it would, of course, not have been practical for the experts appointed by the United Nations to make recommendations for an international fund for economic development to come out in favor of levies which, once internationally agreed, would be compulsory. Their suggestion that, nevertheless, the fund should not be established before there are at least thirty contributing nations is an illustration of their appreciation that aid is "indivisible."

To propose that all aid should be distributed by a United Nations agency, while assuming that the United States nevertheless should continue paying for 90 per cent of it, would be a preposterous and impossible solution. A truly international endeavor must be based on a fair and reasonable sharing of the burden. This is the true challenge to all countries raised by the need in our increasingly interdependent world for international aid.

One reason why I am so adamant on this second reason for organizing international aid internationally, is its relevance to the first one. Only if we reach a universal and equitable participation by governments in international aid can we hope successfully to strive for the elimination of political considerations. From the luxury of his independent status in the academic world and in his efforts towards objective analysis, a scholar can freely criticize the unpleasant sides of pressure politics in an international undertaking. A government has no such independent intellectual recourse; instead, it has power. But in international affairs, even more than in domestic politics, there is no real representation without taxation. A government that does not pay its due share has little voice. It might well hold that the matter is none of its concern. This, however, is a short-sighted view, because we are living together on a shrinking globe, and the way these matters are handled is of considerable interest to all countries—indeed, to all men.

The third reason is that only under an internationally agreed system of widely shared responsibility among the advanced nations will it be at all possible in the present political climate for the aid forthcoming for this purpose to reach any major magnitude and acquire a basis of stability. People in the United States who are conscious of their truly unprecedented international philanthropy in the postwar period—of which, however, very little went to the underdeveloped countries—are now suggesting that aid should stop. The Randall Report states harshly: "Underdeveloped areas are claiming a right to economic aid from the United States. . . . We recognize no such right." When speaking about "right," the commission does, of course, not refer to positive international law, but to natural law, to moral obligations. This statement is important, because it probably expresses realistically the opinion of the majority of the American people, finding themselves as almost the only donors. I believe that the spread of the strategic aid idea, which I criticized above, has also its psychological basis in a feeling in America that the lack of universal sharing is unfair.

The United Nations expanded program for technical assistance—which has no capital to lend or give away—represents on a very small scale an institutionalizing of international assistance, and this is of itself a fact of no small importance. It stands for the recognition of the principle of international solidarity on a really world-wide scale and, indeed, exemplifies an approach towards a sort of international taxation for common ends. But when the United States, in addition to a very much bigger national undertaking under Point Four, promised to match 60 per cent of every other contribution over a certain level to the United Nations program in order to get it agreed upon, and when this was accepted by the other countries, and the whole scheme placed on the basis of yearly voluntary contributions, the political balance of that scheme was destroyed and its possibility of sound growth was circumscribed.[13]

Whatever extra or exclusive responsibility the smaller countries may have found it right and proper to let the great powers carry on behalf of the Arab refugees or the reconstruction of war-damaged Korea—since they felt little share themselves in the responsibility for the policies when the catastrophes were developing—the small scheme for United Nations technical assistance should have been made a really common undertaking. In the same way, the liquidation of UNRRA undoubtedly cannot be discussed without bearing in mind that at the end the United States was paying the totally disproportionate share of 77 per cent of that organization's budget.

THE AWKWARD FACT OF THE UNITED STATES' BIGNESS

At bottom there is, of course, the serious reality that in the non-Soviet world the United States is economically so disproportionately big and its national income so large a part of total income in that part of the world. That is undoubtedly one of the main reasons why it is so exceedingly difficult to build up and sustain truly international organizations.

Under any system of fair shares the material contribution of the United States must be by far the largest of any country. If the United States then wishes to have a say in the control and policy of an organization in relation to its contribution—which from its own point of view may seem reasonable—the other and, particularly, the smaller countries, are apt to slip away and keep aloof. That, however, only tends to make the organization still more dominated by the United States which, in turn, will give more real cause for the others to withdraw still further, and so on in a cumulative fashion.

The United States may then choose to "go it alone" whenever it really matters. The detrimental effects of such a development in the field of international aid are serious and have been commented upon above. In the climate of the cold war the United States may be tempted to use aid as a means of political influence; the receiving countries will anyhow suspect such a purpose, and the new theory, which I have referred to, of strategic aid will only confirm it for them. This will insert still another element of conflict among and within nations. It will, furthermore, tend to destroy the economic norms for giving aid. In the end, it will act as a powerful motive for the United States to get out of it all by cutting down the costs of international aid.

The general problem created by the relative size and power of the United States has not been solved in any of our international organizations, and it is doubtful whether it can be solved in an ideal fashion. Though we do not live in an ideal world, some makeshifts and compromises are, however, better than others. The International Bank has rightly been characterized as "in effect an American lending agency"; but it has been able to carry on its activity with a considerable degree of independence and objectivity. It was set up as an international agency with internationally decided and fixed norms for its operations; if the present trend towards a greater part of the funds being acquired in the capital markets of other countries is continued and strengthened, the Bank could become still more independent.

Likewise, if an international aid agency could be set up and given equally definite terms of reference, and if other countries committed themselves to some real sacrifices—never bigger than abstention from a smaller part of their expected rise in wealth and welfare—it would have a similar chance of independence and objectivity. One of the probable effects would be that even the American contributions would be more regular and larger.

I have quoted above a rather harsh statement from the Randall Report, but it should not be forgotten that there is in the United States, as in other advanced countries, a minority with much broader views; it was actually represented in the commission by the young trade unionist,

Mr. David J. McDonald. This minority would get a better hearing and, indeed, have a more valid cause, if the advanced countries outside the United States would come forward with greater generosity.

The Problem Will Stay with Us

The conclusions we reach are not very encouraging, at least not in the short view. In the last chapter I discussed the defunct international capital market, which is now bringing forth virtually no capital on commercial terms for the development of underdeveloped countries. Whatever happens, the flow of capital will, under any foreseeable conditions, be altogether inadequate from the point of view of the underdeveloped countries' urgent development needs. In addition, we find that the prospects for any sizeable amounts of aid to be made available are bleak.

Before the last war, very few people would have taken seriously a demand for organized measures of redistribution between nations. The principle is now accepted, for instance, in the field of technical assistance, but the actual amounts of international funds involved are infinitesimal. It will probably take a long time before the richer nations are prepared to accept appreciable sacrifices for the sake of the economic growth and the social welfare of the poorer nations as regular and established burdens upon their taxpayers.

Inevitably, though, a policy of international economic sharing will gradually, short periods of retrogression apart, come to involve ever larger amounts of direct assistance. For the immediate future, however, what I have called the solidarity basis—the consciousness of common interests and purposes and the willingness to make sacrifices for the countless families in underdeveloped countries—does not apparently exist to the extent that would make available large increases of economic aid.

Naturally big things can happen. The cold war may subside still further, defense expenditure may decline, and it might then come to pass, as President Eisenhower has suggested and the United Nations envisaged in a resolution, that the advanced nations would be wise and generous enough to devote a large part of the savings from disarmament to aid for underdeveloped countries. Or there may be a depression, with the advanced nations enlightened enough to want to increase the purchasing power of the underdeveloped countries. On the other hand, the reaction to a reduction in armament expenditure or to a depression might just as likely be the opposite; that would regrettably be more in keeping with tradition.

Meanwhile, the United Nations various forums for international economic debate are increasingly being used by the underprivileged countries to launch concerted attacks, demanding reform of the present system of international distribution of wealth. On many occasions the heated controversy on this new front almost succeeds in stealing the show from the political East–West conflict.

One thing is certain: the poor countries will raise their voices louder and louder. They will not recognize as true progress towards international integration a world development under which they remain poor, or even, as has been the case in recent years in some parts of the world, become poorer, while the rich countries become ever richer. They will not recognize our "right" to stay aloof.

RELATION TO INTERNAL INEQUALITIES IN UNDERDEVELOPED COUNTRIES

One last note must be struck before we leave the problem of international aid to the poorer countries. The backwardness and the absence of national integration in these countries is also shown up by the fact that their internal distribution of income and wealth is most unequal. It is, indeed, a regular occurrence endowed almost with the dignity of an economic law that the poorer the country, the greater the difference between poor and rich.

This often creates a paradoxical situation at international conferences. The poorest countries are often represented by very rich, occasionally fabulously rich, individuals, while the richer countries are represented by ordinary middle- and upper-class persons who, for the most part, have inherited little and, though enjoying incomes in some relation to their talents and having assembled funds for modest security, are not at all rich in the oriental or Latin American meaning of the word. This reflects, of course, the socially significant fact that, while we in the richer nations are ruled by governments that are effectively controlled by the masses of people, the poor countries are often ruled by oligarchies of very wealthy individuals and families.

In such a general issue as that of international aid it can be observed that even when the government representing a poor country rests upon such an oligarchy, it will most often voice on the international scene the real interests as they are felt by the nation as a whole—and would no doubt be expressed if the masses were politically conscious and alert and were effectively represented. But there are certain inhibitions natural in the situation and there are certain sour overtones to their pleas for help for their poor citizens.

As for the richer nations, it becomes, of course, impossible for them to avoid a feeling that it would be appropriate if the poorer nations reformed themselves and taxed more heavily their own wealthy individuals, before they come up with demands for the taxation of the nations that are better off. This criticism is seldom voiced openly and almost never in this blunt form; but as an underlying thought it is present in most of the international debates on international aid.[14] There can be no doubt that it represents one of the not unimportant elements impeding its growth.

Aid as Insurance against Revolutions

My purpose in this chapter on the international redistribution problem has been to analyze seriously, coldly, and realistically an increasingly glaring inconsistency in the valuations underlying the main value premise of our analysis: international integration. The valuation conflict is potentially the more explosive, as governments are separate and sovereign, and as there are no political instruments for attaining a common policy other than bilateral and multilateral negotiations and agreements between governments.

It is interesting to note, though, that—in the same way as in the early stages of the development of the advanced nations—redistribution was often justified to the richer classes as an insurance against social revolution, so international aid to the poorer countries tends today in the advanced countries to be regarded as a means of preventing them from turning to Communism.

The insurance theory of social policy in the now advanced countries was in those days never very popular among enlightened people. Nevertheless I often wonder whether it did not contain a kernel of realism. As I showed in Chapter III, the most advanced countries have now reached a stage where the class struggle has been almost tamed and harnessed to democratic institutions of all sorts, in the framework of which interest conflicts are solved by successful collective bargaining. They have moved so far towards social balance because of the enormous strides made in economic progress, crowded into a few decades, and because of an increasing realization of human equality of opportunity. It seems almost superfluous to point out the close negative correlation between the percentage of Communists in the electorates of different countries in Western Europe and the rate of economic progress and attainment of equality of opportunity for the masses of the people.

Nevertheless, I feel some doubt in applying this theory internationally. To begin with, I am not so certain as most of those who take up this theme that the danger is necessarily Communism or economic radicalism generally. I do believe—in later chapters I shall show why—that if the underdeveloped countries do not achieve some real and substantial success in their strivings for economic development, they will be faced with very serious dangers of political cataclysms, and this within a rather short time. But I think a great care should be exercised before suggesting the precise nature of these possible cataclysms. In many cases a further spread of military dictatorships or other forms of Fascist rule seems, indeed, a more probable outcome, at least in the short run; in some other cases the results could be merely social and political decay and bottomless misery, lasting perhaps for decades.

By this I would not want to minimize, however, the very great possibilities, particularly in the long run, for the spread of Communist ideas among both the intellectuals and the masses in many regions where economic development would continue to lag. Neither would I assume that, to a democrat, the spread of dictatorship and Fascism represents under all circumstances a lesser evil.

Pertinent to the problem of international redistribution, as well as to the even bigger problem of reorganizing and improving the regular capital market is, further, the probability that we are not given long to wait, and also that only a rather substantial and stable rate of economic progress in the underdeveloped countries will enable political disaster to be averted. Retarded, slow, and uneven progress may actually be equally or more conducive to these cataclysms than continued total stagnation, assuming the latter were a political alternative. The insurance premium against revolutions abroad cannot, therefore, be a cheap affair. It was the very rapid and great progress in our now well-integrated countries that in very recent times worked the miracle of uniting our nations into real democracies; before that time the world was different and levels of living were never so desperately low.

Professor Ragnar Nurkse has recently drawn our attention to the importance internationally of the "demonstration effect": "the simple fact that in the world today the attraction of advanced consumption standards exerts itself fairly widely, though of course unevenly, among the poorer two-thirds of mankind.[15] As Nurkse points out: "Their concern for economic development is itself, in an obvious sense, a demonstration effect; it would hardly be so pronounced if the high-income nations lived on a different planet." Aid and technical assistance, awarded as at present in homeopathic doses and without any sizeable inflow of capital, while spreading knowledge about our ways of life and our consumption habits and generally contributing to speeding up "the great awakening," will raise expectancies and ambitions that will only be frustrated.

Mr. Paul Streeten, of Oxford, with whom I have been corresponding on these questions, observes: "Sometimes I think it is not so much the absolute level of poverty that makes for Communism as, having become somewhat better off, not growing better off fast enough, particularly if the initial improvement is accompanied by contact with people who are much better off. American aid brings not only goods but also superior American consumption patterns, and the divergence between ambition and fulfilment stirs up revolt. There is also, as you say, the spread of the ideals of equality and brotherhood. A little American aid may be a greater force for Communism than none—which, obviously, is no argument against aid." But it may be an argument for a truly international aid given on a sufficient scale.

CHAPTER X

The Consequences of the Cold War

AN INDEPENDENT VARIABLE

It falls outside the scope of this book to analyze how the present international tension between East and West originated and developed. In the treatment of the problem of international economic integration in the non-Soviet world, which is the subject matter of this book, the whole complex of consequences of the cold war is taken as an independent variable.

If the tension should materially subside, many causes of international economic disintegration in the non-Soviet world would be removed and the fundamental character of the problem would change. If, on the contrary, it should explode into a third world war, all our strivings will have been futile. So much can be said with certainty. It can also be stated that the economic costs of the cold war to the non-Soviet world—as to the Soviet world—are considerable. Nations bear them because they see no alternative, or only an even worse alternative.

Unless we take due and honest account of the effects of the cold war our whole analysis will be illusory. When, however, we come to the problem of assessing more precisely the full costs of the cold war, we come up in most cases against insurmountable difficulties which are inherent in the very magnitude of these effects. "Effects" in this context means logically the difference between the situation that is and the situation that would have been, had there been no cold war. This hypothetical situation, with which we must compare the present, can be regarded as so far from actual reality that in many respects it cannot be determined as a hypothesis should be. To be asked even to guess at some of the effects of the cold war, therefore, is an unreasonable proposal. It is vital to be aware of this limitation upon our judgment, because it is precisely in respect of the economic effects that the difficulties of assessment prove insurmountable.

MIGRATION, CAPITAL MOVEMENTS, AND TRADE

Some of the economic effects of the cold war on the non-Soviet world are certainly minor; for example, the cessation of migration between the two parts of the world—except for the stream of refugees from the disturbed border regions of the Soviet sphere. The almost complete absence of migration over national boundaries is a general situation to which the whole world is becoming adjusted. This fundamental change in international labor mobility during the last forty years is not caused by the East–West tension, and it is unlikely that the cold war has made much difference.

Another point is, however, that the obstacles to travel between the two groups of countries and the breaking down of professional ties, and in many cases of personal and family relationships, have gravely disconcerted people in the Western countries. In its cumulative effects this isolation, together with all the other factors, has undoubtedly contributed to the deep-rooted suspicion and animosity which have replaced the confidence and sympathy cultivated in all the belligerent countries during the war years. Such noneconomic effects are not at all unimportant for the problem of international economic integration, the solution to which must be sought not least on the psychological level.

The effects on capital movements constitute, however, a major factor. Under different circumstances the industrialization of the Eastern countries bordering the Soviet Union could have been partly undertaken on the basis of capital imports from the Western countries; a scheme like that developed by Professor P. N. Rosenstein-Rodan during the war years would have been perfectly feasible.[1] The idea of large-scale credits from America to the Soviet Union was officially envisaged at the end of the war, but was soon dropped in the process of mutual adjustment to rising hostility after the wartime alliance. Its possible direct influence on economic reconstruction and development in the Soviet Union should not be exaggerated, but as an element in building up a spirit of friendly cooperation and giving a momentum to trade it could have been of great importance.

The real effects of the cold war on capital movements go much further. In the non-Soviet world the cold war creates the fear of imminent risks of various kinds, including the risk of a new world war or of localized wars involving regions on the cold war frontier; it also implies the risk of political disintegration of the non-Soviet orbit by a process of secession to the Soviet block—all of which adds to the various other factors, referred to in Chapter VIII, that hamper international capital movements in the non-Soviet world.

It is, moreover, easily the major factor. We have only to cast our minds back to the closing days of the war, when the planning was done for a better and a peaceful world to be guided by the benevolent and confident cooperation of the Allied Great Powers. This hope and expectation of great power cooperation prevailed in all the belligerent countries, and particularly in America; it was in fact the basic assumption underlying all the schemes for international organizations that were then put forward and, in part, given specific shape. It is clear that in such a world even the revival in some form or other of the international capital market might very well have been feasible.

The gradual diminution of trade between the two groups of countries has likewise had very serious effects.[2] The decline of East–West trade has been one of the factors contributing to the acute dollar problem of Western Europe but has, of course, had much wider effects on the economic development of many countries. Certain countries are particularly hard hit by the present situation. It is thus difficult to see how a country like Japan can ever hope to become viable inside the non-Soviet group, if it may not trade with China.

In the context of the cold war the usual comparisons with the prewar level of trade between Eastern and Western Europe are misleading, because the prewar level was itself abnormally low—in the case of trade with the Soviet Union for political reasons, and in the case of other Eastern European countries because of their economic stagnation in the interwar period.[3]

If we mean by the effects of the cold war what we logically should mean, we must compare the present low level of East–West trade—which is down to less than a half of the prewar volume—with the level that could have been reached, were there no political split. That level would be higher, probably very much higher, than before the war, and higher still, of course, by comparison with the present level. Just how much higher is impossible to say.

If the trade barriers between the two groups of countries were lowered and trade gradually resumed on a somewhat bigger scale, there would undoubtedly be some easing of the economic difficulties of the non-Soviet, as well as of the Soviet world. For this reason, all governments—including the government of the United States, so far as Europe is concerned—have repeatedly and persistently declared increased East–West trade to be their policy, and given active support to concerted efforts in this direction.

EFFECTS OF THE ARMAMENT EXPENDITURE

Certain other effects of the cold war on international conditions in the non-Soviet world are of a similar magnitude, though even more incalculable. Fighting in Korea and Indochina has been expensive. Apart from these actual war costs, armament expenditures for military preparedness have assumed very considerable proportions in the United States—and, as far as one can tell, no less so in the Soviet Union—and they are very high in all industrially advanced countries. On the whole, non-Soviet Asia, Latin America, and Africa are as yet hardly engaged in the armaments race. If countries in these parts of the world have increased their military strength at their own expense, it has been for reasons other than the cold war—as when Arabs and Israelis or Pakistanis and Indians arm against each other; the foreign military aid some of them have been able to procure has been motivated in the supplying country by the cold war.

It is, however, impossible to assess with any certainty what the effects of the rise in defense expenditure have been on the economies of Western countries. The primary reason for this is that it is impossible to say what would have been the economic and financial policies followed in the various countries in the absence of this extraordinary armament expenditure and to what extent these policies would have been successful.

One alternative is to assume that, even with a lower level of armament expenditure, the same general level of production and employment would have been kept up. The implied assumption would thus be that, in the countries concerned, an economic policy designed to ensure the present level of activity would have been adopted and successfully carried out. On this assumption we may conclude that the effects of the present level of armament expenditures have been: a slower rate of progress in living standards and social security provisions, curtailment of investment and a slower rate of progress in production in many civilian sectors, and decreased ability to export capital goods to underdeveloped countries.

Theoretically, this assumption is not at all implausible; it would, indeed, be a preposterous thought that during these years our only available means of preserving full employment in our industrialized countries has been to keep up these enormous armament expenditures. This is what Sir Douglas Copland wanted to illustrate when, speaking in the summer of 1954 for Australia in the Economic and Social Council, he touched upon the problem. After having estimated that world expenditure for defense was on a level equivalent to two thirds of the national incomes of the West-European countries, or one third of the national income of the United States, he invited his audience to attempt to realize "the full magnitude of that sum . . . in terms of human efforts and aspirations" and exclaimed: "If two thirds of the labour of Western Europe or one third of the labour of the United States of America would be set aside to promote the economic development of the world as a whole and that of the underdeveloped countries in particular, what a great advance that would mean towards the objectives for the achievement of which the Economic and Social Council has been created!"[4]

The theoretical reasonableness of the assumption that the same level of production and employment would have been kept up even with a lower level of armament expenditure does not, however, imply that this result would actually have been realized. At the other extreme is, of course, the assumption that, with a lower level of defense expenditure, national economic policies would not have been very much different from what they have been these last years. The effects of the increased armament expenditure would then have been the opposite: raising the level of production and employment and generally stimulating business development, without any adverse effects—and probably even the contrary—on consumption levels, investment, and production, whether for home use or for export.

So far as can be ascertained, increased military expenditure within Western Europe and in America has hardly infringed on the possibilities of production for the export market.[5] As a matter of fact, much of the current discussion among economists and in business journals seems to proceed on the basis of the second assumption mentioned above. Corollaries of this way of reasoning—sometimes spelled out, sometimes left as implicit inferences—would be that, if defense expenditures had been lower, countries like Britain and Sweden would have experienced a much more pronounced slowing down of their economic development some years ago, and that the United States would have had its recession much earlier and perhaps lapsed into a serious depression if the Korean war had not broken out.[6]

But as I see it, this common assumption of other things being equal is not convincing. A much smaller rate of expenditure on armaments would have made such a big difference in the situation that other things would not have been equal: another and different economic policy would have been followed. How much different, and with what results, one cannot say.

It is well to remember this, because military expenditure is often blamed for results which are really due to different—and contradictory— policy assumptions; such as, for instance, that rearmament is responsible for having slowed down economic development, while at the same time it is said to preserve the boom.

It is certain that the effect of the cold war in undermining the confidence in the capital market, referred to above, has quite particularly hampered credits to and investment in underdeveloped countries; how much larger the capital stream in that direction would have been without the cold war is, however, impossible to say.

Whether the cold war has decreased or increased the amount of aid given to underdeveloped countries also remains an open question. Apart from the main uncertainty concerning economic policy in general, which has already been referred to and which is naturally also relevant to this problem, there is an additional one. The larger budgets and increased levels of taxation, which in any circumstances are a consequence of increased defense outlays, would normally tend to curtail government undertakings of foreign aid. At the same time, however, the dominant political interest of the United States—which in the world today is the main source of aid—in keeping the non-Soviet block together and strengthening its weaker members has given an extra impetus to aid. It is anyone's guess whether, because of this new motive, and in spite of the financial strain caused by armament expenditure, the actual net amount of American aid is bigger or considerably smaller than it would have been in a less troubled world.

That the cold war has retarded the establishment of the proposed institutions for the internationalization of aid is, however, fairly certain. It is also certain that the cold war has had effects on the distribution of loans and grants as between countries and on their redirection from civilian to military purposes.

OTHER ECONOMIC EFFECTS

There are certain other effects of the heavy military expenditure which can be ascertained, at least as regards their general nature. America and, directly or indirectly, even Europe and the rest of the non-Soviet world, are faced with a situation where a high level of business activity and full employment now depend to a considerable extent on the continuation of a very heavy outlay on defense or, rather, on its not being permitted to taper off more rapidly than other policies can be inaugurated to sustain demand.[7] In present political circumstances it seems little likely that there is any imminent danger to economic stability from this angle.

In all the industrialized countries of the non-Soviet world that have borne heavy defense burdens one further general effect has been to strengthen the secular trend towards the increased importance of the state as a spender of the national income, and so also the trend towards state intervention and central economic planning. This is an effect which is related to the long-term trend, cutting across short-term fluctuations; its importance will increase if the high level of armament expenditure becomes a more lasting trait of our economic system. "This revolution in our national security has had one great effect—one that few of us welcome but none of us can ignore. It has added tremendous weight to the place of government in our economy." I am quoting Mr. John J. McCloy, the Chairman of the Board of Directors of the Chase Manhattan Bank.[8]

Generally speaking, the continuation for a protracted period of such a very high level of defense expenditure will reshape considerably the whole economic and social structure of our national communities. Strategic motives will increasingly play a determining role in the direction of our capital investment and the training of our youth, in the location of industry, in housing policy, etc. The direct allocation of such a large part of our resources for military needs, and the readjustment, according to military ends, of the way in which our other resources are allocated, will naturally imply a distortion of the economy, when considered from the viewpoint of how it could best serve the civilian needs of the population.

Even apart from that, the existing state of tension has exerted powerful effects on the patterns of production and trade by inducing increased national autarky (for example, in shipping and rubber). An adjustment of national economies to the fear of war is also apt to disrupt international economic relations in many other ways. One example is stockpiling. Ideally, stockpiling should act like a stabilizing speculator, buying when a commodity is cheap, and selling when it becomes expensive. The increased international tension resulting from the outbreak of the Korean war made the United States Government act in quite the opposite way— as a destabilizing speculator, buying as prices went up and withdrawing from the market—or, as in the case of tin, even preparing to sell—as prices came down. This policy greatly reinforced the fluctuations of raw material prices and had far-reaching unstabilizing effects on the economies of European countries as well as of countries in Asia and Latin America.[9]

The main conclusion that emerges from this discussion of the economic effects of the cold war is that, according to any hypothesis we make, they are tremendous. The difficulty of forming definite opinions in any less general way stems not from lack of empirical data, but from the very logic of the problem.

EFFECTS ON OUR CULTURE

The psychological and ideological effects of the cold war on Western national communities are also immense. The increasing influence of military *expertise* and the thinking habits of the "military mind," the mobilization of scientists to work on all sorts of "projects" under state direction and financed by *ad hoc* state appropriations, the impetus in social sciences to think in terms of state "power" and state strategic interests, the growth of the state secrecy and loyalty phobias, and the mounting ascendency of state propaganda are only some of the symptoms of these psychological and ideological effects. Gradually they are remoulding our basic valuations; if continued for a prolonged period of time they will alter our entire culture in a direction very contrary to our inherited Western ideals.

Our national communities are already giving reasons for the "impression that we no longer believe in ourselves and that we are prepared to sacrifice the traditional values of our civilization to our fears rather than to defend those values with our faith."[10] Indeed, we are increasingly attempting to exorcise the Devil by worshiping Beelzebub—an old and dangerous game against which our Bible warns us in some of its most golden and sternest passages.

There is unfortunately a good deal of empirical evidence for Mr. Walter Lippman's dictum "that freedom works best in peace and that all war regimes, even cold-war regimes, have to become centralized, illiberal, and arbitrary."[11] Even prior to recent developments of means of total warfare, human sacrifice and material destruction were of such a magnitude that a real war stood out as the supreme horror; it was sensed, though, as something to be gotten over as soon as possible. We should not close our eyes to the possibility that, compared to the pre-atomic wars of the last generation, the psychological and ideological effects on our culture of the frustrating stalemate of a prolonged cold war, stretching perhaps over decades, may be deeper and more lasting. This should be a reason for mobilizing all our strength to conserve our basic values even under the present strain.

Generally, these dangerous effects of the cold war, taking the form of less liberal attitudes on practically all questions, have been most pronounced in America but are also visible in Western Europe. They have an indirect but important bearing on the possibilities of closer economic integration in the non-Soviet world and on the shape international cooperation takes. These effects are highly complex, with many contradictions in attitudes and with curious cross-currents.

To develop this theme further, and to outline how we might save our inherited culture even during a cold war, would require a book by itself.

A Political Effect

There is one political effect, though, that is more direct and that must be especially accounted for. The Soviet sphere represents to the non-Soviet countries a contrast concept, an altogether different type of economic organization. All the countries in the block were underdeveloped, with the partial exception of a few small countries on the European fringe. *This other type of economic organization—the Soviet type—presents itself as fundamentally a system for the development of underdeveloped countries.* This particular point cannot be stressed too much. This important characteristic of the Communist economy is, incidentally, contrary to Marxian predictions, according to which revolution and socialism were assumed to come first to countries with mature capitalism.

The greatest failure of international integration in the non-Soviet world is, as I have emphasized, the stagnation or slow development of the underdeveloped countries and the widening gap between industrially advanced and backward countries. As a social system competing for souls and political power, the Soviet contrast concept has its greatest potential following in the large poverty-stricken regions where the Western system is on weak foundations.

In Western Europe there actually exists a high degree of immunity against the spread of sympathy for the Soviet system, at least at its present stage of development. It cannot obtain much reliable support here as our value structure is so fundamentally different; as is frequently pointed out, but not always understood, the millions who vote the Communist ticket in France and Italy are for the most part not true Communists at all but ordinary citizens who are deeply dissatisfied with what they get out of the national economy and are distrustful of the other political parties, not always without valid reasons.

The same disinclination to the Soviet system cannot be present in the vast underdeveloped areas, where hundreds of millions of people live in poverty and have no other memory than dependence. Many of these countries have recently been liberated from colonial domination and indulge in aspirations about economic development which so far have only faintly materialized, if at all. It is, above all, in non-Soviet Asia, in Africa, and in some parts of Latin America that the Soviet contrast concept can take on the appearance of a promise of liberation and progress. As has often been pointed out in the literature on the cultures of these regions, the autocratic element in Soviet Communism often satisfies a predisposition of the masses in these countries, who have no tradition of Western democracy but for centuries have been conditioned to respond positively to direction from authority.

As a competing method for development of underdeveloped countries the Soviet system has two strong points of appeal, and it is an illusion— and a dangerous one, as are all illusions—to pass over them lightly. For one thing, in its practical application this system has yielded a rapid rise in industrial production and a great expansion of the industrial basis for further increases in output.[12] Upon the completion of its recent Five-Year Plan in 1955, the Soviet Union alone has begun to rival Western Europe in the size of its basic industries, the two areas containing roughly the same population. China is embarking upon development plans with a much steeper rate of climb than other backward countries in the region.[13]

The methods are harsh but not ineffective. By organizing the existing labor surplus for production and by withholding from the population any proportionate increase in consumption, capital is created out of poverty in a cumulative fashion, and so the volume of production is pushed upward along a logarithmic curve. The main emphasis is laid on a continuous strengthening of the heavy industries, at the expense of agriculture and light industries, particularly those producing consumers' goods. Consumers must wait while capital is accumulated. At the same time, personal capital is fast created by a determined literacy drive, supplemented by an organized production of reading-stuff, and by lavish efforts to build up technical education to all levels of responsibility.

These are in rapid outline some of the main elements in the Soviet method of development of underdeveloped countries. To succeed it uses the monolithic state, which implies the one-party system, the extinction of parliamentary democracy, the suppression of a large number of fundamental civil rights and liberties, enforced political conformity, political police, the protecting curtain, a single-minded and unflinching government, an unswerving, trained cadre of administrators and technicians, and an elite group of political followers with religious zeal.

THE SOVIET CONCEPT OF INTERNATIONAL INTEGRATION

The second strong point of the Soviet system as a competing method for development of underdeveloped countries concerns the international relations it builds up within its orbit. There are several elements in this problem that should be clearly distinguished. One is the very obvious ideological and political domination exercised by Moscow. This is one of the things that makes the system most unattractive to people in all countries that are politically fairly developed. In Europe it makes it difficult or impossible for Soviet Communism to attract really reliable adherents, outside of small sectlike groups. In Asia the domination is apparently weaker and, in addition, the political traditions different.

Another element, closely related to the first, is the alleged exploitation of the other countries in the Soviet sphere in the interest of the Soviet Union. This would, of course, be highly unattractive in all countries, regardless of their political maturity. Following these relations with an attempt, as an objective scientist, to reach the truth, I am not yet convinced that this is an important and lasting element in the Soviet Union's relations with its allies, counterbalancing its material and technical assistance.[14]

There is, however, a third main element in the relations between the Soviet Union and the other countries in its orbit that has been given far too little, or no, attention in the general discussion of these problems, and it concerns the concept of international economic integration in its proper meaning. The fact is that astonishingly little appears so far to have been done to form of this group of countries an economically coherent and interdependent whole, so as to take advantage to the maximum of the principle of the international division of labor.

Their national labor markets are thus—except for the systematic exchange of technicians—almost entirely isolated from each other; in fact, they are probably even more isolated than the national labor markets in Western Europe. Although there has been a labor shortage in the coal mines in a corner of Czechoslovakia bordering Poland, where more labor would have been available, labor has not been transferred. The capital markets are equally isolated, except for the swing credits in the bilateral trade agreements and the capital assistance given *ad hoc* by the Soviet Union to needy allies.

Trade is encouraged and recent tendencies have been to give increased emphasis to trade as a means for international specialization and co-operation.[15] Long-term trade agreements make possible a relatively high degree of planned coordination of production and consumption. Technical assistance is developed in a systematic way and is often defined in the trade agreements, and a considerable amount of work is directed to the important problem of standardization.

The fundamental principle seems to be, however, that each country—and, indeed, each major region—should have a well-developed basis of heavy industry. In each of the countries investment and production plans are framed with a view to building from the bottom upwards a rapidly progressing national economy. International specialization has not been given a supreme priority, not even in the recent trend to trade expansion. The stress is everywhere laid on the nation as a unit and on economic nationalism as a legitimate goal. Generally speaking, the unprecedented and unlimited power over all the means of production in this very large part of the world has not been used to integrate internationally the economies of the several countries contained within it—except to an extent on the level of trade.

As an old-fashioned economist in the classical tradition, I am conditioned to find this bad economics, a doctrinal survival of the late Premier Stalin's idea of "socialism in one state," even when the states have become several and when some of them are small. I do see a problem, though. The Soviet theory might be that the marginal adjustments needed for inter-country specialization—which forms part of the *raison d'être* of the price mechanism as a principle of allocation—are of less importance in a highly dynamic process of raising very rapidly total output, and that, further, elements of autarky can even be a means of spurring on this rise in total output. Particularly in the early stages of economic development, the static theory of comparative costs would need to be corrected in order to allow for many positive items of national gains inherent in the process of economic growth. "The economic development plans of Eastern European countries thus show a broad similarity of objectives, and they all repudiate the view that certain countries are inevitably destined for primary production only or for the development of narrowly restricted types of industry."[16]

That to many poor, nonindustrialized nations, who find themselves inheriting a grossly unbalanced colonial economy, designed to serve a metropolitan country on the other side of an ocean and inhabited by another and superior race, this nationalistic element in the Soviet system for the development of underdeveloped countries can have its great attraction, should not be overlooked.

CHAPTER XI

The Drive for Independence
and Development

INEQUALITY

The great inequality in standards of income and welfare in the world is, of course, the main reflection of the failure of international integration. It is sufficient to take a look at the data, albeit imperfect, on national income per capita which the Statistical Office of the United Nations was able to put together for 1949.[1]

The rich countries—mainly our nationally well integrated economies referred to in Chapter III—have only 15 per cent of the population of the world (or more precisely, of the 70 countries considered), but 62 per cent of the world's income; the poorest (under $100 a head in 1949), forming 54 per cent of the population, have only 9 per cent of the world's income (leaving an intermediary group of 31 per cent of the world population with 29 per cent of the income). Even if we refer only to the non-Soviet world, we obtain broadly the same relations: 48 per cent of the population dispose of only 8 per cent of the income.

The statistics underlying such comparisons of national income per head in different countries are extremely frail, particularly those for the underdeveloped countries,[2] and can serve no other purpose than to point to the magnitudes involved in the problem: a broad estimate of the numbers living in various degrees of prosperity or destitution. Only one who has had the opportunity of traveling widely in the rich and the poor regions, and whose eyes have been wide open to unaccustomed sights, can even begin to grasp the stark realities of the manners of living and of the human happiness or misery which are abstractly represented by such average figures.

Implied in them are differences in what and how much people can eat and the degree to which they can satisfy their hunger; implied also is

149

whether they have anything to wear or anything that can be called a home. Behind these bare data are widely differing levels of literacy and culture, standards of health and frequencies of sickness and death, how many mothers succumb in giving birth to a child and how many of the newborn babies die during childhood, and also what length of life a person can expect. I refer to the United Nations Social Survey as an easily available manual on these matters.[3]

The development during and after the Second World War and even earlier has not been towards a lessening of these inequalities, but instead has widened them. Standards in the underdeveloped countries have often been pressed down further. Until recently, agricultural production in the world had not been keeping pace with population increase, with the result that there was on the average some 10 per cent less food to eat per person than before the war. On the whole, the more advanced nations did not eat less; some actually improved their diet. It was the poorest nations, already undernourished, that had to go hungrier.

In the last two or three years world food production has been catching up with the increase in population, but the increased output has been centred almost entirely in North America, while the vast underdeveloped regions in Asia are still lagging far behind.

INDICES OF FOOD PRODUCTION PER HEAD
1934–1938 = 100[4]

	1948/49–1950/51[a]	1952/53	1953/54[b]
North America	118	123	119
Oceania	96	93	93
Western and Southern Europe	94	102	107
Latin America[c]	98	97	96
Near East	95	106	108
Far East[d]	84	85	87
World total[e]	97	101	102

[a] Averages.
[b] Provisional.
[c] If Argentina is excluded, the index for 1952/53 rises to 107.
[d] Excluding Chinese mainland.
[e] Including estimates for the Soviet world.

As these poorer countries do not have the means of paying for increased imports of agricultural produce from America, and as charity has its limits, the United States has now to readjust its state interventions in agriculture in order to check the advance of its production. On a world scale we are back to the tragic dilemma of the thirties: "Plenty of wheat, but no bread."[5]

The postwar era has been one of rapid industrialization. But—outside the Soviet orbit—it has mainly been a continued industrialization of the already highly industrialized regions. Industrial production outside the Soviet Union was in 1952 some 80 per cent higher than in 1938, the last prewar year, but this average conceals the truth that we have just stated. In the United States and Canada, and in Australia and New Zealand, the increase ranged from near 100 to as much as 150 per cent,[6] while in Western Europe taken as a whole it was only around 35 per cent. In the rest of the non-Soviet world, comprising something like three quarters of the earth's population, the increase cannot have been much more than about 10 per cent, thus not even keeping pace with population growth, which has been twice or thrice as fast.

Even within the high-income countries, there has been a significant shift in favor of those which already held the lead. In 1937 the United States contributed about half towards the industrial production of these countries: its present share must be about 60 per cent, with something like one third for the West-European countries included in the comparison, against 42 per cent in 1937.[7]

The secular rise of the United States in economic power is, of course, of the greatest significance. Before the First World War its manufacturing output was somewhat smaller than that of Western Europe as a whole; now it is almost twice as much and accounts for over half of the production of the whole of the non-Soviet world. But this fact should not overshadow the other fact that—with great individual differences—the other industrially advanced countries are also continuing to advance, some as fast as the United States, while the backward countries are on the whole stagnating.

There are some individual spots on the map of the underdeveloped world where rapid economic development is accomplished or where, anyhow, money is flowing in rapidly. Among them are, first, the countries that have large petroleum deposits. Venezuela, which also has iron ore deposits, is today in one sense one of the most prosperous countries in the world. So, too, is Saudi Arabia, which has the financial resources to undertake irrigation schemes that would change the deserts into gardens. In both countries much of the money is not at hand when it comes to the question of raising the level of living and culture of the masses; but the potentialities are clearly there. In the Belgian Congo, the exploitation of uranium and some other nonferrous metal ores has rapidly increased its production and exports; under a tight colonial role of an old type part of the new wealth is spread among the masses of indigenous Negroes in the form of rising levels of living and social welfare measures, carefully calculated so as not to upset the social order.

According to the over-all figures, there has been, both during and after the war, a considerable increase in per capita national income in Latin

American countries and a not insignificant economic development has taken place. This is not true of the whole subcontinent, however. And in some of the countries where a substantial development has taken place it has often been concentrated in a few cities and industrial centers, while large rural areas are left in stagnation and backwardness. Much of the new investment has also gone into providing for the luxury consumption of a minority of rich people. The whole upswing was further founded on the relatively favorable terms of trade that ruled during this period and it is not surprising that the recent deterioration of the terms of trade has tended to slow down the development.

A Latin American economist, Mr. Felipe Pazos, points out that "there is reason to believe that in some Latin American countries, and certainly in some under-developed countries in other continents, the immediate problem is not one of advancement but one of preventing regression."[8] The greater part of non-Soviet Asia has made only slow progress.

Since the beginning of time there have been poor and destitute peoples in the world. The cruel Malthusian checks have operated, and periodically millions have died from pestilence and hunger without the rest of the world being very disturbed. The present worldwide discussion of the existing economic inequalities reflects, however, the fact that a very important social and political change has taken place: these peoples, or those who speak for them, demand "development." The old term "backward countries" is now replaced by "underdeveloped countries," demarcating the change from political statics to dynamics which I commented upon in Chapter II.

The Liquidation of Colonialism

In the wake of the Second World War, practically all Asia was freed from colonial domination and became organized in a number of independent states. As a matter of historical fact, the Japanese conquests in Southern Asia and the Pacific after Pearl Harbor were of great importance in preparing the ground for the liquidation of colonialism in the whole region[9]—among other ways, by their actually driving the former ruling powers from some areas for a certain time, and by destroying over much wider areas the myth of the invincibility of the white man. All armed conflicts on the Asian continent which involve non-Asiatic nations, including the recent wars in Korea and Indochina, will, once placed in their historical perspective, be seen to have had a similar aftereffect on the Asian mind.

The liquidation of colonialism in the non-Soviet world is a historical trend which seems bound to spread over the whole globe and to follow its course to the end. One after another, the remaining colonies and other dependencies, whatever their official titles, are going to win their independence, some of them probably within a comparatively short space of time. The resistance to this trend is feeble. The familiar ideological and political parallelogram of forces is, briefly stated, the following:

The newly liberated states demonstrate their solidarity with the independence movements in all dependent areas, and this policy also has the more or less articulate moral support of the Latin American republics and of all the countries in Europe that have no colonial interests of their own.

The United States is gradually facing a serious moral and ideological dilemma. All its traditions are, of course, strongly anticolonial; but the West-European colonial powers are its closest allies in the cold war. Gradually, the United States is also, willingly or unwillingly, inheriting responsibilities in various parts of the world from these powers, and in some dependent areas it has built military establishments which it now has to protect.

The dilemma of the West-European colonial powers is equally deep, although they are more accustomed to living with it than the Americans. They have now all subscribed to the doctrine that they are only trustees of the peoples in the dependent areas and that their solemn duty is to aid these people faithfully in preparing themselves for self-determination. Colonial domination can now only be defended half-heartedly.

The Soviet Union and countries within its orbit will continue to blow fire under every potential anticolonial issue that enters the international arena. They are thus following emphatic ideological traditions of the Communist movement since its inception, while at the same time exploiting, to their advantage in the cold war, conflicts on the other side.

The anticolonial doctrine has received solemn sanction in the constitution and, indeed, in the very structure of the United Nations, where the ideological and political onslaught has found its international forum. The United Nations operates like a resonance board to the localized outcries in the areas themselves. A few years ago the United Nations was brought to the point of making one of the most backward of these former colonies, Libya, into an independent state. This has had a considerable effect in all North Africa and beyond.

As the ties between the metropolitan country and a dependent area loosen, major conflicts of interests arise in connection with the property and future social and economic status of the white population that forms islands in the sea of indigenous inhabitants and usually controls their most valuable resources. If not handled with the greatest wisdom and foresight, these conflicts may bring about serious tragedies. In many cases the conflicts become complicated by disagreements between the governments and administrations in the metropolitan countries—which often

are becoming prepared for large-scale reforms and for political settlements—and the European settlers who stick to their privileges.

In this great chain of events not only are nations born, but a new and
intense nationalism is fostered. The political leaders of the new countries
have to arouse ambitions among the masses, if for no other reason than
that, under the circumstances, this is their means of acquiring power.
The aspirations which they know they can arouse successfully are the
cravings for political independence and for economic development and a
rising standard of living and culture.

Once more the old adage is validated that nothing is so easily popu-
larized as nationalism. The whole of the intelligentsia and the tiny middle
class will naturally be unanimous in their intense nationalism, however
varied their other political inclinations and interests; but the pliant,
illiterate masses can also be roused by nationalist appeals.

Unfortunately, these nationalistic appeals are usually more successful
if they are given a negative spicing. It is a common trait with all of us—
going back to the way we are educated and the frustrations in all our
lives—that it is much easier to be aroused against something than for
something. From this point of view it is a remarkable thing, and a
fortunate one, that in Southeastern Asia, where we find so many of the
new states, the rising nationalism has so far been kept relatively free from
xenophobia and particularly from hatred against the nations that formerly
ruled them. This is a good testimony both to the former rulers and to
the new leaders who took over. As is well known, this is particularly true
of the former British dependencies; but even in Indonesia, for instance,
the aversion to the Dutch is not violent.

Whether that will be a lasting situation is, however, uncertain. Besides
the relative success or failure of their internal policies, there are personal
factors entering into this problem. Almost everywhere the helm is now
manned by individuals who had their education in Europe and America.
They are strongly Western in all their moral and intellectual allegiances.
Often they are rationalists and many are outstanding personalities. In
India and the other former British dependencies, native civil servants who
had been educated under the old regime have kept their positions, and
in the present scarcity of trained personnel they have a monopoly of
influence. The new generation of leaders will have a different background
and is almost bound to be different in outlook.

Meanwhile an expectation has been created, and still prevails, of
economic development and rising living standards. If the economic
development should be slow, which is probable in almost all these
countries—and still more if per capita consumption should fall, which
is possible in at least some of them—attitudes might change rather
abruptly.

In the Near East the trend of frustration, suspicion, and xenophobia is already apparent. In Africa there are obvious changes taking place that are liable to spread hatred against every white person. In all Southeastern Asia a milder variety of antiwhite feelings is giving its flavor to public life. In China a violent and sickening anti-Americanism—fed by successive events over many years—is now almost a main emotional and political basis for the government. These are social facts that we have to face; they do not disappear because we think the attitudes are unfounded or desire them to be different.

The Impact of Color

There is one fundamental fact in these countries which all concerned are usually too discreet to talk about, but which will increasingly play on the minds of the peoples: the correlation between poverty and color. All the high-income countries, and some in the middle-income groups, have almost unmixed populations of European stock. Most middle-income countries have mixed or colored populations. All the poorest countries are colored according to the social definition of the term laid down by the nations that have European origin.

In countries where there are both colored and white people, the whites are always at the top and the colored at the bottom. This is true in the United States, where the many Negroes and the few Mexicans, Asians, and aboriginal Indians are together a small minority—just over 10 per cent—but it is also true in South Africa, where the native blacks are the great majority, even without counting in those of mixed bloods and the Indians, who are also discriminated against on the basis of the color concept. In the Catholic Latin American countries, where a definite color bar is not openly recognized, there is nevertheless a social tendency that expresses itself in a fairly persistent correlation between color and social and economic status.

This correlation is such a powerful social reality that it cannot but influence even the colored peoples. A lighter shade of skin becomes a social and economic asset, particularly for women. This is true in North America and also in Latin America. In India the caste structure is not unconnected with ethnographic differences reflecting both historical origins and selective forces during later developments. The Sanskrit word for caste, *varna*, originally meant color. But there is a tendency for even body size to mean something, particularly when smallness is connected with a darker shade of color.

Consciousness of color and its social impact have consequences for all attitudes to life, even in minor matters. When I recently visited the capital of one Asian country, I came across two society journals: even in details they showed revealing likenesses to similar publications for upper-class American Negroes. The dolls bought by ordinary Chinese parents in Singapore or the Indian ones in Bombay and Calcutta do not have black hair and eyes, but fair hair, blue eyes, and rosy cheeks, like English babies.

Most people in the world are colored in this sense; most people are poor. Invariably it is the colored people who are the poorer. The fact that shades of color are a determinant of social and economic status even among the colored people themselves does not help to overcome the feeling that this whole correlation is a fundamental injustice, crying to Heaven. Neither is it much of a consolation to the colored peoples that the situation 1000 or 2000 or 4000 years ago was different, most whites, or all whites at that time being barbarians. Drawing attention to this fact is rather a typical expression of colored nationalism.

There is at present almost a conspiracy of silence around this question. Most colored people who are not Negroes usually want to avoid discussing the issue—but it lives on as a powerful complex. I have myself observed how near the surface this complex is and what a potentially tremendous load of emotions it carries. It tends to systematize and to aggravate all other tensions. It gives its strange undertone to all social and political problems, internally as well as externally.

Part of the international impact of the South African *apartheid* policy is due to the fact that it irritates and feeds this complex all over the world. As Indians are involved, and as their rights cannot be pleaded in very different terms than would also cover the Negroes, there develops a tendency to generalize the conflict white–Negro into white–nonwhite, *i.e.*, white–colored. There are many other such conflicts brooding just now in other parts of the world which are white-dominated but have a large colored population, such as British Guiana, and more of them are bound to arise as time goes by. They will all stimulate the color complex globally, as does also the mere fact of the color bar against immigration into the advanced white-dominated countries, quite independently of whether there is any actual desire to migrate.

One factor that has smoothed matters over, or at least avoided an additional irritation of international problems, is the very favorable course that race relations in the United States have taken since the Second World War. This trend, which stands out in contrast to many other less liberal trends in the United States of today, is of an international importance that should not be underestimated, and I can on this point reiterate my conclusions in the last chapter of my book, *An American Dilemma*.[10] Few Americans, even among the most internationally versatile, can really appreciate the tremendous positive effects in international relations of the recent Supreme Court decision outlawing educational segregation.

The most important direct effect of the breaking down of color prejudice in a white-dominated country is on this country's own international policy. Professor Clarence E. Glick, of the University of Hawaii, observes: ". . . if the climate of opinion, a public conscience, and action patterns are created in these countries which will make possible the enjoyment of full political equality by all their citizens of multiracial origins, then the climate of opinion, public conscience, and action patterns would exist which would reduce the role of racial sensibility in the international relations of these nations with 'nonwhite' nations of the world. The two realms of race relations in the politics of the modern world—intranational and international—appear merely to be two aspects of a larger whole."[11]

This is the first condition for an improvement of the situation. To obtain, thereafter, a politically significant decrease in the racial sensibility in international relations on the part of the nonwhite nations, who are now winning back their independence and whose minds are filled with the resentful memories of the subdued role pressed upon them for generations, is a more distant goal. It would also require some substantial rise in their living conditions and confidence in their future progress. To my mind there is no doubt that for the time being—things being as they are, and even assuming that we continue to reform ourselves rapidly—the tide of racial resentment will be rising in the underprivileged world.

In the struggle for the souls in these vast backward areas, the Soviet system for development of underdeveloped countries can exploit a third strong point, which should be added to the two already noted in Chapter X, namely, the undeniable fact that the Communists have succeeded in exterminating racial prejudice in their minds and in their dealings with colored people. To overlook this fact is another of those dangerous opportunistic illusions.

This pattern of thinking and living in the Soviet orbit has, incidentally, a much older and firmer basis than Marxian ideology. Except for much ugly anti-Semitism, the old Russian culture was considerably cosmopolitan and broadminded in racial relations, actually even more so than the Roman Catholic cultures in Southern Europe and Latin America, which have always been superior in these matters to the Protestant cultures. Pushkin would have been a Negro, according to the social definition in the United States.

Russia was a great Asian power long before Communism reigned. Quite apart from new China, the Soviet Union has within its boundaries millions of people with the religious and cultural traditions of Asia and non-European facial features. This becomes the more important, the faster the development process in the Soviet Union moves its dynamic centers eastwards and southwards.

A WORLD IN REVOLUTION

The emergence of all these new nations in the international concert, the intense and growing nationalism in these countries, the foreseeable continuation of the liquidation of colonialism in other parts of the world, the fact that all of these new nations are colored and very poor and that they are developing a growing feeling of solidarity among themselves and with other poor and colored nations, who for similar reasons are paying back with their solidarity[12]—all these are emotional elements in the chorus of demands for the development of the underdeveloped countries. There are potentialities for national as well as regional integration in these trends—and in the end also for general international integration, if matters were dealt with on all sides by supreme courage, wisdom, and devotion to human ideals. But, undoubtedly, the immediate result of the appearance of so many more independent political and economic units and so much more released nationalism is in itself a force making for international disintegration.

"Great movements and forces, springing from deep wells, have converged at this mid-century point, and I suspect we have barely begun to comprehend what has happened and why." So did Mr. Adlai E. Stenvenson open his lectures at Harvard University in the spring of 1954. ". . . In the background are the opaque, moving forms and shadows of a world revolution, of which Communism is more the scavenger than the inspiration; a world in transition from an age with which we are familiar to an age shrouded in mist."[13]

From one important point of view this whole development is nothing else than the victorious spread of Western ideals. We are finally conquering the world spiritually. This is the reason why we have not the capacity to fight this development, except in the form of halfhearted, opportunistic and, in the end, self-defeating moves. Everything we say or do is apt to strengthen the hold of our ideals over the disadvantaged nations.

The West is not consciously cynical. Generally speaking, nations as democratic cultural entities have not the intellectual ability to be cynical to the same degree as individuals, unless they go bluntly Fascist. This is the secret of the functional hold of ideals in a democratic society. The awakening of the underprivileged peoples is bound to be a cumulative sequence; and the advanced nations, whether they intend it or not, will steadily feed new energy to the process.

Our whole literature propagates these ideals; they are preached in the churches and taught in the schools; they are voiced by every speaker we send out to bargain for goodwill. All studies we make have the same effect and so has our influence on their students who come to our universities. The ambitions of the underdeveloped countries are written into the constitutions of our international organizations, the activities of which, whether or not so planned, will propagate still further the revolutionary Western ideals. Our political and cultural propaganda—nay, even the "psychological warfare" of recent years—however cleverly we try to contrive our pleading, will almost of necessity be an influence strengthening the drive for the general ideals of independence, development, equality, and justice; for we regularly attempt to use these ideals as rationalizations for our strivings, even when they have a less elevated origin or purpose.

THE ATTEMPTS TO ACHIEVE DEMOCRACY

To our Western ideological heritage also belongs the belief that political democracy is the right road to progress and that progress will strengthen democracy. The non-Soviet world—and quite particularly the underdeveloped part of it—has unfortunately still to be characterized in the same way as when the American lawyer and diplomat—who from before the turn of the century until the outbreak of the First World War was Assistant Secretary of State—the late Mr. John Basset More, looked out over the world from his office in the old State Department building in Washington and sighed: ". . . a motley procession: governments liberal and governments illiberal; governments free and governments unfree; governments honest and governments corrupt; governments pacific and governments even aggressively warlike; empires, monarchies, and oligarchies, despotisms decked out as democracies, and tyrannies masqueraded as republics—all representative of the motley world in which we live and with which we must do business."[14]

But in this field, too, Western ideals are making their impact. Even the Communist countries furnish themselves with democratic constitutions framed according to our established concepts, and most dictatorships in the non-Soviet world also observe certain elements of democratic form and vocabulary. The international organizations all have constitutions that are imbued with the idea that democracy is a supreme value.

A more substantial gain, however, is that many of the newly liberated countries in the non-Soviet sphere, and some of the major ones, actually attempt very earnestly to carry on their affairs on a democratic basis. Since the large majority of the population in most of these countries is illiterate and little experienced in self-government even on the local level, this attempt is truly heroic. India's and Indonesia's recent national elections, as well as Turkey's break with the one-party system and many other similar accomplishments in other underdeveloped countries, demarcate great and real advances for the ideals of parliamentary democracy—in spite of all possible reservations about their actual application. In many more of the underdeveloped countries the vision of the leaders and the expectancy of the peoples are definitely directed towards freedom and political democracy, and present practices are recognized to be imperfect.

After the First World War, when Europe was still considered almost the only problem in the world, because Asia and Africa were not yet roused, an important result of the peace conference was the setting up of democracies in all the new countries in Central and Eastern Europe. As we know too well, almost all succumbed to totalitarianism, long before the outbreak of the Second World War. With these memories fresh in mind, it is difficult not to feel apprehensive in watching the continuing trend towards dictatorships of one type or another in some countries in each of the major underdeveloped regions. It is also disquieting to hear thoughtful and right-minded citizens in other underdeveloped countries express their doubts whether their country is really mature enough for political democracy.

One thing is certain: the underdeveloped countries that are still bent on political democracy need above all a reasonable degree of economic progress and national integration in order to keep to the road they have chosen. As Mr. Eugene Black, President of the International Bank, put it when speaking to a 1954 session of the Economic and Social Council: "static economics may be explosive politics."

ECONOMIC DEVELOPMENT: THE DEMAND FOR A SHORT CUT

The strong emotional relationship of the drive for economic development to the fight for national political independence is a very important fact, distinguishing it from the historical industrialization process in the now advanced countries. It is one of the reasons—though only one, and I discuss others in the next chapter—why economic development in underdeveloped countries becomes from the start an intensely political matter, a business for the governments.

Indeed, the very fact that there is a political drive for economic development is a new and different thing. Economic development is sold to these peoples as a national goal to be attained, as a government program, or a state plan. In our countries economic development was mostly something which at a given time just happened to take place. Our governments and parliaments became deeply involved in the process, it is true, but in the rather diversified manner that was usual for state operations of this period. The main captain of economic progress was the individual entrepreneur.

Still more important is the fact that in the underdeveloped countries economic development is motivated by the desirability or necessity of raising standards of living. Since the days of Adam Smith the textbooks in economics have developed the idea that consumption is the only purpose of production, but in real life this abstract concept never played a major role. The practical goal was production for immediate profit, and production was not primarily the business of the state. "We are faced not with the private entrepreneur adding to the supply of goods by the application of revolutionary technologies—the model of earlier development—but with the problems confronted by governments trying to give effect to a desire for higher consumption by introducing and adopting new techniques from other countries."

Dr. H. W. Singer, from whom I quote,[15] rightly points out that this is a "non-Schumpeterian world." "In the Schumpeterian model of economic development the rise in real incomes is originated by a lowering of real-cost functions, that is by innovations on the supply side."[16] "Innovating individuals are not motivated by any desire to improve general standards of consumption. They desire only to improve their own standards, by means of profits, and there is only one way of doing that: by changes on the supply side."[17] As I said, governments were involved from the beginning in our countries, too, but their aim was to "support industry," to facilitate foreign loans, or to safeguard certain principles of fair play and justice as rules of the game. No central planning was attempted. Any random sample of the parliamentary papers of any of our advanced countries in the years of early industrialization will reveal the use of a totally different vocabulary, reflecting a totally different ideology, compared to the present vocabulary and ideology of development of underdeveloped countries.

As a matter of fact, in our countries the levels of living of the masses were mostly not raised at all for decades, or raised very little—at least, this was so in Europe; in the new countries the more favorable relationship between working population and natural resources made it possible to have very high profit levels concomitant with high wage rates much more quickly. Study of the miserable living conditions of the workers in the early stages of industrialization served as a primary basis of the revolutionary doctrines of Marx and Engels and was also the source of indignation and inspiration for Zola, Dickens, and a host of other social novelists of the nineteenth century in all countries. The gains of industrial progress were canalized into profits; the unequal income distribution arising therefrom made possible very large savings which were largely ploughed back into investments; they, in their turn, resulted in ever larger production; the growth of industrial production was provided with the plentiful and cheap labor supply it needed from the overpopulated rural areas; the population pressure was kept up not only by the fall in death rates but also often by agrarian reforms and technical advance in agriculture, which at the same time increased agricultural production sufficiently to feed the growing industrial population. With individual variations in the several countries, this sequence was the very essence of our development process.

The political basis for this individualist and acquisitive society of the industrial revolutions was "orderly government" and the rule of law, as those countries had inherited them; but these governments and parliaments did not have a democratic basis in the modern meaning of the term. Income limitations withheld the votes from the great masses of the people. In the New World, where universal suffrage was older, other circumstances protected the hold of the political power by the wealthy—in particular, the continuous stream of pliant immigrants, the appearance of the political machines, and the open access to free land on the frontier which served also as an escape for the unruly.

Only after decades of hard fighting were trade unions permitted to exist; only gradually did they thereafter build up real bargaining power for the workers. Universal suffrage was finally won—but only after a long and ardent struggle over decades. The political power basis was thus created for the big strides towards the welfare state that were gradually made by the introduction of progressive taxation, labor legislation, and social security systems. By that time, however, production had already grown to such an extent that it could support the burden of all this new equalization and provide high living standards for the masses of the people.

Ours is a "derived welfare," to use Singer's expression. It was built upon decades of accumulated capital wealth and productivity, by which production could continue to grow. There are well-known reasons why, at that higher level of productivity, the welfare state became even a necessary basis for continued growth by supporting demand and thereby preventing stagnation on account of "overproduction" or "underconsumption."

In this respect, the Soviet system for economic development follows closely the old capitalist pattern, and it is naturally with those early stages of industrialization that its results should be compared, both in regard to industrial growth and to the advancement of welfare for the people. The motives and the social mechanisms are very different in this, a century-delayed industrial revolution. A higher speed is demanded and the monolithic state and its salaried technicians have replaced the individual risk-taking entrepreneur; but there is this essential similarity that at the expense of a delayed rise in consumption standards large savings are squeezed out from the population and used for heavy investment, with a view to the further rapid growth of production. Elements of very advanced social security and popular education are singled out for early realization; for the rest, the welfare state has to wait while the productivity basis is being laid.

Japan had earlier carried out a state-induced industrialization process on fundamentally similar lines. Incidentally, the *Wirtschaftswunder* in Western Germany, implying a very rapid recovery from the economic ruins of the Second World War and the immediate postwar years, was also carried out according to the old formula: high profits, large savings and investments, low wages; the millions of destitute refugees from the East substituted for the labor surplus in the overpopulated rural areas of the earlier industrialization experiences, keeping down wages. In a similar fashion Finland worked itself out of the morass after its defeat in the war —without much financial aid from abroad, but having to pay a heavy war indemnity to the Soviet Union. It could not, however, prevent inflation from becoming the main means of ensuring a high rate of savings and investment at the expense of consumption levels.

ARE WE EXPORTING A REVOLUTION?

The underdeveloped countries today are bent upon creating "initial welfare" directly out of poverty. By the political situation and by their ideology they are driven to attempt to skip that delay in raising consumption standards which all advanced countries have experienced. To them, in fact, development means primarily rising standards of living for the masses.

This cannot, of course, be done; by some means or other the capital must be created and consumption standards kept low, while the rise in productivity is attained; otherwise there will be no economic development.[18] As Professor W. Arthur Lewis points out: "the central fact of economic development is rapid capital accumulation (including knowledge and skill with capital). We cannot explain any 'industrial' revolution . . . until we can explain why saving increased relatively to national income."[19] In the underdeveloped countries, the definition of the development problem in ideology and propaganda as a drive for raising the standards of living for the masses increases immensely the difficulty of accomplishing the necessary accumulation of capital.

They also have much less preindustrial wealth to start off from than our countries had; while our countries had a long period of development and rise before the coming of the economic and technological revolutions, most underdeveloped countries are sunk in a tradition of accentuated stagnation.[20] They are usually desperately poor, with a per capita income usually less than half—and in the largest part of the underdeveloped world probably much less than half—of what it was in most of the now advanced countries prior to their industrialization.[21] They are faced with many other additional difficulties compared with those other countries that once started to industrialize; some of these additional difficulties were enumerated in the introduction to Chapter III and will be analyzed more fully in the two chapters that follow. As we have seen in Chapters VIII and IX, they do not have anything like the easy access to cheap foreign capital that countries like Sweden and the United States had in their time, and the prospects for substantial capital aid from the richer countries are for the time being almost nonexistent. It is an understatement to say that the task the underdeveloped countries will be trying to perform is a different one and vastly more difficult than any our advanced countries have ever faced.

If the richer countries do not furnish capital, what they do render is a powerful spur to the underdeveloped countries' craving for a quick rise in their consumption levels—to their demand for "initial welfare" without the delay for savings and investment. They do it, first, by accepting without much reservation the definition of economic development as a drive for higher living standards for the masses of the people in these countries. Almost the whole literature on economic development of underdeveloped countries starts out from this definition of the problem. This is, indeed, not unnatural when we remember the very low levels of living in these countries. Often it is argued that this more humane approach is what distinguishes economic development under democratic conditions from what would take place under a Communist regime—in my opinion a rather dangerous assertion if, realistically, living standards will have to be kept low in order to allow development.

Second, as was pointed out in Chapter IX, the richer countries exert an influence in this direction by the very fact of their own high levels of living and by the wide publicity about these made possible by modern means of communication. For this reason, merely to start later makes things very much more difficult.

Third, the advanced countries are actively rationalizing their own situation—and their social policies at home, based on a national solidarity which has no counterpart internationally—by the formulation, built upon elaborate and impressive research, of minimal standards for various items of consumption, like food, housing, health, and education. These normative standards that are attainable in the advanced countries and thus appear sensible to them, are all sky-high above actual levels of consumption in the underdeveloped countries and above anything these countries could possibly realize in the foreseeable future. They are thereby giving the authority of science to social discontent and further encouraging the definition of development in terms of rising consumption levels.

The International Labor Organization labored for a quarter of a century to reach international agreements built upon the principle that working conditions should conform to the same standards all over the world—an excellent principle from the point of view of the value premise of the present study, except for the reservation that such agreements must necessarily remain a dead letter and almost a slightly cynical joke, until the differences in levels of labor productivity are diminished. The organization is now devoting its major practical efforts to rendering technical advice to countries that need it, adjusted to their actual industrial situation. The advice given cannot fail, however, to have the same effect of raising normative living standards above the actual ones.

The World Health Organization and UNESCO are spreading knowledge of standards of health, culture, and education; neither can these standards be given immediate reality, except as primitive and rudimentary beginnings. I am the last person to want to minimize the eminent importance of the practical accomplishments of these organizations in the underdeveloped countries, but in this connection my point is merely that they, too, are contributing to setting standards for these countries which imply an increased upward pressure on consumption levels.

"Technical assistance" is becoming the unanimously hailed means of aiding the underdeveloped countries in their drive for economic development: never has an expenditure of twenty-odd million dollars a year—the scope of the United Nations expanded program for technical assistance, and corresponding, if I am correctly informed, to a tenth of the cost of one of the modern giant bombers—earned so much eloquence in return. By the propaganda that has to be kept up in the developed countries to get that money appropriated, the feeling is created also in these nations that something substantial is done to help the underdeveloped countries. But the truth should not be concealed that the technical assistance program is, as Lord John Boyd Orr puts it, "hopelessly inadequate"[22] and, furthermore, that a main reason why it has become so relatively popular in the richer countries is exactly that it is so cheap a means of helping the poorer ones. The implication is, however, that in the underdeveloped countries that type of technical advice is the one thing most of them could afford to buy themselves—if they had the capital for development. Again, I am eager to stress that I am the last person who would wish to minimize the real contribution of this program to economic development, even in its present diminutive scale and without the accompanying capital. My main point in this connection is merely that one of its major effects is to raise expectations that are not fulfilled and to make a great number of beginnings that cannot be followed up.

The underdeveloped countries' drive for "initial welfare" is thus powerfully prodded by the advanced countries, and for the best of reasons, while at the same time their economic development is not being supported by the material means by which it could be realized. Our various policies towards these countries, considered in conjunction and as a whole, are framed as if we wanted to intensify the dilemma in which they are finding themselves. And undoubtedly we do it out of idealism, though without letting it impose on us too great sacrifices.

Our modern welfare state, which is the crowning result of decades of heavy savings and rapid industrial development under the most favorable conditions, is becoming a revolution exported to the stagnant, poverty-stricken regions. And I do not see how it could be otherwise. This is, in fact, a major contradiction in our economic policies and in our attitudes to the world problems, on the same level of importance as the general conflict between national and international integration which I analyzed in Chapter IV. At bottom both have the same origin: too little international solidarity; and there is similarly only one effective cure: more solidarity.

The underdeveloped countries themselves have very little choice in this matter. Given the political forces, as they have been reviewed in this chapter, and the relations with the advanced countries, as determined by the policies of those countries, the underdeveloped countries are driven, as if by immutable destiny, to attempt the almost impossible. Many of these countries, for example India, want to perform this near-miracle under a fully democratic system of government, giving the majority power to the poor masses and—equally important—with the freest contacts with the entire world, and fully exposed to all the currents of knowledge and ideas in the world.

CHAPTER XII

National Integration
in the Underdeveloped Countries

DEFINING THE PROBLEM

Most of the underdeveloped countries have deeply disintegrated national economies. All sorts of social and economic barriers stand in the way of realizing equality of opportunity for individuals. At the same time, these countries are desperately poor; many of them have been economically stagnant for a long time. The two-way relationship between national integration and economic progress has been stressed in Chapters II and III. In all the underdeveloped countries the economic development problem is primarily a problem of seeking national integration in its necessary combination with economic progress, the one being both the result of and the condition for the other.

If the underdeveloped countries were to succeed in really setting out on the road to national integration, this would undoubtedly, in the general manner described in Chapter IV, strengthen forces which are not favorable to international integration—at least until policies for international cooperation have been inaugurated on a much larger scale than is at present within our horizon. But it cannot seriously be maintained that international integration should be bought at the cost of preserving the underdeveloped countries in economic disintegration and stagnation. Further, as was pointed out in Chapter I, these countries are not, and certainly were not in the pre-1914 period, an integral part of the world economy in any sense that can make the internationalist happy. The long way they have to go to reach national integration and, in particular, their concomitant dismal poverty are themselves the most blatant expressions of international disintegration.

This concept of their problem as primarily one of national integration and development is also consistent with the nature and direction of the political forces that are now powerfully at work in the underdeveloped countries and that were analyzed in the last chapter. It gives its due to the new nationalism and, if the implications of this concept are pursued successfully, gives nationalism its positive and constructive outlet.

With the emotional and ideological changes now taking place in the underdeveloped countries, the inevitable alternative to national integration and development is not simply continued stagnation, but probably political cataclysms of one sort or another, as was hinted at in Chapter IX. Several countries in the Near East, for instance, are close to the brink. There is clearly no way to prevent internal and external tensions mounting in the underdeveloped countries, other than their, too, becoming consolidated internally and setting out on the road to national economic development. Of political as well as economic necessity, international integration can be reached only through national integration, and it would be grossly superficial to treat the problem in any other way.

It is also superficial to believe that the problem is simply one of economic change. This bias is the stronger, because it is in line with powerful vested interests. In many of the underdeveloped countries policy is dominated by oligarchic groups; as Mr. H. L. Keenleyside has pointed out, "in comparing the various nations, there would seem to be an almost direct relationship between the concentration of political power and the immaturity of the national economy."[1] Those in power are often all out for economic development in a narrow sense but would want to see it happen without changes of the social structure within which they are privileged.

Whether they make it clear to themselves or not, they are then, in fact, following the traditions of colonial times. In that historical epoch economic development—characterized by the growth of plantations and other enterprises of the enclave type—was also conceived of in isolation from any broader political, social, and cultural aspirations on behalf of the population at large. In Chapter VIII I stressed that all the metropolitan powers, however differently they framed their colonial policies, found it politically expedient to strengthen, support, and use for their own purposes the oligarchic groups who had their own interests in preserving the political and social *status quo*. In a sense, this mechanism of reactionary political expediency is the main explanation why colonialism implied economic stagnation almost by necessity.

When discussing the development problem in several of the underdeveloped countries with their officials, I have often observed a bias for economic development in terms of dams and industrial plants. The horrible vision often enters my mind of the ultimate results of our continuing and rapidly speeding up the practice, well established in some countries during the era of colonialism, of tossing together ever bigger crowds of illiterate proletariats—these new proletariats being even more uprooted than they were in the stagnant villages, where they had lived in the remnants of some culture and some established mores.

THE NEED FOR RAPID SOCIAL REFORMS

At this point it is useful to recall that the economic progress we have witnessed in the now advanced countries was associated from the very beginning with fundamental changes in all social relations. In fact, as I pointed out in Chapters II and III, the gradual attainment of national integration had its essential base in these noneconomic changes: increased social mobility both locally and within the entire national community, which opened up the avenues for competition and individual advance; intensified social cohesion and practical solidarity in the nation as a whole, which formed the basis for the coming into force of rules that applied to the entire community and for the sharing within the whole nation of the burden of common expenditure; increased participation by all the citizens, on local and national levels, in the political responsibility of controlling the social processes. It was through such changes that greater equality of opportunity was gradually attained. Economic development was in many ways a driving force, but it was itself made possible and continuously sustained by all the other socially integrating changes.

In retrospect economic progress and national integration seem largely to have developed as the almost automatic outcome of a process of cumulative causation, where one change continuously induces others, which in turn react and give a new momentum to the initial change. The term "industrial revolution" seems itself to overdramatize what actually happened in the economic field; socially, in any event, the process was more one of evolution. Legislation, when it was enacted, was most often introduced in order to catch up with a situation that had gradually come about, and was sometimes simply a legal sanction to an established state of affairs. By a sequence of a great number of mostly small changes established patterns and social structures were remolded into new social forms, allowing increased mobility and individual advance under conditions assuring people's experience of mutual solidarity within a widened circle, stability in social relations stretching ever further outside the local community, and an increased measure of social and economic security.

This view is apt to lead us to forget how much political struggle preceded some of the changes, and also that serious social frictions and tensions often developed and reigned for long periods before the adjustments were finally accomplished. But even if due account is taken of these reservations, it remains true that by and large economic progress and national integration went hand in hand as a rather peaceful, all-embracing, and gradual process of social adjustment. The general climate was, from the beginning and increasingly, one of rationality, belief in advancement, and confidence in the future. And it took about a century to accomplish it.

The major explanations of how this was possible have been referred to in several connections in earlier chapters. The initial impediments to social change were much smaller than in most underdeveloped countries today. These now industrially advanced countries had had for generations a considerable preindustrial economic development, with the result that they started out from a position of greater wealth and much higher levels of income. They were also leaders in the contemporary world and formed a partial international community with considerable migratory movements; as, one after another, they entered the industrial era an effective international capital market furnished them with capital on cheap terms.

Further, they had long traditions of political independence and of the rule of law, and even at the onset of industrialization social conditions were more egalitarian and less frozen. These nations had been the homes of the great modern intellectual movements towards spiritual freedom and rationality, beginning with the Renaissance and the Reformation and culminating in the Enlightenment, and their universities nursed the developing sciences. For all these reasons they were intellectually and morally much better prepared for social change.

In some of the underdeveloped countries that are relatively better off economically and where economic stagnation, foreign domination, and population pressure have not created such social havoc, it is quite possible that under otherwise favorable circumstances—including the development of international relations—a successful process of economic and social adjustment can take place, rather similar to the one the advanced countries have gone through. I am thinking of countries like Israel, Turkey, the underdeveloped countries in Southern Europe, and of many countries in Latin America. But in most underdeveloped countries, some with very large populations, economic progress and national integration will not get under way in this easy manner. Stagnation will not be overcome before the deeply entrenched social impediments to change are removed. The result of the forces for change pressing from without and within might otherwise be only the negative one of destroying existing social norms and forms without new viable ones taking their place.

Dr. Eugene Staley has well formulated the situation as it confronts the planner of economic development in most underdeveloped countries: "The social obstacles to development are tenacious because they are deeply imbedded in habits of millions of individuals, in the accepted social arrangements we call institutions, and in the system of values by which people decided that some things are good and others bad, some more important and others less important."[2] In countries where the economy has long been stagnant, people have a strong natural conservatism because their culture is so traditionalistic and contains virtually no elements of scientific and technological experience and, consequently, no habit of experimentation.

When economic change hits a society of such closed minds and entrenched social rigidities, social values are destroyed almost of necessity. It cannot be expected to embark more or less as a matter of course upon an almost automatic process of adjustment to economic changes which, by their cumulative repercussions on all social factors, will carry it through the early industrialization phase towards our modern welfare state of mutual solidarity and commonly shared high living standards. *To prepare the way for economic development such countries need initial reforms of the social structures on a vast scale*; without them there will be no national integration and so no economic development. Without them the only result will be an end of the security and solidarity of the stagnant, isolated, local social compartments.

THE VIEW OF CULTURAL ANTHROPOLOGISTS

Long before the development of underdeveloped countries became a dominant problem in international politics, cultural anthropologists were making a thorough study of the social life in the stagnant local communities of these countries. Recently they have often had occasion to criticize as superficial the writings of economists on the development problem. Following their old theoretical tradition of ignoring the noneconomic factors, on the ground that they fall outside economic analysis, economists have often simply assumed that the national communities would become adjusted psychologically, socially, culturally, and politically to the economic changes as they occurred; and they have done so with few qualms of conscience, since such an assumption has proved not too unrealistic in the case of the historical development of the advanced countries from the preindustrial stage and onwards. They have, however, usually failed to observe the big difference in the initial readiness for change just referred to.

By and large the critical points made by the anthropologists are pertinent and well taken. We now have a big literature which stresses this difference and shows how this or that economic change, under the special circumstances ruling in a particular underdeveloped country, had such and such unexpected, and regularly detrimental, effects. The anthropologists are usually much less explicit and precise and, incidentally, also less well in accord with each other, when the practical question is raised: how, then, shall we go about achieving economic development? Often, their only answer is to give vent to a conservative bias: that economic development should not be hurried. This answer is not very satisfactory, for, as I shall argue in this chapter, there are compelling reasons why. on the contrary, development will have to be speeded up to the maximum possible degree.

There are new political dynamics in the situation that scientific study can shun only at the danger of becoming unrealistic and inconsequential. Professor Jacob Viner puts it this way: "Most countries, if their people are to be satisfied with their rate of progress, will have to move forward at a much more rapid rate than did in the past century those countries which are now the most advanced; and many of these countries have disadvantages of poor natural resources, unfavorable climates, and populations already dense, which neither Western Europe, the British Dominions, nor the United States, had to face."[3]

For obvious reasons the scientific study of the cultures and the social relations of the peoples in underdeveloped countries was initiated mainly in the universities and other agencies—including the missionary establishments—of the colonial powers; it was only with the permission of their governments that the cultural anthropologists could carry on their field work. Even today these countries are leading in this field of social research —with the exception of the United States, which, however, is gradually acquiring the responsibilities of a metropolitan power. The American anthropologists have recently made outstanding contributions to knowledge, but in one particular respect they have only rarely broken with traditions: they have not made place for a new, thoroughly dynamic, and practical point of view in their studies of the cultures of underdeveloped countries.

The economic interests of the old colonial powers were not to promote economic independence and industrial diversification in the colonies but to preserve them as extensions of their own home markets, to establish and protect their colonial enclaves, mainly in the extractive industries, and to promote the interests of their settlers. Their political interest was primarily to preserve peace and stability and to avoid social upheavals.

It implies no reflection on the moral integrity of the individual scholars, but only a legitimate inference concerning the influence of the social and political setting upon intellectual life, when I venture to express the opinion that this power situation made it natural for research to concentrate on social statics rather than social dynamics. Though the cultural anthropologists were occasionally taken into counsel by their governments, it is easily understandable that the advice sought concerned problems of how to avoid tensions rather than how to release the dormant capacities for cultural growth and development to economic and political independence of indigenous populations. This historically close relation between colonialism and the evolution of cultural anthropology is, incidentally, one of the reasons why I personally consider it of prime importance that research institutes under truly international auspices be created for the scientific study of social problems in underdeveloped countries.

There were other, and independent, ideological interests which animated cultural anthropologists; those interests were all in our old Western liberal tradition but did not conflict with their fundamental conservative bias in regard to social change. One interest was to refute European ethnocentrism: to teach, and to demonstrate to the Western world, that these peoples in the underdeveloped countries were not simply barbarians but had a culture, though different from ours, and to show that under existing conditions their way of life and their social organization contained elements of functional rationality. They seldom attempted, however, to develop their science into a social technology, which would have meant utilizing their assembled stock of knowledge about the social facts to prescribe how social change could be induced and controlled in a rational and wholesome way—though they did point out to the economists who, split up into their various sects, nevertheless all stem from a fighting church of reformers, that their economic analysis was superficial and that the policies they propounded could cause harm when they argued for economic development.

But the drive for economic development in underdeveloped countries is not the feeble brainchild of scheming economists; it is a living political force of immense and irresistible power in our contemporary world. I believe that under the influence of the changed political situation in the world the next stage in the development of cultural anthropology will necessarily be its orientation towards social technology. I believe, further, that the whole of our social science, when faced with the tremendous problems that economic development of the underdeveloped countries is raising, will be forced into interdisciplinary research of a type and on a scale that we have hitherto only talked about but not accomplished. And I believe that our work will be increasingly directed to giving the answer to the urgent, directly practical problems—though I hope that the deeper fundamental research will not be neglected.

SOME MAIN ASSUMPTIONS

Conscious of the weak foundations, I shall nevertheless now attempt to formulate a few summary judgments which I need in order to proceed with my exposition of the social issues raised by the development problem in underdeveloped countries; they will be enlarged as these issues are taken up for separate treatment later in this chapter.

Strong forces for change are operative from without and from within these countries. The political forces were analyzed in the last chapter.

Population pressure, to name only one other force for change, will tend to increase, partly because of the availability of cheap means of bringing down the death rate even without a rise in standards of living; the relative pressure will become stronger, the less economic development there is. *In this situation there is no choice open between wanting a slower or faster rate of economic development. Every government will have to do its utmost to push on as fast as possible.* A slow rate of economic development implies grave social and political dangers.

Advice not to hurry economic change has, therefore, to be rejected. The anthropologists are right, however, in saying that the cultural and social effects of economic change may be disastrous—and that, further, these effects may also soon frustrate economic development. They are then assuming, however, that these effects are left to take care of themselves. If the political necessity of rapid economic development is assumed, the obvious conclusion is the opposite—that the cultural and social changes have to be planned and controlled; to a certain extent they have even to be induced.

In fact, we are compelled to accept the necessity of radical initial reforms of the social structure, opening the way for economic development and steering the social changes towards wholesome adjustments. I believe —and I would like to have more research centered on this particular point—that in a stagnant community some of the bigger social changes, if they are well prepared, intelligently directed, and explained to the people, will often meet no more resistance and have no greater adverse effects than smaller social changes in popular beliefs, social etiquettes and patterns of behavior. In planning the induced changes it should be recognized, however, that there is supreme sense in the anthropologists' caution that careful consideration should be given to the actual conditions in every particular country that experiences economic change and the consequent necessity of large-scale social reform. Generally, the scope and speed of change has to be taken as more or less given by political and economic necessity, while the form and the detailed direction of change are open to a variety of alternatives that require careful study before a choice is made.

The anthropologists are also right in warning against Western ethnocentrism: there are social values in these cultures very much worth preserving and there are impediments to change which, in the interest of preserving those values and avoiding cultural breakdowns, should be circumvented and not brutally overcome. Mr. Tarlok Singh states as the criteria for the principles of economic reorganization of India, which he has been trying to work out, that they "should be in accord with the character, traditions and genius of Indian rural society, and should at the same time lead, over a period of years, to economic efficiency, social justice and democratic freedom."[4] This is in a nutshell what must be the approach.

We should therefore not expect as a result of the development process mere replicas of Western communities. Instead, we should hope for the enrichment of the world's civilization by the creation of new social forms for progressive national cultures. We should not assume that our particular "way of life," our patterns of business organization or public administration, and our various brands of representative democratic government are suitable social forms in the underdeveloped countries.

In the ideal case the development of an underdeveloped country should thus be steered towards a society which in many important respects would be different from our Western societies: there are historical roots that should not be cut, inherited mores that need adaptation but not abolition. Many of the valuations in these countries contain great possibilities for a social development towards good human societies, though moving in other directions than those of our Western civilization.

When all this is said, however, it must be remembered that certain of our basic Western valuations will have to be imported, together with our techniques, if the underdeveloped countries wish to achieve a harmonious industrial civilization. For one thing, they will have to implant desires for efficiency and material advance and inclinations toward rationalism, experimentalism, and enterprise. Since modern industry needs a national frame—because of technological development, even more so than the advanced countries needed it a hundred years ago—they will have to break down barriers between the local communities; they will have to create the conditions for wider social mobility and lay the basis for national solidarity. They will have to instill respect for the principle of the rule of law and stamp out arbitrariness, corruption, and inefficiency in public administration.

That industrial society needs social forms other than a stagnant, self-contained peasant society is only another way of stating the demand for social adjustment. Broadly speaking, the direction of these adjustments is given and they cannot be very different in underdeveloped countries from what they were in the advanced ones. As I have already pointed out, the "awakening" of these nations and their drive for development imply that they are making way for these particular Western ideals. This movement is reflected in the fact that their students come to our countries to study, while we send out our experts to teach.

In one particular respect, the acceptance of our Western values has been made an explicit assumption of the present study. My general value premise is the desirability of political democracy. A Communist dictatorship would rapidly and effectively carry into effect the initial eradication of impediments to change that I have shown to be necessary—though in a way concomitant with other changes which are undesirable according to my general value premise. Under the assumption of political democracy these initial changes will instead have to be given the form of social reforms to be decided upon by due political process. The majority will have to be in favor.

The reforms have to be carried out against tremendous forces of social inertia: conservatism among the masses and vested interests of the privileged few. Democracy is no easy short cut to national progress, but rather an exacting moral imperative. It is our faith that only under democratic rule will people's innermost strivings be protected and a basis laid for attaining the distant goal of a "free world" of liberty, equality, brotherhood, and, therefore, peace. So far as democracy is concerned, we *are* ethnocentric on behalf of the inherited values of Western civilization.

But democracy takes many forms, and other forms than ours are not inferior, if they are better adapted to the community values of the underdeveloped countries. Apart from this, we should not expect a perfect democracy to spring forward as a fiat of national decision in countries where authoritarianism has been the tradition, usually strengthened during colonial rule. It is also appropriate in this connection to recall that in the advanced countries, in spite of much more favorable conditions—including the presence of well-established Western ideals of liberty and equality and century-old traditions of political independence, orderly government, and the rule of law—the more perfect forms of democracy developed only late and as a result of a slow process. Even now they are not everywhere perfect.

In Sweden universal suffrage was not won until after the First World War and under the impact of the Russian revolution. In Switzerland women are still deprived of the vote. In the United States, though the last ten years have seen a rapid improvement in the situation, Negroes are in some regions still disfranchised and experience difficulties in obtaining equal protection and justice. More generally, the low percentage of voters in the United States and other indications point to the continuation of a relatively low degree of citizens' participation in political decisions. Corruption and graft continue to be a problem, particularly on the state and local levels.

The group of experts appointed a few years ago by the United Nations to study the economic development problem of underdeveloped countries saw very clearly the problems referred to in the preceding pages:

The people of a country must desire progress, and their social, economic, legal and political institutions must be favourable to it. . . . There is a sense in which rapid economic progress is impossible without painful readjustments. Ancient philosophies have to be scrapped; old social institutions have to disintegrate; bonds of caste, creed and race have to be burst; and a large number of persons who cannot keep up with progress have to have their expectations of a comfortable life frustrated. . . . In our judgment, there are a number of under-developed countries where the concentration of economic and political power in the hands of a small class, whose main interest is the preservation of its own wealth and privileges, rules out the prospect of much economic progress, until a social revolution has effected a shift in the distribution of income and power.[5]

As is made clear by their concrete proposals, the experts do not mean by "social revolution" the violent overthrow of existing institutions, but their adjustment to make progress possible by exactly the kind of initial, large-scale reforms of the social structure, the necessity for which I am arguing. On this point I should like again to cite Tarlok Singh:

We are confronted . . . with a society harbouring a number of false values, in which the new wealth is not passing to those who need it most, in which the bulk of the population remains poor and ignorant, and in which resources are not efficiently organised and developed in the interest of the community. In a situation of this character, there is danger that when, through instinct and suffering, the masses begin to interpret for themselves their state of poverty, the entire social order and the economic system which sustain it may alike collapse. It is necessary, therefore, to think and act, in good time, in terms of new principles of social action.[6]

Social Cleavages

One important and immensely difficult problem of national integration arises from the fact that many of the underdeveloped countries have in-herited ethnic, cultural, or religious chasms, splitting off population groups which had stubbornly resisted, and equally stubbornly been denied, social and economic integration. They have not only different standards of living but different ways of living and attitudes to life. The groups do not mix in work and still less do they share in other social ac-tivities. The most fundamental thing is that their loyalties do not con-verge. This problem is present in Asia, in some countries of the Middle East and Southeastern Europe, in many Latin American countries, and also in parts of Africa.

The winning of national independence among formerly subject peoples has, as a short-term effect, often only released and intensified internal animosities and tensions. In some parts of the world more or less forced migrations have been taking place, such as the exchange of populations between India and Pakistan, or the similar exchange between Greece and Turkey after the First World War; after the Second World War Bulgaria expelled its Turks. In such migrations, vast human suffering is involved and serious refugee problems are created. The migrations are seldom complete and, instead of settling the problem, they often increase tension not only among, and around, those who have gone to be settled in a new country, but also among those who are left behind. As the plight of the Arab refugees and the expulsion of the Germans from East-European territories illustrate, explosive international problems often smolder in the wake of population shifts.

Forced migration is a hideous process. Whenever it has taken place in modern times, it has been during or immediately after a war, while the conscience of rulers and peoples could be silenced. It is therefore not a practical solution if we are planning for a world which we pray should gradually settle down to peace. In most cases there are, in any event, no open spaces where an unwanted population scrap can be dumped. Moreover, people are rooted in their surroundings even if they are not integrated with the rest of the nation. The large Chinese minorities in several East-Asian countries, for instance, cannot possibly just be pushed out.

So there remain dual populations, with dual cultures and often with dual economies. Segregation inevitably brings with it discrimination: the out-group is kept away from certain activities, functions, and occupations. In self-defense, the out-group does what it can to exploit the in-group. The Chinese, for instance, like the Jews once in Europe, undertake functions of moneylending and commerce which are more or less taboo in the indigenous populations or which represent activities where the in-group is for other reasons less effective. Sometimes the out-group may seem to perform socially useful functions and the split in functions due to segregation and discrimination may appear a not irrational division of labor. But it is not voluntary; it is the effect of extreme social rigidities which are irrational and, therefore, in their total effects hamper national integration and economic progress. It is, more particularly, irreconcilable with the growth of an industrial civilization and is deeply incongruous with the development of democracy.

The dual economies and, in the end, the cultural isolation must be broken to achieve integration; but there is no simple and easy way. In most cases it is bound to be an arduous gradual process and, if successful, it will have to include the breaking down by law of dissimilar economic mores and of segregating and discriminating practices, especially in the availability of schooling and other public services and in the labor market. Contract will have to be substituted for status. A deliberate effort will have to be made to train persons from the majority group to perform functions earlier monopolized by the minority group; in exchange, persons from the minority group will have to be permitted to do the things reserved for the majority group. At bottom it is a process of consciously directed education, and this education must accept the tenets of a wider concept of nationality, including the minority group, and of mutual tolerance. It can only be successfully pursued in the general milieu of economic progress and rising living standards widening the elbow room for all.

This is, of course, the "melting pot" solution, and I do not believe there exists another. We should not overlook the very serious difficulties involved. And when we are giving this advice to the underdeveloped countries with their heritage of stagnation and deep social fissures, we should not forget that in America it worked only with considerable friction when the South- and East-Europeans began to swarm in, and that until recently it never effectively included colored people—this in spite of the rapidly expanding economy, the universal conditioning in the Western ideals of equality and dignity of the individual human being, and the consciousness of the unique fact that in America, as Franklin Delano Roosevelt once put it: "We are all the descendants of revolutionaries and poor immigrants."

What can as yet be observed in most of the underdeveloped countries is only mounting tension between the separate groups; this is certainly true in Asia and the Middle East. My impression is nevertheless that, at a deeper level of social causation, integration is gradually and slowly beginning to advance. There is no contradiction between these two assertions; for nobody should expect that these many-centuries-old population fissures could be healed without friction and tension. Advance is even more noticeable in some countries in Latin America. Yugoslavia has an ugly tradition—demonstrated as recently as the Second World War —of bloodstained conflict between closely related but distinct peoples; yet it has recently given one of the most remarkable examples in world history of how a nation can, by its own organized efforts, rapidly become politically and socially integrated; and it has only done so by giving equal rights to all ethnic groups and promoting the development of backward areas. In India, though unfortunately only after the tragic dismemberment of the two Pakistani territories and after much bloodshed and migration, Pandit Nehru and his friends succeeded in calming down the storms of emotions and building up in the remaining part of the country a state guaranteeing equal rights and protection to the large minority of Moslems who remained.

Into this context fall also all other inherited social cleavages in the underdeveloped countries as, for instance, the Hindu caste system. It is a very remarkable thing that on the ideological level this problem is now solved in India, and its solution is probably Gandhi's greatest contribution to his nation's spiritual and material development. In India today there is practically no public writer or speaker who does not urge the liquidation of the caste system. But to get this ideal carried into effect in the villages will take considerable time. There is a whole pattern of social taboos—concerning the access to wells, the entrance to occupations, the availability of education, the choice of marriage partner, etc.—that will have to be broken down.

Even if in most cases time will be required for integration to reach its completion, the decisions of governments and legislators to embark upon it, the beginning of a popular education aimed at changing attitudes, and the initial outlawing of certain flagrant patterns of segregation and discrimination will open up new vistas in national societies even where minds are stagnant. The mental climate will change. The democratic process itself, bringing together representatives from different groups for deliberation and decision on common problems, works powerfully to bridge the chasms. This is, incidentally, one of the reasons why centralized democratic government is not enough but must be complemented—or, rather, underwritten—as rapidly as possible and to the maximum extent by effective democracy in revitalized local self-government.

THE CLASS STRUCTURE

Economic progress requires, however, a much more general loosening-up of the rigid class system in the stagnating national communities.

The very unequal distribution of incomes and wealth that characterizes most underdeveloped countries was referred to in Chapter IX. In fact, only the smallest part of the cumulative inimical results for economic development of these gross inequalities is related to their direct economic effects. By themselves, equalization measures in these countries could achieve only an infinitesimal rise in income levels for the masses of the poor. Furthermore, in these countries, where capital formation is so necessary and has such severe limitations because of the great poverty, an unequal income distribution could be defended with more justification than in our rich and industrially advanced countries as having the social function of creating savings—provided that the high incomes are not spent on conspicuous consumption, and sometimes conspicuous capital construction, which unfortunately they often are, or else detracted by capital flight or gold hoards.

These inequalities in the distribution of income and wealth have, however, wider social and political ramifications. They are most often related to a system of landownership and a superimposed social class structure that kill the ambitions of the peasants. The very fact that such inequalities endure suggests a state of passive acceptance on the part of the masses which is itself a basic cause of political, social, and economic stagnation. But these attitudes are, in their turn, conditioned by the tenancy system of landownership and the entire social structure founded on the grossly unequal distribution of income and wealth. This vicious circle has to be broken; no national integration and no economic progress is possible without vast redistributional reforms.

The situation in which most underdeveloped countries find themselves with respect to the economic class structure and the distribution of income and wealth bears little resemblance to conditions in the advanced countries before their industrialization. A few of those countries, like Sweden, had in fact never succumbed to feudalism, as the farmers had succeeded through repeated minor revolutions in nipping it in the bud; for different reasons the same holds true for the historical latecomers in the New World, insofar as they did not come under the domination of feudalism's more recent capitalistic incarnation, the plantation system. Many other countries carried out agrarian reforms before they entered the era of the industrial revolution or in its early stages. At the time when they approached their economic development none of the now industrially advanced countries had the extreme economic and social inequalities and the very rigid class structure of most underdeveloped countries today.

One very considerable political difficulty in carrying out these reforms is the poverty of these countries and the compelling necessity they are under to prevent consumption of the masses from rising very much and very fast, if they want to secure the savings they need for economic development. The reforms can therefore not be given the popular motivation of soaking the rich to feed the poor—apart from the fact that, as I pointed out, there would be very little to distribute.

Consumption levels can, in fact, not be permitted to rise at all, except subsequently to, and corresponding to only a part of, a rise in production; as I shall later point out, it is possible that a temporary result of the redistributional reforms may even be a decrease in productivity which would make attempts to raise consumption levels even more disastrous. Redistributional reforms that do not protect national savings not only fail to open up any advance to economic development but will even bring about a deeper and more widespread poverty.

In addition to land reform these countries will need progressive taxation; for the time being their tax systems are regularly regressive and, in particular, spare the rich from any considerable burden.[7] But they will have to tread this road with utmost care in order not to destroy the forces for economic development. They should discriminate in favor of savings and of enterprise; shifting some of the rents from land to the profit-earning sector may often be a rational policy. They, much more than the advanced countries, need "incentive taxation." Their redistributional social security systems bear as yet only the faintest resemblance to those of the industrially advanced countries;[8] and I think we should in all frankness advise them that they will not be able to afford much more in the near future. The advanced countries had very little of this type of redistribution until they had reached a much higher level of productivity.

Their redistributional reforms should thus have the purpose of breaking down rigid class structures and improving the incentives for, and the conditions of, enterprise and production—such as land reform—but for the rest should aim at siphoning off income from consumption, particularly luxury consumption, to savings. To give effect to such rational but austere principles under conditions that prevail in underdeveloped countries would be a hard task for mature democracies and their experienced administrations. The underdeveloped countries must try to do it within the frame-work of their much frailer political systems and with weak and sometimes even corrupt administrations; to these additional difficulties I shall return. If they do not try or do not succeed, they are in danger of losing all possibility of giving a spur to national integration and economic development.

LAND REFORM

With the overwhelming dominance of agriculture in the national economies—which is one of the indications of an underdeveloped country—land reforms naturally take first place among the redistributional reforms. Local conditions vary widely and no generalization can apply to all areas. The most common social and economic defects of the agricultural system in underdeveloped countries are, however, well summarized in a United Nations study in the following way:

> For many countries the agrarian structure, and in particular systems of land tenure, prevent a rise in the standard of living of small farmers and agricultural laborers and impede economic development, both by preventing the expansion of the food supply and by causing agriculture—usually the major economic activity of the country—to stagnate. Among the features of the agrarian structure which have most serious effects are the uneconomic size of farms; the maldistribution of land ownership with concentration of large estates insufficiently utilized and the landlessness of a large part of the rural population; the fragmentation of holdings; the high rents and insecurity of tenure characteristic of many tenancy systems; indebtedness and lack of adequate credit facilities for the small farmer; absence of settled title to land and water; plantation economies which offer low wages and no share in management to the cultivators; taxation policies which impose undue burdens on the small farmers and farm laborers; and in general an unsatisfactory set of incentives for a rising and sustained agricultural production.[9]

Land reform is, furthermore, a primary condition for industrial growth. A main obstacle to industrialization in underdeveloped countries is the lack of a large and expanding market; this in turn is a consequence of the poverty and the low living standards of the people, most of whom are living from agriculture. It is of the same importance in countries where ownership of land is divorced from its cultivation that land is traditionally an object for investment and speculation by the tiny class of people who are better off. The very fact that land then becomes a symbol of wealth, power, and prestige is apt to decrease the incentives for enterprise in manufacturing industry.

Redistribution of land, which breaks up large holdings and allocates them in plots of a few acres to peasants living at the subsistence minimum, may in the shorter run tend to reduce total agricultural production, because the new owners lack capital and often also experience in rational cultivation. It will almost always reduce temporarily the marketable surplus of agriculture, and it is easy to imagine cases where sheer starvation in the towns may be the result. The old system represents with all its imperfections a functioning social organization that furnishes the peasants with credit, seeds, and sometimes fertilizers, and that compels them to market their products.

To overcome these short-term dangers, land redistribution has to be combined with very determined efforts in other directions, mainly in the field of education and organized cooperation of all kinds. The freed farmers have to be taxed in order to make up—and, if possible, more than make up for—the savings of the formerly rich landowners. In other respects the new organization of agriculture can take many social forms and will have to be adjusted to the conditions existing in the different countries and to the valuations among their people.

However difficult, land reform has nevertheless to be tackled; otherwise the vicious circle will never be broken. Attempts at lifting the level of education and enterprise of landless peasants who are not given the land are almost certain to fail.

NOT WITHOUT STRUGGLE

All these things are obvious to any serious observer, and for several years now decisions have been taken at various United Nations meetings recommending land reform and setting it in its proper relation with other efforts to improve agricultural productivity and the living conditions of the farming population. As the years have passed, the resolutions have tended to become ever longer and more comprehensive; the several specialized agencies have the problems under study. Ordinary well-meaning newspaper readers in our advanced countries might be led to believe that things are happening on a large scale.

But land reform is a much more serious thing. It is a matter for internal politics, and it implies in almost each of the underdeveloped countries a struggle for power and wealth. Professor J. K. Galbraith has this to say:

Unfortunately, some of our current discussion of land reform in the underdeveloped countries proceeds as though this reform were something that a government proclaims on any fine morning—that it gives land to the tenants as it might give pensions to old soldiers or as it might reform the administration of justice. In fact, a land reform is a revolutionary step; it passes power, property, and status from one group in the community to another. If the government of the country is dominated or strongly influenced by the land-holding groups—the one that is losing its prerogatives—no one should expect effective land legislation as an act of grace. . . . The best assurance of land reform, which I for one hope can be orderly and peaceful, is a popular government by those who really want reform.[10]

The United Nations experts previously referred to, in considering the problem of land reform, make the following assertion: "Private enterprise will not yield its best results unless legal and social institutions are such that the private initiator secures the fruit of his own effort." They suggest, first, tenancy legislation to protect the tenant against arbitrary disturbances and to compensate him for improvements which he has effected, and continue:

In many cases, even more radical reform is needed than legislation protecting tenants. In many under-developed countries, the cultivators of the soil are exploited mercilessly by a landlord class which performs no useful social function. This class contrives to secure to itself the major part of any increase in agricultural yields, and is thus a millstone around the necks of the tenants, discouraging them from making improvements in agriculture and, in any case, leaving them too little income from which they might save to invest in the land. In such countries land reform, abolishing this landlord class, is an urgent pre-requisite of agricultural progress. . . . Land reform in these countries would be the first step necessary for releasing the productive energies of the people.[11]

The experts take an equally stern line with respect to the moneylenders: "The burden of private debt upon the small farmer comes within the same category. Where this is so large as to discourage initiatives, governments have sometimes to create machinery for wiping out excessive debt."[12]

We would deceive ourselves if we did not face the fact squarely that land reform is not simply just a good and wholesome scheme that the underdeveloped countries have every reason to hurry and adopt in order to make economic development possible—it goes against powerful and deeply entrenched vested interests. The same is true of all other economic and social reforms that tend to disturb the *status quo*. Galbraith, taking as a point of departure the argument that economic development assumes popular government, comments:

In the past few years we have somehow managed to persuade ourselves that all of the governments of the world want economic progress. This is undoubtedly true of the great masses of the people of the world. But we should not suppose that the lip service that members of their governments pay to these aspirations reflects, in all cases, a genuine desire for change. In important parts of the world—in much of South America and the Middle East and elsewhere in Asia with such great exceptions as India—governments are still the property of the puppets of small groups whose future security may be not with progress but with stagnation. It is idle to hope that these groups will misinterpret or ignore their own short-run interest and become reliable partisans of progress.

. . . Material progress is to the advantage of the masses of the people. If they are in command of their political destiny, or if they are of sufficient political consequence so that dictators can remain in power only by their claim to serve mass welfare, there will be progress. But progress does not necessarily reward the colonial power or the domestic oligarchy. It may, on the contrary, be positively damaging and even dangerous to them. Landlords in backward countries, if they see clearly their interest as some have the undoubted capacity to do, will not welcome the industrialization that will make their labor independent and expensive. The merchants who man the tollgates at the ports of the Caribbean and South American countries do not want modern methods of mass distribution which would promptly bypass them. The soldiers who infest the political life of the South American republics would be quickly returned to barracks by the business classes and the labor and farm movements that effective economic development would bring.[13]

Staley likewise observes that in underdeveloped countries small groups of privileged people, enjoying exceptional wealth, political power, and prestige, and privileged also as regards health and education and so possessing more than average energy and social skills, are often likely to be apathetic, if not actively hostile, to many of the measures required for economic modernization. But he adds this important qualification:

Many acquire loyalties to their nation, or perhaps to humanity, stronger than their loyalties to the supposed interests of their class. . . . The notion that social origin determinates a man's political views, and especially his attitude toward the changes requisite for successful economic development, no doubt has a good deal of validity in terms of statistical averages, but in any society where new ideas have begun to percolate there are bound to be a considerable number of individual deviants, mutants, who do not follow the average pattern. It is precisely these individuals who are the key to social and economic change.[14]

This is true and should not be forgotten; but even so, the reforms are not likely to be handed down to the poor masses of people merely because of the rationality and benevolence of the privileged classes; as always before in history, reforms have to be fought for and won against the fierce resistance of most of those who have to accept sacrifices. And without minimizing the importance of outside advice and pressure, as exemplified in the resolutions of the various organs of the United Nations, the decisive struggle has to be waged on the homeground. The reforms will have to come as a result of a gradually more effective domestic political process.

This process is cumulative in character and, from the opposite viewpoint, nothing is more apt to strengthen the basis for the frail beginnings of political democracy in underdeveloped countries than the successful embarking upon the reforms necessary to break down the social and economic inequalities. As the United Nations experts put it: "Attempts to control the consumption of the rich have real political value if the government is trying to win the confidence and the co-operation of the low and middle income groups for its development program."[15]

EDUCATION AND HEALTH

The molding together in a liberated national unity of ethnic, cultural, and religious groups and social castes, the land reform and generally the loosening up of the rigid economic class structure are only a part, in a sense only the outward part, of the great initial social adjustments necessary for releasing the forces for national integration and economic progress. Within this framework a great number of other social changes must take place, and in the cumulative process of adjustment they are all interdependent, being causes as well as effects. The entire social system must be moving.

Perhaps the most important single element in a national integration program is educational reform, and, in my view, the most important single element in educational reform is a determined literacy drive.[16] The literacy drive should be backed up by the establishment of a high priority for the production of reading matter—a derived demand which is often not catered for, with the result that the whole literacy drive comes to naught.

Something tremendously vital to his spiritual integration into the nation and into the world happens to the peasant when he can read the names of the streets as he goes to town and when he can start to make out the syllables in the local newspaper—especially if the process goes further and he also obtains easy access to reading material that is of personal importance to him. All other education—in government, health, more rational methods of production, etc.—becomes relatively hopeless without this basic condition of literacy. To start on a national development program while leaving the population largely illiterate seems to me to be futile.

A literacy drive—like the whole educational reform, if it amounts to anything—will most certainly introduce a new complex of tensions in a backward country, and will contribute to all the other factors breaking down the mores of a stagnant community. This community, however, will already be under the influence of all the other factors tending to loosen up existing attitudes and institutions; and in this dynamic stream all other elements of national integration policy, and not only the literacy drive, are influences of change. The policy influences should so far as possible be directed towards building up a new and stable system of social relations. It is the particular characteristic of literacy that it will tend to increase the ability of individuals to seek and follow a rational adjustment to the changes that occur.

In addition to the literacy drive, there is need for a radical reform of higher education. I am thinking not so much of the level of higher education in most of the underdeveloped countries—low as it is—as of its direction. What these countries need is an increased output of administrators, doctors, engineers, agronomists, and all sorts of technically trained people on different levels, as well as primary school teachers.

Yet almost without exception their higher education is now oriented towards turning out young persons trained in law, philosophy, languages, and literature—an eighteenth-century ideal from the Western world, which has become a dangerous cultural lag. Even within the so-called useful professions students from the underdeveloped countries are often likely to choose the more esoteric and least practical branches. A colleague from an American university told me that their graduate school is rich in aerodynamicists from one Asian country, a profession for which this nation as yet has little need. A young man from another Asian country, sent to study taxation, was inevitably attracted to the more abstruse mathematical branches of "welfare theory."

In spite of the crying needs for trained personnel in all these countries, we find that in many of them there now exists an academic proletariat. As a matter of fact, one of the politically most unstable elements in many underdeveloped countries consists of the intellectuals and semi-intellectuals who have received the wrong type of training and are maladjusted. They are doomed to remain without roots, the more so since these countries lack the social basis of a large and stable middle class. The more important fault in the present system is, however, its failure to produce the badly needed technicians.

A reform in the field of higher education in the underdeveloped countries has to overcome many cultural pretensions and to struggle against many vested interests. The pretensions as well as the vested interests often dominate not only the teachers but also the national educational authorities; they have their deeper causes in the inherited class and caste structure of society. However great the resistance, this struggle has to be waged and won; it must be put among the urgent necessities. A practical and financial difficulty is connected with the fact that technical education often requires expensive laboratory equipment and a higher ratio of teachers to students than do art subjects or law, in which faculties there is also more "idle capacity" as a result of established tradition.

A determined drive for educational reform on a broad front, stretching from a general literacy drive to the widening and modernization of training centers on the university level, will not be inexpensive. As has often been observed, this type of consumption is productive; it is really capital formation, though invested in people and not in the material tools for production. There is no easy way of measuring its marginal productivity or how far it can be stretched without implying an unbalanced allocation of the resources of national savings, which are mostly very scarce in underdeveloped countries. But without doubt, and as a general rule, these countries would be well advised to switch considerably more of their savings to education.

The same is true in regard to health. Productivity is kept down by preventable illnesses. But again, the question of the most remunerative direction of efforts is a crucial one in the underdeveloped countries, whose only chance of economic development depends upon the most careful husbandry of scarce resources. And again, it is a question of overcoming vested interests, rooted in the great economic inequalities in these countries and in the class structure. In many, if not in most, underdeveloped countries doctors are concentrated in the cities, where they earn comfortable incomes from catering to the few rich, while there are virtually no doctors available for the masses of people in the villages. Generally, there is also a tendency to spend relatively too much on curing sickness and preventing death and too little on public preventive medicine.

The health problem presents several dilemmas. One is that economic considerations of costs cannot be excluded when deciding how far society should go in curing sickness. Indeed, even the richest country could spend a much greater proportion of its national income on doing even more to keep its weak and old citizens alive a little longer. The problem has recently been discussed as a very practical one in England. The problem in an underdeveloped country, though considerably different from that in England, is different only in degree: it has to draw the line for its investment in the nation's health and longevity within very much narrower limits.

Another dilemma, which is now rapidly disappearing in industrially advanced countries but is tragically real in the underdeveloped ones, concerns the relation between health and the level of consumption. In the latter countries people are undernourished and underhoused, and their working conditions are inferior; with more food, better houses, and more hygienic working conditions they would be healthier.

For a long time to come this dilemma will be unavoidable. The national communities cannot afford a much higher level of consumption, if they are bent on economic development. They must seek the maximum improvement of the health of the population which can be bought at a price they can afford to pay, that is, without permitting a rise of consumption very much or very soon.

POPULATION PRESSURE

By far the gravest of the social problems facing most underdeveloped countries concerns population policy. "Population increase hovers like a menacing cloud over all poor countries. It can offset, and more than offset, the contribution to economic prosperity which all other factors can make."[17]

While there are great variations in the relation between population and natural resources, many of the underdeveloped countries are densely populated; it is in the logic of things that these densely populated ones together account for by far the larger proportion of the total number of people living in underdeveloped countries. Most people in non-Soviet Asia live in very heavily populated areas, such as India, East Pakistan, Ceylon, Java, Japan, Formosa, and the Philippines. The larger part of the populations—two thirds or three quarters—live crowded on the land, which often tends to be depleted of its natural fertility.

Southwest Asia, with its large desert tracts, and some countries in the Near East have a lower density of population. So have generally—again with large variations—Latin America and Africa. Even in such regions, however, the people often live cramped together on the land; and a rapid change towards better utilization of the resources would usually require both more enterprise and more capital than are at present available.[18] As a matter of fact, the distribution of trained skills and capital equipment is even more unequal, to the disadvantage of underdeveloped countries in general, than the distribution of natural resources.

The populations of all underdeveloped countries are rapidly increasing; the approximate rate of annual increase is 2.3 per cent for Latin America, 2.0 for the Near East, 1.4 for Africa, and 1.3 for the Far East. Since prewar times the total population of underdeveloped countries has increased by something like 30 per cent; as industrialization in most of these countries has proceeded very much more slowly, the very largest part of the population increase has had to be absorbed by the already overcrowded agricultural sector.

Present trends point to a rise in the rate of population increase in the underdeveloped countries. India's population is estimated to have increased by about 44 per cent between 1921 and 1951, as against slightly more than 5 per cent between 1891 and 1921. The consensus among the experts is that this rise in the tempo of population increase in the underdeveloped countries must be expected to continue—unless very radical changes in population policy occur.

The main reason for this judgment is the spectacular development in medical science, especially since the war, which makes it possible to reduce death rates drastically by means which are relatively inexpensive and do not assume a rise in standards of living. In many countries of Latin America and in some parts of Asia and Africa, the death rates at present are only about one half as high as they were prior to the war and lower than they were in the advanced countries in the childhood of the older generation. There is every likelihood that within the next decade or two this condition will spread throughout the underdeveloped regions of the world.

The birth rates in underdeveloped countries, on the other hand, are as high as ever; improved health conditions and the more favorable age distribution of the population resulting from lower mortality rates in early childhood will tend to raise them further.

Professor Frank W. Notestein, who is no alarmist, sums up the situation by stating plainly that "it is clear that in the long run high birth rates are incompatible with low death rates." Leading up to this conclusion, he reasons as follows:

Fertility is apt to yield rapid growth if low death rates can be attained. Whether they can be attained for a substantial period of time depends in large measure on whether economic development can come rapidly enough to forestall catastrophes. A sober consideration of the existing situation leads one to expect that catastrophes will in fact check rapid growth. It points to the urgency of rapid economic development on a broad front to forestall such tragedy. It also points to the urgency of giving attention in regional planning to those changes which bring pressure on the birth rate. Today's problem arises in large part from the absence of such planning in the vast agricultural development of these regions. . . . First of all, we need to know how to reduce birth rates in an agrarian society. The problem is too urgent to permit us to await the results of gradual processes of urbanization, such as took place in the Western world.[19]

In several respects the situation was very different in the advanced countries when they embarked upon their industrialization process.[20] For one thing, populations were small, considerably smaller than we usually realize. The sheer magnitude of the development problem in the underdeveloped countries today is immensely larger.

Not only the relatively empty countries in the New World, but also the older European countries, had therefore a much more favorable initial relationship between population and resources than have underdeveloped countries today, particularly those with the largest populations. In recent decades the populations of the latter countries have been growing at much higher rates than the modern industrial nations in their preindustrial stage, and the prospect is that they will grow still faster in future, while there are no clear signs that their industrialization will speed up very much.

In the now developed countries, the large growth of population that eventually occurred was, in fact, merely a consequence, not an antecedent, of industrialization. There, as in the underdeveloped countries today, the rise in the rate of population increase was a result of a fall in the death rates, while the birth rates usually remained high until towards the end of the nineteenth century. The difference is, however, not only that in the underdeveloped countries the fall in the death rate tends to precede industrialization, but also that it tends to occur rapidly, while in the developed countries it took several generations. Thanks to the new discoveries a fall in the death rate has become "autonomous" and can take place even when living standards are not rising or, indeed, when they are falling.

A reminder is here in place that the advanced countries' industrialization and the rise in population increase occurred in the era of free migration. Europe today, assuming the same history of natural increase, would have had some hundred million more people if the emigration to other continents had not taken place. A corresponding outlet for population surplus does not exist for the underdeveloped countries today. Cross-boundary migrations have generally been checked; the emigration that takes place is highly selective and discriminates against emigrants without capital and skill; most of the people living in underdeveloped countries are colored and are kept within their own countries anyhow by the color bars.

Also, a system of multilateral trade permitted many of the countries which became industrialized one hundred or one hundred and fifty years ago to follow a course of development that was not closely dependent on their natural resources. They found markets for their manufactured goods in less developed areas and could import food and raw materials from there. Such a line of development is hardly possible today for underdeveloped countries.

We should also recall that there was then in existence an international capital market from which the industrializing countries could borrow money on relatively very favorable terms. We have seen in Chapters VIII and XI that the underdeveloped countries today have no such easy access to foreign funds, that governmental loans, loans from the International Bank, and foreign aid do not in any substantial way substitute for the defunct capital market, and that there is little prospect that they soon will.

At bottom are, of course, all the other differences referred to earlier in this book and, in particular, the differences in initial wealth and levels of income.

THE ECONOMICS OF POPULATION GROWTH

The fact that the populations in underdeveloped countries are rapidly increasing and the prospect that they will increase still faster within the near future, are naturally reasons why it is so urgently necessary that their economic development be speeded up. But this population development is itself, at the same time, a tremendous impediment to economic development. This is so primarily because of the poverty of these countries, their low levels of income, and their great difficulty in producing fresh savings.

In a rich country the extra spur on the demand side, caused by population increase, may even be needed in order to keep up consumption and investment and thus to maintain full employment. I am inclined to believe that the high birth rates in the United States and most other advanced countries after the Second World War—probably, in their turn, an effect of full employment and the recently much perfected systems of social security—have been one of the factors preserving the protracted postwar business boom. I find it probable that over a much longer range of years the absence of population increase in France has, on balance, been a factor contributing to the social and economic stagnation of that country.[21]

In underdeveloped countries, if they keep at all to the road to economic development, neither consumption nor investment needs any extra stimulus, and both have constantly to be held in check in order to avoid inflation. In the reactions of their economies to population changes the underdeveloped countries are different from the richer countries just as radically as they are different in regard to the effects of import restrictions, a problem I deal with in Chapter XIII.

In fact, underdeveloped countries can ill afford the structural growth of the economy which a population increase would require only in order to preserve existing levels of income—before there is any development at all. The investment in feeding and bringing up a considerably larger new generation and, thereafter, the proportional increase needed for producers' equipment may in most underdeveloped countries leave little or no net savings for any economic development in terms of higher productivity per capita.

There are dynamic factors in this equation which should not be forgotten.[22] Economic development in terms of higher productivity depends not only upon higher capital intensity but also on the introduction of new techniques. But improvements in production techniques depend in their turn on the availability of more and better tools; stagnation of productive investment will also hamper technical progress. It is also true that when the rise in the rate of population increase is caused by a lowered death rate, this will correspond to a general rise of health standards in the population. As the lowered death rate reflects particularly a decrease in deaths during early childhood, it will also tend to raise the proportion of the population reaching the productive age. Both these changes will tend to raise productivity and levels of income—but they are bought at the price of a more rapid rate of population increase, which raises demand for consumption and investment before any investment in development can take place.

In evaluating the effects on economic development of a population increase, and an increase in the rate of population increase, it is necessary to bear in mind the existing situation of population pressure. In one sense practically all underdeveloped countries are "overpopulated"— in the sense that they have surplus labor which is not put to economic use. This is, in fact, from one point of view the basic cause of their poverty. Regularly from a third to a half of their manpower in agriculture, in which most of the population earns its livelihood, is superfluous, in that—even without any special labor-saving devices, but with a better organization of production and a few more and better tools—they could maintain existing production with a much smaller agricultural population; in the cities there is at the same time unemployment and still more "underemployment." The surplus population would assume even larger proportions if new production techniques were introduced and there were substantial productive investments.

Economic development must consist of putting more workers into economic production and gradually also of improving the techniques and raising capital intensity—thereby increasing production, facilitating savings and capital formation, and, in time, making possible also rising living standards for the masses. When there already exists so much surplus labor that needs to be provided with economic employment—usually enough to tax all that the national communities can mobilize in the way of capital, enterprise, and organizational ability for decades ahead—a large population increase will only maintain the surplus and make it more difficult to work off. The growth of working population, caused by population increase, does not therefore usually result in a proportional rise in production.

On these points we should recall the definition of economic development in terms of raising the standard of living for the masses of people; this is a political premise of immense importance in all the underdeveloped countries. It has been a recurring theme in this book that governments in these countries will have to check rises in consumption most severely in order to allow for investment in the growth of production. As low as living standards are in these countries and as extravagantly as the hopes have been raised—for which a heavy responsibility falls on the advanced countries—this necessity of raising savings for investment represents one of the greatest political difficulties facing all underdeveloped countries.

Providing for a population increase diminishes the available savings for investment in higher levels of productivity; the prospect of a still higher rate of population increase is bound to accentuate this dilemma.

Even if there is some development, which usually assumes some savings above what is needed to take care of the population increase, the increase in production which can be used either for savings or increased consumption will be smaller than it could have been with a similar sacrifice but without population increase. If such a country decides nevertheless to press on with economic development, the population will have to wait still longer for any major rise in standards of living or, perhaps, even take a cut in consumption. If, on the contrary, it falls for the temptation of following an easier policy, development will be checked and future living standards will be endangered.[23]

The danger is, naturally, continued stagnation. We know too well from the colonial era that if the population is constantly increasing, stagnation of average levels can well be concomitant with considerable development of individual enterprises and localities. As Notestein points out: "If gains in production only match those in population growth, 'improvement' may result principally in ever larger masses of humanity living close to the margins of existence and vulnerable to every shock in the world economic and political structure. Such 'progress' may amount to setting the stage for calamity. Much of Asia seems to be perilously close to this situation."[24]

POPULATION POLICY

The end result of the application of modern medical methods to underdeveloped countries may thus be only to strengthen the hold of poverty over their peoples. This dilemma cannot be solved by slowing down the health reforms. The urge to prevent illness and death cannot be inhibited; it is planted too deeply in our Western system of ideals, which is now strengthening its hold all over the world.

For women to bear children and lose so many of them before they have grown up means such human misery that we cannot possibly abstain from attempting to save their lives; and as I have pointed out, the progress of medical science makes it ever cheaper to do so. High mortality in early ages and poor health at every age in the population also imply a great waste of productivity which we must try to combat. This is, in fact, a very important part of any effective plan for economic development. But it all becomes self-defeating if we cannot at the same time bring down the birth rate. Reduction of birth rates in underdeveloped countries is no substitute for economic development, but rather an essential condition for its success.

There is no rational ground for believing that this problem will solve itself. In the Western world birth control came late in the development and only when—on account of very exceptional circumstances, which cannot be expected to recur in most of the underdeveloped countries—living standards had reached a level considerably above what we can possibly hope for in the underdeveloped countries in the foreseeable future. In most of them, indeed, the level may even tend to fall, if the rapid population increase should continue.

The spread of birth control in the advanced countries was not a result of any technical development of contraception. On the whole, it did not—and to an astonishingly high degree, does not today—utilize any developed technique, but instead is carried out by one precaution or another, usually coitus interruptus, which must have been known ever since there has been an awareness of a causal relation between coitus and conception. Birth control, when it spread, was thus directly and solely the result of changed attitudes. It is very difficult to believe that in these poor countries such a rationalization of attitudes will come as a natural development. As always in poor societies, children are not such a large extra burden *to the individual family.* To have many children is, on the contrary, often the only available means of social security *for the individual.* In a quantitative sense this will tend to change somewhat, but hardly radically, when many more are surviving.

There is, however, one weighty reason why the historical analogy should not lead us to take a too desparing view of the problem. Even though it is extremely probable that the population problem will not solve itself in the underdeveloped countries, it would be very different indeed if birth control became part of public policy. In the Western world birth control had to spread in the beginning against the very explicit and powerful resistance of the organized community: law, religion, the medical profession, the whole educational system, and the press. Undoubtedly it would have spread much earlier if these powerful forces had remained neutral, as they mainly do today, and still earlier if they had favored it.

The one hopeful thing is that there are signs in many underdeveloped countries that the community is preparing itself for an effective public policy of propagating and spreading birth control. This is, incidentally, one of the points where the countries in the non-Soviet world may be able to inaugurate a policy that—even aside from the fundamental question of civil liberties—is rationally superior to that of the Soviet system. The Communist opposition to birth control is an example of the strong doctrinal determination of policy in the Soviet orbit—even if it is conceded that the relatively very favorable relationship between population and natural resources in the Soviet Union makes this doctrinaire attitude less expensive; it will be interesting to follow the development in China, where for obvious reasons opposition to birth control will be really expensive. The opposition goes back to Marx, who had a strong dislike for Malthus and everything associated with him, directly or indirectly, partly because Malthus had provided the basic argument for the "iron law of wages."

In a recent article Professor S. Chandrasekhar put the practical problem in clear terms: "Unrestricted population growth and a rising standard of living in the present economic context cannot go together. . . . The present task is to carry this reform to the millions of mothers in Asia, Africa and Latin America who desperately need it. Fortunately, by and large there is no organised cultural, institutional or religious opposition to family planning in the under-developed countries."[25] Many field studies recently carried out have, furthermore, demonstrated that poor people out in the villages respond positively to the suggestion that the number of future births could be checked. Pandit Nehru has time and time again put his immense popular authority behind the movement for birth control and the Indian Government has begun to sponsor educational and other actions to support it. Other governments in Asia as well as, for instance, the government of Egypt, are gradually moving towards a similar position.

Such a policy would have to overcome immense difficulties. While birth control in the advanced countries usually spread first in the upper income groups and in the cities and only slowly reached the lower income groups and the rural areas, underdeveloped countries cannot wait on such a slow sequence but will have to attempt by conscious policy to get birth control applied at once among the tradition-bound, illiterate, poverty-stricken masses in the rural villages. We have little experience in social history of any conscious attempt to spread birth control among poor people, and none at all related to such very poor people and on such a massive scale.

With the implementation of such a policy, even technical contraception would come to play a role which it never played in the advanced countries. To be effectively used it would have to be very much improved and made available systematically and free of charge. Possible future discoveries leading to the provision of inexpensive, completely harmless tablets or injections for temporary sterility could have international social and economic effects of the same magnitude as, or even greater than, those which may follow the splitting of the atom—and would make for progress and harmony with much more certainty and without at the same time horrifying the entire world by the prospect of total destruction.

THE NEED FOR LARGE-SCALE FRESH RESEARCH

All the pressing problems of social reform to which I have so far referred in this chapter have in common that they do not seem to be very amenable to quick solutions; yet time is of the essence. By a combination of a long-standing heavy population pressure and general stagnation, most of these countries have not only economically, but also in their various social adjustments, reached a situation that cannot continue for long and yet can only be changed with the utmost difficulty. That is a major dilemma facing all underdeveloped countries.

Should these big populations continue to increase rapidly, should they remain much longer illiterate and divided by internal chasms and gross economic inequalities, and should economic integration and progress for these and other reasons be slow or nonexistent, a situation will develop ever more different from any yet faced by our now highly integrated democratic nations in their preindustrial stages. Internal tensions and the violent forces for change in the world at large, pressing from the outside, may then well be transformed into political action by an often dissatisfied and maladjusted class of intellectuals and semi-intellectuals.

The method of progress in the advanced countries was through a gradual development that left much to natural forces and was steered only by piecemeal and occasional interventions by the state and other public or quasi-public organs, these interventions themselves mostly being in the nature of adjustments that had matured to the point of realization within the social process of cumulative causation. Applied to the underdeveloped countries, this method needs radical amplification if it is to have any chance of success. Reforms must be pushed faster and harder, both in the social and in the economic field. Otherwise there is a clear danger that stagnation will only change into decomposition or that society will break up violently.

An extra urge to speedier reforms—and also a guide to them—is the present image of the highly integrated and progressive countries. The underdeveloped countries naturally fix their attention more on the social and economic results that are finally accomplished than on the rough road the advanced nations have traveled to reach them—and rightly so, because why should they repeat all their errors and try again all the blind alleys? As a matter of fact, this is the one great advantage that the underdeveloped countries have today in comparison with the developed countries in their early stages of development. They have at their free disposal a vast accumulated capital of knowledge and a highly advanced technique, not only in the economic but also in the social field.

Being a latecomer and being able to take over and utilize the entire fund of know-how that has been assembled by the industrially advanced nations are, however, not unmixed blessings, and there are very specific inherent difficulties. For one thing, there is an imponderable stimulus from the very fact of running ahead of others, and countries that are lagging behind and trying to catch up may have to overcome a corresponding feeling of defeatism. There is, further, the actual difficulty of standing up to the competition of the advanced, rich, and rapidly progressing countries; Western Europe has been experiencing it in its relations with the United States, but the situation must be immensely more difficult for the underdeveloped countries. It is probably no accident that not only the Soviet Union but also, in its time, Japan, when starting out on the road to economic development, found it desirable not only to use very strong protective measures but also to apply a curtain of secrecy to shield herself from all influences from the advanced countries other than those they decided were beneficial to their economic development and easily controlled.

Thirdly, as Singer has pointed out, the awkward fact is that it is very much easier to transplant the fruits of economic development, or at least to go through the motions of doing so, than to transplant the seeds:

It is fatally easy to transplant them [the fruits], not as end products but in isolation, divorced from the process which has created them in the industrialized countries. Treated in such fashion, these fruits of economic development have a way of putrefying and even checking development itself. Transplant medical improvements in isolation, and you increase the population which is being maintained at stationary standards rather than raise per capita standards. Transplant advanced social legislation and it either remains a dead letter or proves positively detrimental to economic development; create a desire for luxury consumption, and the foreign exchange resources available for the import of capital goods are reduced; set up an elaborate machinery of state planning, and under the conditions obtaining in many underdeveloped countries such machinery often becomes absurdly irrelevant to real needs and possibilities.[26]

The underlying difficulty for the underdeveloped countries in putting to their greatest advantage the accumulated wealth of knowledge, available as a result of the development in the advanced countries, is that the actual techniques in which this knowledge has been embodied are not adjusted to the particular circumstances. Usually they cannot be simply copied, for the circumstances in which they are to be applied are so different; and if copied, they do not achieve their maximum results and might be positively disadvantageous. All the problems have to be thought out afresh and new techniques invented which, if the basic fund of knowledge is drawn upon, will be vastly superior to the present techniques in the underdeveloped countries.

This is most definitely true in the field of social reforms, with which we have so far dealt in this chapter. Not only are the initially existing outer circumstances—including the geological and geographical setting, social stratification, and various standards of education, incomes, consumption, and production—vastly different, but the inherited valuations are unique. I have already stressed that, even if some broad valuations, mainly relating to social mobility and equality of opportunity, will have to be imported together with the machines, in order to fit an industrialized community, we should not expect the underdeveloped countries to become social and political replicas of the advanced countries. Not only the priority to be given different reforms and the speed of their application, but also the entire manner in which they should be worked out in order to fit a particular underdeveloped country are important problems. They cannot be solved by simply attempting to reproduce what the advanced countries have accomplished.

For this reason the underdeveloped countries are in urgent need of fresh large-scale social research, concentrated on their own practical problems as they appear in the setting of their actual living conditions and based also on insights into the valuations and aspirations of their own peoples. Much of the literature on the problems of these countries produced in the advanced countries is superficial and strangely irrelevant; the present political and strategic preoccupations in some of these countries and particularly in the United States also give much of this literature a coloring that to the underdeveloped countries is extraneous and suspicious.

The industrial production techniques will also need adjustment. In the advanced countries, these techniques have been developed and have resulted in more or less standardized equipment, which is now offered for sale to the underdeveloped countries. They are the outcome of a long development which, as a result of economic progress itself, has been increasingly dominated by situations of scarce labor and abundant capital and, furthermore, by high standards of education and technical ability among the engineers, foremen, and workers. In underdeveloped countries the abundance of labor, the scarcity of capital, and the low level of education and technical skills would make it economically advantageous to use much less capital-intensive equipment, fewer labor-saving devices, and, generally, much simpler techniques. Many of these countries are, furthermore, in the tropical areas of the world, whereas all our modern industrial techniques are appropriate to the conditions in the temperate zones.

This is not the same as saying that their production methods should be old-fashioned and outmoded; they must benefit from all existing or new scientific knowledge, but adapt it to the actual factor proportions and other existing conditions in their countries. This would again require fresh industrial and scientific research on a large scale; for natural reasons they cannot expect that the advanced countries would do it for them as a regular part of their own programs.[27]

Further, the administration techniques of operating a production plant and a business firm and, indeed, the whole social organization of production and distribution in the national community is something that cannot simply be taken over from the advanced countries and applied in under-developed ones. Fresh research will again be needed to work out patterns of organization that are best suited to the very different conditions obtaining in these countries.

Failure to think out old problems anew will constitute not only a heavy disadvantage in every field of competition with the advanced countries but also a serious impediment to economic development.

Without the initial social reforms all efforts are, however, futile. As the United Nations experts point out:

The first major obstacle to the general advance in technology in under-developed countries is . . . the lack of an educational and administrative structure through which the producers can learn the new technology. . . . Neither must education be conceived merely as a process of transmitting techniques. For what is required is a radical change in the outlook of the peoples of the under-developed countries. The progress in technology in Western Europe and the United States of America is based on a long scientific tradition, a conception of nature leading to a spirit of exploration, discovery and experimentation. A further obstacle to the absorption of new technology is the social structure of some countries. The people of these countries will not be receptive unless the basic social and economic institutions are such as to stimulate incentive and initiative. . . . In many countries, social reform is as much a prerequisite of technological progress as is change of outlook.[28]

THE ROLE OF THE STATE

In this connection, it is interesting to note the unanimity with which central economic planning as a policy is pressed upon the underdeveloped countries. "It has been a minor irony of the postwar experience of the United States," Professor W. W. Rostow observes, "that its agents, both in Europe and in underdeveloped countries, have found themselves urging an increased role for government planning in the economies of the areas where the American interest was engaged. This was the consequence of no conspiracy among New Dealers or Socialists who found their way into American foreign operations. This was a realistic response to the nature of the societies where a sustained rate of economic development was sought in the American interest."[29]

Professor Norman S. Buchanan makes this assessment of the situation: "The nineteenth-century sequence will probably not be repeated. The state rather than the drive of private enterprise in pursuit of profits will determine the major features of industrial development in the [now] low income areas. Domestic savings and investment, labor training and mobility, imports and exports, foreign borrowing and home finance will be guided by the visible hand of the state in the quest for higher incomes through industrialization."[30] Professor John H. Williams again and again repeats his belief that "the kind of development program now needed for a better balanced world requires planning, whether or not we like that word, because it would not be at all certain otherwise how the parts might fit together";[31] he is then thinking of the problem of international relations but would, of course, find still more important reasons for internal planning in the underdeveloped countries.

Even Professor Jacob Viner—though somewhat grudgingly, for reasons which I partly share—finds himself among the planners, having to admit that "what the proper division is between government initiative and private enterprise must depend largely on the extent to which the general public is able and disposed to exercise the needed initiative, enterprise, and skill. In some countries the masses of the people are probably too poor, too ignorant, and too bound by old patterns of behavior to do much for themselves; and, if there is to be progress, it must be initiated and, for a time at least, largely conducted from above."[32]

All special advisers to underdeveloped countries who have taken the time and trouble to acquaint themselves with the problems, no matter who they are—teams of experts from the International Bank or other international agencies, including the Colombo Plan; officials of the American Point Four Program; private foundations and consultant firms; independent social scientists; journalists or visiting politicians—all recommend central planning as a first condition for progress. Implicitly they all assume a different approach to the social and economic problems of the underdeveloped countries today than that which historically was applied in the advanced countries. They all assume a very much greater role for the state.

Most of the advisers from the advanced countries who are now urging the underdeveloped ones toward central planning of their social and economic reforms are not doctrinaires, sold on planning as a panacea, but on the contrary usually more at home among the critics of central planning. Yet, faced with the peculiar problems of the underdeveloped countries they nearly all become zealous planners.

If governments of underdeveloped countries have gone far in central planning and in preparing for large-scale state interventions, it is rarely because of the earnest advice of the experts from the advanced countries. As I pointed out in Chapter XI, the very definition of economic development as an attempt to raise living standards for the broad masses of people —which is common in all underdeveloped countries and generally accepted in the entire discussion of the problem—and the further concept of this attempt as a political drive, strongly associated emotionally with the cravings after economic and political independence, identify economic development as the pursuit of a government plan or program.

Behind this general trend of thinking is also the appreciation of the desperate situation of most of these countries and the need for speedy reforms. I have just shown this in regard to the population problem where, if grave and imminent dangers are to be avoided, natural forces cannot be left to work themselves out and a policy is therefore urgently required. More generally, there are compelling reasons to achieve a much more rapid economic development than could be hoped for without central planning and government initiative. There is also a comprehension of the opportunities for using the more powerful technical knowledge now available and which will not be exploited fully if development is left to take an undetermined route. There are many other reasons for central planning and large-scale state intervention in underdeveloped countries which, however, are all included under these general formulas.

Thus, to exploit effectively modern technical possibilities, investment and production projects will nowadays often have to be larger in scope than private initiative in these countries can handle. For the same reason, initial investments will have to be directed more to the sphere of external economies, in the provision of power, means of transport, etc., and to various social purposes, from schooling to housing. Technological development has changed the basic conditions for industrialization during the last hundred years.

If rapid development is desired in a low-income, stagnating peasant economy, geared to self-sufficiency—unlike a progressive industrial one— so much more attention needs also to be given in the initial stages to balancing the growth of different industries, so that the increased supply of various goods meets an effective demand. Leaving economic development to natural forces means in most cases continued stagnation or unnecessarily slow development. A progressive economy can take better care of itself because it has momentum; a stagnant economy must first be given momentum.

In most of these countries the social chasms and the inequalities of distribution have considerably hampered the growth of the commercial middle class, which in the advanced countries played such an important role in economic progress. As Rostow points out, "it is easy to forget that, before the industrial revolution came to Western Europe and the United States, it was preceded by several centuries of commercial and early industrial development, which had formed a class of private entrepreneurs prepared morally, intellectually and technically to exploit the potentialities of the innovations that came forward. The middle class, in a sense, was the most important of the economic innovations of modern times; and it is not susceptible of rapid diffusion throughout the underdeveloped regions of the contemporary world."[33]

It is, further, highly characteristic of all the underdeveloped countries that their business classes are bent upon earning quick profits not by promoting long-term real investment and production but by buying and selling, moneylending, and other easier ways of making money, which also often escape taxation. Profits tend to be invested in land, or else hoarded or transferred abroad, when they are not dissipated in a costly display of wealth and social status. There is a low propensity to save and to invest productively in new enterprises.

In these countries there is everywhere a relative lack of the entrepreneurial spirit. As Staley points out: "Private enterprise fails to function effectively in most underdeveloped countries, not so much because it is repressed or interfered with as because it does not yet exist in the modern sense in which Americans automatically think of it."[34] The problem is not merely to release it but to cultivate it. The real task is one of "institution-building."

If there is to be economic development, the state will almost inevitably have to take the initiative. The Secretariat of the Economic Commission for Asia and the Far East, when discussing this problem, concluded that "the experience of the last few years suggests that only in Japan and Hong-Kong is private business fully capable of developing the economy by its own resources and on its own initiative."[35]

THE PROBLEM OF ADMINISTRATION

This urge to central planning and the necessity for the state to be the initiator and promoter of business projects—at least in the beginning, until the social and economic conditions have been created for private business on a larger scale—confronts all the underdeveloped countries with a major problem: that of efficiency and incorruptibility in government and administration. This is another thing about which there is *consensus sapientium.*

It is a quite common complaint in the reports on the development problems of underdeveloped countries, which now abound in the publications and archives of international agencies, that one of the important obstacles to development is the state of public administration: it is ineffective, untrained, incompetent, and often corrupt. In all programs for international technical assistance improvement of public administration plays a prominent role.

But here, too, the underdeveloped countries are faced with a much more difficult problem than that once solved in the now advanced countries. In the countries of the northwestern corner of Europe, which have gone furthest in cleansing and rationalizing politics and administration and have often succeeded in making public enterprises models of efficiently organized business, there was, to begin with, an age-old tradition of legalism. Since heathen times these cultures have shown a fanaticism in explicitly regulating the relations among individuals and between individuals and the community in terms of honesty and fairness and equality under the law.

The inefficiency and corruption that nevertheless did creep into the politics and administration of these countries were finally cleaned out at a time, a little more than a hundred years ago, when the state had still few economic functions. The strong state—in the sense of being incorrupt and efficient—was in these countries the accomplishment of economic liberalism, and the job was so well done that the state could later gradually enlarge the scope of its activities by taking on more and more functions without becoming corrupt and inefficient. The paradoxical truth is that it was economic liberalism that perfected the main instrument for central economic planning and public interventions in the modern welfare state.

Underdeveloped countries have to attempt to create an efficient and honest political and administrative machinery without much in the way of legal traditions. And time does not allow them a purgatory era of economic liberalism; *they have to reform their politics and their administration at the same time as the state is increasingly compelled to handle vast public funds and run business on a large scale.* From this point of view, too, one of the most valuable heritages the British Empire has left to its former colonies is the tradition of the British civil service.

As "it takes good administration to improve bad administration," here is another vicious circle that creates deadlocks and obstructions, if it is not broken by vigorous and successful action.

Development requires good administration, yet good administration is itself a result of economic development. It is not, of course, a necessary result, for some highly developed countries have very bad administrations. The difference is that once development has been achieved, bad administration can be afforded as a luxury, while where administration is poor from the beginning, economic development is made more difficult if the government becomes its main agency, whether by choice or because of the absence of innovating entrepreneurs.[36]

The United States is, of course, the main example of a developed country which has not attained the highest standards of administration. If the Americans are far ahead of us all in business and production, this is entirely due to their productive efficiency on the farms, in the factories, and in the stores. Their politics and public administration, at all times and under all parties, have suffered, and still suffer, from serious shortcomings. In administration there is waste of effort, overcentralization, lack of uncomplicated delegation of authority, etc., which are related to insecurity of tenure and of social status and many lingering traditions from primitive democracy and the spoils system, as well as many other peculiar traits that have developed fixed patterns. Economic liberalism never carried out its purges in politics and administration in the United States.

It is an interesting sociological problem why the nation which has so successfully rationalized its private economic life and accomplished the highest level of labor saving in production and distribution, has tolerated so much waste and inefficiency in administration and politics. What has to be done is usually done, though mostly in a very cumbersome and expensive way. Even a good administrative unit in the United States spends several times the manpower on a specific task that a Swede or Dutchman would employ.

The United States can, of course, afford a more cumbersome and therefore relatively expensive administration; the underdeveloped countries cannot. American administration can also to a large extent stay out of economic life as its business is efficiently organized. As a matter of fact the relative inefficiency of public administration in the United States is in that country an important and rational motive for the state to stay out of business as far as possible—as indeed it also was in Adam Smith's Britain. The underdeveloped countries, on the contrary, are dependent on the administration to perform a great number of functions that in the United States can be left—and had better be left—to private initiative.

Not unconnected with its less efficient administration, the United States has, however, the large and often valuable scientific literature, the great university institutions, and the legions of experts on administration. Nearer home we have, incidentally, a similar division of practice and theory: some European countries, for instance, are distinguished by a highly efficient and inexpensive system of tax collection, while others have the professors of public finance and fiscal administration.

I have often reflected on the consequences of the fact that the underdeveloped countries get so much of their advice on administrative reform from American experts. There are clear advantages in this: an American expert has experience and training in how to fight various shortcomings in administration which a British or Scandinavian expert may lack. On the other hand, an expert from the rich and exuberant United States may by his upbringing be less disturbed by the wasteful habit of having too many officials on a job, which is a common vice in all underdeveloped countries. Because of the great scarcity of trained personnel and the larger scope of administrative responsibility, it is much less tolerable there than in the United States.

BALANCING THE ECONOMIC DEVELOPMENT PROGRAM

It is in the setting of these most difficult social and political handicaps that the underdeveloped countries in the non-Soviet world have to start an attempt to pursue their economic development. The plan of economic development they have to follow has to be very delicately balanced for reasons already discussed and also because they are excluded by our general assumption, from using many of the efficient but harsh methods of the Soviet system for development of underdeveloped countries. In particular, they cannot—and do not want to—press so hard on their consumers. As Pandit Nehru points out: "The difficulty comes in always between the needs of today and the demands for tomorrow. A poor country, poor in resources, has not got large resources for investment for building up tomorrow. And if you want a surplus, well you have to be strict with yourself in the present generation: and democracy does not like stinting the present. . . . But that is a tremendous advantage, from that limited point of view, which an authoritarian government has, which can build for tomorrow, not paying too much attention to things of today. . . . We cannot do it."[37]

The next chapter is devoted to a more intensive analysis of one aspect of this model of economic growth, one that directly concerns international relations: the financial and commercial problems of underdeveloped countries. At this stage of the argument our interest is confined to their internal policies.

In the underdeveloped countries by far the greatest part of the population—often well over two thirds—is agricultural. With the high rate of population increase in these countries, industrialization has to be very rapid in order to absorb the rise in agricultural working population and still more rapid in order to effect a slow decrease of it. Under the best of conditions they will for decades ahead be countries with very large agricultural populations. For this reason alone, a major problem of economic development that immediately faces underdeveloped countries is, therefore, how to raise the productivity of the land and of the peasants. "Industrial expansion without agricultural reorganization will leave the bulk of the people in a state of poverty. . . . In other words, we can plan against mass poverty only if we set out to create the conditions of a rapidly expanding and efficient economy both in agriculture and industry."[38]

In most underdeveloped countries, improvement of productivity in agriculture is, furthermore, an essential precondition for industrialization. The expansion of employment, absorbing those previously unemployed or underemployed, and the relatively higher wages paid to industrial workers—one of the essential results to be gained by industrialization and, in fact, a necessary inducement for workers to move out of agriculture—will cause a rise in total demand; since absolute incomes will remain low, this will mainly express itself in a higher demand for food. At the same time, this development process will also involve somewhat rising income demands in agriculture and, in particular, a higher level of food consumption. With the tight foreign exchange situation in which these countries ordinarily find themselves, if they are pushing on with industrial development, the only way of avoiding inflation is a substantial increase in total agricultural production, allowing an increasing proportion of it to be supplied to the nonagricultural population. In addition, if there is not an expanding market among the agricultural population, created by the purchasing power they acquire by their greater sales of agricultural produce to the towns, industry will not have the growing market it needs to go on expanding.

In Italy and in Southern Europe generally, low productivity in agriculture is a main limiting factor to all attempts to push ahead with industrialization.[39] In Latin America several countries have been hampered in their economic development because it has been too confined to the growth of a few modern cities and some islands of industry, leaving agriculture, and thus the main part of the economy, in decay and backwardness. This has undoubtedly been one of the main causes of the constant pressure of internal inflation and also of the foreign exchange difficulties. The determination to tackle the problems of the village is, by contrast, one of the hopeful things in India, where space and natural resources are so pressed upon by its dense population, and where for these and other reasons the beginning must be so hard. Many of these problems are basically political and social—land reform, the abolition of the caste system, literacy, fundamental education—and have already been referred to.

A third important reason for giving agriculture a high priority in the development plans of every underdeveloped country is that only thereby can the integration process be given that solid start at the "grass roots" which is required if it is to take the form of a steady, peaceful, but rapidly accelerating social growth. A large literature, devoted to this problem of community development and partly spurred by the practical experience gained from the economic development policy in several countries and from the international technical assistance efforts, is already beginning to appear.[40]

The general economic, social, and cultural situation in underdeveloped countries is very far from the type of national integration that industrially advanced countries have reached; community development must proceed well in advance of the ultimate creation of the larger national solidarity that is the goal of, and the necessary condition for, a modern industrial society. Meanwhile, local integration and the attainment of social mobility and equality of opportunity, as well as economic diversification in the local community, represent a preliminary stage of advancement. But they are, in addition, an important element in national integration when this is finally achieved. For the larger part of the population, the local community is and will remain the agricultural village. Great importance for the intelligent approach to this building up from the grass roots of a more developed state of economic and social conditions attaches to the time-sequence or, from another point of view, the scale of priorities given to different efforts.[41]

Economically, a main limitation on expansion of production in agriculture is that, on the whole, the scope for labor-saving devices is restricted as long as there is a surplus of labor. Efforts will have to be directed towards laying more land under cultivation and to increasing farm yields. The existing know-how will have to be used for applying a new technique, rationally adapted to existing factor proportions, which is not the same thing as carrying on with an out-of-date technique.[42]

Agricultural reorganization will reveal a large surplus of workers which had previously remained concealed. Part of this labor surplus can be drained off by stimulating cottage industry, again with a technique that takes account of the fact that for the time being labor is a factor of production that has little or no social scarcity. All sorts of capital-producing work on country roads, dams, local irrigation systems, public buildings, or other communal amenities can be carried out for the same purpose; improvements in rural housing and sanitation can be stimulated. This type of investment usually requires little else than labor—which is in plentiful supply—and locally available resources. It represents a sort of direct saving and will raise productivity and standards of living. To be economical from the social point of view those undertakings need not have the full value of market wages for the labor employed, as the population has to be sustained in any case.

This is not a process that starts or continues through the simple operation of the price mechanism. It has to be initiated by the state and nourished by government direction and, to an extent, government subsidies; a large-scale educational and training effort is also involved that will not be undertaken by private enterprise. It will never make real progress, however, if the active cooperation and enthusiasm of the peasants themselves is not enlisted.

As I mentioned, the result of part of these investments is an immediate rise in the living standards of the rural population. The further development aim is to advance production by gradually raising capital intensity, improving techniques, and increasingly drawing the surplus labor into economic production. Standards of consumption can then again be raised.

To be a self-perpetuating process the rise of consumption standards must not be allowed, however, to swallow up the whole of the increase of production, but must continuously leave a substantial part for capital accumulation in the form of new investments. In the perfect model the saved portion of the production increase would soon have to be increased by taxation, designed first to pay for the subsidies involved and gradually also to provide for an additional volume of investment outside the agricultural sphere, from which more agricultural labor could then be siphoned off to industry.

Even if the degree of mechanization in agriculture remains low until the far-off day when labor begins to be scarce, there will from the very beginning of this process be a rising demand for tools. The gradually increased consumption standards in agriculture will also raise the demand for industrial goods. This creates an expanding market, the importance of which for industrialization in underdeveloped countries has recently been stressed by Professor Ragnar Nurkse.[43]

Meanwhile, and as an autonomous part of the development program, substantial investments outside the narrow frame of community development are assumed to be made in railroads, canals, irrigation schemes, power installations, and other forms of essential overhead capital. This part of a development plan is the one that creates the heaviest demand for capital, particularly as it usually has a long maturity period before it yields higher production. While its major objective is to create the basis for a further industrialization, it creates at the same time, if planned as a continuous expansion, a demand for industries producing materials and equipment.

If, as is assumed to be an urgent necessity in the underdeveloped countries, the movement towards industrialization is to be pushed ahead, the state will have to intervene in the field of manufacturing industry too, not only creating the external economies and supplying transport and power, but often also organizing the marketing of the produce of the expanding industrial sector, providing facilities for training workers, foremen, and technicians on all levels, as well as business executives, giving managerial advice, making capital available, often subsidizing or protecting new industrial enterprises, and sometimes actually establishing and operating them. At the same time it must have as its principal objective not only the development of industrialization to its practical limits, but also its direction, so that the growth is balanced and met by effective demand.

The abundant supply of labor means that in industry, as in agriculture, a technique other than that used in advanced countries will have to be applied; while based upon modern knowledge of technology, it should take into consideration the fact that capital is very scarce while labor is plentiful. Again, as in agriculture, to be worth while from the social point of view, an industry does not need to be profitable enough to cover fully its wage costs, as long as there is a surplus of workers, who must in any event be kept alive, or external economies emerge as an important by-product.

Even more than in agriculture, however, investments are necessary to keep this process moving. Capital must be created and accumulated by voluntary savings or taxation out of the rising production. As capital is scarce, the utmost economy in its use is necessary. In underdeveloped countries it becomes even more important than in developed countries to assure full utilization of capacity. More often than in developed countries will there be good reasons to organize shift-work in order to allow a factory to be run day and night.

From one point of view the poverty of an underdeveloped country arises from the fact that its labor is not used at all or not used in an economic way. It is from the fuller and better use of the idle resources—represented mainly by surplus labor—that both the rise in living standards and the increase in capital formation must ultimately come; in their turn, these two effects become the basis for still further advances.

From another point of view the cause of poverty is the lack of capital. To squeeze out the necessary savings from a population that, even after the development process has gone a long way, will still be living on very low and only slowly rising levels, is a formidable task for a government that seeks its basis in popular support. There is, however, no alternative for a country that wants to speed up the process; outside credits and aid will never suffice. Only if we remember this, and also pay due regard to the need for a very delicate balancing of all the elements in the very involved dynamic process that I have sketched above, can we fully grasp the magnitude and the immense difficulty of the task that is facing underdeveloped countries in their strivings for economic development.

THE STAGE SET FOR A GREAT HUMAN DRAMA

However difficult the task, one thing stands out: the hope for economic development of underdeveloped countries depends very much on the state's being able to plan and to direct, and even to invest and to produce. If this is to be done wisely, the government will have to do its utmost to avoid overcentralization and to exploit every possibility of pushing responsibility onto the specialized organs and local authorities. It must preserve with utmost care whatever voluntary industrial and other organizations and local self-government exist and, at the same time, do whatever it can to nurture their growth; a firm central control must, of course, be exercised in order to enforce broad directives and to prevent exploitation and corruption. It is in these difficult matters of decentralization that the underdeveloped countries could derive the greatest advantage from studying methods and practices in Northwestern Europe.

If the underdeveloped countries are to succeed, their national economies are going to contain, even in an early stage of their development, large elements of socialism, larger even than in the nationally highly integrated and industrialized countries. Leaving aside the old doctrinal issues, the fact is that "capitalism" as an economic system—modified, as described in Chapter III, in a fundamental fashion as a result of a reorganization under collective, public, quasi-public, and private influences and containing substantial elements of socialism—has today perhaps a greater momentum than ever in the highly industrialized countries. There it is youthful, robust, expanding, and anything but in decay. In most of the underdeveloped countries, however, the main danger is continued stagnation. There, capitalism and private enterprise are weak, and show only the most feeble tendencies to develop by themselves as they did in the earlier history of the industrially advanced countries. Only as a result, and within the general framework, of state planning and large-scale state promotional activity from the very beginning is there any hope at all of eventually fostering some kind of capitalism and private enterprise in these countries.

Central economic planning in the industrially advanced democracies has until now been far from completely successful.[44] The underdeveloped countries are compelled to attempt a reasonable success of planning and state direction, though they do not have at their disposal our apparatus of administration and planning.

On one point I am less pessimistic than at least some of my colleagues: I believe that a considerable amount of central planning and state direction is quite compatible with democracy and a free society; I do not believe that the advanced countries, because they give ever greater scope for planning and state direction, are moving towards a society with less personal freedom and less democratic participation: quite the contrary. I find no example in history where democracy has been lost because of too much planning and state intervention, but plenty of examples of the contrary.

"Planning . . . need not necessarily be imposed arbitrarily from above" —I am quoting the Indian philosopher and administrator, Professor Humayan Kabir, who on many points has attained a more succinct formulation of some of our general experiences in Northwestern Europe than most of our own writers; he continues:

Just as the political decisions of a democracy are the result of the interplay of the inclinations, wills and decisions of a multiplicity of individuals, the planning of the welfare state can be the result of the interplay of the wishes, desires and hopes of all its citizens. The fact that society and the state are organisms in which the individual members act and react on one another and determine the nature and direction of their development makes such democratic planning not only possible but the only form of planning that can serve the real interests of the individual and the community.[45]

Our whole discussion of planning and state direction in the industrially advanced countries and particularly in Northwestern Europe has, however, related to a gradual development and, much more important, has always assumed that there exists as a basis a highly integrated national community with well-entrenched legal traditions, a vast network of organizations for protecting economic interests and/or social ideals, a vigorous democracy in local municipalities and provinces, an effective and incorrupt civil service, and an educated, politically mature, and public-spirited citizenry with long-established traditions of freedom and self-government on the national and local levels—things which are fortunately a reality in that part of the world. But these assumptions are obviously not fulfilled in any of the underdeveloped countries.

The dilemma is that in most of the underdeveloped countries, without planning and state initiative there will be at the most only very little development and national integration, and then most surely will democracy be in jeopardy. This dilemma only gives added stress to the urgent necessity of giving high priority to large-scale initial social and political reforms of the structure of society that could assure as quickly as possible the realization of the fundamental assumptions enumerated above.

The stage is set for a great human drama. Taking into account all that has been said in this and the preceding chapter, and also the virtual certainty that foreign credits and aid from the advanced countries will continue to be relatively insignificant in relation to needs, it is difficult to avoid the conclusion for most of the underdeveloped countries that, looking at the matter objectively, the most probable outcome is failure and consequent social disintegration and political upheavals.

A reservation has to be made, however, for an imponderable in the problem: the faith and devotion of their intellectual and political leaders.

THE CAPACITY TO ABSORB FOREIGN CAPITAL

Their task would naturally be easier, and the outcome less uncertain, if they could reckon on a greater human solidarity on the part of the industrially advanced countries. If more substantial amounts of credit and capital aid were forthcoming, economic progress could be secured with less hardship for the population in terms of suppressed levels of consumption, or a speedier progress won with unchanged savings efforts on the part of the population.

The rapid economic development of the Soviet Union got off to a start virtually without foreign loans, except for some medium-term commercial credits; the same was also true, on the whole, of Japan several decades earlier. I am, however, assuming in this book that the goal is to accomplish economic development without the harsh internal disciplines of the monolithic state. As Buchanan points out, it implied in the USSR among other things "keeping the output of consumers' goods at exceedingly low levels, and even exporting grain to pay for needed imports, despite the fact that some people were even starving at home. This will be precisely the difficulty in some low-income areas of today. The level of consumption is so exceedingly low that any reduction will force starvation, or at least hardship, upon many millions."[46] But the alternative to the Soviet way of reaching economic development should not be economic stagnation.

By far the greater amount of capital formation needed for economic development in underdeveloped countries will under any circumstances have to be provided from domestic savings out of the rising productivity following economic development. It has been calculated that to supply all Asia with a modest average of $2000 worth of machinery and tools per worker would cost an amount three times the national income of the United States; to raise the average output per worker in the major part of Asia to the level that Japan had reached before the Second World War would cost more than one and a half times this amount.[47]

A capital inflow even approaching such figures is unthinkable and would even be unnecessary. It is indeed quite natural and in line with all earlier historical experiences of the development of a country that foreign capital should only be marginal and serve to give a start and keep up a momentum. If, however, that much were forthcoming—say, something corresponding to what in earlier times the capital market was prepared to furnish countries like Sweden and the United States when they were developing—this could in many of the underdeveloped countries signify the difference between success and failure.

It has, however, to be admitted that the experience of the International Bank and all other international and national agencies in the credit or aid field has shown it to be extremely difficult to find really well-prepared investment projects in most of the underdeveloped countries. It is not only the supply of capital that is severely limited, but also what we might, with some broadening of the term, call "effective demand."

The main explanation of this is the very fact of the vicious circle which is holding down these countries in poverty and stagnation. As Nurkse has pointed out, while a country's capacity to absorb foreign aid for current consumption is presumably unlimited, there exist fairly definite bounds to absorptive capacity if the aid is to be applied to capital formation. These bounds arise from an underdeveloped country's backwardness and from its lack of various overhead facilities and from many other bottlenecks. At the same time a very strict monetary and financial control is required in order to hinder it from spilling over into consumption, and this is a very exacting demand on an underdeveloped country.[48]

In his analysis of the same problem, Professor S. Herbert Frankel reaches down to a still more fundamental level when he stresses that capital formation involves "the evolution of a different art of living and working." "The 'poorer' a country in skilled labor and in national resources, the less capital it is likely to have, *and the less it can afford to have,* until the whole social and economic complex of its activities has gradually evolved patterns of economic behavior suited to its use, reproduction, and further accumulation."[49]

When all this is said, it nevertheless remains true that a substantial capital inflow of capital from the advanced countries is an almost necessary precondition in most underdeveloped countries if they are to witness a rapid rate of economic development; the social and political dangers inherent in their failure should also be borne in mind. In spite of the limitations to their absorptive capacity—which, viewed from another angle, are nothing else than their staggering difficulties in initiating and sustaining economic development—there is no doubt in my mind that if the advanced countries approached this problem with the same seriousness and zeal which they ordinarily devote to their own affairs, not to speak of their attitudes to defense and national security, they would not fail to find productive outlets for a considerably increased stream of capital to the underdeveloped countries.

In view of the nature of the underlying causes of the limited absorptive capacity of underdeveloped countries, the advanced countries should, further, be aware of their crucial responsibility for doing their utmost to raise or, in any event, not to lower standards of morale and efficiency in these countries by the way in which they furnish capital assistance and the conditions attached to it. As I have pointed out in Chapter IX, the danger is particularly that in the general climate of the cold war the advanced countries are tempted to inject politics into capital aid and use their hold over the purse strings so as to force the underdeveloped countries to accept the role which Professor Jacob Viner characterized as "pawns in the play of power politics."

There is, indeed, a very real danger that the advanced countries may become in this way accomplices in preserving and fortifying exactly that type of political and social system that is characterized by a limited capacity to absorb and utilize to any real advantage capital assistance from abroad. The United Nations experts on economic development had their eyes on this danger:

> Some countries are ruled by corrupt or reactionary cliques whose régime might be overthrown by the people if there were no foreign aid, and who may be settled in their rule because foreign grants have become available. Members

of the United Nations will not wish to have had any hand in fastening such governments on peoples. They might therefore wish to lay down certain minimum conditions before an under-developed country was admitted to the list of those eligible to receive grants.[50]

ACCESS TO KNOWLEDGE

Providing a modest stream of capital as credits or in aid is, however, not the only proof of human solidarity on the part of the industrially advanced countries that could condition very considerably the chances of underdeveloped countries to avoid a disastrous failure. It is perhaps even more important for them to obtain real access to the wealth of knowledge that is assembled in the industrially advanced countries.

Knowledge can be imported.[51] Denmark is a country where relatively few new technical discoveries have ever been made, but few nations have ever exploited new ideas from the entire world as rapidly and effectively as the Danes. In spite of a relative scarcity of natural resources, and with no colonies to exploit, Denmark also had, until the Second World War, the highest standard of living in Europe. Similarly, the United States depended until recently almost entirely upon the fundamental research work done by scholars in the great European tradition, while they became prominent much earlier in applying science industrially.

But this transmission of knowledge was never a mechanical one. Knowledge cannot be imported in bales or barrels. There must be competent receiving centers; each of the two nations that I have singled out as having been particularly successful in exploiting knowledge from abroad had from the beginning effectively working research organizations, specializing in keeping abreast of what was done abroad and adapting it to conditions in their own countries.

The radically different circumstances in the underdeveloped countries make the task of adjusting to suit their own needs the wealth of assembled knowledge abroad a particularly difficult one. I have stressed above that they will have to think all problems through afresh in order to make the best use of this knowledge. This means that they urgently need large-scale research in all fields: neither the techniques of political and social reform, nor the industrial techniques, nor the techniques of business management and administration can simply be copied. If copied, the new techniques will not work well; in some cases the effects may be damaging to economic development and integration. In the next chapter I stress their urgent need of large-scale market research.

That is the reason why, in addition to training schools on all levels, which I have mentioned above in discussing educational reform, the underdeveloped countries need to build up research institutions on the university level. Ultimately they will need a substantial staff of their

own people competent to work constructively and intensively in all
sciences.

From many points of view it would follow logically from all our ideals
that the advanced nations should lend a helpful hand in accomplishing
this great task. If they had the vision and understood the supreme
significance of it, they could on this immaterial aid spend very productively several times the amounts now paid for national and international
technical assistance; it could improverish no one, since it would amount
to an insignificant and minute percentage of the national incomes of
these countries and would hardly be noticeable on our levels of consumption and savings. Apart from its results for the underdeveloped
countries, I would expect that this enlargement of research would quite
incidentally render also more general results that would make the
investment directly worth while even to the advanced nations.

Building upon the heritage of the Middle Ages, our universities of the
Western world after the Renaissance took an important part in the
widening of the provincial cultures and the building up of the national
solidarity upon which our modern national welfare states have been
founded. The real situation in the world today, as it has been shaped by
the material and spiritual changes that make us now all so interdependent,
would indicate that we should be ready for the final step to truly international universities.

To a degree the medieval universities were international; it was the
hegemony of the Church that gave them this character. From that time
on, in spite of the often very nationalistic tendencies in many countries,
the idea of the International Academic Republic has been preserved, not
only in our basic assumption of the oneness of truth, but in many academic
patterns, policies, and institutions. The new waves of nationalism after
the First World War and, lately, the impact of the cold war have, however,
brought a reaction. Particularly in America, but gradually also in
Western Europe, the state loyalty phobia and many other influences, to
which I referred in Chapter X, and comment upon further in Chapter
XIV, are narrowing the horizon for scholars and strengthening the nationalistic tendencies of the universities.

I am convinced, however, that the scientific personnel in our universities and other learned institutions, who are under the influence of the
inherited tradition and feel higher loyalties than to a particular state,
are much more prepared for internationalism than the nations at large
or their instruments—whether the governments or the university administrations—in countries where the universities are not entirely under
the authority of the faculties. The challenge to harness all our knowledge
to the development needs of the underdeveloped countries could furnish
the spiritual catalyst for a change of trend towards internationalism

instead of nationalism. The coming into being of even a few really international institutions, free according to our cherished tenets, recruited from all countries, and under the aegis of international agencies, which would be constitutionally bound to respect and preserve this freedom and this openness, would be eminently important for the problem I am here discussing. But this dream of the internationalist has perhaps for the time being little possibility of realization.

The Role of Technical Assistance

In recent years national and international technical assistance programs have on a small scale attempted to overcome this problem of how to make the knowledge assembled in the advanced countries available to the underdeveloped ones. First, there is the United States' Point Four Program, which is much bigger than all the others taken together. There are, in addition, a few other very minor national programs sponsored and financed exclusively by one country. In Asia the Ford Foundation is making significant contributions, particularly in community development and education, and other American institutions of a similar kind are financing projects in different parts of the underdeveloped world.

A more substantive and collective program is handled by the Colombo Plan—within the framework of which there is also distributed some capital aid—and another by the United Nations and its specialized agencies. In addition to its own Point Four Program the United States also contributes to these two international ones, to the extent of almost two thirds in the case of the United Nations.

The problem of the very unequal sacrifices borne by the different advanced countries, for technical assistance as well as for capital aid to underdeveloped countries, has been discussed at some length in Chapter IX, where I suggested that the inadequacy of the funds available for technical assistance is not an unrelated fact. There are, as I pointed out, very strong reasons why a greater part of this activity, as of all international aid, should be the responsibility of the United Nations. In the case of technical assistance there is, in addition to the reasons referred to in Chapter IX, the further advantage in organizing the work internationally that the choice of experts is not then limited to nationals of one state.

But increased international responsibility for technical assistance clearly implies a greater readiness on the part of advanced nations other than the United States to contribute financially—as I pointed out in Chapter IX it would never be a question of real sacrifices. The present financial share of the United States in the United Nations' technical assistance program is far too large; it takes the balance out of its control and direction and hampers its further growth. In any case, as long as the United States is contributing 90 per cent or more of total world expenditure on technical assistance, it would be totally unreasonable and, indeed, damaging to the whole spirit of international work, to propose that it should all be handled by an international organization.

Even though the funds are inadequate and the contributions disproportionate to the financial means of the various countries, the appearance on the world scene of technical assistance to underdeveloped countries is still of dramatic importance. It signifies a recognition—given, so to speak, in principle—of international solidarity on the part of the richer countries with respect to the destiny of the poorer ones. As such it is a decisive step forward, and to withdraw would be psychologically and politically impossible.

Technical assistance is bound to become an expanding activity—how fast and how steady is difficult to say. Thousands of missionaries of rationality, experimentalism, economic and social advance, and a generally better life are penetrating and fanning out in the vast backward regions. This has been, indeed, one of the rare examples in postwar years of an effort towards international cooperation which is commonly felt to have been a real move forward. Though still on a very small scale, its success is unquestionable.

The funds from the various technical assistance programs that have so far been devoted to the building up of solid research organizations and of equally urgently needed training schools are insignificant. Both these streams of activity fit well into a rational long-range plan for furthering the development of underdeveloped countries. A very considerable redirection of the available funds to be used for building up and supporting regular institutions for research and training is probably the most urgently needed reform among all technical assistance activities. The fellowship programs, useful as they are, should really be considered as only an extension of such efforts.

The little money for technical assistance that has been channeled through the United Nations has nevertheless meant very much to its various specialized agencies and the ideals they stand for; to some of them it has almost given a new lease on life. Not least on account of the cold war—though not only for that reason—their possibilities of acting as vehicles for reaching intergovernmental agreements on important matters have been limited, and without the responsibility for a technical assistance program some of those agencies would have been hard put to perform really worth-while functions in the present state of international relations.

The underdeveloped countries, with their pressing problems at home, their scarcity of trained personnel, and their cultural distance from the advanced countries, would have been rather on the fringe in most of the international agencies and would, anyhow, have had good reasons to look upon them and their doings as things of little concern to them. Technical assistance has not only given the international organizations a new and important purpose and function; by sending experts to those countries that most needed their advice, they have drawn these same countries into active cooperation, at least in technical matters. They have, in fact, acquired a practical importance for those countries which, it must not be forgotten, make up the majority of their members.

This strengthening of the international organizations is by itself not unimportant in the present situation, which, as I have noted in Chapter IV, is characterized by a great and growing disparity between institutional weakness on the international and strength on the national level. Technical assistance has, indeed, become an important part of their regular activity; and this extrabudgetary replenishment for technical assistance has been particularly important in a period when their ordinary budgets were severely curtailed.

It is generally agreed that the World Health Organization and the Food and Agriculture Organization have been relatively the most successful in their technical assistance. Difficulties have been greater in the industrial field; only a very minor part of the funds and the efforts have taken this direction. One reason for this is naturally that there is no worldwide international organization for industry, which could incorporate technical assistance into its normal work program, as the FAO has been able to do for agriculture. That is why it has been suggested that an international industrial development authority be established as a specialized agency and that the United Nations regional economic commissions, which already operate in the industrial field, be engaged in the technical assistance activity in their respective regions.

There is, however, a much more fundamental reason for the greater difficulties in the industrial field, one which is also relevant to the national technical assistance programs. The need for technical advice, when building up new industries, is much more diversified and of such a very large scope that it cannot possibly be met by sending a few experts for a short time. In the industrial field the underdeveloped countries undoubtedly need much more intensive and regular relations with the industries in the advanced countries. This, in the main, can only be established on a business basis.

Nevertheless, even in the industrial field there is a real job for technical assistance to do and this is, of course, the reason behind the suggestions to establish a firmer institutional basis for it within the United Nations. A technical assistance program can sponsor those initial explorations of resources, markets, and other technical and economic conditions, which businessmen or governments may be equally reluctant to pay for before it is established whether a project is feasible or profitable, but which are so necessary in order to avoid waste and failure.

If there were an institutional framework for technical assistance work in the industrial field, similar to that in agriculture or in health, uniting efforts which are now frail and dispersed, one further service it could render to the underdeveloped countries would be to act as a really businesslike, and scrupulously fair, international employment agency—nonpolitical and also independent of private business interests—to aid the underdeveloped countries in the very difficult problem of drawing upon the resources of expert manpower in the whole world to their best advantage.

It could also act as a sort of consultative business agency which, by establishing a link with business firms, private consultative engineers, and other available experts, would assist on request an underdeveloped country to make the most advantageous purchase of the technical services it needs for carrying forward its industrial development projects. These services might include the concrete blueprinting of the plants, analyzing accurately the supply market for equipment, comparing delivery terms, other contract conditions, and credit facilities, hiring management assistance, and placing their own people in apprenticeship with industries abroad. This would assume direct contacts with private business and private individuals; the foreign office and, indeed, governmental administration in the several countries are often not the most useful intermediaries. Again it should be underlined that the agency would need to be managed on straight business lines and be so directed and controlled that its absolute impartiality and, in particular, its political independence of individual governments and private business interests, were unquestionable.

In the industrial field, the available resources—which, even under the most favorable circumstances, will be small compared with the needs—should thus be reserved mainly for the preliminary, preplanning explorations, where they could, however, play an important role. For the rest they should be devoted to providing an institution through which unrestricted access to the entire market supply of technical personnel and services would be acquired, so that the underdeveloped countries could really exploit this market to the full. *In the main, the underdeveloped countries will have to pay for the industrial techniques and know-how they need.* If they had sufficient capital for development, they could absorb this extra cost. These purchases would figure as regular cost items and would not, comparatively speaking, constitute a very large portion of their total investments.

In Chapter XI, I observed that technical assistance has acquired its popularity in the industrially advanced countries largely because it appears as a cheap means of aiding the underdeveloped countries to accomplish economic development. This is a self-deception. It is no substitute for credits and capital aid to underdeveloped countries; the advanced countries cannot buy off the need for capital export by offering technical assistance. On the contrary, technical assistance is apt to mobilize the latent needs for capital, to spell them out in concrete projects. The more technical assistance that is made available and the more effectively it is applied, the bigger, the better prepared, and the more articulate will be the demands for capital.

Mr. Jonathan Bingham—who has his heart in the matter and who, as former Deputy Administrator and Acting Administrator of the American Point Four Program, has some practical experience of what technical assistance really means—has expressed his belief that "although at the present time, interest in the program is at a new high, and far more requests for help are received than can be filled, the time is not far off . . . when the less developed countries will have had enough of experts able to furnish nothing but advice."[52] From one point of view, the real importance of technical assistance will be to help overcome the limited absorptive capacity for capital import of the underdeveloped countries, to which I have just referred, and to make their demand for foreign capital "effective." If this demand is not met, the only result in many cases will be frustration.

In the broad historical sequence of events, the technical assistance programs are continuously giving new momentum to the political drive for economic development of underdeveloped countries; they are thus, by themselves, anything but a solution of the development problem. Even in its proper and limited field of attempting to bring to the underdeveloped countries the assembled wealth of the advanced countries' knowledge—that is, apart from the need for capital for investment, which technical assistance only accentuates—and even if the funds available were considerably larger, technical assistance could only tackle this broader problem in a makeshift way and on a very small scale. As I pointed out, the problem can only be solved by greater internationalism in our university life and by gradually building up a large number of research and training institutions in the underdeveloped regions themselves. The magnitude of this larger problem should not be lost sight of.

What, finally, advanced countries could do for the underdeveloped countries in the field of international trade, but which they in recent years more and more definitely have been retreating from doing, will be discussed in the next chapter.

CHAPTER XIII

Commercial Policy
of the Underdeveloped Countries

AN INTELLECTUAL SUSPICION

In a discussion of the commercial policy of the underdeveloped countries the simpler and more reasonable approach is to base the argument directly on a consideration of these countries' own development interests, rather than to start out from a general theoretical model or a philosophy of world trade. The argument set forth in this chapter will lead to certain more general considerations, but they will be in the nature of conclusions and not premises.

In the complex of tensions between the peoples in the underdeveloped countries, on the one hand, and the industrially advanced ones, on the other, there is an important intellectual element: a suspicion by people in the former countries that in their only recently challenged monopoly of advanced economic analysis, the economists in the latter countries have viewed matters too exclusively from the point of view of their own nations' circumstances and interests, which are not always those of the peoples in the underdeveloped countries.

Professor Raúl Prebisch, in the essay[1] which served as a prologue to the remarkable series of studies by himself and his group of economists in the Secretariat of the Economic Commission for Latin America, pointed out that "one of the most conspicuous deficiencies of general economic theory from the point of view of the periphery [*i.e.* the underdeveloped countries] is its false sense of universality."[2] More specifically, he stressed that "it is not surprising . . . that the studies published on the economy of Latin American countries often reflect the points of view or the experience of the great centers of world economy. Those studies cannot be expected to solve problems of direct concern to Latin America. The case of the Latin-American countries must therefore be presented clearly, so that their interests, aspirations and opportunities, bearing in mind, of course, the individual differences and characteristics, may be adequately integrated within the general framework of international economic co-operation."[3] And he adds the comment: "An intelligent knowledge of the ideas of others must not be confused with that mental subjection to them from which we are slowly learning to free ourselves."[4]

The truth, which Prebisch has expressed with an unusual bluntness, is that most of our economic literature is influenced by the fact that economics, like all other sciences, has developed in the industrially advanced countries and—according to a psychological mechanism well known to students of the sociology of knowledge—has been apt to generalize from their prevailing conditions and interests. This is now accepted as almost a commonplace among the intellectual and political leaders in all underdeveloped countries. It is, indeed, a tenet from these nations' spiritual revolt for independence and development which Professor Jacob Viner has seen:

The great changes which have occurred since the First World War in economic and political conditions have brought with them marked changes in the questions which the public asks answers for and for which the economists attempt to provide answers. The growth of the political importance and the articulateness of so-called underdeveloped countries made unacceptable, at least to them, an economics which takes its tone, selects its problems for attack, and conducts its analysis solely in static terms and solely or overwhelmingly in the light of the conditions and the concerns of the industrially most advanced, the socially most stable, and the economically most prosperous countries.[5]

To Viner's observation, to which I fully subscribe, I would like only to add the further point that when economists, without explicitly accounting for it, treat the commercial policy problems of underdeveloped countries within the framework of general theories that are fitted to the conditions and interests of the advanced countries, they are following a procedure which is intellectually false. With a view to avoiding this theoretical pitfall *I propose, in discussing the commercial problems of the underdeveloped countries, to tackle the subject, deliberately, from the viewpoint of their own interests.* I shall try to establish and make quite explicit what that viewpoint is. It is my opinion not only that this principle is methodologically correct, but also that its observance by economists in the advanced countries would increase the practical usefulness of their analysis of the problems of underdeveloped countries and the weight their advice would carry among the experts and political leaders of those countries.

One more preliminary clarification is necessary. I shall continue to assume that the underdeveloped countries have chosen the more difficult road of attempting to solve their economic problems without recourse to the harsher methods of economic development applied under the Soviet system.[6] More particularly, I assume that they preserve a significant role for the price mechanism in bringing about internal adjustments both to their own policy measures and to exogenous changes.

In utilizing the price mechanism as a servant of their policy, they will, however, have reasons to change very considerably the conditions under which it operates and thus also change its outcome in terms of production, factor allocation, prices, costs, profits, and the distribution of incomes. I do not generally concede to the free trade doctrine its traditionally asserted status as the rational norm, in relation to which interferences have to be proven to be advantageous exceptions.[7] Applied to the severely unbalanced situation in which the underdeveloped countries find themselves as the result of history, such a pretence on the part of a non-interference policy has even more obvious logical flaws.[8]

In rereading this chapter before printing, I realize that the title given to it is very much too narrow, though I have let it stand as I can not find a more adequate one. What I am really trying to do is to analyze the entire economic policy of an underdeveloped country from the point of view of its trading relations with the outside world; in this connection I have felt free to include a discussion of the developed countries' policies towards the underdeveloped ones as setting many of the conditions for its own policy. The chapter has thus become a long one dealing with many topics; to aid the reader in following the argument I have permitted myself to split it up under several main subheadings.

UNBALANCED ECONOMIES

The starting point for an attempt to formulate a rational commercial policy for the underdeveloped countries should be a clear recognition of the important fact that their economies are unbalanced and that there are in most cases, therefore, valid and strong reasons for a vigorous policy of industrialization. This is merely one aspect of their underdevelopment; what it implies more specifically from the point of view of commercial policy will be analyzed in later sections of the present chapter.

Mr. Folke Hilgert has recently pointed out that "the fact that many underdeveloped countries do not derive the advantage from modern transportation and commerce that theory seems to demand is one of the most pertinent facts in the present international situation and cannot be easily dismissed."[9] He develops his thought in the following way: "But trade does not tend to equalize the supply of such factors [of production]. Rather, where trade creates openings for profitable production, the existing facilities utilized in such production will tend to be further expanded. . . . The original disparity in the distribution of facilities for production may thus be further increased." What Hilgert is here pointing to, though he does not develop his thought, is that fact that instead of an equilibrium, as the theory of international trade would demand, we are facing *a cumulative process away from equilibrium in factor proportions and factor prices, engendered by international trade;* and the reference he makes to Europe's rapid industrial development during the last century and the dependence of this development upon its trade relations with the backward regions is, in fact, a good illustration of this.

In the newly liberated countries, this fact that their economies are unbalanced has its specific historical background in the political circumstances which we call colonialism. These countries were backward and poor even before they were subjected to the political domination of a metropolitan power, and this initial backwardness cannot, of course, be blamed on colonialism. Nor do I wish to assert that the metropolitan powers deliberately and regularly followed a policy of hampering industrial diversification in their colonial empires, though there are many examples of that, too. Much more generally their present condition is the natural outcome of the working of the prevailing political, social, and economic forces of the time, a process which I sketched in Chapter VIII.

Quite understandably, the governments of the metropolitan powers, responsible to their parliaments at home and not to the peoples in the dependent territories, were unable to undertake any great sacrifice in order to promote a general and balanced industrial development of their dependencies. However, they did conceive a clear interest in building up economic enclaves there, related to their own economies at home; in promoting and safeguarding their own settlers; and, more generally, in treating their dependencies as protected extensions of their home markets for their industries. Even countries that were formally independent were often, and with a similar result, under the economic domination of one or several industrially advanced countries. The cumulative process of international trade towards greater disequilibrium, hinted at above, was everywhere in operation.

The "awakening" of the underdeveloped countries has one of its focal points in their increasing consciousness of their unbalanced economies and in their determination to change this situation. Most of these countries have a very high foreign trade ratio, in relation to their national product or income. Contrary to the teachings of classical theory, however, this high foreign trade ratio is not a healthy sign of their vigorously exploiting the economic advantage of an international division of labor. It is rather one of the indications of their underdeveloped status and, more precisely, of the fact that their total production and income are very low.

The greater part of their population is rural and lives overcrowded on the cultivated land, even in sparsely populated countries; they gain their meager livelihood from backward, mostly self-subsistence farming, often under the curse of a feudal system of landownership and indebtedness. There are generally few manufacturing industries producing for the needs of the domestic market, but many establishments for producing the primary goods that make up the bulk of the exports; these may or may not be organized with modern efficiency but usually pay the indigenous workers extremely low wages. The system is completed by the dependence of such a country on imports not only for capital goods but also for most manufactured consumer goods and sometimes even for part of its food.

The craving of all underdeveloped countries for industrialization should be viewed and understood against this factual background of their very unbalanced economies as inherited from the era of colonialism and economic dependence. "Thus there exists an obvious disequilibrium, a fact which whatever its explanation or justification, destroys the basic premise underlying the scheme of the international division of labor. Hence, the fundamental significance of the industrialization of the new countries. Industrialization is not an end in itself, but the principal means at the disposal of those countries of obtaining a share of the benefits of technical progress and of progressively raising the standard of living of the workers"—I am again citing Prebisch.[10]

Manufacturing industry represents, in a sense, a higher stage of production. In advanced countries the development of manufacturing industry has been concomitant with these countries' spectacular economic progress and rise in levels of living; many of its products are indeed almost symbolic of a high living standard. Not least in the underdeveloped countries, the productivity of manpower in industry tends to be considerably greater than in the traditional agricultural pursuits. Industrialization, and the growth of that part of the working population that is engaged in industry, is therefore a means of raising national income per capita. In countries like India and Japan, with a high ratio of population to natural resources and, in particular, to land, manufacturing industry represents virtually the only hope of greatly increasing labor productivity and raising levels of living, however much is done to improve agriculture. But even in countries where the population pressure is lower—as, for example, in many Latin American countries—the successful exploitation of a more favorable relation between population and natural resources requires mostly the growth of manufacturing industry.

There are noneconomic or borderline arguments, too. Thus modern civilization in almost all its more sophisticated forms is rooted in, and depends upon, city life; urbanization is not possible without some measure of industrialization. Indeed, a broad association seems to exist between industrialization on the one hand, and social and economic change on the other. As Professor J. K. Galbraith points out, "a purely agricultural country is likely to be unprogressive even in its agriculture."[11] Industrialization creates a technology which can then be applied to agriculture but not vice versa.

On different layers of the social structures of their national communities, there are thus facts and causal relations which in underdeveloped countries provide powerful reasons for the urge towards industrialization. It is wrong to characterize this urge as an unreasonable obsession, as some economists in the industrially advanced countries have occasionally come very near to doing. Added to the sound logical reasons there are also the resentful memories of colonial exploitation, focused on plantations and mining for export and on dominating their domestic markets for the metropolitan powers' own industry. This historical fact of earlier economic dependence is undoubtedly bound to heighten the emotional appeal of industrialization projects, which take on the character of important symbols of national independence.

The urge in underdeveloped countries for industrialization is thus a complex one, composed not only of rational motives, but also of irrational and emotional impulses which constitute overtones in the discussion of their economic problems. Without denying the paramount interest of these countries in pushing forward with their industrialization, it is therefore important that they be reminded that, as I pointed out in the last chapter, there are important reasons why, at the same time, they should make vigorous efforts to raise productivity in agriculture.

However rapidly industrialization proceeds, the great masses of their working populations will for decades and, perhaps, generations be employed in agriculture, and the levels of living of the rural masses will mainly be determined by their productivity there. Also, the whole national integration process will have to be focused on cultural, social, and political advances taking place in the rural villages, where most people live; these advances require a gradual release from the utter destitution in which they are now held. And the general rise in money incomes accompanying economic development will, in very poor countries with low nutritional standards, mainly materialize in an increased demand for food; if agricultural production does not rise correspondingly, narrower limits will be set for the possible rate of economic development.

In many Latin American countries, the ever-accentuated disparities in standards of income and culture between regions, occupational groups, and social classes naturally counteract national integration and, consequently, hamper economic development, while they jeopardize the possibilities that might otherwise exist of approaching more mature forms of political democracy by peaceful social processes. At the same time the helpless yielding to continuous inflation also points to the fact that the development of manufacturing industry and the rise of modern cities have not so far been everywhere accompanied by equally ardent and successful attempts to raise productivity in agriculture. This should perhaps not surprise us too much; for, as I stressed in the last chapter, effective measures to raise productivity in agriculture are bound up with land reform, literacy drives, and other fundamental political and social changes that turn against the entrenched vested interests of the privileged classes in society.

The "industrialization" the underdeveloped countries need is, indeed, a much broader social reform than one concentrated on the growth of manufacturing industry. The "industrial revolution" in the advanced countries was preceded by, or concomitant with, radical advances in agriculture and transport; it was never concentrated on manufacturing industries. This is worth stressing since, in particular, the memory of economic colonialism is apt to cause underdeveloped nations to feel a certain contempt for primary production; part of this reaction is undoubtedly irrational.

In many of the most advanced countries agriculture and the mining and preparation of raw materials have remained very important. More particularly, their foreign trade is often still based largely on the export of the products of those sectors of the economy. As a matter of fact, the successful industrialization of these advanced countries was to a large extent achieved through a rationalization and expansion of those extractive industries. What coal production and coal exports formerly meant for England is well known. Sweden receives continuously over 40 per cent of its export income from wood products and 10 per cent more from iron ore. The United States, Canada, Australia, and New Zealand are other examples confirming the thesis that successful industrialization need not mean a decrease, and may even imply a substantial increase, in the output of agricultural products and raw materials for export.

What is true, however, is that *primary production in countries that are developing, usually even at times when this production is rapidly rising, employs a smaller and smaller proportion of the working population, while manufacturing industry, transport, public services, education, and various other occupations engaged in providing services of different types employ a growing proportion.* Almost three quarters of Denmark's relatively very large exports consist of products of its highly industrialized agriculture which, however, does not now directly employ much more than 20 per cent of its total working population, and the position in the Netherlands is similar.

THE ROLE OF HIGH EXPORTS IN ECONOMIC DEVELOPMENT

An underdeveloped country has powerful reasons for maximizing the total value of its exports; for its ability to export will always be the main determinant of its capacity to import the capital goods which it needs in order to build up, *inter alia,* its manufacturing industries.

Owing to its present unsatisfactory state of industrial development, an inheritance from previous history and a part of the conditions to which it has to adapt its economic policy, it can produce very few capital goods at home. Its exports will determine the rate at which it can import them and, therefore, the speed by which it can push ahead with industrial development. Inevitably, the exports of an underdeveloped country will consist almost entirely of foodstuffs and industrial raw materials, these usually being the only commodities which it can bring forth in any great quantity.

Prima facie, the proper approach to exports for an underdeveloped country would seem to be in the nature of a general and uncomplicated policy of export promotion. In order to increase its ability to import the capital goods it needs for economic development, its interest would seem to be the simple one of selling abroad its export goods as much and as dearly as possible, while exerting itself at home to produce them at the lowest real costs.

The industrialized countries are themselves engaged in a continued industrialization which, on the whole, ought to increase their need for imports of primary products. On this score, therefore, the interests of the developed and the underdeveloped countries of the world would, again *prima facie,* not seem to be in conflict. What interest conflict there is relates to agricultural products and is a conflict between two developed regions of the world. Western Europe has an interest in buying more of such products from the underdeveloped countries—in order to diminish its dependence on imports from America and thus relieve the dollar shortage, and in order to improve its competitive position in the import markets of these countries.

The underdeveloped countries are, however, dissatisfied with what they get out of this exchange in the international markets, i.e., with their terms of trade, and this is another element in the growing tension between them and the industrially advanced countries. Their dissatisfaction relates first to the general level and the long-term trend of the prices of these agricultural products and raw materials, in comparison with the prices of the mainly manufactured goods which they import. It also relates to the very large short-term fluctuations of their export prices that continuously put their exchange balance, the stability of their economy, and their development planning in jeopardy. I shall take up these two problems one after the other.

THE TERMS OF TRADE

LONG-TERM PRICE TRENDS

A general comparison between the long-term development of prices of primary goods and manufactured goods cannot be very relevant to our problem, as the one sixth or so of the non-Soviet world's population that lives in the industrially advanced countries produces not only nearly three quarters of all manufactured goods but also more than two thirds of the industrial raw materials, including those emanating from agriculture, though a much lower proportion of all foodstuffs. As the underdeveloped countries, contrary to the advanced countries, use relatively little themselves of what they produce in the way of industrial raw materials and as their nutritional standards are low, their share as exporters in the world market for primary products is greater than their share as producers, but still considerably less than one half. The rest of the world trade in primary products takes place between the advanced countries. But exports of primary goods account for nearly 90 per cent of the foreign exchange earned by underdeveloped countries.[12]

The trend of relative prices of primary products has not been the same for all products. We can note, for example, that prices of forest products —making up about one quarter of the total output of industrial raw materials—have for several generations been moving upwards in comparison with other primary prices. This is one of the factors explaining the spectacular economic development during the last century of a country like Sweden. It contributes also to explaining why Finland succeeded in fighting her way through many vicissitudes from poverty and dependence under Tsarist rule, through two world wars where she was out on a limb, a world depression between, and a reconstruction period at the end, during which she received practically no outside aid but had to pay war indemnities and resettle refugees from lost territories. It is one of the factors explaining Austria's remarkable upswing after the Second World War. The underdeveloped countries, however, have as yet very little in the way of forest products to export, and many of them are, in fact, instead importing large quantities of timber, pulp, and paper.

Likewise, a country like Belgium, favored in heavy industry by natural resources as well as by national traditions of enterprise in this field, has witnessed a favorable trend in its terms of trade. The underdeveloped countries, on the contrary, are often not well endowed with natural resources for producing those primary materials which enter into steel production or not well placed for importing them, and those who are have in any event not yet gone far in developing these resources.[13]

With individual exceptions, the underdeveloped countries have had rather bad luck in the historical development of international prices of their typical export articles, which have not, on the whole, been the

dynamic industrial raw materials, essential to modern industrial development. On the rare occasions when they have had such export articles, as
in the case of rubber or nitrates, they have often encountered the discovery of industrial substitutes. There are exceptions to this: oil is one,
uranium may develop into another. But most of the underdeveloped
countries are saddled with a basket of traditional export goods—like
copper, lead, raw silk, tobacco, tea, tin, zinc, and various foodstuffs—the
prices of which have been lagging behind.

This is naturally one of the explanations, though hardly one of the
more important ones, why these countries have remained underdeveloped.
On the other hand it is, of course, equally true that it is their underdeveloped status, with all that that implies of rigidity and lack of enterprise,
that explains why they have been sticking so tenaciously to the bad risks
in production and export and not been reorienting their economy and
shifting their resources more rapidly to adjust to the changing opportunities. When we are discussing their unsatisfactory terms of trade we are,
in other words, only studying another aspect of the vicious circle of relative stagnation in which they have been caught.

A United Nations study has ventured the generalization that from the
latter part of the nineteenth century to the eve of the Second World War
there was a secular downward trend in the prices of the primary goods
the underdeveloped countries exported, relative to the prices of the manufactured goods they imported. The result was that, on the average, at the
end of this period—which was, however, in the late years of the Great
Depression—a given quantity of the former would pay for only 60 per
cent of the quantity of the latter that it could buy at the beginning of the
period.[14] This figure has been widely quoted as an index of the deterioration of the terms of trade of underdeveloped countries during this period.

The trade positions of different underdeveloped countries vary, however, substantially. More basically, the very definition of the concept
"terms of trade" as applied to a long period—during which the quality
of different commodities has changed in different ways and to different
degrees—is a most complicated matter and its statistical measurement is
exceedingly difficult and uncertain. The last word on this problem will
in any case be said only after much more research, and it is extremely unlikely that it will be possible to give it the form of a neat average figure
to which a reasonable degree of meaningfulness can be applied.

THE GENERAL LEVEL OF EXPORT PRICES AND THE QUESTION OF
INTERNATIONAL DISTRIBUTION

More fundamentally—and apart from the moot question of the historical trend of prices—what the underdeveloped countries are concerned
about is the general level of their export prices, which they consider to

have been, and to be, very much "too low." The exact meaning of such an assertion is difficult to clarify as there is no objective norm of comparison available. It is partly nothing else than an expression of a general dissatisfaction with the facts that their countries are poor and that the remunerations to the factors of production, including those engaged in export production, are inferior.

It is also, however, partly an inference from certain facts and from theory. The rise in productivity has generally been very much greater in the advanced countries than in the underdeveloped ones. According to economic equilibrium theory, gains from higher productivity in one sector would be passed on to the whole trading community in the form of lower prices for the produce of that sector. Within the industrially advanced nations, taken individually, this equalization process in the market has undoubtedly had a considerable, and growing, effectiveness, aided and directed, however (as I explained in Chapter III) by an ever more comprehensive public economic policy. But internationally it does not seem to have been operating. While it should have improved the underdeveloped countries' terms of trade substantially, quite the contrary seems actually to have occurred.

The plight of the underdeveloped countries stems mainly from a low level of productivity and a slow rise—if any—of this level. The point here is, however, that this fundamental disadvantage has not been counterbalanced by favorable changes in the terms of trade. It is this point that the authors of the United Nations study, just referred to, have in mind when they argue that: " . . . the under-developed countries helped to maintain, in the prices which they paid for their imported manufactures relative to those which they obtained for their own primary products, a rising standard of living in the industrialised countries, without receiving, in the price of their own products, a corresponding equivalent contribution towards their own standards of living."[15]

Prebisch goes one step further: ". . . it is evident that in the centre the income of entrepreneurs and of production factors increased relatively more than productivity, whereas in the periphery the increase in income was less than that in productivity"; and: "the great industrial centres not only keep for themselves the benefit of the use of the new techniques in their own economy, but are in a favorable position to obtain a share of that deriving from the technical progress of the periphery."[16]

The main fact that could be brought forward to sustain this conclusion is, of course, population pressure and the existence of surplus labor in underdeveloped countries. As long as there is no scarcity of labor—at a price that exceeds only by a conventional margin the subsistence level— rises in labor productivity would tend to be transferred to the importing industrial countries while any similar productivity rises in the underdeveloped ones would be entirely preserved for increases in the remuneration of their factors of production.[17]

If the discussion along this line were to be carried further, there are a number of general observations concerning forces and conditions—besides the general condition of the surrounding subsistency economy in underdeveloped countries and the population pressure—which would need quantitative analysis within the framework of a dynamic theory of international price formation. Among these observations are the following: that for many exports the underdeveloped countries are competing with advanced countries, where productivity has been rising rapidly—even, and not least, in primary production; that the larger part of foreign enterprise in, and capital inflow to, underdeveloped countries has been, and continues to be, directed almost exclusively towards enlarging their export industries; that at the same time the industrially advanced countries have protected and subsidized their own primary production—particularly agriculture; that an element of the vicious circle of economic stagnation is rigidity, hampering the adjustments to changes in the relative prices in the international market that would be necessary in order to exploit advantages and escape disadvantages; that, on all levels of the economic processes, efforts toward the monopolistic organization of markets are bound to be much more effective in industrially advanced countries than in underdeveloped ones; and, more generally, that because of their poverty, the precariousness of their narrow exchange margins, and their desperate need of continuing large exports in order to be able to import both essential consumer goods and capital goods for their economic development, the bargaining power of underdeveloped countries has been, and remains, relatively very weak.

These things and many others would have to be taken into account in order to explain the long-term development of international prices and, more specifically, why the results have been so unsatisfactory for the underdeveloped countries. Because of its paramount importance in intensifying the political tension between the underdeveloped and the industrially advanced countries, this problem warrants large-scale, penetrating, empirical research which would have to go far outside the field of international trade statistics.

After completing such comprehensive studies to explain why the terms of trade for underdeveloped countries are as they are and have developed as they have been doing, we might become able to ascertain whether, in what sense, and to what degree the general level of their export prices is "too low." Definitely, however, the present terms of trade form part of a general situation where these countries are very poor. And whatever the explanations, the immense importance of the terms of trade for the underdeveloped countries should be recognized. I have already noted the high foreign trade ratios that are typical of most of these countries. Even minor changes in their terms of trade have, therefore, financial consequences many times larger than the availability, even after any possible increase, of foreign credits and aid; in comparison with credits a favorable turn of the terms of trade has, in addition, the same advantage as aid in that it does not require future resources in order to service the loans.

The United Nations study, already referred to, contains the calculation that a 10 per cent change in the underdeveloped countries' terms of trade would modify their capacity to import by as much as 1500 million dollars a year.[18] The Secretariat of the Economic Commission for Latin America has estimated that the improvement in the terms of trade for Latin America from 1946 to 1952 made available to that continent more than 11,000 million dollars—that is to say, about 4.3 per cent of the aggregate product of the area for the whole seven-year period.[19]

What the future trend of the terms of trade for underdeveloped countries will be is difficult to forecast. Some experts have thought that with the limited openings for extension of primary production in new areas of settlement, the foreseeable rapid continued growth of industry in the advanced countries, and the drift of labor out of agriculture, there will be a greater relative scarcity of the world supply of primary products, the profits of which will partly fall to the underdeveloped countries. Others have reached the opposite conclusion by pointing to the very great scope for improved agricultural productivity (not least in the advanced countries themselves), technical progress in making further economies in the use of raw materials in industrial production, discoveries of new synthetic and other industrial substitutes for a number of primary products, and the invention of new technical processes of producing such substitutes at ever lower costs.

In the general trend towards autarky in the advanced countries, accentuated as an effect of the cold war, the underdeveloped countries have also to reckon with the probability that even in the future their products will suffer from discrimination in favor of national products or industrial substitutes and that the degree of discrimination might increase. This judgment refers to the underdeveloped countries generally; a few of them that are in possession of natural resources for the production of strategic materials—particularly if they happen to be relatively safely situated on the map from the point of view of possible future military action—will instead meet an extra, noneconomic interest on the part of the great powers in aiding them to develop these resources.

THE POLITICAL ISSUE

The assertion of a general bias in the distribution of the gains from technical improvements made by Prebisch as well as by the authors of the

United Nations study implies, of course, a serious criticism of the actual operation of the international trade mechanism. I have selected the quotations above primarily because of their great political importance. Without any doubt, this is the way people in the underdeveloped countries think about the way the distribution of advantages from international trade disfavors them when they rationalize their bitter sense of frustration. Prebisch himself immediately adds:

The pointing out of this disparity between prices does not imply passing judgment regarding its significance from other points of view. It could be argued, on grounds of equity, that the countries which strove to achieve a high degree of technical efficiency were in no way obliged to share its fruits with the rest of the world. Had they done so, they would not have reached their enormous capacity to save, without which it might well be asked whether technical progress would have achieved the intense rhythm which characterized capitalist development. In any case the productive technique exists and is at the disposal of those with the capacity and perseverance to assimilate it and increase their own productivity.[20]

This last statement represents, however, a sort of "good loser's" gallantry which is scarcely representative. As in all questions of distribution, there is a moral and political element involved and I have already hinted at it. If during this period the underdeveloped countries had been able to sell their exports and buy their imports at more favorable terms of trade, they would have had a larger share of world income. The industrialized countries would have been somewhat hampered in their economic progress. On the other hand, the underdeveloped countries—and, in particular, those that, like the Latin American countries, were politically independent—would have had a better chance to start earlier, and pursue more effectively, their advance to economic development. At least they would have enjoyed higher levels of living.

As Dr. H. W. Singer says: "Thinking along these lines, one is bound to conclude that the failure of the underdeveloped countries to come closer to the levels of the industrialized countries and to approach them more rapidly should not be laid entirely at the door of domestic weaknesses or handicaps implicit in the economic structure of the underdeveloped countries. Hence, the increasing inequality in the distribution of world income need not be accepted as inevitable, given the present economic structure of underdeveloped countries."[21]

This is, of course, precisely the type of situation that in our modern national welfare states in the advanced part of the world has given cause to large-scale and far-reaching corrective state interferences with the operation of the price mechanism. In fact, as these policy interferences—changing radically the terms of trade of different industries and regions and the very conditions underlying them—were restricted to the national states, some of these policies have contributed to keeping down the terms of trade of the underdeveloped countries and thus worsened their plight.

As I observed in Chapter IV, economic solidarity stops, however, at the state boundary. In the industrially advanced countries, giving support to those of their own citizens who do not come up to a recognized level of national subsistence standards is now a generally accepted norm, and these countries are now all committed to economic policies aimed at protecting and subsidizing regions and industries that are lagging behind in economic development and levels of living. But it is equally an accepted norm that outside the national state no such obligations exist.

In December 1952 the General Assembly of the United Nations adopted a resolution dealing with, among other things, "financing of economic development through the establishment of *fair and equitable* international prices for primary commodities."[22] The resolution—which is only one in a series of resolutions that is bound to grow as the years pass by— first noted the ability to obtain *"adequate"* proceeds from exports as one of the most important sources of financing economic development for underdeveloped countries; it therefore wanted attention given to the "correction of *maladjustments"* resulting from, among other things, secular movements in the value of primary goods in terms of manufactured goods. The resolution expressed the opinion that "wherever governments adopt measures affecting the prices of primary commodities entering international trade, they should duly consider the effect of such measures on the terms of trade of countries in the process of development, in order to ensure that the prices of primary commodities are kept in an *adequate, just and equitable* relation to the prices of capital goods and other manufactured articles so as to permit the more satisfactory formation of domestic savings in the countries in the process of development and to facilitate the establishment of fair wage levels for the working population of these countries with a view to reducing the existing disparity between their standards of living and those in the highly industrialized countries." The governments were asked to cooperate "in establishing multilateral as well as bilateral international agreements and arrangements relating to individual primary commodities as well as to groups of primary commodities and manufactured goods" for the purpose of, among other things, ensuring an *"adequate, just and equitable relationship"* between prices of primary commodities and manufactured goods.

This is exactly the vocabulary and the ideology of national welfare state policy, but applied to the world at large. The two-thirds majority of the General Assembly that was needed to carry the resolution was made up of the many underdeveloped nations; each of the much less numerous industrially advanced nations voted against the resolution; Pakistan was moved to join the advanced countries for this occasion, while Nationalist

China, Greece, Haiti, and Turkey found it appropriate to abstain; the Soviet block countries also abstained but have in similar later encounters joined their forces with the majority party of the underdeveloped countries. This roll call vote is reproduced here as it is of considerable political interest.

It is easy to predict with almost complete certainty that in the foreseeable future nothing whatsoever will result from this resolution or similar ones that are now being adopted regularly at every year's meetings of the Economic and Social Council and the General Assembly of the United Nations. We are not living in the World State; there is no World Government in existence and no World Legislature. A majority vote in an organ of the United Nations can have effect only as a demonstration of opinion; it may be useful for propaganda at home and may exert some slight political pressure upon nations and governments abroad.[23] The richer nations, who are a tiny minority but exercise most of the real power in the non-Soviet world and are expected to make all the sacrifices, are not prepared to go along. The basis of human solidarity does not exist that would lead them to permit the extension to the poorer rest of the world of the solidarity principles of their own happy and progressive national welfare states. To most of their peoples the very idea is absurd.

The group of economic experts appointed to consider the subject and prepare practical proposals also skated round the clear meaning of the resolution: that redistributional intent was to be a norm for the practical proposals. "The Committee is agreed that price can be called 'fair,' 'just,' and 'equitable' as well as 'reasonable' as long as it does not perform extreme upward and downward gyrations which are caused by abnormal and transient conditions or serve no useful economic purpose."[24] The experts thus identified the redistributional norm with the norm of price stability, which was also a main subject of the resolution. This was not, however, the intention of the majority of the representatives of the poor countries who voted for the resolution; they meant, as farmers in our countries who plead for higher agricultural prices, that the prices they were getting were "too low." And the demand for distributional justice will continue to haunt international gatherings.

The experts went on to explain, however, that "it is a plausible hypothesis that the bargaining strength of the under-developed countries is in general inferior to that of the wealthy industrial countries." They also added that "governments may agree on operational definitions of what 'fair' or 'reasonable' prices should be. Yet to advance such definitions is not a matter of expertise and hence not within the province of experts. It must rather be based on a set of values which governments share and— to the extent that they disagree—on their relative bargaining power."

Finally, they gave, however, their obiter dictum: "We believe it to be

preferable in general that prices should be left free to perform their function of allocating productive resources and that 'unfairness' should be
compensated by direct income transfers."[25] Apart from the fact that, as I
have shown in Chapters VIII and IX, very little in the way of transfers
takes this direction, or can be expected to do so within the foreseeable
future, the main and interesting observation to make is that this principle
is not applied within the individual states. On the contrary, extensive
economic policies have been inaugurated in all industrially advanced
countries with the purpose of influencing the national economies and
effectuating redistribution without direct income transfers—for example,
in agriculture.

I have quoted this political judgment of the experts and the somewhat
halting reasoning behind it, because it renders a realistic characterization
of the world political situation. This situation is, quite simply, that in the
international field there is virtually nothing akin to the solidarity demonstrated in the national welfare states towards people in the underdeveloped regions and industries of those states.

To this hard fact the underdeveloped countries have to adapt their
national commercial policy as best they can. I shall return to this problem
after dealing with the second main grievance of the underdeveloped countries against the working of the international price mechanism: the short-
term instability of their markets.

INSTABILITY OF MARKETS AND
STABILIZATION POLICIES

WIDELY FLUCTUATING REAL EXPORT PROCEEDS

The products that make up most of the exports of underdeveloped
countries show large price fluctuations from month to month and year to
year. This is mainly due to the generally low demand elasticities for many
of those products and to the low supply elasticities in primary production
everywhere, which tend to be still lower in underdeveloped countries
because of the general rigidity of their economies. At the same time, instability of supply on account of the weather is a characteristic of agriculture, especially when production techniques are inefficient. Primary
commodities are also more influenced by speculative buying and selling,
and changes in inventories often tend to aggravate instead of dampening
fluctuations in demand. In many fields the imports of primary commodities, thought weighing very heavily in the trade balance of the exporting underdeveloped countries, constitute only a marginal supply
to the importing countries and are in danger of being cut more than
proportionally when demand falls.

A United Nations expert study of the problem[26] shows that during the period 1901 to 1950 the year-to-year price changes of 18 primary commodities, which represent the major exports of 47 underdeveloped countries, averaged about 14 per cent; fluctuations within the year averaged about 27 per cent as between the high and the low point of each year. But primary producers' vulnerability to price fluctuations is greatly increased by the fact that year-to-year movements tend to be in the same direction for two to three years at a time; so that in the sample studied cyclical price declines averaged about 27 per cent for individual commodities much more.

The changes of export volume showed up as even larger than the price changes and for the sample studied averaged between 18 and 19 per cent on a year-to-year basis. Usually they did not run counter to the price changes—except in the case of foodstuffs—but reinforced them. The fluctuations in export proceeds, therefore, tended to be still wider. Even when measured on a year-to-year basis and averaged among all the commodities studied, the figure was calculated to be as high as 23 per cent. Again, it should be recalled that changes tend to proceed in the same direction for several years. The average percentage is actually raised to 37 if calculated for either the upward or the downward phase of the cycles.

To this should be added the fact that the secular trend seemed to be rather towards wider price fluctuations. Also, a larger sample of 200 varieties and specified grades of primary commodities gave generally still higher percentage changes than the standard sample referred to above of 18 main commodities. It should, of course, not be forgotten that the period under study included two world wars and the Great Depression which, on the other hand, must have tended to give higher figures for price fluctuations than would correspond to what would have happened if conditions had remained more "normal." Whether the future development is going to be in this sense more "normal" is anybody's guess.

Many of the underdeveloped countries rely almost exclusively on the export proceeds of one or two commodities. This lack of diversification naturally tends to increase the fluctuations of their total export earnings. Underdeveloped countries show generally, as I pointed out, a high degree of dependence on foreign trade for their national income. Many of those countries that have their exports concentrated on one or two commodities have at the same time very high foreign trade ratios, the export proceeds in some countries being responsible for half the national income or more.

Prices of most capital goods also show marked instability. On the average, manufactured goods have, however, a narrower range of variation. For this reason, but also because prices of primary and manufactured goods do not move in an absolutely synchronized pattern, the fluctuations of real export proceeds of underdeveloped countries, in terms of the goods they buy for their exports, were still very high, about 13–14 per cent on a year-to-year and 22 per cent on a cyclical basis.

While the terms of trade for industrialized countries tend to move inversely to the business fluctuations and thus mitigate their effects to some extent, the contrary is true for underdeveloped countries. There the changes of the terms of trade tend to intensify the effects of general business fluctuations.

What there is of capital inflow to underdeveloped countries follows the same pattern. It tends to broaden when business is good and to shrink when business is bad and when capital influx is most dearly needed; capital flights tend to move in inverse relation to the business cycle and thus also to accentuate that cycle.

From the point of view of the need to import capital goods for economic development it should also be noted that a large part, usually more than a half, of the export proceeds are needed for the import of essential consumer goods. In a downward movement, this usually results, of course, in the cutting down of imports of capital goods much more than proportionally to the total fall in export proceeds.[27]

These are well-known facts. The situation naturally varies considerably from country to country. The average figures quoted above from the United Nations study have only an illustrative significance in suggesting the relative proportions of the magnitudes involved. Our argument in the following pages would not be substantially invalidated if another study using more or different statistical material arrived at somewhat higher or lower figures for the average fluctuations of prices and export proceeds.

INFLATIONARY PRESSURES

One main and general effect on the economies of underdeveloped countries of this instability in their export markets is to increase the economic risks of devoting productive resources to production for export. This will make investment and production for export relatively less advantageous and less attractive. It gives an extra and powerful motive for adoption of an economic policy of self-sufficiency. As these nations are now increasingly becoming masters of their own house and have begun attempting to plan rationally with their own permanent interests as the guiding norm, this motive will come to play an increasingly important role. There are, however, other considerations, and I shall leave this question for the moment, merely emphasizing the fact that in solving the policy equation of allocating resources between production for export and for the home market this effect will have to be given its due weight.

More specifically, this exposure to violent shocks in their international trade is apt to create a continuous danger for these countries' monetary and financial stability and, in particular, to engender strong and recurrent inflationary pressures. There are, as I shall point out later, rational though very difficult national policy measures by which this danger can be averted, partly at least. But the "natural tendencies," against which those national policy measures would have to be directed, lead to increased inflationary pressures both when the export proceeds turn upwards and when they turn downwards.

In the former case, if new fiscal and monetary disciplines aimed at increasing national savings are not applied, the income increases accruing from the larger export proceeds will—according to the well-known mechanism of the Wicksellian cumulative process and via reactions in consumption demands, other incomes, tax yields at unchanged rates, public expenditures, investments, etc.—start an inflationary spiral. The new extra space created in the exchange balance, which initially materializes in an increased exchange reserve, will then easily be filled by rising demands for imported goods; the checks against imports which at that point will have to be introduced will give new force to the inflationary movement. The relatively low elasticity of domestic supplies, which is a characteristic of underdeveloped countries, plays an important role in spurring this process of internal inflation.

But a downward turn of export proceeds is also conducive to inflation in a poor country with low levels of living and where the "natural tendency" is never to acquire much of an exchange reserve. The initial effect of lower incomes from exports will be, it is true, to engender deflationary forces in the economy. But wages and other incomes in the export industries, as in other occupations, are always sticky to some extent and anyhow do not react instantaneously; demand will also, at least initially, be kept up by the use of what there is of available liquid funds. As tax-yields decrease, public expenditures, which can usually not be adjusted downwards quickly, will as a matter of fact become financed by budget deficits. Investments had been decided upon and begun; they can rarely be stopped very rapidly, which also will keep up incomes. In these various ways the edge will be taken off the initial deflationary impact, particularly if the fall in export proceeds sets in during the course of an inflationary process.

Now, part of consumers' demands, which have not fallen, or not fallen enough, is directed towards imported goods, and the investments require payment for capital goods bought abroad. If then, with falling export proceeds, imports of consumers' goods have to be cut down severely, and more severely in order to make room for some import of capital goods, this by itself will induce an inflationary effect. If there had been some influx of foreign capital before, this will tend to shrink or to stop—or even to reverse itself into a net capital outflow—which aggravates the situation.

A devaluation of the currency, if that road is chosen or if the country is forced to take it by the pressure of events, will tend, by its effects upon prices, to intensify the inflationary forces and might, in addition, worsen the terms of trade. This will have the effect of wiping out altogether the widened exchange margin which should have resulted from devaluation.

Around this main theme of perpetual inflationary pressures in good as well as bad times there are innumerable variations, as, for example, a study of most Latin American countries' monetary history reveals. Indeed, in that type of society any change of demand and supply, in whatever direction, will tend to have inflationary effects; but the changes in the trade field are much the biggest and least controllable. The industrially advanced countries, with their very much wider margins in all respects, have not been too successful in managing their internal balance of total demand and supply. My main point in this connection is that the exceedingly wide variations in the underdeveloped countries' real earnings in international trade, on which they are usually much more dependent for their incomes, must make for them the task of preserving monetary equilibrium a vastly more difficult one—particularly because of their poverty and because of their drive to economic development, which implies a political necessity of attempting to hold investments at a high level.

Disruption of Economic Planning

From another point of view, this great instability of real export earnings makes national economic planning, which the underdeveloped countries are now urged on all sides to undertake and which is so essential for their success in economic development, a much more difficult thing. In particular, investments should rationally form a continuous economic process and not proceed by fits and starts. Insofar as capital goods imported from abroad are needed for economic development, a rational programming must be able to count on their availability at a planned time and not when the foreign exchange happens to be at hand. The real costs of investments are also increased when they cannot be planned and executed without constant consideration of the availability of foreign exchange.

Investments must be kept on a high level over the years to give any real basis for a steady economic development. Attempts on the part of the governments to keep up investment in the interest of economic development, if not accompanied by measures to increase savings correspondingly, will only strengthen the inflationary forces; and the result may indeed in the longer run be a level of investments lower than if they had not been pushed so hard. Further, inflation, together with its consequences for the operation of the foreign exchange balance, is one of the strongest deterrents to the inflow of foreign capital; lessening of this flow, or the increase of capital outflow, will, in its turn, compel the governments to a more restrictive import policy which again tends to strengthen the inflationary forces.

The government of an underdeveloped country is placed in an almost impossible dilemma, where its attempts to keep up the level of investments feed inflation, and where then, because of the inflation, investments have to be cut down. The end result of its actions during various phases of the cumulative process may very well be both inflation and low levels of investment. As the United Nations experts pointed out: ". . . it is precisely those sectors of their economy upon which the drive towards economic progress most depends which are vulnerable to the shock of external and internal instability."[28] The earlier expert group who wrestled with the same problem put it this way: "Their margin of consumption above subsistence requirements is very small, and the main brunt of any drop in their export receipts must therefore be borne by their development programs, which are vital to their future."[29]

When investments are made in an inflationary climate, they often take an unrealistic direction; any existing plan for the use of available capital will be distorted. In the postwar years and until recently many Latin American countries have on the whole been rather favored by the general level of their terms of trade, their national income per capita has been rising considerably, and their rate of capital formation has been rather high. But nevertheless, as Professor Ragnar Nurkse points out, "Under the influence of inflation and luxury import restrictions . . . investment has tended in recent years to concentrate on residential construction, largely for the upper income groups, and on luxury industries, while essential public installations such as railways and ports have in some cases tended to fall in disrepair. It cannot be denied that economic development is going on, but it is taking a needlessly painful and contorted form."[30] If the present lower level of their terms of trade, or still lower ones, should come to prevail for a number of years, that would not by itself cure inflation. Other things being equal, it would indeed give a further spur to inflation, at the same time as investment and development would be curtailed, not necessarily steered into more productive lines.

To all the evil results of fluctuations in export proceeds and inflationary climate I would add their influence on business mentality. Speculation, which an inefficient central banking system is unable to check, becomes one of the major forces in the development of foreign-induced inflationary pressures. But besides this, the wide price fluctuations have deterrent effects on recruiting brains and initiative for industry and enterprise. Speculation and the gamble of trading under conditions of high risks and high profits will attract venturesome youth, while the prospects of laboring for mass production with low profits, which must be the goal for successful industrial development, will become unattractive. This is the more damaging, since in most underdeveloped countries there is the recognized difficulty of changing the traditions of whatever small business class there is from seeking easy profits through trade and speculation to embarking upon sustained enterprise. Trade has always and everywhere been the breeding ground for industrial entrepreneurs, but when prices fluctuate widely and inflation becomes a major business factor, sufficient industrialists of the most desirable type are not forthcoming.

NATIONAL STABILIZATION POLICY

It has been a recurrent theme of this book that one of the most difficult tasks of the governments in underdeveloped countries is to force national savings up to the level of the investments that are necessary for the desired rate of economic development. The primary effect of the great variations in the underdeveloped countries' export earnings is to put their monetary and financial stability under recurrent strain to permit the "natural tendencies" to work themselves out free from government interference, which would lead to increased inflationary pressures, both when the earnings increase and when they decline. The task of balancing savings and investments would be exceedingly difficult even if the export proceeds did not fluctuate so widely—because of the low levels of income, the undeveloped structure of financial institutions, the prevalent attitudes to savings, enterprise, and investment of the tiny well-to-do classes and, above all, because of imperfections in the machinery of government and administration. Under these circumstances, the fluctuations of real export earnings and their consequences on the entire economy confront the government of an underdeveloped country with the choice of either controlling national savings or else losing its grip over the development problem almost entirely.

The government must somehow—by taxation or other means—manage to immobilize effectively the increases in export earnings when they tend to rise; it may then also be able to mitigate somewhat the hardships when earnings fall. As Nurkse has stressed: "An improvement in the terms of trade will make no significant contribution to capital formation unless the increment in export proceeds, and hence in people's income, is directed into saving, voluntary or involuntary."[31] In order to secure the holding up of investments, when later the export proceeds turn downwards, this extra effort is, indeed, essential.

The degree of pressure on savings that has to be applied should depend on a primary decision about the level of investments that the government wants to assure, *i.e.*, how fast it dares to push the rate of economic development. Any rational policy of internal stabilization must thus be founded on a development plan which establishes the major objectives of economic policy in general. Such a plan must have the entire economy within its focus but must at the same time have regard to the conditions in the various sectors. The difficulties faced by an underdeveloped country in producing such a plan in a realistic fashion, in adhering to it against difficulties, and in altering it as circumstances change, do not need elaboration.

By what means the stabilization policy should be carried out is a technical matter which I must pass over in this very general sketch. I agree with Nurkse that in a poor underdeveloped country the control of the savings ratio must become to a great extent a matter of taxation of one form or another. I should like to add, though, that if such a country really succeeds in preserving a reasonable degree of internal monetary equilibrium for a number of years, and if at the same time real economic progress gets under way and care is given to the building up of various savings institutions,[32] it may well be that over a period of time a growing portion of the necessary savings can be on an individual, voluntary basis.

Measures to control national savings in the face of widely fluctuating export earnings should result in the accumulation of foreign reserves when export prices move up and their gradual exhaustion when they move down. This policy may be combined with, or rather partly consist of, an internal income-stabilization scheme, expropriating export earnings when they are rising and paying out subsidies when they fall.

The operation of such a scheme is an extremely delicate matter; if, as is natural enough, it tends to take on the character of a general income support, it will not prevent inflation. It should be recognized that from the point of view of a long-range production and export-promotion policy the guaranteeing for a number of years of relatively high and stable prices for one or several of its major export commodities may be an entirely rational device. If not counterbalanced by a stern taxation policy, it will, however, almost automatically lead to inflation as, for instance, Turkey has recently found out.

The internal income stabilization policy may be combined with a systematic attempt to manage national buffer stocks with the intention of carrying over supplies from periods of low to periods of brisk demand. The stocks of export commodities then replace the reserve of foreign exchange which otherwise would accumulate and fluctuate in the same way. If a number of countries followed a similar policy, the latitude of price fluctuations on the world market would tend to decrease. Again, it should be noted that it is a delicate and risky operation, which also requires substantial financial resources. A national economy is easily forced to carry a much higher burden of investment in stocks than is healthy either for its exchange balance or for its economic development, which needs foreign exchange for buying capital goods.

Lastly, one important point should again be stressed. The advanced countries have not been too successful in the past in controlling their level of savings and in keeping their economy in balance. The under-developed countries are compelled to attempt to stabilize their economies more successfully, though all their levels are very much lower and their reserves scantier, the exogenous impulses very much stronger, their invest-ment needs much more urgent, and their governments and administra-tions incomparably weaker.

THE CONVERGENCE OF INTERESTS

It is against this background that proposals for concerted international action to stabilize commodity prices should be viewed. The paramount interest of the underdeveloped countries in international price stabiliza-tion is evident from my analysis above. The politically important fact is that these wide fluctuations of the prices of primary products are also not in the interest of the industrially advanced countries.

They increase their difficulties, too, in maintaining internal monetary stability. The speculative stocking boom in primary products and their rising prices during the early phases of the Korean war brought, for in-stance, many countries in Western Europe into a bout of inflation which had later to be followed by a period of relative stagnation of their indus-trial progress. Even when monetary balance is preserved, the economic risks in trading and stocking primary products will have to be paid for, which must tend to raise over the years the level of their prices to indus-tries and, finally, to consumers. Also, the instability of the underdeveloped countries' import demands for capital goods is, of course, disadvantageous to the industrial countries. It is, furthermore, apparent that the wide variations in the market for primary products and their consequences for the underdeveloped countries' import demands add another difficulty to all the others mentioned in Chapter VI, hindering the attainment of a more reliable system of balanced international trade and payments, which is a commonly shared goal.

Nor are such wide variations necessary in order to adjust the supply of primary products to the usually very gradual and continuous changes of consumption and production. The prominent economic experts who, under the chairmanship of Professor James W. Angell, wrote the United Nations report, *Measures for International Economic Stability*, concluded that "it is hard to believe that to achieve these objects, price fluctuations need be nearly so great as they are in fact. Much smaller changes would, on the contrary, obviate unnecessary and wasteful fluctuations in investment in primary production and in the use of primary products. There can be little doubt that they would, on balance, be better for all concerned."[33]

To this statement—which represents, so far as I know, a unanimous view among economists—the later expert group on commodity trade and economic development added this reflection:

It is possible to surmise, therefore, that the desirable results of price changes—the encouragement of a better allocation of economic resources—ought to be capable of achievement without violent instability. Indeed, if prices really had to change by 15 percent or 20 percent from year to year in order to achieve minor alterations in resources allocation, this would raise serious doubt about the effectiveness of this method of securing a desirable allocation. In any case, we do not believe that the large price fluctuations are in fact serving useful allocative purposes.[34]

We are thus for once in the happy situation where economists are unanimous and all national interests converge.

To sum up, we have no doubt that industrial as well as economically underdeveloped countries would be better off—in terms of real income and its balanced growth—if the gross instability in primary commodity markets were moderated. It remains for all countries to recognise and fully appreciate this coincidence of interest. If they do, the basis for joint action is established and the problem becomes one of choosing the proper means.[35] . . . We prefer to think that the many solemn declarations by official and unofficial spokesmen of industrial countries, voicing their concern with the development of economically backward countries, were prompted by a measure of sincerity.[36]

FAILURE TO REACH PRACTICAL RESULTS

The wide variations of the real export earnings of underdeveloped countries are partly related to the general business fluctuations. International cooperation to stabilize business conditions in the world at large would undoubtedly mitigate the harmful effects caused by the price instability discussed here. In Chapter VI I pointed out that international efforts in this direction, which at one time enjoyed very general support by economists and statesmen alike, have now been almost given up.

The very small capital influx to underdeveloped countries—and, in particular, the tendency to vary in correlation with real export earnings—also aggravates the adverse effects on the economies of underdeveloped countries of price instability. In Chapters VIII and IX I reached the conclusion that there is no likelihood that foreign capital will, within the foreseeable future, be made available to these countries in any substantial amounts. In the present chapter I have also pointed out that the changes in terms of trade caused by price fluctuations have effects on national incomes of such great magnitude that they cannot possibly be bought off by any practical increase in foreign credits or aid.

Nevertheless, if measures could be taken to uphold and perhaps to increase capital inflows during periods when real export earnings of underdeveloped countries were low, this would naturally be helpful. Arguments for organizing such compensatory capital movements have frequently been put forward by economists, and concrete proposals in this direction have been worked out by the various United Nations expert groups that have been dealing with the stabilization problem. In supporting their proposals, they have all pointed out that such compensatory capital movements would be in the interest of the advanced countries as well, since their exports of industrial goods to the underdeveloped countries would be kept at a higher level.[37] However well founded in logic and in the converging interests of all countries, these proposals have as yet not led to any practical action.

Even if there were an organized international system of concerted measures to counteract general business fluctuations and to stabilize the capital flows in and out of underdeveloped countries, this would minimize but by no means solve the problem caused by the instability of prices of primary products. Since, however, there is no such effective cooperation within sight, measures for price stabilization are even more important and urgent.

This is the problem that is dealt with under the title "commodity agreements" or "commodity arrangements." It does not concern the issue of improving the long-term level of prices of export products from the underdeveloped countries, referred to earlier in this chapter, but only the problem of how to counteract their wide short-term variations.[38] As I pointed out earlier, even if international cooperation to solve the former problem is for the time being excluded, a solution of the latter problem, where interests so widely converge, would, of course, be of tremendously beneficial importance, in the first place to the underdeveloped countries.

Long before the war there were, besides the international cartels, a series of various multilateral and bilateral arrangements, mostly between producing countries, aimed at stabilizing prices. During the war, such arrangements were given an impetus by the successful operation of the coordinating supply agencies on the Allied side, set up to allocate resources and regularize trade, mutual aid, and prices. Another important stimulus was, naturally, the international idealism nurtured in this time of great stress, when thinking was so uninhibited and binding policy commitments so far off.

Various schemes for price stabilization became important elements in the planning for peace; in particular, the safeguarding of the interests of the underdeveloped countries was held up as a moral imperative for the cooperation between nations in the new world which was to emerge after the victory over Fascism. Often large-scale international economic planning was envisaged as the general background to price stabilization policies.[39]

John Maynard Keynes gave his authority to the feasibility of accomplishing international price stabilization and offered practical suggestions as to how it should be done. The postwar discussion was given a good send-off by a report, published in February 1945, on *Economic Stability in the Post-War World*,[40] worked out under the auspices of the League of Nations by a committee of economists headed by W. W. Riefler and proposing the setting up of buffer stocks within an international framework.

The Food and Agriculture Organization started out under John Boyd Orr with a magnificent scheme for a "World Food Board," presented to the first conference of the organization in Copenhagen in 1946. The Board not only would have stabilized prices of agricultural commodities but also would have financed and directed the disposal of surplus products at reduced prices to needy peoples and, in addition, run an emergency world food reserve.

The scheme was somewhat ambitious in certain respects and badly needed to be carefully worked over. This was partly done during the next few years and resulted in a change of the proposed Board to an "International Commodity Clearing House." This change was, in fact, only one of the steps in the slow but, in the end, effective destruction of the entire scheme, which naturally had created suspicions among all "sound" and orthodox representatives of governments, particularly those of the richer countries. Sir John himself, who stubbornly stuck to the ambitious aspirations of wartime idealism, preferred to resign and was given a peerage at home and the Nobel Peace Prize by the Norwegians, who appreciate great and generous thoughts.

Some such scheme with broader terms of reference than price stabilization would certainly have had important functions to fulfill in the field of the production, trade, and consumption of food; the technical difficulties of operating it could have been overcome—*if* the world were a better one, more like the one people expected when war was still being waged. The agency could have dealt not only with foreseeable problems of food supplies but also, and more generally, with the large disparities between rich nations under pressing tendencies in burdensome surpluses and poor nations always risking starvation or near-starvation; but I do not think it could be brought into existence and function effectively in the nationalistic climate that since then has hardened progressively with each passing year.[41]

On the general international trade front, Cordell Hull, President Roosevelt's Secretary of State, and a distinguished group of devoted economic experts working under his direction, made preparations towards the end of the war for an International Trade Organization; rules for commodity agreements were part of the plan. These ideas were further elaborated during the long discussions of the Preparatory Committee set up by the United Nations and the results were incorporated in Chapter VI of the Havana Charter. The International Trade Organization never came into being; but long before its fate was clear, and because of the passage of time, an Interim Co-ordinating Committee for International Commodity Arrangements was created to sponsor and guide the calling of intergovernmental conferences on particular commodities.

Very little practical action followed, however. The whole movement for stabilizing international prices of primary products has, in fact, been petering out and has achieved very little.

THE DEEPER EXPLANATION OF THE FAILURE

It is worthwhile reflecting for a moment over the deeper causes of this discouraging development. For one thing, there are very difficult technical problems to be solved if the world price of a commodity is to be effectively stabilized. Insofar as the scheme involves stocking, it would also require quite considerable financial reserves. My own personal experience of multilateral intergovernmental negotiations convinces me that it is unwise to underestimate these technical difficulties and the very laborious and time-consuming staff work that is required to reach practical results. I am, like the majority of economists who have studied the problem, nevertheless convinced that the technical difficulties could be overcome—if there were a positive will on the part of the governments to overcome them.

I believe we should not confuse the matter by offering an unnecessarily complicated explanation of our failure to do anything effective about international price stabilization. The main explanation is quite simply that the basis of human solidarity between nations does not yet exist for a large-scale settlement of such a big economic problem. It is not only, as I have repeatedly pointed out earlier in this book, that the international machinery for international cooperation is weak; the machinery is weak mainly because it lacks a solid foundation in people's allegiances and expectations.

The fact that in this case, as I have also stressed, there is a clear convergence of national interests in favor of a settlement does not contradict this proposition. It is a routine experience of every international civil servant that, almost as a rule, government representatives arrive at their meetings with instructions to oppose initiatives. Legislatures, governments, and administrations are usually more narrowly nationalistic than the enlightened sections of their general publics. All the earlier conditionings of negotiators in the international economic field have taught them to do their utmost in fighting fiercely for the national penny while losing the commonly desirable pound.

I have often reflected over the lack of enlightened generosity that characterizes intergovernmental bargaining and differs so widely from the way in which big business makes its deals: in a spirit of much more largess, mutual faith and confidence, with a sense of the true proportions, and a ready preparedness to make small concessions to secure big profits. Another comparison, equally disadvantageous to intergovernmental negotiations, is with organized collective bargaining in the labor market in some of the highly integrated national communities.

In questions of price stabilization a government is asked to make a commitment to pay more for a commodity at certain times in the future and less at others; in addition it is perhaps asked to contribute to the financing of buffer stocks. The natural tendency is always to suspect that the other partners get away with an "unfair" advantage. It is usually realized that there is a common gain to be made and shared, but it is feared that the others get it all and perhaps more than that. I mean it quite seriously when I say that, however many statistics and technical formulas we pile up at the conference table in order to give objectivity to as many elements of an issue as possible, the essential difficulty to overcome in intergovernmental negotiations of this type is very simply the restrictiveness of national governments and their suspicions about each other.

Even if the general national interest to cooperate in reaching an agreement is clear in the abstract, this becomes easily confused in national discussion. A government represents different groups with different interests: in advanced countries there are primary producers as well as consumers; in both types of countries there are many middlemen who earn their profits by speculating in unstable prices. These are special interests and the public interest is, of course, different and should be overwhelming. But in the advanced countries with their accomplished systems of representative democracy the public interest in an international issue of this type is apt to go by default amid general apathy; nobody is ready to wage a fight for it as there are usually no clear and immediate group interests involved and as the special interests can harp on the nationalistic sentiments that are always present. Governments in the underdeveloped countries are often even more directly the prey of special interests.

Further, we will have to remember that even if the issue is defined as the limited one of price stabilization, the underdeveloped countries are, as a matter of fact, also dissatisfied with the general level of prices of their export goods and they are under a very strong temptation to try to get additional protection for this other interest under the cloak of price stabilization. They will anyhow always be suspected of trying to do so by the representatives of the advanced countries. On their side, they are conscious of their weaker bargaining position and will suspect the advanced countries of taking unfair advantage of this by trying to use the agreements to depress more generally the long-term level of commodity prices.

The agreements would usually depend in some way and to some extent on how the prospects for the future price development and, indeed, the general trend of the world economy, are regarded; at least the governments' interest in reaching a certain agreement at a given time will depend on these factors. As these prospects are always exceedingly uncertain and not susceptible to objective assessment, opportunistic impulses on both sides will tend to hinder a common assessment. Usually, both importers and exporters are reluctant to give up possible chances of lower or higher prices, respectively. Nevertheless, all these difficulties could be overcome if there was a real will for a settlement.

Such a will undoubtedly exists as a general attitude and is steadily becoming more articulate among the leaders in the underdeveloped countries, where the interest in price stabilization is greatest. They are joining forces in general complaints and declarations; but it must be said that they have done very little in practice to obtain international agreement on stabilization schemes for the specific commodities in which they are chiefly interested. Partly, this is just one more indication of the lack of practical cooperation between underdeveloped countries themselves, which has often been referred to in this book—when it comes to negotiations, they are interested in different commodities and, even in regard to the same commodity, their interests vary. Partly it is caused by the general inefficiency of their governmental machines.

Meanwhile attitudes in the advanced countries have gradually turned more and more definitely against the idea of international price stabilization. As concerted international action to stabilize their export prices would undoubtedly be one way of really helping the underdeveloped countries—and of doing it on straight business lines, without incurring much expense, but actually benefiting the advanced countries—this is a rather sad reflection.

In the United States, the President's Materials Policy Commission presented its report, *Resources for Freedom*,[42] as late as June 1952—it is usually referred to as the Paley report, after its chairman—and came out clearly for the earlier established policy line in favor of international price stabilization, recommending both multilateral agreements and the device of buffer stocks. Since then there has been a general hardening of hearts in the United States which has coincided with a less anxious out-look on the scarcity of industrial raw materials needed in that country. The majority of the Randall Commission[43] took an entirely negative attitude on the issue, and most advanced countries have followed this development in the United States.

Undoubtedly to some extent as a reaction to this, the underdeveloped countries have become ever more vociferous in demanding price stabiliza-tion. The dividing line between two political parties, as it were, in the world, the rich and the poor, has become more clear cut.

Most underdeveloped countries are weak and dependent—economi-cally, politically, and militarily. While some of them nevertheless make it a point of honor to demonstrate a high degree of national integrity, it can be noticed that when an issue comes up in an organ of the United Nations many others tend to be lined up for voting by one or several of the big industrial powers. Increasingly, however, the underdeveloped countries are declining to toe the line in economic questions of vital importance to them. A sort of collective disobedience is spreading; the fact that it is so widespread—and also, of course, the realization on all sides that the passing of a resolution does not cause any real immediate change—gives a sort of protection for a more independent voting on these questions.

And so a poor countries' party in general economic questions has be-come established. The decision of the Economic and Social Council last summer to set up a new commission to tackle the price stabilization prob-lem was, for instance, made by the votes of the underdeveloped countries —now joined by the countries in the Soviet bloc—against the votes of all the industrially advanced countries.[44]

I feel certain that no competent and objective observer of the interest-ing political development I have sketched will disagree with me when, hereafter, I base my argument on the conclusion that for the time being no substantive progress will be made in solving the problem of inter-national price stabilization.

FACING THE WORLD MARKET

NATIONAL EXPORT POLICY

The following analysis of the problem of the underdeveloped countries' national commercial policy is based on a number of major premises that I have sought to establish in this and the preceding chapters:

1. The underdeveloped countries are under the political necessity of pressing on with their economic development plans as rapidly as they can—in the very difficult internal circumstances that were analyzed in the

last chapter and the great handicaps to their international trade relations that have been the object of study so far in this chapter.

2. For most underdeveloped countries, no really substantial amount of foreign credits or aid is likely to be forthcoming; likewise no major reforms are on the way to introduce an effective compensatory cycle of capital inflow in order to ease their payments situation when real export proceeds are falling.

3. No large-scale international agreements are in sight to improve the underdeveloped countries' terms of trade or to stabilize the world prices of their exports; nor are there any prospects that effective action will soon be taken for international control of industrial cartels.

The almost complete lack of progress in international attempts to ameliorate the conditions under which the underdeveloped countries are laboring in the field of international trade naturally makes it even more important that their national commercial policy be handled with wisdom. The following observations, like the rest of this book, are only in the nature of a broad sketch, but I would like to state in advance my opinion that this subject is one of crucial importance. The underdeveloped countries' way of handling their commercial policy will be one of the most significant factors in determining whether they will fail or succeed in their drive for economic development.

As they are the poor and the many, this problem should, according to the philosophical traditions of political economy, rank very much higher in our discussions than it usually does. If these countries were to succeed, a more correct and democratic international balance of economic power would be created. Then, perhaps, even the efforts towards international cooperation in the trade field would be given a better chance than now, when their bargaining power is so frail. Perhaps even our international economic organizations could be revitalized.

A useful starting point for the discussion of the national commercial policy of underdeveloped countries may be to recall that these countries have a vital interest in high exports in order to enable them to raise their necessary imports of capital goods for economic development. But this does not imply simply that it is in their interest to press on with their traditional exports. They should rather take a good look at the composition of these exports and at their prospects in the world market and then make up their minds about which exports they should try to increase and which they should rather leave alone or reduce. They should seek out for themselves the dynamic commodities with rising demand trends and with high income and price elasticities and try to get away from those with a doubtful future.

Unfortunately many, if not most, underdeveloped countries are firmly established in lines of exports in regard to which the world demand is not very elastic and the demand trend is not rising. By raising its output of such commodities, one underdeveloped country may gain some advantage at the expense of its competitors—who are also to a large extent underdeveloped—but if all underdeveloped countries did their utmost to increase their present staple exports, they might end up poorer than they were, while the advanced countries would reap the benefits. In some cases a single underdeveloped country occupies so important a place in the world market in respect to one commodity, that an increase of its supply would bring down the price substantially and, consequently, increase its export proceeds less than proportionally—perhaps even reduce them.

If there is one generalization that can safely be made from comparative studies of the development of the terms of trade of different countries it is that—besides factors beyond a single country's own control, such as its natural endowments and the trends of world production and consumption—it is a country's ability to adjust rapidly and continuously and to shift its resources to the most advantageous uses that determines how it fares in, and what gains it reaps from, international trade.[45] Great flexibility is, however, a result of economic development and high levels of production spread out in different directions; the rigidity of an underdeveloped country's economy is one of the marks of its underdeveloped status. To break this vicious circle, deliberate efforts are necessary. If they should succeed, then these efforts would be an important element in its economic development.

More than other countries, the underdeveloped ones need to have penetrating studies made concerning development trends in world supply and demand. And they cannot restrict themselves to the fruits of the studies the advanced countries are making for their own use, nowadays often with narrow and very special strategic perspectives. Here is another field where the accumulated knowledge in the world cannot simply be taken over, but where the underdeveloped countries need to have fresh thinking applied in stating their specific problems and solving them.

They need independent research into the existing openings in the world market, taking into account their special opportunities and difficulties, their natural resources, their labor force, and their available capital. Insofar as they are not able to carry out this research themselves, or to do it all rapidly enough, they have good reasons to put pressure on the international organizations of which they are members, to do the market studies for them.[46]

DIVERSIFICATION OF EXPORTS

One important purpose of these market studies should be to give rational guidance to the diversification of their exports that most underdeveloped countries urgently need. As I pointed out, the exports of many of these countries are concentrated on one or two main commodities; all come to the world market with much too narrow a range of export goods for sale.

One important interest in spreading the exports over a wider range of commodities is naturally to even out risks. With the violent fluctuations of the prices of the export goods of underdeveloped countries, this interest is by itself very considerable.

Another interest is to strengthen their bargaining power. A country like Greece, trying to earn half its export proceeds by finding markets for its tobacco, is continually forced to accept a number of concessions regarding its imports, which it would not accept if it had a freer position since they run counter to its development policy. Often it is compelled to open its boundaries to the import of a number of consumption goods while there is idle capacity at home to produce them. Some Latin American countries, in a similar situation in regard to their exports, have likewise been forced to make commitments with respect to their tariff policy which they would not have chosen to make if their bargaining position had been stronger and if they had been free to consider more exclusively their own development needs.

A third, and main, interest in spreading their exports over a wider range of commodities is that this is the only practical means of overcoming the basic weakness of underdeveloped countries in international trade, which is rigidity, and of acquiring the flexibility in their economy which is a precondition for greater success in exploiting the new opportunties and releasing themselves from the less remunerative lines of export. The only way of doing so is continually to seek out new products for sale and so build up gradually a greater number of export outlets.

In this field—as, indeed, generally—they must overcome tradition and acquire the pragmatic and experimental habits of modern business. Insofar as underdeveloped countries in general succeed in doing this, their exports of many commodities with low income and price elasticities and stagnant demand trends would naturally shrink or develop less rapidly. This would, therefore, be the surest way of improving their terms of trade with respect to traditional exports as well.

All this will require extensive government intervention and must be the result of far-sighted government policy and planning. We should not conceal from ourselves the fact that the natural play of forces in the market will simply mean continued rigidity and stagnation. As always, the good planning needed is aimed at breaking rigidities, increasing flexibility, and liberating forces and not at straitjacketing the development.

And here we are, of course, again up against the real and serious bottleneck that in many, if not most, of the underdeveloped countries will

retard progress: the lack of a progressive, competent, incorrupt administration under a stable government, a vigilant and enterprising business
class, and a plentiful supply of skilled technicians and economic experts.

Exports of Manufactured Goods Also

If the diversification of exports were to be limited entirely to primary
products, the opportunities may perhaps not everywhere amount to very
much. A word should be said here about the taboo existing in most of
our thinking against the export of manufactured goods by underdeveloped countries. It is gradually becoming recognized that it is a rational
element in their economic development policy that they should build
up industries and increase their production of manufactured goods;
but it is taken more or less for granted that these should be for domestic
consumption only and not to compete in the world market.

When the advanced countries industrialized they were in the fortunate
situation of being surrounded by an underdeveloped world which they
could use as a market for cheap manufactured goods and as a source of
supply for food and industrial raw materials. This was one of the in-
estimable advantages in being ahead of the rest. The latecomers are obviously not able to follow the same simple pattern. So far as exports of
manufactured goods are concerned, the underdeveloped countries meet
on the world market well-established, highly productive competitors
whom in most branches they cannot undersell. In attempting to reach a
better balanced economy they will certainly need to industrialize, but for
a long time they will have their hands full in trying to meet the demands
of their domestic markets. Meanwhile they will have to acquire the
capital goods they need for development—and often additional food and
many manufactured consumers' essentials—mainly by selling primary
products, the only ones they are presently able to produce in large
quantities.

But recognizing these facts in the situation certainly does not imply
that the industries they can build up should be relegated altogether to
the protected home market. From the point of view of international
division of labor this would be entirely unsound, and many opportunities
of coming into such export lines where price and income elasticities are
great and demand trends rising would be lost. The development of industrial exports is generally apt to instill more of a dynamic spirit of
enterprise and competition into a stagnant economy.

Japan in its time never accepted this taboo and indeed could not
possibly have done so, given its development aspirations and the relations between the trend of population increase and the confined space of
its homeland; Japan can still less accept it today with a population nearly

thrice as large as in 1870. India is already one of the major world ex-porters of textiles and, in Southern Europe, Yugoslavia is attaining some success as an exporter of manufactured goods and even of machinery.

More generally, if economic development is to amount to anything—if stagnation is going to be broken—one underdeveloped country after another will have to enter the world market for manufactured goods in a big way. India might very well in time find it advantageous and perhaps necessary to become an exporter of manufactured products, perhaps even of capital goods, on a large scale. It would be in line with the efforts to establish a more permanent international trade balance in the world, if industrially advanced countries adjusted their ways of thinking and their commercial and industrial policies to these new possibilities.

The advanced countries will, however, probably try to close their markets to "dumping" from the underdeveloped countries. The history of Japan's long struggle to get into the world markets with its industrial products—which, incidentally, has entered into a new acute and crucial stage—makes it possible to forecast the kind of difficulties that will be placed in their way in order to uphold the taboo. It makes it also prob-able, however, that the discriminatory measures applied in order to keep them out of international trade in manufactured goods will in the longer run have only limited success.

On the ideological front, the underdeveloped countries will have to press for a clarification and, indeed, a redefinition of the odious popular term "dumping," with all its emotional content, which will be thrown at them as new competitors on the international market for manufactured goods. They will have to bring Ricardo's old battery again to the firing line. And they must insist that there exists a relevant difference between, say, an international industrial cartel lowering temporarily its prices in a particular country long enough to liquidate sprouting competitors and a poor country with low wages and levels of living which succeeds for this very reason in producing and selling export articles at lower prices. They will even have to defend and gain recognition for the fact that it may be entirely sound economics for a poor country with a large surplus working population to subsidize an industry to encourage its growth and to make it competitive. The workers who thereby become employed would have to be sustained in any case and the real cost of labor is thus lower to the nation than the wages paid.

Both because the underdeveloped countries are backward in skills and technology and because the character of their basic home markets is determined by poverty of the wide consuming public, the manufactured goods in which they will more easily become competitive in the interna-tional market will usually be of the low-quality, cheaper variety; they will for the greater part consist of semimanufactured, but also of more finished goods. The adjustment of international trade that will be needed is, first, a preparation by the advanced countries to move out of these production lines. They had originally, and have still, a considerable export production in those lines that they sold mainly in their colonial empires and other underdeveloped countries. It has been one of the first demonstrations of economic independence of the former colonies to begin to squeeze out these imports from the metropolitan countries and substitute for them the produce of domestic industry; the recent history of world trends in the production and trade in textiles provides a clear illustration.[47]

Rationally, it cannot be expected to end in self-sufficiency, however. Even in the advanced countries there is a limited market for this type of cheaper product. A natural trend would be a reversal of the established direction of international trade, so that the advanced countries, instead of exporting them, became net importers.

The bigger market is, however, in the underdeveloped countries themselves. For the long period ahead while they all have very incomplete industrial structures, a most interesting possibility is opened up of a "second-grade international specialization" growing up among these countries, particularly in regard to cheaper qualities where the industries in the advanced countries could be effectively undersold.

From this point of view, one of the most damaging policies the advanced countries are following in the interests of their own industries is to protect the markets of their colonial dependencies against imports from other underdeveloped countries. These dependencies represent very important potential markets for the kind of cheaper manufactured goods I am here discussing and would be natural participants in the international specialization of the kind I have in mind between underdeveloped countries. This is, incidentally, one of the motives for the underdeveloped countries' keen interest in gaining independence for the colonies and dependencies, though there admittedly are other motives which are politically more important.

Cooperation Among Underdeveloped Countries

What I am here suggesting is, in fact, a cooperation in international trade among the underdeveloped countries or groups of them, focused particularly on trade in manufactured products. The scope for such a cooperation is naturally limited, as almost by definition partnership is more natural between underdeveloped and developed countries than between underdeveloped countries by themselves. But in one field such cooperation would be of special importance and, indeed, almost a precondition for successful industrialization, namely for industrial goods the economic production of which assumes a larger home market than a single underdeveloped country can offer, at least until production and consumption generally have reached much higher levels.

The present situation in many underdeveloped countries is that, as they proceed with industrialization, they reach a situation where in many new industries they have idle capacity, not only in terms of potential manpower but also in terms of plant and equipment. Such idle capacity is an almost criminal waste in an underdeveloped country; it owes its existence to a combination of a small home market and various indivisibilities of modern methods of production. Where the choice of technology is limited and the opportunities of trade small, an underdeveloped country is placed in a dilemma. It has to decide whether it is prepared to tolerate some idle capacity, pay the considerable additional cost involved, and still go ahead with industrialization in a particular sector, or whether to abandon the attempt. International cooperation of the type suggested would have the task of reducing such idle capacity to a minimum and thus of enlarging the field for economically productive industrialization.

The Secretariat of the Economic Commission for Latin America has presented plans in several studies for this type of cooperation in its region. In its latest publication it again discusses the problem under the heading "Liberalization of Inter-Latin American Trade."

Industrialization is developing in "water-tight" compartments of national economies, and trade in industrial products between Latin American countries is very rare. While industrialization merely covered those goods for which the national market permitted enterprises of sufficient size to be established, this industrial isolation was no cause for serious concern. But when, to meet the needs of development, industrialization is extended to goods which can only be economically produced by mass production methods which exceed the demand of the domestic market, it is imperative to organize reciprocal trade between the Latin American countries.[48]

For this purpose the authors propose reciprocal trade liberalization and other measures in order to encourage trade between certain Latin American countries "in goods which are not at present being produced, which are only being manufactured in small quantities or which are alone produced on a large scale in some of the countries and not in others."[49] The idea is, in fact, that, especially when the technical conditions for economic production require a large home market, a regional group of underdeveloped countries should go ahead together in order to accomplish for themselves the growth of industry behind a protective wall against the industrially advanced countries, the general motivation for which I shall discuss later with respect to a single country. It is pointed out that this liberalization of trade between the Latin American countries need not influence either the United States or Europe more than the effects of a tariff with which either of these countries might attempt to protect its domestic output[50]—it only makes possible the use of more efficient production techniques and, of course, enlarges the scope for possible industrialization in the region with a minimum of protection.

The idea deserves more serious and sympathetic study than it has had so far and may have its application in other underdeveloped regions as well. The difficulties of carrying it out are, however, considerable. It would require cooperative planning and not only cooperative discrimination. On the basis of such planning, one country would allow preferential terms for imports of a particular product from another country in exchange for a similar treatment on the part of that country in regard to another product; and this agreement would then have to be followed up by a planned increase of the investments for production of the two products in the respective countries. It is difficult to believe that a customs union or anything similar, without cooperative planning, would be likely to lead easily to much specialization of any beneficial kind.

It should also be realized that such a cooperative policy between underdeveloped countries would imply a radical breakdown of all their traditions. In all regions there has been very little economic cooperation between underdeveloped countries. In fact they have had very little mutual trade; interregional trade in Latin America is extremely low and interregional transport is very undeveloped. "Once again a vicious circle occurs. The means of transport are deficient and there is a lack of trade owing to transport difficulties."[51]

Trade and transport have been developed among the advanced countries, between them and individual underdeveloped countries, but not among those countries themselves. Governments and businesses in underdeveloped countries are conditioned and trained to negotiate and cooperate with their opposite partners in advanced countries but not with governments and business in other underdeveloped countries. To break this formidable tradition, founded upon generations of history, and to open up new parallel relations between governments and businesses in underdeveloped countries in a region, is a very difficult undertaking.

Nevertheless, I believe there is still a good chance for such a development. The abnormal isolation that has existed for so long and become part of the tradition, itself implies the existence of large, unexploited opportunities for trade and economic cooperation. This is true, indeed, even in the underdeveloped part of Europe, in spite of the relatively much more intensive trading relations there. The Secretariat of the Economic Commission for Europe recently had the opportunity of working on the common development problems of Southern Europe in close cooperation with experts nominated by the governments of Greece, Italy,

Turkey, and Yugoslavia. During this work all were struck by the unexplored possibilities for trade between these countries and, generally, for cooperation and mutually beneficial assistance in many detailed fields which come to light as soon as their development problems are viewed together as a whole and not isolated into their national compartments.

So far, the most successful demonstration of a beginning of economic cooperation between underdeveloped countries is offered by the Central American states, working under the auspices of the Economic Commission for Latin America. In spite of great internal weakness and a troubled political situation, the governments have recently been eager to enter into active cooperation. The reason is partly that the very small size of some of the Central American republics turns economic cooperation between them into a matter almost of life or death; it is their only hope for laying a basis to their efforts of gaining an economically more independent status.

MONOPOLISTIC COOPERATION

At this point it is natural to raise the question as to whether the underdeveloped countries could do something together in order to improve the prices of the staple commodities which make up the bulk of their exports and in many instances will continue to weigh heavily even after considerable diversification. The characterization I have given above of the market situation for those commodities would, of course, seem to be an argument not only for a careful calculation of demand elasticities and market trends separately for each country, but also for monopolistic cooperation between several exporting countries.

Naturally, the underdeveloped countries would be well advised to consult together. Each country by itself will anyhow have to study the market prospects carefully in order to decide on its own production and export policy for various commodities. To give each other the benefit of sharing in a group what they know, how they think, and in what direction they plan to move can only be to the common advantage. Whether the result could ever be a reliable agreement on concerted action is more doubtful.

To begin with, concerted action between the underdeveloped countries in the trade field would meet with suspicion and resentment on the part of the advanced countries, and, of course, the former are all very weak and susceptible to political pressure.[52] Furthermore, for many commodities the underdeveloped countries control only a part, sometimes only a small part, of the total world market supply. Even when they are the chief suppliers, it would be difficult, as the history of rubber and coffee in the period between the two world wars is apt to show, to get several underdeveloped countries to agree on a common policy.

Their positions as sellers on the market is varied. In particular, the big and small producers do not easily keep together. Colombia and Nicaragua were the chief beneficiaries of the Brazilian coffee valorization schemes, and the small producers played havoc with the schemes to restrict output of rubber. This lack of solidarity on the part of the smaller producers is, incidentally, one of the crucial difficulties that meet all international commodity agreements that operate by restricting output.

Although underdeveloped countries have often been at a disadvantage when entering into competition in world markets with the advanced countries and may often suffer from particular subsidy policies followed in these countries, there are also examples, and important ones, of situations where the edge of the advanced countries' competition becomes blunted because of their more effective protection of producers' interests. One rewarding field for diversification of exports from underdeveloped countries has in recent years been precisely in those fields where the lobbies around the United States Congress have been successful in keeping world prices relatively high—as, for instance, in the case of cotton and copper. This is an uncertain basis for the long-term export policy of an underdeveloped country, as there is always the risk that the United States will change its policy—for instance, by giving a greater scope to export subsidies.

Similarly, as long as the United States and Canada succeed in keeping wheat acreage restricted in their countries and wheat surpluses manageable, and in disposing of those surpluses abroad without disturbing the regular world market—which, of course, just now is a big question mark —wheat producers everywhere in the world reap some of the advantages together with the North-American farmers. Likewise it has been primarily the interest of preserving oil prices in America on a remunerative level that has led the big, closely linked oil companies to adopt policies designed to keep up high oil prices in the rest of the world too.[53]

What I am here exemplifying is not a real cooperative partnership between industrially advanced and underdeveloped countries but the fact that sometimes, and indeed often, the collusion of interests in the former countries will have effects which are beneficial to some interests in the latter countries. More regularly, the effects from protectionist policies in the advanced countries can, however, be assumed to be detrimental to the producers in underdeveloped countries.

This is certainly so in regard to monopolistic regulations of supplies and prices of commodities which the underdeveloped countries have to import. Particularly as their own possibilities of exerting monopolistic pressure in regard to their exports are exceedingly limited, one important cause of deep suspicion and dissatisfaction in the underdeveloped countries is their feeling that as buyers they find monopolistic conditions in the markets for most manufactured goods, but especially for capital goods that they need to import for their economic development.

On this point it should be recalled that, as a sort of counterpart to the commodity agreements to stabilize the prices of primary goods, the programs for postwar international cooperation also included a proposal for effective control of industrial cartels. Like all other big wartime schemes, this proposal, too, has come to naught.

The question then arises whether the underdeveloped countries, if they kept together, could accomplish anything by themselves to improve their situation as buyers. The answer must be probably no. They are too small a part of the market for industrial goods and they have too precarious a bargaining position to do anything very effective in order to countervail monopolistic pressure.

But, individually, they would all be in a much stronger position as buyers if they could spread their purchases more evenly over the world. Since colonial times and as a result of economic dependency generally, they have been too settled in traditional lines of business contacts in only one or a few industrial countries and have rarely fully surveyed the entire supply market. Here again, they would need more organized market research.

Quite apart from monopolistic elements in the ordinary sense of the word, the supply market for manufactured goods and particularly for heavy equipment has in the postwar period tended to change towards lower supply elasticities. When, for example, a favorable move of the terms of trade makes it possible for a number of underdeveloped countries to come out as buyers of capital goods to an increased extent, they are now likely to find a situation in the exporting countries of full employment and high utilization of industrial capacity. As they often represent only an apparent marginal market to the industrial countries, and particularly because they have been forced by the fluctuations of their export proceeds to be very irregular customers, they may not always receive the most favorable price conditions and delivery dates. This is another reason for an internal stabilization policy that can also stabilize their import demands for capital goods. But it also stresses the importance for them of bringing their custom to the entire market, for supply conditions will usually be different in different countries. One special reason for their weak bargaining power is often their dependence on credit which is supplied together with equipment. Whatever they can do to strengthen their financial situation will make it easier for them to buy their development goods cheaper.

The facts are not easily available but my feeling is that—apart from their having to pay the price for being irregular customers with insufficient knowledge of the supply markets, too limited business contacts, and need of credits—the monopolistic practices in the markets for most capital goods (and, in particular, engineering products) are much less effective than is usually thought in the underdeveloped countries. There is probably much more competition among the suppliers than they now are in the position to exploit properly.

My feeling is, however, also that there are certain fields where the monopolistic practices are more effectively applied. One such field is probably in shipping. Another one is in the sale of chemicals, a group of products usually left out of the category of development goods. And yet chemicals have an important part to play in all economic development even if they usually represent production expenses rather than investment costs.

Not least important are the pharmaceuticals. The prices charged for some of the drugs are prohibitive to the common people in underdeveloped countries because of the cartelized organization of the world's chemical industry. A greater supply of pharmaceuticals at cheaper prices would contribute greatly to increasing the welfare and the productive efficiency of the population of backward areas. As we have no bright prospects in our general plans for international control of cartels, the World Health Organization might find it very rewarding to look a little closer into the special situation created by the monopolistic organization of the pharmaceutical industry.

The problem of the priority to be given to health work in the general development plans was touched upon in the last chapter. In this connection I would like only to express the opinion that for the time being the effective way open to the underdeveloped countries of dealing with monopolistic practices in the sale of pharmaceuticals would be to start up production of these goods themselves. In some important fields, at least, it should not be impossible for a number of underdeveloped countries, if they cooperated, to go much further in producing the necessary pharmaceuticals both effectively and economically; to keep down the costs they would have to concentrate on a few specialities, carefully selected from the point of view of their health needs, and go in for real mass production to serve the mass consumption they need. It would be difficult to withhold the technical know-how from such enterprises for public welfare in the underprivileged countries; there *does* exist a world opinion, if it is not left sleeping. Some of the world's great scientists might be willing to make their services available. The investment costs would be high, but the investments would have a great degree of security as the governments could plan and guarantee the demand.

A beginning has actually been made—with the active cooperation of the United Nations Technical Assistance—by the construction of factories for the production of DDT in Ceylon, India, and Pakistan and by the projected creation of a penicillin factory in India, designed to serve the Southeast Asian region. Several other projects in underdeveloped countries are under way; but there is still a long way to go before underdeveloped countries more generally acquire, for their defence, a reasonable control in this small but important industrial field.

COMPETITION AND COOPERATION

Some general conclusions of our analysis so far, which has mainly been confined to the problems of export policy of underdeveloped countries, may be worth emphasizing.

Underdeveloped countries have too little bargaining power to hope ever to gain much by resorting to monopolistic practices. Their great hope of pushing ahead is in competition. If ever the world political climate again improves sufficiently for the issue of an international control over industrial cartels to be fruitfully discussed, the underdeveloped countries should belong among its strongest proponents.

At home they must exert themselves to loosen up rigidities and gradually build up a system of production that adjusts as rapidly and completely as possible to the opportunities of the market. Abroad they have to attempt to break their way into new trading fields, including those of certain manufactured goods, by being able to sell at competitive prices. Their only way of gaining the upper hand over foreign monopolistic practices in their import markets is, first, to liquidate the important elements of factual monopoly which are based on their traditionally very narrow business contracts and, second, to be prepared to substitute competitive home production for the import of foreign products when the foreign products are kept at excessively high prices.

I have in the preceding sections touched upon the various possibilities that exist in the field of trade for the underdeveloped countries to join forces in order to reach these policy goals. Those possibilities should not be overestimated; everything is difficult for the underdeveloped countries, not least their mutual cooperation. But neither should they be underestimated. Since so little can be expected for the time being from more general international cooperation within the United Nations and elsewhere, it is even more important that, at least regionally, the underdeveloped countries avail themselves of the opportunities for increasing their strength by united action.

For centuries these nations have been isolated most unnaturally from each other, and all their relations—political, cultural and economic—have usually been restricted to individual intercourse with the advanced nations or with one metropolitan power. This situation, which is reflected in the way business is done, tends to prevail even after the colonial bonds have been thrown off by the formerly dependent nations and after all of them have conceived the vision of economic development.

This isolation is unnatural and frustrates their opportunities, like all the other rigidities which are the mark of their underdeveloped status. Most definitely they need to come closer to their own peers in the region and in the world at large, to integrate themselves more fully with other nations whose conditions most closely resemble their own and who have the same aspirations. From one point of view, the otherwise seemingly pious resolutions in the organs of the United Nations may play an important role in bringing together governments who share the same interests and ambitions.

They will need to cooperate in order to win countervailing power, as the poor classes had to do in the new highly integrated, advanced, and democratic countries. Individuals do occasionally, but nations, like social classes, almost never give up existing privileges, except under pressure. As I have repeatedly stressed, the underdeveloped countries can cooperate among themselves with a clear conscience, as the rise in their bargaining strength can only be in the interest of world democracy. If by keeping together they could strengthen their bargaining power, this would, as a matter of fact, also make their cooperation with the advanced countries more possible and more fruitful. For, without any doubt, the greatest difficulty for that cooperation is the present inequality in economic strength which makes real partnership difficult or impossible.

But so deep and traditional is the isolation of the underdeveloped countries from each other and so many other impediments stand in the way—including the internal social and economic disparities within each one of these countries—that for a long time to come their concerted efforts will be weak or entirely futile. In the commercial field they will mostly operate entirely alone, on a national basis.

COMMERCIAL POLICIES AND ECONOMIC DEVELOPMENT

MAIN CRITERIA FOR IMPORT POLICY

Most underdeveloped countries have abnormally high foreign trade ratios though, as I observed, this is more a consequence of low productivity and low national incomes than of a really high level of foreign trade. Their economic development goal is to raise the levels of productivity and national incomes, not necessarily the level of foreign trade.

Nurkse puts the argument for a higher degree of self-sufficiency in the following terms:

To push exports of primary commodities in the face of an inelastic and more or less stationary demand would not be a promising line of long-run development. If it is plausible to assume a generally less than unitary price elasticity of demand for crude foodstuffs and materials, it seems reasonable also to conclude that, under the conditions indicated, economic growth in under-developed countries must largely take the form of increased production for domestic markets. . . . Under these conditions, if there is to be any development at all, it must concentrate at least initially on production for local requirements; and so long as this development increases the level of productivity and hence of real purchasing power, it will tend in the long run to help rather than hinder the growth of international trade.[54]

We have seen that, in addition, the underdeveloped countries have to put up with a great instability of export prices that tends to put their economies under a constant strain. This must also diminish their interest in increasing their exports and strengthen their desire for greater self-sufficiency. The same thoughts are basic to the important studies of Prebisch and his collaborators in the Secretariat of the Economic Commission for Latin America.

On the other hand these countries are all in dire need of importing capital goods on a large scale for their economic development; in the main, these imports must be paid for by their exports. Neither is this point missed by Nurkse and Prebisch.

The two propositions are not irreconcilable, though practical policy is always in the nature of a compromise, even when it is rational. The general terms of the compromise are the following:

1. The important aim is, as I have shown, not so much the negative one of reducing nonprofitable exports but the positive one of seeking out new lines of exports of dynamic commodities with high income and demand elasticities and rising demand trends. Exports will thereby be spread over a wider range of goods, thus spreading risks, strengthening the country's bargaining power, and making the whole economy less rigid and more easily able to shift resources according to the exogenous economic changes. The unstabilizing effects of the price fluctuations should, furthermore, be met by monetary and fiscal methods. Few underdeveloped countries will be in a strong enough financial position to afford making a shrinkage of the less advantageous exports a first aim of policy; but such results will follow as an effect of competition if the positive export-promotion policies in regard to the more useful export goods are successful. Meanwhile, the total export volume will be kept up in order to procure the maximum imports of capital goods for development.

2. The development of domestic industry should be pushed in order to substitute domestic for import goods and eventually to furnish new exports; both effects will again provide increased resources for imports

of capital goods. More generally the increase of industry represents an important element of national economic development towards higher levels of productivity and income.

So far, I have discussed only the first point, which concerns mainly the export policy. I now turn to the second point, the import policy. I assume, on the basis of my previous argument, that exports are held at a high level.

Nevertheless, in order to push its development, an underdeveloped country will normally be bound to restrict imports of consumption goods in order to devote as much as possible of its available foreign exchange to buying capital goods. To maintain and eventually to raise the standard of living among the people, the import of some consumption goods will have to take precedence over the import of others and, in particular, the import of luxury goods will have to be restricted. More generally, however, it will seek to produce at home and substitute for imports everything it can produce at costs that are not too much higher than the prices of corresponding import goods.

These are in the very broadest terms the main criteria for the import policy of most underdeveloped countries that want to speed up their economic development—and, incidentally, to a large extent also of developed countries bent upon developing still further and doing it more quickly than the capital resources available at home and from abroad would permit. To suggest that an underdeveloped country should abstain from establishing priorities in the budgeting of scarce resources of foreign exchange would be tantamount to denying it the use of one of the most important means of planning for national development.

I wish to stress that I am assuming a policy of economic expansion. Capital goods are preferred to consumption goods in the imports, not because they are better in any intrinsic sense, but because they are more urgently needed for the economic development the country is bent on accomplishing.

My argument for protection does not, therefore, apply to the score or more of underdeveloped countries whose governments for the time being seem to be satisfied with the existing relative stagnation or, anyhow, have not yet got down seriously to the task of starting on their economic development. They usually have plenty of import restrictions which, however, cannot be justified by the reasons accounted for below. Some of them succeed in preserving monetary equilibrium. This is, however, an easier task; some do not, in spite of the relative absence of the pressure of economic development. Neither does my argument apply to some of the oil-producing underdeveloped countries which are now getting, as their share in the oil profits, almost more foreign exchange than they can make good use of.

Some of the arguments have a lesser bearing for a country like India which is exceptional in that its foreign trade ratio is low.

CREATING THE DOMESTIC CAPITAL FOR DEVELOPMENT

A policy of economic development—as compared with an earlier stage of economic stagnation—creates a whole series of new and additional demands on the foreign exchange resources. The need for the imported capital goods is only one of them. By far the larger part of the total costs for the new real capital to be created is, however, expenditure in payment of domestic labor and various materials and manufactures provided at home; later, when the capital is incorporated in the national economy, usually a still larger part or often practically the whole of the operating costs are payments to domestic factors of production. Indeed, the justification for economic development is from one point of view precisely that it draws surplus or uneconomically employed labor and other resources into productive employment. This cannot be done without creating at the same time new incomes and causing old incomes to rise, with the consequence that consumption demands will also rise. Part of the increase in demand falls upon imported consumption goods.

Under these circumstances it should, perhaps, first be said that there must be something wrong with an underdeveloped country that does not have foreign exchange difficulties. But it must also be stressed that the problem cannot be solved simply by protective methods, applied with the purpose of holding down imports other than those necessary for feeding the development process. The most important contribution of Nurkse in his recent book on economic development and capital formation is his lucid and convincing demonstration that the problem of creating the necessary domestic savings for economic development is not solved by preventing foreign imports from coming into the country.[55] It can only be solved by creating a large enough difference between domestic production and consumption.

If the difference—savings—is not created, or if it is not large enough to support the investments, pushing ahead with economic development will give rise to internal inflation. By itself, the raising of protective barriers and, more fundamentally, the very need to raise them, as there is not enough foreign exchange to pay for the increased demands for imports, accelerates rather than hampers the internal inflationary process.

A certain mild inflationary climate may be conducive to greater economic efficiency—by loosening up all sorts of rigidities, speeding up various processes, raising the effective utilization of plants and labor, etc.; by its effect on income distribution inflation also creates some forced savings.[56] But if the inflationary movement is permitted to gather speed, if it becomes cumulative and enters into expectations, it tends instead to lower the level of voluntary savings so much that the rate of total increase in savings declines and may become negative. At the same time inflation falsifies and distorts all the economic norms in the community, including those determining the direction of investments. It then also becomes extremely difficult to stop without causing a crisis.

Moreover, as Professor V. K. R. V. Rao has shown, "the existence of disguised unemployment, household enterprise, production for self-consumption, dominance of agriculture, and deficiency of capital equipment and of technical knowledge—all characteristics of an under-developed economy—create conditions analogous to those of full employment. . . ."[57] The point where inflation becomes cumulative is much nearer. "The case for investment supported by deficit-financing for the purpose of inducing a given increase in output is . . . much weaker in an under-developed economy as compared to that in a developed economy."[58]

There are two ways of creating the necessary equilibrium between investments and savings—other than by watering down the investments—and they have to be applied simultaneously: one is to increase as much and as rapidly as possible national production, particularly along lines that provide an increased supply of consumption goods to meet the increased demand;[59] the other is to apply pressure on private incomes and demand in order to increase savings.

I have already noted, in the previous chapter, the necessity for a vigorous campaign to raise productivity in agriculture and achieve thereby, not only higher food standards among the agricultural population to meet the rise of per capita demand, following the effects on incomes in agriculture of the exodus of labor and the repercussions there of the higher earnings of those who leave; but also a substantial increase in food supply to the industrial population, which is growing and receiving gradually rising wages. A one-sided industrialization policy that neglects to provide for a simultaneous—or, if possible, earlier—development of agriculture is almost doomed to frustration by inflation.

For the same reason an underdeveloped country—which is assumed to be unwilling to place its consumers under the very harsh discipline of the Soviet system for economic development—will direct a major part of its investments to building up manufacturing industries for producing consumers' goods and will strive to get these new or enlarged industries to deliver the additional consumption goods to the domestic market as rapidly as possible.

This undoubtedly often implies a compromise with the long-term development interest. What such a country particularly needs in order to make headway in economic development are investments that take a long time to mature in the form of an increased supply of consumption goods: all sorts of overhead capital, like transport facilities, power plants, and other means of raising the level of external economies and often some heavy industries. The investment plans have, therefore, to be most carefully weighed. In a sense, investments in rapidly maturing consumption industries are much less of an exertion; they can be raised to much larger volumes without intruding more on the savings balance than a much smaller volume of the other type of investments.

At the same time as efforts are made to increase production of consumption goods, monetary and fiscal means will have to be applied in order to hold down private incomes and to increase savings. The larger the relative share of investments that do not immediately increase the supply of consumption goods, the harder have the income- and demand-repressing policies to be fashioned.

A PRECARIOUS BALANCING

Very much depends on the sequence of events. If there is a reasonable initial balance between total supply and demand, the government may take the risk of allowing investments to run ahead of savings and cause a certain amount of inflation to create the necessary short-term equilibrium between demand and supply—provided that it has things firmly in hand and can prevent the process from becoming cumulative. However, this in its turnr assumes, first, that it pursues energetic policies to raise productivity in agriculture and that conditions there are such that a rapid rise in the supply of agricultural products can be expected; and, second, that its industrial development plans are so fashioned that they will result within a short space of time in rising supplies of manufactured consumer goods for the domestic market.

Generally speaking, the fact that playing with inflation is an invitation to a Wicksellian cumulative process stresses the crucial importance of the time factor. The whole operation is, indeed, an extremely delicate adventure and particularly difficult in an underdeveloped country where supply elasticities are low. It implies the simultaneous application of, on the one hand, strong expansionist measures in the form of investment—and every underdeveloped country bent on development will want to expand in this way as far and as fast as it dares—and of, on the other hand, balancing repressive measures of keeping down incomes and demands, in the form of taxation and other means.

The first part of the development prescription would not seem to meet great difficulties per se. To spend money is always easy. If, however, the government wants to make a large expansion in investments without raising impossible demands on the effectiveness of the repressive measures, referred to in the second part of the prescription, the investments will have to be most carefully selected with a view to obtaining quick results in increased domestic supplies, though with due regard to the no less vital, long-term need to increase overhead capital and improve external economies. This is, indeed, a tall order; it needs intensive expert planning of the highest caliber.

It is, however, the second part of the prescription that in a poor country with low levels of consumption raises the most serious difficulties, the more so as again the lack of political stability and administrative efficiency is in most cases a bottleneck. The low degree of supply elasticities in the economy of underdeveloped countries decreases the limits for productive deficit spending and increases the necessity of measures to keep down income and consumption to match the investments. "The old-fashioned prescription of 'work harder and save more' still seems to hold good as the medicine for economic progress, at any rate as far as the under-developed countries are concerned"—I am again citing Rao.[60]

It is, indeed, appropriate that we show some indulgence towards the many governments of underdeveloped countries that succumb under the pressure and permit inflation. If this accomplishes the forced savings that are necessary to close the gap—and this may be possible, at least for a time, though at the cost of serious social damage and a distortion of the economy, including the kind of investments undertaken—it can be argued that, under the circumstances, this was the only means of preventing a dangerous slowing down of the economic development process. But the point is very soon reached—earlier in underdeveloped countries than in industrially advanced ones—where this type of development policy is self-defeating, and many examples could be cited.

THE FOREIGN EXCHANGE FRONT

Taking these risks is more prudent if the crucial foreign exchange position is so strong that it can last while things work themselves out in agriculture and the new consumers' goods industries. It is in this connection that foreign capital influx increases the "international space for national expansion." An improvement of the terms of trade, if it should occur, has the same effect.

By themselves, however, neither of these fortunate events—even to the extent that they really happen—can substitute for domestic capital formation in an underdeveloped country. "Domestic action is essential for the effective use of external contributions as well as for the tapping of potential domestic sources. There is no solution of the problem without steady and strenuous efforts on the domestic front. In a sense, therefore, it all boils down to this: capital is made at home."[61]

What an easing of the foreign exchange balance does, is to increase the international space within which the government of an underdeveloped country can operate without being compelled radically to raise import barriers or to accept devaluation. Both new barriers against imports and devaluation are apt to increase internal inflationary pressure; devaluation might in addition tend to worsen the terms of trade and thus shrink the international space available. An inflow of foreign capital can mitigate internal inflation by making it less necessary to restrict consumption.

The dangers on the foreign exchange front provide a reason for directing investments in industry towards the production of commodities that are substitutes for imports, and are also an extra inducement for planning the investments so as to give quick results in increased supplies. From the exchange point of view an underdeveloped country has an interest in pushing exports and even directing a considerable part of the new investments into export production, particularly if this will give quick results in earning more foreign exchange. In any well-balanced development plan the expansion of export production along lines where new supply is likely to meet high income and demand elasticities and rising demand trends must be given its place alongside the building up of import-competing industries by protection. This interest is so important that, even with a large surplus of labor, an underdeveloped country might rightly assign considerable priority to capital-intensive industries for export— such as mining and mineral refining—at the same time as it generally seeks to develop industries that are more labor-intensive.

Underdeveloped countries that have an import of foodstuffs, which they can decrease, or an export which they can increase, have also, of course, in the development of higher productivity in agriculture, an opportunity to increase the international space for their industrial development. Again, this time from the foreign exchange angle, agriculture stands out as having a strategic role in economic development.

From the point of view of foreign exchange—as well as from that of internal inflation—investments in overhead capital and external economies represent a sacrifice that has to be taken in the long-term development interest. With that exception, therefore, an underdeveloped country that is not applying the Soviet system will not generally be interested in attempting at an early stage to produce complicated machinery or other products that require initially the large-scale establishment of an integrated structure of many branches of industry. Foreign exchange considerations are bound to give primary importance to reaching as directly as possible an increased supply of export- and import-competing commodities; the interest in preventing internal inflation motivates primarily investments in agriculture and consumer goods industries.

There are, however, borderline cases of capital goods industries that can materially aid in building up industries to provide, or save, foreign exchange and that are needed to raise productivity in agriculture or consumer goods industries. If development within an underdeveloped country thus creates a sizeable and calculable demand for special kinds of machinery—say, pumps for irrigation schemes—that in the normal course of events would imply a considerable increase in import needs, and if their production can be undertaken without a wide and complicated industrial basis, such a country might very well have good reasons to embark upon producing these engines, if necessary behind a protective wall of import restrictions. The same is generally true of the production of agricultural tools.

Then there is the big field of industrial raw materials, such as coal, cement, and pulp. Industrial development will rapidly increase the domestic demand for these commodities, several of which have high freight costs when imported. If natural resources permit, an obvious element of the industrial development plan will be to begin producing them for the domestic market and the calculated future market, in spite of the fact that they are relatively capital-intensive.

Special Reasons for Protection in Underdeveloped Countries

My argument so far has led to the conclusion that *import restrictions in underdeveloped countries are primarily necessitated by the effects on the foreign exchange balance of the increased demand for imported goods. This, in turn, is the direct or indirect result of the increased investments implied in an economic development policy.* The pressure to apply import restrictions can be minimized by directing as far as possible the development process towards increasing exports and substituting for imports and, in the fortunate case, by capital inflow or improved terms of trade. I believe that this way of looking at the problem is realistic and gets down to the fundamentals.

Quite apart from any interest in protection of domestic production, even a rationally conceived and executed development policy will need to apply import restrictions—complemented by strong monetary and fiscal measures to minimize a rise in domestic incomes and consumption, but intent upon exploiting to the limit the existing possibilities of economic development. Some rise in incomes and consumption demands is inescapable and some is needed—for instance, in order to induce workers to move to the growing centers of employment. And the rise in imports of capital goods is by itself an additional and desired demand on the exchange reserves. It is clear *a fortiori* that a less firm hand on the monetary and fiscal levers will lead to import restrictions, but that is not the real point.

The general character of these import restrictions—and I include under this term customs duties as well as exchange and other quantitative restrictions—is also determined by definite exchange considerations. They will have to give free entrance to imports of capital goods but clamp down on imports of consumption goods and, in particular, of luxury goods. None of this implies protectionist motives. If the advanced countries want to relieve the underdeveloped countries of this necessity of applying import restrictions—without, of course, putting a brake on their economic development—it can be done. The means of doing it are also clear: lifting any barriers they have erected against imports from underdeveloped countries and inducing a capital flow to those countries.

In addition, however, to this immediate reason for applying import restrictions, in order to preserve the foreign exchange balance, the underdeveloped countries have quite a number of other sound reasons, based on their peculiar situation, for using these restrictions for protective purposes. Without going into details I shall briefly discuss what these special and additional protective interests of underdeveloped countries are.

I have already stressed that one of the difficulties of industrial development in underdeveloped countries, and one of the great hindrances to giving real momentum to a development policy, is that internal demand must be built up simultaneously with supply. The unlikelihood or, anyhow, the exasperating slowness of any self-engendered process of "natural growth" offers a main explanation why sustained stagnation becomes a sort of natural equilibrium and why policy interventions are called for. Indeed, the entire idea of a policy of economic development is to break away from this low-level equilibrium.

Now, import restrictions afford a means of by-passing altogether this process of "natural growth" and creating at once the necessary demand for a particular domestic industry. They create a sizeable internal demand for a specific commodity, without the necessity of waiting for the slow and difficult growth of the entire economy. This particular means of creating the demand basis for a new industry has the further advantage that it is relatively simple to operate and can be adjusted from time to time to the actual expansion of domestic production.

On this point it should be noted, however, that the export market affords a similarly available outlet for increased production which neither assumes waiting for the "natural growth" of the entire domestic economy, nor necessitates the creation of demand by import destrictions. And also from the foreign exchange angle it does the job equally well.

The second special reason for protection is the important fact that an underdeveloped country is characterized by the absence of an industrial basis which implies a great difficulty in economic development. For this very reason, however, the external economies to be gained from an individual investment—the advantage accruing to other and mostly future industrial enterprises—is relatively large. This advantage, which does not appear in the business calculation for the investment, is also a rational motive for subsidizing industries, including the export as well as the import-competing industries. The national calculus should be a dynamic one, taking into account not only the new external economies in the narrow sense but also the improvement of the productivity of labor (effected by higher consumption levels and by the greater number of workers receiving training in mechanical work) and, indeed, the regional change of the entire climate for enterprise which may follow the start of a new industry.

Third, an underdeveloped country nearly always has a large and permanent labor surplus, which makes it economically advantageous to draw labor into production, even when in terms of international market prices the products can be bought cheaper abroad. From a national point of view the differences between what the workers actually produce—measured in terms of the prices of the excluded imports—and the decrease in total production caused by their withdrawal from their previous unemployed or underemployed status (which might be zero or even negative) is a clear gain, though part of the gain will be a higher level of consumption of the workers drawn into employment.

The existence of surplus labor in the export industries as well as in the import-competing industries will motivate an extension of investment and production beyond the limit where wage costs are fully met by the export proceeds. This becomes important in seeking to develop new export lines in directions where demand elasticities are high and the demand trend rising.

Fourth, the structure of internal costs and prices in an underdeveloped country tends to be lopsided as between industry and agriculture in a way that hampers industrialization, if industry is not protected and encouraged by fully compensating import restrictions and export subsidies or by a system of multiple exchange rates having that effect. Though there is a lack of comprehensive and detailed statistics on wages and remunerations, the generalization holds true that a very wide gap between real earnings in industry and agriculture is a distinctive mark of an underdeveloped country. Such a gap existed in all advanced countries in much later stages of development and served as a force in causing labor to move from rural to urban districts and from agricultural to industrial pursuits; as a matter of fact, the disappearance of this gap has only occurred in a few countries as they have gradually reached a very high level of development and a very low proportion of the labor force engaged in agriculture. In underdeveloped countries this gap tends to be exceedingly wide.

A basic factor underlying this phenomenon is, of course, the existence in all underdeveloped countries of surplus labor in agriculture. This does not explain, however, why real wages in industry tend to be so much higher. Systematic empirical labor market studies are lacking and the following remarks are conjectural. There are probably a large number of elements of inertia in underdeveloped countries hampering the readiness to move from agriculture to industry and thus preserving an artificial difference between the level of effective labor supply in agriculture and industry. Not only skilled but also unskilled labor with that minimum of sophistication that render workers useful at all in industry remains relatively scarce. Industrial workers have also an opportunity which is almost totally lacking in subsistence farming to organize and join in concerted action in order to defend and improve their earnings. Moreover, labor legislature and social security policies become naturally focused on the welfare of the industrial workers.

But quite apart from its explanation, this gap in real wages and, consequently, labor costs between industry and agriculture, affords a rational reason for industrial protection. The Secretariat of the United Nations Economic Commission for Europe has in several of its publications touched upon the problem and has in one of them stated it as follows:

> The case for industrial protection in the relatively retarded countries of Southern Europe goes beyond the traditional "infant industry" argument. It has rather to do with the fundamental lack of balance between industry and agriculture in those countries. The existence of vast surpluses of manpower in agriculture creates a situation where money costs of production in industry are higher in relation to agricultural money costs than is warranted by comparative real costs in the two branches of the economy. Under such conditions, the exchange rate at which the foreign account tends to be in balance would be one at which industrial costs tend to be systematically noncompetitive with foreign costs, and *vice versa* for agriculture.[62]

Both the two last mentioned special reasons for protection refer to the allocation of labor. In both cases the argument really is that the social costs for labor are lower than the money wages. This does not apply to capital, however. In an underdeveloped country the exact opposite is true, most of the time. Nationally, therefore, substitution of capital for labor should not be driven to the point indicated by the money wages or —which amounts to the same thing—in calculations interest should be charged at a rate higher than the market. Otherwise investments in industry would be excessive and wasteful in a social sense because they produce a smaller return on capital than is possible elsewhere. This important point can also be taken care of by a systematic effort to subsidize rapid and simultaneous improvements in agriculture.

This all adds up to the conclusion that "the maximizing of private profit provides poor guidance for investment particularly in less-developed countries."[63] It does not imply, however, that the price mechanism could not be used for reaching the adjustments, but that the mechanism has first to be conditioned by deliberate policy interferences.

The explanation why various lines of investment and production are not taken up in an underdeveloped country is, of course, that they are not profitable. The reason why labor is unemployed or underemployed is that it cannot compete on the market. In fact, the essence of the situation of an underdeveloped and stagnating economy is that the market forces do not themselves engender development. Therefore, interferences in the price system are called for in order to make investment and production along selected lines profitable. If successful, those interferences will release a cumulative process with a momentum to continued development.

In theory, these incentives applied in order to start and sustain the development process can be given many forms; they can, for instance, be direct subsidies out of the state treasury. From many points of view direct subsidies represent the cleanest solution; no advanced country, however, has ever followed this prescription in regard to the major part of its interferences in the price mechanism. An underdeveloped country would have more initial inhibitions against doing it because of its greater difficulties in raising taxes to pay for the subsidies. Even more important, however, is the fact that, as I have shown above, an underdeveloped country bent upon development will, in order to preserve its foreign exchange balance—and quite apart from any motives of industrial protection—be compelled to take measures to restrict imports and push exports. These measures, which actually all must imply protection and subsidy, are already within the system for exchange reasons; as motivated by these reasons they are regularly big enough to take care also of the protective interests.

APPLYING THE TRADE CONTROLS

INCREASED SELF-SUFFICIENCY

The four special reasons for industrial protection in underdeveloped countries—the difficulties of finding demand to match new supply, the existence of surplus labor, the large rewards of individual investments in creating external economies, and the lopsided internal price structure disfavoring industry—amount only to a spelling out in more specific terms of the characterization I gave in the introduction to this chapter of their economies as grossly unbalanced.

In spite of the high priority that I am assuming will be given to

export production, it is natural that in all underdeveloped countries industrialization should take the path of attempting to reach increased self-
sufficiency in an increasing number of production lines. This natural
tendency becomes strengthened as a consequence of the fact that—for
not very rational reasons—export subsidies are apt to meet more dislike
abroad than import restrictions. Even if the total exports should be kept
up and increased, the foreign trade ratio will fall while the total national
product will rise. To a large extent this will, indeed, be a mark of their
success.

This drive for self-sufficiency in underdeveloped countries should be
judged from this broader point of view. It is basically only an approach
to a more balanced situation in their international trade and internal
economies and should to that extent not hurt the feelings even of the
ardent free-trader if he has thought through the dynamics of the theory
of comparative costs. As an objective for economic policy in underdeveloped countries, self-sufficiency has, indeed, a long way to go before it
can rightly be put in the same category as the autarkic tendencies that
have dominated for many decades the commercial policies of the industrially advanced countries—particularly the bigger ones—that I
analyzed in Chapter IV.

It should not be concealed that balancing the interventions in trade is
a difficult problem but, if my analysis above is correct, it is a problem that
cannot be evaded except by relinquishing the ambition for economic
development. Interferences there have to be for exchange reasons alone;
it is merely a question of where and how to apply them. They can most
certainly be applied well or badly from the point of view of long-run
development, as well as from the point of view of the immediate welfare
interests of the population. Capital is exceedingly scarce in underdeveloped countries and it has to be carefully considered where the investments should be made. In the cases, or to the extent, import restrictions are imposed without having a protective purpose but in order to
save foreign exchange by curtailing consumption, they have to be imple-
mented by, and coordinated with, internal taxes and controls of domestic
production and consumption.

These problems of economic planning and of policy implementation are
partly additional to the difficulties mentioned above of preserving internal
and external monetary balance in spite of a vigorous development policy.
A most delicate system of considerations is assumed: what particular industries should be protected and to what extent; how to prevent demand
from spilling over from the foreign goods that are kept out to alternative
domestic products—for example, luxury products; and, more generally,
how to prevent the diversion of resources from the lines they should
follow according to the development plan. The element of surplus labor,

which is a valid reason for subsidy, has to be looked into carefully; there may be alternative uses where the relative productivity is different. Likewise, the effects on external economies must be carefully estimated and compared.

It is, indeed, quite possible for a not very stable and efficient government and administration to mismanage its foreign trade policy, as it may other economic policies, and many warning examples could be cited. But the point often missed in the literature on these dangers, which usually ends up by piously warning the underdeveloped countries against interfering in foreign trade, is that this warning cannot possibly be heeded—the interferences are there, and are a necessary result of embarking upon a development policy. The real and practical problem is only how they should most effectively be planned and most wisely carried out.

TARIFFS AND QUANTITATIVE RESTRICTIONS

From a purely technical point of view, import restrictions of one type or another seem to offer a simple way of creating the demand basis for a new industry. The consequent increase in the internal price of the products provides the necessary subsidy in an uncomplicated way which involves neither direct taxation nor the actual disbursement of funds. Such restrictions require a minimum of direct interference with the price mechanism and this is, of course, the explanation of their great popularity as a means of economic planning in all countries at all times. It should be a particularly important advantage in an underdeveloped country, as one of its many weaknesses is in the field of administration.

The suggestion has sometimes been made of achieving, at least in part, the broad policy goals of import savings and industrial protection by introducing a flat-rate ad valorem duty, applied uniformly to all manufactured products that could reasonably be expected to be produced in the country;[64] the purpose could equally well be served by a higher exchange rate to be applied when paying imports of industrial goods. This would throw to the maximum extent the responsibility for the adjustments of the economy onto the price mechanism, and it would tend to preserve in an automatic fashion the country's share in the general interest of international specialization of production.

Such a policy would quite particularly fit the fourth special reason for protection—the lopsided cost and price structure in underdeveloped countries as between industry and agriculture—but would in a general way accommodate the others too. It would also ease the exchange situation by applying an indirect tax on a large number of import goods; it would not worsen its terms of trade as a devaluation often would. Its purpose would be to offset to some extent the general handicap of underdevelopment and provide a general momentum to industrialization, while removing the responsibility for discriminating between different industries from the government.

It could, of course, be supplemented by special levies on luxury imports—and corresponding internal taxes on home produce—not only in order to carry out a desired redistribution of real incomes and discriminate against certain consumption, but also in order to make the system sufficiently effective in bringing down imports.

If import restrictions are necessary and protection desirable, this would perhaps be the sophisticated free-trader's dream of how to accomplish it. The most effective and least expensive way of doing it would probably be by a system of multiple exchange rates.

I do not believe, however, that any underdeveloped country would be prepared to confine its entire import policy to such a simple device. Even considering only the long-term interests—and forgetting for the moment the variety of short-term interferences necessitated by its widely fluctuating export proceeds—no underdeveloped country would leave so much of its development policy to the free play of market forces; and we should note that no developed country has ever done it. An underdeveloped country must be the less willing to do it, as one of the common weaknesses of these countries is the absence of an enterprising business class that can be expected to behave as economic theory assumes. The government of such a country will feel that they must themselves judge how the development process shall be directed and make all the major decisions and take the initiatives. They are usually well aware of the shortcomings of their administrations, but consider their business groups even weaker.

This being admitted, I am nevertheless of the opinion that underdeveloped countries have reasons to consider carefully whether they should not have a simple, flat-rate discrimination in favor of manufactured products as a basis for their commercial policies.

The next best choice from a free-trader's point of view would be regular tariffs, fixed at different levels but embodied in semipermanent legislation. They would seem superior to quantitative controls of various types, which can be changed by administrative ruling and are subject to constant pressures from interested parties at home and abroad.

The greater stability of tariffs would also normally increase the stimulating effects on the entrepreneur who contemplated entering a protected industry. This would have special importance with respect to foreign enterprises, if the country wishes to stimulate direct foreign investment behind its protective walls. For that matter, even the competing foreign exporter, however much he dislikes protection, would normally prefer the stability that tariffs provide to the uncertainty of quantitative restrictions. Moreover, quantitative controls have the defect that, if the import licenses are not auctioned on a free market, they create unearned windfall profits for importers—or for those who in the first place acquire import licenses—whereas by tariffs these profits would be expropriated at the source. This must be considered a big advantage in favor of tariffs, particularly in underdeveloped countries, where taxation of profits is always an uncertain process.

These are very solid reasons for attempting to carry out the import restrictions by means of tariffs; a system of multiple exchange rates, if it were given the same stability, would have similar advantages. If the international trade were more stable, these reasons would count even more. However, with the very wide fluctuations of export earnings to which underdeveloped countries are prey, and given the added dynamic influences of the development process itself, the effects of which on the exchange balance will not always be smooth, it must be assumed that to a considerable extent the underdeveloped countries will have to rely upon direct trade and payments controls as quite regular means of commercial policy.

Managing such quantitative controls, the rules for which easily grow into a complex tangle without really diminishing the intrinsic arbitrariness of the entire operation, has not been such a success in advanced countries; it has everywhere to some extent, and sometimes to a great extent, destroyed business morale. In many underdeveloped countries, particularly where a firmly coordinated economic policy has not been laid down as a general basis and where the administration has been inapt and partly corrupt, the damaging effects have been serious.

The system tends easily to create cancerous tumors of partiality and corruption in the very center of the administration, where the sickness is continuously nurtured by the favors distributed and the grafts realized and from which it tends to spread out to every limb of society. Industrialists and businessmen are tempted to go in for shady deals instead of steady, regular business. Individuals who might have performed useful tasks in the economic development of their country become idle hangers-on, watching for loopholes in the decrees and dishonesty in their implementation. This is all the more dangerous as a general weakness in underdeveloped countries, inherited from a long history of stagnation, is that their business classes are too much inclined to look for easy profits in place of sustained enterprise.

I believe that this is a very important problem in the underdeveloped countries. It can easily influence the economic, social, and political climate and destroy the psychological foundation for development planning and its efficient and economic execution. It gives a quite unnecessary advantage to the competing Soviet system of economic development, which at least stamps out petty graft and corruption. The advanced countries—which often have not cleaned out their own houses—do the underdeveloped countries a disservice by not reacting more strongly against some of their business firms' connivance with these weaknesses.

Though I have come to the conclusion that underdeveloped countries will be compelled to rely upon quantitative controls as a regular means of restricting imports, I am bound nevertheless to recognize the serious difficulties they create for economic development. I therefore draw the further conclusion that, even at the sacrifice of a degree of much-needed flexibility, import restrictions should be carried out to the greatest possible extent by the regular means of tariffs or multiple exchange rates, which are easier than *ad hoc* administrative rules to protect from the worst type of mismanagement. The more successful a government is in maintaining and enforcing monetary stability, the larger the part that can be played by tariffs or a stable system of exchange rates.

For the rest, serious study and relentless efforts should be devoted to simplifying and rationalizing the direct controls and to getting them administered with scrupulous honesty. As part of the national economic planning, a budget for the disposal of foreign exchange should be worked out, and the handling of this budget should be as important a matter as the handling of the fiscal budget. The entire matter should be dealt with as a most crucial object of statesmanship—indeed, as a matter of political survival.

Often a foreign partner is involved in the "grey deals"; therefore much could be accomplished by international cooperation. This is, indeed, one field where the advanced countries, by participating in such cooperation and by demonstrating firmness even in regard to events that only just touch the limits of their own jurisdiction, could render the under-developed countries an important service at no real sacrifice.

Bilateralism

A note incidental to the main line of the argument should be added, concerning the distinct possibility of a certain trend towards bilateralism in underdeveloped countries' trade relations with the industrially advanced countries.

Owing to the acute necessity of making the most discriminatory use of its foreign exchange, an underdeveloped country is bound to seize eagerly every available opportunity of receiving more foreign credits. One possibility occurs in connection with buying equipment from abroad.

American business has conquered markets in Latin America and elsewhere partly because of its greater ability to grant credits in connection with its exports; practically all United States government credits are tied to exports. In Chapter VIII it was pointed out that Japan and Western Germany in particular have recently carried out similar export drives, and reasons were given why European countries more generally should be prepared in their own interest to improve their facilities for giving credits in connection with actual export purchases. It was also stressed that this could result in a fairly considerable increase of credits available to the underdeveloped countries.

Such credits—even if small compared to the development needs and even if not on a long-term basis—undoubtedly influence the import situation of these countries and must generally encourage them to conduct their trading relations along bilateral channels. Import deals, partly financed by tied credits, often already are—and may increasingly become—a not inconsiderable portion of the underdeveloped countries' total imports of capital goods.

Sometimes they form part of wider agreements on export deliveries by these countries. As failure to reach multilateral commodity agreements becomes more or less final, the desire for price stabilization might also gradually induce the underdeveloped countries to seek long-term bilateral export agreements. There is a distinct possibility of relating such export agreements to agreements on imports of industrial equipment, partly financed by tied credits, and this line of policy is being opened up by Japan in relation to some of the underdeveloped countries in Asia, at least in limited fields.

West-European countries have a general interest in increasing their trade with underdeveloped countries outside the dollar sphere and might increasingly become interested in similar bilateral agreements over a number of years, linking equipment exports, partly financed by credits, with imports. Here the interests of the primary producers seem to run parallel with those of the manufacturers dependent on imports of primary products. The trend has been in the opposite direction recently, but that might not be too reliable a guide to the future.

However, the underdeveloped countries have to watch their step carefully, lest by such bilateral agreements their hands are too firmly tied. They may miss their chance of broadening their business contacts so as to exploit to the utmost the market possibilities, in particular as buyers of capital goods. It is possible for comparatively small credits, and a measure of price stability for a part of their exports, to be bought too dearly.

NOTE ON COLONIAL BILATERALISM AND THE ROLE OF BIG COMPANIES

The urge to keep free from hampering bilateral relationships and to strive instead for an extension of their business contacts to the entire world market in regard to both exports and imports—which I have stressed above as a main commercial interest of the underdeveloped countries—should have firm psychological and political roots in the memories of former colonies' recent history of political and economic dependence on a metropolitan power. For one important aspect of economic colonialism was—and still is—enforced bilateralism and the consequent restrictions on the choice of partners in international trade.

I have already referred in this chapter to the way in which European colonialism restricts the scope for the type of cooperation between less developed countries. This "second-grade international specialization" in the production of cheaper commodities, as well as in other joint efforts to decrease their economic handicaps, is, of course, also effective in curtailing trade with other advanced countries, besides the metropolitan country, and this has until now been discussed as the main problem.

The methods traditionally used for enforcing bilateralism on behalf of the business interests of the metropolitan country have varied considerably; they were not limited to discriminatory measures applied to foreign trade and payments. The whole system of colonial laws and regulations was adjusted to this purpose. Behind this massive protection an institutional structure of business was built up, controlled from the metropolitan country, which, even when there was considerable competition between individual business houses of this country, functioned to keep out intruders from other trading countries.

Often large companies, usually with their headquarters in the metropolitan country—though sometimes with vast international affiliations—acquired a firm grip over important branches of the colony's economic life: they had either obtained a government concession or enjoyed a *de-facto* monopoly through having undertaken the "opening-up" operations, acquired ownership of land, and built large-scale establishments. The spheres of activity of these companies varied considerably from the exploitation of mines or plantations to running comprehensive export-import enterprises. Big companies also operated in politically independent countries; in some cases they held such a dominating position that they gave to a country's economic and, in particular, its commercial relations a quasi-colonial character.

These companies were often able to count on powerful political backing from their home governments and had usually close ties with persons in the governments and administration of the country where they operated. The considerable risks involved in this type of enterprise were balanced by high rates of profit, founded upon their monopoly position. The activity of these companies was by no means entirely inimical to the interest of the country which became dependent upon them. The historical alternative would, in fact, often have been the absence of the enterprise. But by their monopolistic power they tended to enforce and strengthen the colonial—or, in politically independent countries, quasi-colonial—bilateralism in the country's international trade relations, and that is my point in this connection.

In the many colonies that were recently liberated most of these institutional ties have been or are being dissolved. More generally, the enforced bilateralism of earlier times is, of course, a main explanation of the tendency in underdeveloped countries for their business contacts to be limited in scope. In the remaining political dependencies enforced bilateralism is still the rule.

Other countries that are discriminated against by the trade and payments regulations, by the entire institutional structure of business in the colonies, or by the monopolistic powers of the big companies, do not, of course, like this situation. The United States is disturbed by the restrictions imposed in British and French colonies against Japanese trade and would also like to see many African dependencies less closed to its own business interests; while the activities of some American corporations, operating in certain Latin American countries, are at the same time causing resentment in that region and are looked upon with suspicion by the rest of the world. The Germans and Italians are increasingly referring to their loss of colonies as an economic handicap and demanding greater access to other countries' dependencies; meanwhile the idea is gaining support in France that it could perhaps strengthen its position in North Africa by inviting the Germans and Italians to participate in a joint exploitation of the potentialities of the French dependencies there.

In response to the gradual awakening of the colonial peoples and the general spread in the industrial countries of the feeling that colonialism is doomed and has eventually to be liquidated, policies and methods are being adjusted, though with different speeds and in different ways. Greater respect is often now shown for national ambitions in the dependencies; colonial governments and big companies are now more and more prepared to shoulder greater costs of welfare work and to share profits with the indigenous peoples. Considerable capital flows are initiated and industrial development plans are often drawn up so as to provide a somewhat greater industrial diversification in order to lay the basis for a more balanced economy. In some instances moves are made towards self-government; usually a main interest of the metropolitan government is then, though, to protect the inherited bilateralism in commercial relations. At bottom, the explosive issue is, of course, the one of final political authority over a country's freedom to decide upon its own destiny, including its economic policy and its commercial relations with the outside world, and there are latent conflicts brooding in various parts of the world.

By these hints I have only wanted to point out the place in our analysis of the enforced bilateralism under political and big-company colonialism; this problem would deserve intensive study as an important part of the general problem of the tensions occurring in the present phase of the rapid world development towards the liquidation of political and economic colonialism. The argument in this chapter has been proceeding under the assumption that the underdeveloped countries are independent politically and free to frame their commercial policies to serve their own best interests.

THE RATIONALITY OF A DOUBLE STANDARD OF MORALITY IN INTERNATIONAL TRADE

THE VERY SPECIAL TRADING POSITION OF UNDERDEVELOPED COUNTRIES

Finally, one main conclusion from our analysis should be stressed. All underdeveloped countries have a major interest in maintaining and increasing their exports, though as far as possible along more remunerative lines. All of them, furthermore, are compelled to use the whole of their export proceeds, foreign credits, and aid so as to keep imports up to the highest level. From this point of view import restrictions in underdeveloped countries are simply a shift of import demands from some commodities to others, and generally to goods needed for economic development. They do not imply a diminution of total imports. *Their import restrictions and export subsidies do not, therefore, decrease total world trade.*[65]

Their dependence on high export proceeds and their need to use them all for imports are caused by the political necessity of economic development. Import restrictions are forced upon them as a consequence of the development policy; their seriously unbalanced economies provide additional motives for import restrictions, which are, however, mainly operative only in the directing, weighing, and implementing of the restrictions which they must anyhow apply because of the scarcity of foreign exchange. In a sense, the underdeveloped countries, when they have once gone in for economic development, are forced to be protectionists. They could not avoid it except by relinquishing economic development.

This, and the closely related fact that their protection does not cause a fall in their total imports, should make it easier for the rest of the world to recognize as legitimate the desire of underdeveloped countries to apply a policy of protectionism. I believe the time is ripe for a general acceptance of these facts and causal relations, which will anyhow and inevitably determine the commercial policy of these countries.

Protection in an advanced country with no foreign exchange worries will, however, restrict total world trade, since in such a country there is no mechanism whereby a restriction of the imports of one group of commodities is automatically compensated by an increase in imports of another group. A secure foreign exchange situation implies that there is no continuous, acute pressure on the exchange reserves and a self-sufficiency policy in such cases really means cutting down total imports and decreasing world trade, which is simply not true of underdeveloped countries.

THE TRADING POSITION OF THE UNITED STATES

In this connection it is impossible to avoid making the observation that the United States has succeeded in following a protectionist commercial policy on its own behalf—though such a policy actually reduces world trade—while urging the entire world to liberalize trade, in the specific sense of abolishing import controls. And it has extended this advice to the underdeveloped countries, which do have a rational and vital interest in strictly budgeting their imports (in fact are compelled to do so) and whose restrictions do not reduce world trade.

The Secretariat of the Economic Commission for Latin America has devoted a section of a recently published report to this problem under the heading: "The United States and Trade Reciprocity."[66]

The position of the United States as the principal dynamic centre of the world economy contributes very special emphasis to the concept of trade reciprocity. . . . Thus the tariff concessions granted by the United States to countries in course of development act as a counterpoise and world purchasing power generated by greater United States imports will tend to transform itself directly or indirectly into greater international demand for United States' exports. . . . If the principle is recognised that the volume of Latin American imports is not determined by tariffs but by exports, it would not be difficult to find an agreement of interests. . . . This ability of the United States to obtain spontaneous reciprocity for its tariff concessions is a result of the fundamental changes that have taken place in the short lapse of one generation. Interested as it is in a vast peripheral development policy, the trade policy of the United States should also be modified in accordance with its new international situation.

The short and simple meaning of these perhaps slightly involved sentences is this: the United States should entirely reverse its commercial policy; like Britain in its time of plethora of foreign exchange resources, it should unilaterally reduce its own import restrictions, which would have very wholesome effects all around; but it should stop pressing the underdeveloped countries to reduce theirs, because they need them and they do not cause a shrinkage of trade.

This is, of course, seen by many Americans too, even outside the fold of the economists. Thus Mr. George F. Kennan states his opinion: "Economic protectionism is not only an anomaly, but it is a ridiculous and ignominous expedient for a nation of our vigor and stature. What was right and necessary for a struggling underdeveloped country can be a form of infantile escapism for a strong and ostensibly mature one."[67] This would not be exactly my way of putting it but in substance I quite agree with Kennan.

Professor Jacob Viner is equally blunt: "We should not use foreign aid as conscience-money payments for our tariff," and: "A reduction of our trade barriers, which after fifteen years of being whittled away still remain formidable, can be of greater benefit to other countries than all the much-advertised grants, loans, and technical aid."[68]

That an American trade liberalization is very strongly in the interest of the rest of the world is not to be doubted. It is only on the basis of this interest that it can be effectively motivated; both the prominent American authors I have cited are, of course, ardent internationalists in the great tradition. Whether—leaving out of account the interest all countries, including the United States, have in a stable, prosperous world —a decrease of American import restrictions of various types can also be motivated on narrowly national, purely selfish grounds, is much more uncertain.

It may be that there is a long-term economic net advantage to be gained for the United States by readjusting its production and consumption so that a number of commodities are imported on a larger scale against a rise in export of others—this is the free-trade argument. But for various reasons—and, in particular, because of the size of the country and its variegated resources—it is my belief that if this qualitative consideration were translated into quantities, the gain would be small compared with the national product the United States has reached under present conditions, and also compared with its normal annual growth. The richer a country, the less important is an additional dollar and the more easily can it pay for pampering vested interests. The United States can easily afford its protection in the same way as it can afford to have an expensive, cumbersome, and less efficient administration, a fact to which I referred in the preceding chapter.

This conclusion is the more important as the readjustment to freer trade undoubtedly would cause certain temporary disturbances and losses. These are also small compared with the large changes the American economy is continuously and successfully undergoing. But particularly as they would be, in a sense, self-inflicted, and as the whole matter is anyhow not a tremendously important one from a narrowly national point of view, it is quite natural, and from this point of view also rational, that the United States should be reluctant to touch the more sensitive parts of its trade restrictions.

I am making this concession because I want to be candid in my reasoning. American national interests, narrowly interpreted, do not in my opinion warrant a large-scale trade liberalization. The only real justification is the international one: the interest of the world as a whole, in which the United States certainly has a share. *Only as an act of international solidarity does American trade liberalization make sense. But in that wider setting a unilateral action would be appropriate.*

A FALSE PRINCIPLE OF EQUALITY

My interest here is, however, the commercial policy of the underdeveloped countries. In regard to them, it cannot be stated that it is in the interest of the world that they relinquish import restrictions and abstain from export subsidies. On the contrary, it is in the general interest that they should be able to develop their economies as rapidly as possible; shortage of foreign exchange and, consequently, interferences with their foreign trade, are incidental to a policy directed towards this goal.

Looking back, we in the advanced countries have good reason to ask ourselves whether one policy line—basic, in a sense, to both the Bretton Woods agreements and the abortive attempt to create the International Trade Organization—was not downright wrong, and whether this is not one explanation of why our strivings failed to the degree they did. I mean the idea that all nations are equal, and that the international community should be based on principles and rules that are applied to all. It is an ideal that they *should* be equal but if, in fact, they are not, equal treatment becomes inequality.

Sir N. Raghavan Pillai, Indian Under-Secretary of Foreign Affairs, speaking in the recent session of GATT, said this emphatically: "Equality of treatment is equitable only among equals." And he added: "All that the under-developed countries ask is that in the name of reducing barriers to international trade, they should not be denied the fullest opportunity to develop their economy and to choose and decide for themselves the most appropriate measures for the purpose."[69]

This thought and the underlying basic facts are gradually being recognized. In GATT and the International Monetary Fund the underdeveloped countries will probably have a special status—*de facto* they already have it and now it is only a question of giving it to them also *de jure*—which will leave them sufficiently free to handle their commercial and exchange policies as they find they must do. They are, indeed, in no position to bind themselves in the way the existing agreements assume.

Their freedom will be connected with obligations to observe certain formalities and with some delays and paper-shuffling. But a much more difficult handicap—which, on account of their weak bargaining power, they cannot so easily overcome—will often be bilateral undertakings that they will continue to be pressed into against their development interests in order to achieve an outlet for their exports.

Indeed, *one of the substantial aids advanced countries could give underdeveloped countries would be to use their bargaining power against them with greater consideration* and, in particular, to stop virtually forcing them to import goods which they do not want, either because they can produce them at home or because they feel that they have no place in a national program of imports for economic development. Such a consideration in commercial policy would be a substitute for the aid and credits which they are not getting. But it would assume a totally different philosophy in the industrially advanced countries concerning their commercial relations with underdeveloped countries, in fact an adaptation of the approach they take as a natural thing towards underdeveloped regions within their own boundaries.

My main point is that these countries are in a quite special situation as long as they have not caught up with the developed countries; for this reason a double-standard morality in international trade is rationally motivated. They not only have good reasons but are virtually forced to control their imports and subsidize their exports—indeed, to practice systematic protection—if they are not to give up their drive for economic development. Their contribution to raising the level of world trade is to do everything they can to increase their exports along the most promising lines in order to make space for greater imports—which they are also bound to try to do—and to handle all their economic policies, including commercial policy, in such a way as to secure the maximum rate of economic growth.

Traditional but still current generalizations in the field of international trade that do not take into account the special situation of these countries would, if they were heeded, necessitate a slowing down of their economic development. But, since their interests are so clear and strong, and the political necessities so imperative, the advice given will usually not influence their actual policy. It does, nonetheless, create international irritation: unnecessary dismay on the one side, and confusion of thoughts, half heartedness, and, ultimately, suspicion and anger on the other side.

THE TRADING POSITION OF THE REST OF THE WORLD

If it is established, first, that, so far as their commercial policy is concerned, the underdeveloped countries belong to a special category and not only have an interest but are virtually compelled *to control and in-*

crease their foreign trade; and, second, that the United States is in the absolutely contrary position on both these scores, it is still necessary to find a place in this scheme for the rest of the world.

I am disregarding the several underdeveloped countries that, as I noted, are not troubling themselves with any ambitious development plans but are quietly surviving in relative stagnation. Many of them have plenty of old-fashioned protection; a few of them preserve a reasonable monetary equilibrium; none of them has any reason to find this impossible. As ideas from the outside penetrate their boundaries and they, too, are aroused by "the great awakening," and as the population pressure grows, they will also have to make serious efforts to rise out of mass poverty and economic stagnation. Their place will then immediately be in the separate category of underdeveloped countries that try to develop.

But what about countries other than the United States in the group that we defined as industrially advanced in Chapter III? Canada for one must be placed almost side by side with the United States. It is true that it carries on an industrial development policy requiring more capital than is provided for by domestic savings, but the extra capital flows freely from its big neighbor. Switzerland is, of course, a clear creditor-country, partly because so much foreign flight capital seeks refuge with, or passage through, her financial institutions. Some other industrially advanced countries in Western Europe are approaching, and may soon pass over, the borderline to the same upper division where there are no acute worries about foreign exchange and where, therefore, every import restriction tends to decrease world trade.

In all these countries, as in the United States, there are local and special interests calling for protection. There are, furthermore, general reasons for protection, including the social and economic ones for aiding agriculture and other industries with remuneration rates generally lower than the national level, or for influencing national distribution more generally by altering the supply of various consumption goods and their relative prices. There are also reasons for protection related to business cycle policy, those directed towards making gains through influencing the terms of trade and, of course, the infant industry argument, etc. More recently, under the influence of the cold war, strategic reasons for self-sufficiency in various lines of production have come to the fore.[70]

On all these matters I refer to the literature on international trade, and I would add that in general I share the liberal tendency that has permeated the main body of this literature from the time of Adam Smith and Ricardo; thinking through the peculiar problems of the underdeveloped countries in preparing this book has mainly strengthened my conservative inclinations in regard to trade policy. In Chapter IV, however, I have analyzed a whole system of psychological, ideological, political, and economic forces that, even in those developed countries that are undisturbed by foreign exchange worries, induce autarkic policies.

North America emerged from the Second World War richer and with rising levels of living—the main explanation being, of course, not only her distance from the scene of military action, but also the Great Depression during the thirties and the relative failure of the New Deal as an economic policy and a cure for the depression. Western Europe however, was ravaged, lost most of its foreign assets, and saw its entire position in world trade radically altered. This time the West-European countries decided upon rapid reconstruction and development. Their changed position and their policy of speedy recovery had the effect of throwing them all temporarily into the category of underdeveloped countries, having to face all of the monetary and financial problems that I have analyzed in the latter part of this chapter.

This was true not only of the really underdeveloped countries in Southern Europe; as a matter of fact some of these countries, like Portugal, Spain, and, for a time, Italy, tended to adhere more to the group of underdeveloped countries that were slow in coming to grips with their development problems and that I have left somewhat on the fringe of my analysis. France—on a higher level of production and consumption but bleeding white from vastly overextended political commitments overseas (which were well beyond her capacities to sustain) and with severe rigidities in her economic life caused by a long history of inflation and stagnation—is a borderline case, particularly in regard to the western provinces.[71]

Turkey and Yugoslavia are clear examples of underdeveloped countries that are laboring faithfully on with their economic development and therefore struggling with the problems typical of such a situation and such a policy. Greece is in a similar situation, though handicapped by scantier natural resources, by having recently fought a civil war, and by other causes. The geographical position of these three countries on the cold war front has, on the one hand, secured them much more capital aid for development than other underdeveloped countries but has, on the other hand, compelled them to devote much more of their national product to defense expenditures. From the point of view of our analysis above it is not astonishing that they have had acute difficulties with their balance of payments, while Portugal, for example, has not.

But I am more particularly thinking of the highly industrialized, rich, and progressive countries in the northwestern part of the continent. In particular, a country like Norway, that courageously raised its investment ratio higher than any other country in Western Europe—but that did not secure a position like that of Canada in the United States capital market—was naturally caught in the position of a struggling underdeveloped country trying against odds to push ahead with economic development. To a varying degree the same was true of all the industrially advanced countries in Northwestern Europe. At a later stage of the process and, more precisely, after the outbreak of the Korean war, all these countries also undertook heavy rearmament expenditures which, of course, raised the same problems as investments for development, except that as investments they are unremunerative even in the longer run.

There was this important difference, however, between their situation and the one in which the underdeveloped countries now find themselves: outside capital was made available. The massive Marshall aid represented a solidarity among the advanced countries—or, more precisely, of one of them to the others—for which there is at most only an insignificant comparison in the broader world setting between advanced and underdeveloped countries. Essentially, the Marshall Plan, as it worked out, was merely a complex of national investment programs financed to a degree by the United States.

The capital inflow made it possible for these countries to carry on their development programs with relatively less internal inflationary pressure and relatively fewer import restrictions than would otherwise have been necessary. The existence of the sterling area, the relative cohesion even in Western Europe, founded upon a high and unique degree of trade interdependence, and American indulgence (and, in fact, positive urging) made it possible increasingly to reduce import restrictions within the region and transform them into trade discrimination against the United States.

There is another important difference, too. The import restrictions were motivated solely by exchange considerations and, of course, the traditional reasons for protection referred to above. None of the special and additional powerful reasons for protection in underdeveloped countries, discussed earlier in this chapter, is valid for countries in Northwest Europe. There the existing markets are in general large in relation to new units of production; in cases where they are not—as when modern technology prescribes units of production too big for the national market —this can usually not be overcome simply by keeping out foreign goods but only by international integration, which is the opposite of protection. Full employment has been successfully preserved and there is, anyhow, no surplus labor. The lack of external economies is not a serious difficulty as it is in the underdeveloped countries; the gain from external economies in ever new investment is usually much smaller. Their price and cost structure is not lopsided as between industry and agriculture. More generally it can be asserted that their economies have had a recent history of industrial expansion and are not unbalanced because of prolonged stagnation and economic colonialism; when the postwar emergency is overcome, the need for ready adjustment to changes and the ambitions for continued growth and development have become important elements in their national life; but these aspirations have almost nothing in common with the gross lack of balance in the economies of under-developed countries.

How "Financially Sound" Is Western Europe Going To Be?

In Chapter VI I expressed the opinion that the industrially advanced countries in Northwest Europe, as a region, should now be able to manage their internal affairs and their international relations so as to take their proper place as creditor countries in a more closely integrated world economy. Compared with the underdeveloped countries in the southern part of the region and in the world at large, which have to squeeze savings out of utter poverty as a necessary condition for economic development, the industrially advanced countries all have relatively high levels of income. They should be able, by appropriate economic, monetary, and fiscal policies, to maintain savings high enough to ensure a strong continued development at home and, in addition, a capital surplus that could be the basis for both trade liberalization and a substantial outflow of capital to the underdeveloped countries. These policies would have to be fashioned in such a way that the higher savings quota would not dampen the forces of economic progress: by including new elements of investment stimulation and, equally important, by abolishing existing disincentives to investment.

Were this happy state of affairs to become a reality, the industrially advanced countries in Northwest Europe would naturally take their place beside the United States as countries whose import restrictions would tend to decrease world trade. They would, together with the United States, Canada, and the advanced countries in the British Commonwealth—assuming that they too followed such an import policy—form the sort of world that is usually referred to in the literature on commercial policy. There would be another division for the underdeveloped countries, which we cannot possibly expect to come into this kind of situation within the present epoch of world history.

In Chapter VI I came, however, to the conclusion that this level of "financial soundness," even for a limited number of countries, is not just around the corner. The convertibility that might be reached will probably be founded on a considerable capital autarky and, perhaps, quite a lot of discriminatory protective restrictions on trade and payments. There are differences even in Northwest Europe, and individual countries may move towards the sterner level of "financial soundness" where they become completely free from exchange worries and can even open up their foreign exchange boundaries to capital export. The other countries would remain in the category of underdeveloped countries or in some intermediary category created for their convenience.

The basic issues should not be confused, however, by false pretenses of equality. An industrially developed country does not become an underdeveloped one merely by mismanaging its currency, or by raising its level of investments higher than available savings, including those its government is willing or able to procure by taxing its citizens, without having recourse to outside financing.

There is, first, the continuing difference that such a country does not have the special and additional reasons for protection which underdeveloped countries have, precisely because the latter are industrially underdeveloped. It comes into the same division solely because it has not assured itself a safe and comfortable exchange situation, and its interferences with its foreign trade can have only this reason.

Second, there exists and will probably continue to exist a certain degree of solidarity between the relatively rich and advanced countries, which through centuries of vigorous intercourse have become related in culture and sometimes by blood ties—a solidarity which the underdeveloped countries neither have among themselves nor share with the advanced countries. This solidarity between the advanced countries is, as we have seen, not strong enough to form the basis for a constructive policy of economic cooperation. Even in their internal relations the trend has for a whole generation been towards increased autarky. But it is probably large enough to permit in various forms a certain minimum of capital assistance. In particular, the United States will probably feel a continuing responsibility for keeping them financially viable.

Also, as these countries are all relatively well off in spite of their exchange difficulties—which will continue to be referred to as temporary—and if, as we can assume, they are not merely squandering the money but building up ever higher productivity, then they do represent better debtors, even when their currencies are inconvertible and they keep up trade restrictions motivated by exchange considerations.

The southern part of Western Europe is underdeveloped. The countries in this subregion can, however, probably count on continuously higher credits and international aid than other underdeveloped countries, partly because of the greater strategic importance in the cold war that will be given Europe and partly because of cultural and blood ties. Insofar as Northwestern Europe does not really step over into the category of creditor countries and as, anyhow, the countries in that part of Europe have other outlets for their capital exports—which for various reasons, and contrary to the idea of West-European integration, will be given priority—most of these credits and aid to Southern Europe will have to come from the United States. If the capital inflow is large enough, it will, of course, to the same extent make it possible for the underdeveloped countries in Southern Europe to keep up a certain rate of economic development with less interferences in foreign trade.

One final remark: all tendencies to capital autarky in advanced countries and all import restrictions, to the extent that exports from underdeveloped countries are involved, will increase the difficulties of those latter countries, hamper their economic development, and/or push them further in the direction of foreign trade control and self-sufficiency.

CHAPTER XIV

The World Adrift

DRIFTING TOWARDS A DESTINY

A study of trends and problems in the field of international economic integration ten years after the end of the Second World War must invest us with humility and even anxiety. This is, indeed, the effect which the marshaling of the data and the inferences under the various chapter headings have had upon the present author. It is not possible to conclude that the non-Soviet world is now on the way to a higher level of economic integration. In most respects the trends are definitely in the opposite direction.

The practical problems facing us, if we want to change these trends, are momentous. Like all problems they can be solved on paper, and as my interest is constructive and primarily practical such paper solutions to the specific problems are presented in the various chapters. But my analysis has led me to conclude that translating these paper solutions into practical action would assume radically changed attitudes in all nations, and honesty requires that this crucial conclusion be put before the reader constantly. As the problems are urgent and as I fail to see what can induce such large changes in attitudes quickly enough, I finally emerge with what amounts to a string of almost insurmountable difficulties. I have not set out to write another utopia but a factual and practical tract: not to describe what could be done in a dream world but what we can reasonably expect to happen in the world in which we live. And such an analysis of international integration problems at the present time is bound to be disheartening if it is at all realistic.

In fact, I know of no government and no political party in any country which is really facing up to these problems. There are small groups, like the Quakers in the Anglo-Saxon countries and some of the quiet scholars of the Roman Catholic Church, who, because of their religious preoccupation, have acquired the strength to see beyond the more immediate

299

things. And there are in all parts of the world many individuals in the great humanistic tradition who also see what the inevitable conclusion must be. When such persons accept political responsibility—and some of them have responsibility of the highest order—a condition for continuance in power is that they accept and recognize the practical possibilities at hand in their several countries, determined by their fellow citizens' present attitudes, and so reserve their profounder insights for general pronouncements that do not upset practical affairs.

The social scientists have all the facts under study. None of the data and few of the detailed inferences in this book are in any way original; indeed, for the larger part the book can claim only to assemble and present well-known facts. This time, however, I have sought not so much to increase detailed knowledge as to use existing knowledge to attain a broader understanding.

And then I get the feeling—and sense the anxiety—that the world is drifting towards a destiny that it has not charted in advance and for which it has not been deliberately steering its course. World history has probably always evolved in this way; the lack of foresight will always be apparent in retrospect. This is how crises and wars come about—and our personal financial bankruptcies and divorces. Something is under way that at one stage, if it had been analyzed squarely and faced courageously, could have been stopped by relatively minor sacrifices, intelligently applied, but at a later stage cannot be stopped at all, even by very much bigger sacrifices.

My historian friends tell me that the world has always been heedlessly drifting. In this respect there does not seem to be much difference between our age and the period of the Crusades. They agree with me, though, that nowadays history is made at a very much higher speed—a result of modern technology, which, together with its cultural, social, economic, and political consequences, has not been given enough serious and detailed research in the social sciences. The dangers of this reckless course are telescoped and thus magnified.

In the Greek tragedy the fateful conflict that in the last act brings defeat and death to the hero raged in his own breast. This has ever since been the fundamental theme in great literature. The cheaper variety of dramatists have instead always had recourse to the villain and his plots when they constructed a melodrama—whether small and private or huge and public. And so most often do the journalists, the politicians, and, indeed, the general public when attempting to explain to themselves why things go wrong. The religions in their more primitive stages likewise provided their faithful with a devil and his following.

This is, however, a superstitious view. The great literature is right: the real element of tragedy in human affairs is that people, who have the propensities for good, do wrong and thus cause misfortune to each other and to themselves.[1] Such was—as we can see now when the contemporary storm of blindfolding emotions has abated—the origin of the first modern great war a hundred years ago, the American Civil War, which had been portended by decades of cold war. Such is the background of many trivial court cases every day in every place.

In our general thinking it was the philosophy of the Enlightenment that finally did away with the old superstition of the villain by proclaiming that man was good and that our misery was not due to human nature but to man's environment in the widest sense: to social institutions and to opportunist ignorance[2] when living in them. In a very fundamental sense this thesis is basic to the practical ideals of liberty and equality; on the intellectual level it is parallel to the moral axiom of the dignity of the individual human being. This ideology became ingrained in the social sciences, which at that time began their modern development. All research on historical or contemporary social relations has since then confirmed the environmental hypothesis of the basic philosophy.[3] This does not mean that the old superstition of bad men is eradicated from popular thinking; it continues to give its heat and afford a motivation to human action in private as well as public affairs.

This view, which is the view of the social scientist, is on one level a deeply pessimistic one, since it assumes that good people, as they are conditioned by their environment, can make life a hell for each other and themselves and all the time honestly plead to their conscience that their intentions were good; they do it often in a family, in a neighborhood, in a nation, and in the world. On another level—and this is our great inheritance from the rational philosophy from which the social sciences branched two centuries ago—this view is fundamentally optimistic.

It holds that truth is wholesome and that a catharsis of the public mind is possible. As man is good and has the power of reason, he can attempt to dispel the clouds of his emotions, overcome the opportunism of his ignorance, reach a fuller and more dispassionate knowledge about himself and the world and, indeed, *change his attitudes so that they become more rationally related to the existing facts and to his deepest valuations, his ideals.* The social scientist in this great tradition is also an uncompromising adherent to freedom of thought and expression because they create a social situation where maximum possibility is given to the individual citizen to make this great attempt towards rationality. In the end this represents our only hope.

The same revolutionary faith that man is good and has reason, which we in the Western world associate with our inheritance from the Enlightenment, was in India the ancient wisdom upon which Gandhi built his trust that truth will prevail, having a momentum stronger than all temporal powers, all political persecutions and impossible to contain within state prison walls, which would crumble like card houses.

The Impact of the Cold War

At the present time when more than ever we need the freest and most virile thinking in testing out new approaches to all international problems; when, in the end, the request to our nations must be to change our attitudes to world problems; and when, therefore, we need all our moral and intellectual powers, a mental inertia is descending upon us, caused by the cold war. To all the other social forces, which I analyzed in Chapters III and IV as having driven our civilization for many decades in the direction of nationalism, has now come this new exigency, a main impact of which has been to narrow the horizon of public discussion and to attach penalties to intellectual disagreement.

From the beginning, an ideological effect of Communism in the Western world has been to strengthen political reaction. I think it can be shown that Nazism would have had much less chance of exerting a hold over the German people after the First World War had it not been for the activity there of the German Communist Party. But it has been left till after the Second World War for us to realize the fact that in many parts of the Western world Communism in the Soviet Union can drive people to intellectual stupor by a sort of telekinesis.

Many of us remember the practical joke, played by the American journalist who wanted to see how the man in the street would react to the revered formulations of the Declaration of Independence and the Gettysburg Address without being told their origin, and found that people believed them to stem from Communist propaganda. This story has a sinister implication for the mental state of our nations. It is wrong for us in Europe to feel unduly haughty and believe that these telekinetic effects of Soviet Communism are confined to America, for similar things can happen even in the other advanced countries of the Western world if we do not erect our fences of critical alertness.

Very widely, indeed, the situation is becoming one where Soviet Communism needs only to give verbal homage to one of our cherished inherited symbols for us to give it up in utter defeatism as if it were contaminated. Several years ago an Austrian friend confided to me that in his country it was dangerous to state that one was for peace because peace was a Communist propaganda slogan. Also several years ago, I heard that an international organization, with which I was connected, had a large edition of posters that could not be used because the biblical dove of peace figured on it—the story was fortunately apocryphal but the serious thing is that it could be told as a story which might be true.

Only the Communists' antireligious prejudices have until now hindered them from compromising seriously the central parts of the Bible. But in many countries on many occasions even the word democracy has been in danger of becoming leprous. And unfortunately it is a fact that in recent years—during the time when the United States Supreme Court made its historical decision to declare racial discrimination in schools illegal—it actually happened during the American loyalty investigations that the presence of public officials at a party where some Negroes were also invited could be used as ground for suspicion of disloyalty—by the logic that Communists preach and practice racial equality.

When the Soviet Communists take a stand for an idea, not as a very sophisticated form of studied propaganda but as a natural policy of a minority party in the world—and often on the basis of tenets of faith which Soviet Communism adheres to in line with the Western doctrinal origin of its creed—this idea tends to become "Communism" not only for the halfwits who in our strained international situation often play a role they have not played for at least two centuries—except occasionally, as in Nazi Germany—but often also for the circumspect and cautious good citizen.

In this climate of creeping intellectual hysteria it must be feared that the urgently necessary reorientation of our thoughts regarding international cooperation may be inhibited. I fear that the Soviet Communists will not need to exert great ingenuity to compromise seriously the whole issue of aiding the underdeveloped countries in their development efforts and make it taboo in the West. This would then be a result, not of their intellectual and moral strength, but of our weakness. The situation is already that, at least in the United States, this issue of cooperation for economic development is on the verge of becoming no longer quite respectable, unless dressed up in a way the underdeveloped countries will never accept: as a political device for fighting Communism.

I fear a similar fate for the anticolonial attitude that in the United States—itself born in the earliest revolt against a ruling metropolitan power—has been a cherished part of the national creed throughout its national existence, and that to all honest liberals in Europe has been a self-evident principle for a century and more, even if not enough serious efforts were made on its behalf in national policies. The eager search for Communist instigators of anticolonial movements, wherever conflicts occur in the world and very often on the most scanty evidence, is gradually compromising in the public mind the anticolonial movements in a way that reminds one of how, in a recent referendum in the canton of Zurich in Switzerland, a proposal for enfranchising women was defeated—mainly, I understand, because the initiative had come from the Communist Party. If this development should continue, the Western democracies will gradually take the position of defenders of an indefensible *status quo.*

The disheartening fact is that today so few people are prepared to stand up and explain in simple, straightforward words the obvious proposition that a truth does not become less true and a moral principle not less valid for us because the Soviet Communists also acclaim it, and that to forget this amounts to losing our intellectual and moral integrity and the freedom of our minds, and to giving up ideological independence and initiative.

Serious damage to the integrity and therefore also the strength of our culture is being inflicted by this intellectual cowardice. It is essential to democracy that the spectrum of ideas be as wide as there are rational grounds for honest differences of opinions. This was once self-evident but is so no more. It must instill us with humiliation and serious concern for the future when we experience the present spread of ideological conformism. We cannot, and should not, rely upon youth to stand up for spiritual independence. They have never experienced the full freedom of Western civilization as it once flourished when there was inner security, and they are under the handicap of having to build for themselves a career in the world as it actually is. The duty falls upon the generation that represents the tradition and has the security of status, acquired by earlier accomplishments, and of a relatively shorter life expectancy which should anyway make them freer of anxiety.

An Emotional Cycle

All this can, of course, be explained in psychological terms. There are undoubtedly reactionary groups that have an interest in this development and their influence should not be underestimated. It is perhaps also natural that the good citizen feels in a confused way that in these difficult times he should not take any stand far removed from the middle of the crowd, if the Communists have made a move to occupy a particular position, since he does not want to aid them. On a much lower level of moral standards is the egoistic motive that he feels afraid of being branded as Communist by the people who are using the opportunity of our ideological ailment to enforce *Gleichschaltung.*

To understand this dangerous mental inertia, it is also necessary to go back a few years and see clearly how the present reaction to the cold war is only the last phase of a violent emotional cycle: on the upswing, during the later years of the Second World War, of feelings of close alliance with, and sympathy for, the Soviet Union, and now, on the downswing, of revulsion, hatred, and fear as the illusions about cooperation after the war have been shattered. I am referring to the belligerent nations and, in particular, to the United States. In a country like Sweden, which succeeded in preserving her traditional armed neutrality in the war till the end, and which can also build upon more than a thousand years' experience of wars, commerce, and cultural relations with Russia, this emotional cycle has naturally had a much smaller swing in both directions, and a Swede can perhaps, without any intrinsic merit of his own, for this reason more easily have an independent and stable viewpoint enabling him to gain a clearer perspective of this particular phenomenon.

Undoubtedly, and again particularly in America, many of those who during the upward phase of the emotional cycle felt warmest towards their country's great ally, the Soviet Union, were in the glorious tradition of liberalism and enlightened internationalism—though whole nations were not far behind them. This is important, as the obligation to do the fresh thinking and work out the new approaches to the world problems would now naturally have fallen on them. Undoubtedly, too, during the downward phase of the emotional cycle in the cold war and because of the memory of their own attitudes a few years ago (and almost in self-defence and self-justification when pleading to their own conscience) they have often felt compelling reasons to out-Herod Herod in the popular revulsion against Soviet ideology and policy. Quite apart from any pressure of McCarthyism and other forms of crude retroactive thought control, it is easily understandable if, after their emotional history of the last fifteen years, the liberals have become a little dazed and uncertain. To a considerable extent they share this experience with the rest of their nation.

The most damaging and intellectually most unsettling effect of the emotional enthusiasm for the Soviet Union during the upswing in the cycle was the tendency during this period to rearrange opportunistically knowledge about the Soviet Union and one's own thinking about these facts in order to justify the sympathy.[4] A most interesting volume, using as source material highly respectable publications from this period, could be written about this. Such a volume would be an important one, if it could help to prevent in the present phase of the cycle an opportunist tendency in the opposite direction, in arranging facts about the Soviet Union and drawing inferences.

In the fall of 1943, when I visited America, I was disturbed by what I then looked upon as signs of faltering intellectual integrity. "The admiration for the Soviet Union tends generally to bring Americans to the attitude that the ends justify the means and that might takes precedence over right. This tendency, even if yet not so strong, towards a dilution of the American liberal idealism might turn out to be one of the most important, and most fateful, of the developments we are now witnessing."[5] I am convinced that several of the roots of the present weakness of liberalism in America—which in its entire history has been the great and, as a trend, the dominant moral force—go back to confused thinking and opportunistic choosing and manipulating of facts during this period at the end of the Second World War.

IN THE SOCIAL SCIENCES

The ideological effects of the cold war cannot, of course, leave the social sciences unaffected, where the objects of study are the facts and causal relations around which opinions and ideologies are formed. It is, indeed, only natural that the impact of the cold war even on the social sciences should be serious. They are essentially only an element of our culture and share its fate.

All our intellectual exertions are now taking place in a strange political climate. Anyone who is in a position to make firsthand observations in a limited area of international events soon becomes very much aware of the powerful opportunist bias in the selection and evaluation of news for the general public, not only in the Soviet orbit, but increasingly also in the non-Soviet world. In the social sciences it is especially our most general ideas, our implicit assumptions, and our way of stating and facing problems that are apt to be sensitive to this continued and systematic bias in the reporting of events and in their interpretation. For these things determine the mental climate in the national communities where we are living and working.

The cold war also has a more direct impact on our thinking, as increasingly certain beliefs become commonly recognized as the right and respectable ones and certain others as wrong or deviously dangerous. This is, of course, contrary to the very spirit of science and if this situation proves to be a lasting one it is bound to have fateful effects. I have in another connection commented upon two tendencies that are visible: the first, to seek an escape into details and technicalities; the second, to avoid in particular questions that are highly controversial.[6] Partly, at least, this is a sort of defense on the part of the social scientists against the ideological pressure of the community in which they are living.

I do not want to be misunderstood on this point. It is natural and commendable that in the social sciences we should strive for ever greater specialization, ever more intensive search for variations in minor matters, and ever more refined methods of ascertaining the manifold facets of our increasingly complicated world. With these strivings I am, of course, entirely in sympathy. To seek verification of all the relevant detail is true progress in social sciences in their present stage of development, and the larger part of our exertions should take this direction.

But it cannot be concealed that this direction of our work opens up the possibility of dropping an analysis of a practical problem at the point when it exceeds mere technicalities, without venturing to draw the essential inferences. The widely dispersed nature of modern research also makes it possible for us, almost without even noticing it ourselves, to avoid asking the awkward questions. I am not so much complaining that more and more labor is devoted to less and less interesting things, for everything is in the final analysis interesting and important. My complaint is rather that we do not venture to devote more effort to what really matters and, not least, to what is controversial.

I am not unaware of the large output of general books devoted to problems of great practical importance; indeed, in many cases I rather feel that some of them have not been based on enough investigation of the facts and enough hard critical thinking and that they might have fared better with less intellectual enterprise. But my main point about our generation's practical generalizations is that under the terrific pressure of public opinion, as it manifests itself under the impact of the cold war, these studies tend to draw the horizon for valuations too narrowly and, more specifically, to reason too much from popular political valuations in a particular national community at a particular time; sometimes they simply agree tacitly to follow out the national propaganda line in the "psychological warfare."

In the advanced countries we are, for instance, producing a large literature on the underdeveloped countries. This often is not based on value premises corresponding to our basic inherited ideals, those which we to a large extent share with the nations now experiencing the "great awakening." Instead, it reflects much narrower political and sometimes even strategic national interests. I am afraid this opportunism in the selection of value premises for scientific study of world problems will in time result in our spiritual isolation from the intellectual life of the underprivileged countries and, in the most unfortunate case, spur them on to an even greater defensive nationalistic coloring of their own scientific work.

One general bias that our milieu is constantly pressing upon us is unfounded optimism. Particularly in America it has become a popular belief that this is the way of fostering courage at home and abroad. The nation is inclined to demand of a scientific analysis of a practical problem, as of a film, not only a happy ending but also a positive title and a reassuring content. Some problems are, however, too loaded with difficulties to permit of such a treatment, except by distortion. I am inclined to agree with my old friend Professor William E. Rappard, who attacks the comfortable habit of building up our own morale by stimulating our congenital optimism—"that terrible mental disease which makes one confuse hopes and prospects. Easy intellectual optimism is for the mind a dangerous habit-forming drug. As such it may well be compared to the narcotics that at first seem to exalt, but in the end never fail to sap the vitality of the body."[7]

The Western world, and most surely not only America, is thus constantly deluding itself with certain policies—and paying for widespread publicity to do it—such as imperfect degrees of currency convertibility, minor cuts in tariffs, emphasis on getting private capital to move where it does not want to go, very partial and largely unreal efforts towards economic integration among some West-European countries. These policies, even when they are commendable in themselves, only nibble at the fringes of the big pressing problems. The social scientists come under the ideological pressure not to deprive the general public of its illusions, i.e., not to inform it of the true proportions of facts, issues, and accomplishments.

But the courage that our nations need in our time is not the cheap and, in the end, unreliable one of false optimism and the whipped-up belief that everything will finally turn out to be going our way. They need, rather, the courage of desperation which all the time seeks and exposes the cold truth and which is strong enough to face serious dangers squarely and even to accept calmly reverses and retreats and which urges us to work on nevertheless, even against all odds, and to stick to our basic ideals. Turning the tide would, indeed, require changed attitudes within and between all nations. The social sciences have, of course, not the duty of reformers to be the actual agents of this change of attitudes. But opportunist pressures are tending to divert us from our real duty of analyzing relentlessly the facts and thereby preparing the ground among our peoples for that realism in their world outlook, which is the first condition for the needed change of attitudes.

If the world ever returns to sanity, it will be immediately apparent that many of our scientific exertions during recent years have been illusory. This is a matter that comes within the broad realm of the still undeveloped sociology of knowledge; its crucial importance, not only for the social sciences themselves, but also for the general formulation of ideas and ideals—and, consequently, also for political development—would warrant penetrating and pitiless study. The general value premise upon which the sociological study of the social sciences will have to be based, is given: in a democracy it is in the public interest that the truths—not least the uncomfortable ones—be established and disseminated as widely as possible; illusions—and particularly the opportunistic ones—are a public danger. This value premise is implied in the great motto with which Columbia University entered in 1954 the celebration of its two centuries of existence as a force for rationality in America and in the whole world of learning: "Man's right to knowledge and the free use thereof."

THE MAIN LINE OF THE ARGUMENT

We started our study by defining the problem of international economic integration in terms of the Western world's inherited ideals of liberty and equality (Chapter II). In our cultural setting there can be no competing value premise. Though perfection is distant and our vision blurred, we all know at heart, though vaguely, what we are talking about, for this is the essence of sharing in a common civilization.

In the industrially advanced nations, which form a tiny minority of mankind although they exert a disproportionally large power over world events, the internal development has been approaching integration in terms of these ideals with an accelerating speed in a process of cumulative social change (Chapter III). Relatively speaking, these nations have become ever richer, their common expectancy is that the future holds in store for them both greater equality of opportunity for the individual and higher average levels of consumption. We have studied how progress in production has been a condition for this higher degree of national integration, but also how integration was a condition for economic progress; progress is, in fact, interwoven in the cumulative social process of national integration and is an element of it.

In our study of international economic integration we first focused our interest on the mutual relations between the advanced countries. During the last forty years these relations have been forcefully influenced by an uninterrupted sequence of violent international crises culminating in three periods of great world calamity, the First and the Second World Wars and the Great Depression between them. There were continuous minor crises between these three major culminations as well as after the last one; the most recent crises being the Korean war, which threw all countries—except the United States and a few others—off their economic balance. It would be surprising if this sequence of crises had now finally reached its end; anyhow, there no longer exists in the Western world, as there did immediately after the First World War, a commonly shared assurance that we are on the way "back to normalcy." It is clear that the trend to international economic disintegration, which stands in such dramatic contradiction to the development towards national integration in the individual advanced countries, has obtained much of its momentum from this sequence of violent crises.

This trend has, however, also deeper causes and this explains why the effects of the crises continually pile up, one on the other, and thus permanently change our societies. We have seen how the integration process in the national states strongly tends to turn inwards the interests of the citizens, whereby international allegiances are weakened. We have also studied in some detail how a great number of economic policies, devised to realize national economic stability and equality, have an inherent tendency to cause international disintegration (Chapter IV). This is true not only of the large number of irrational policies, which we have in all countries because our democracy is not sufficiently alert and intelligent, but also of policies which are rational from the exclusive viewpoint of national interests. This is the deeper causal mechanism behind the growing institutional disparity between ever strengthened national states and weakened international institutions.

As our value premise is international, and not only national, integration, we have inquired into the practical means of overcoming this flagrant contradiction in all our policies and found that, theoretically, the contradiction could be resolved by an international cooperation directed towards coordinating, though not liquidating, the national policies in the service of commonly felt interests. As an international community does not exist, except in its barest and most rudimentary beginnings, whereas the national communities are strong and getting ever stronger and are also instilling a continuously growing allegiance to national at the expense of international values, we have to face the fact that, practically, attempts to realize the international goal meet overwhelming resistance. The trend has been, and still is, in the nature of a continuous retreat to economic nationalism.

This conclusion was reached on general grounds from a study of the social forces operating within the machinery of the welfare state, which for long has been the well-established form of national community in all advanced countries, and was then verified with special reference to labor and capital movements (Chapters VII and VIII). We found that international factor movements, which had played such a very important role in the process of national and international integration of the advanced countries before 1914, have now been relegated to tiny streams diverted from their natural courses.

Thus in most cases the states have virtually sealed the boundaries of their national labor markets against any intruders—even from neighboring and closely related nations. The international capital market has almost ceased to function, except for the reinvestment of profits or for direct new investments in the imperial outlands, where they can be closely controlled as auxiliaries to the economy of the home country. Government credits, mostly granted by the United States, and the operations of the International Bank, have not to any material extent become a substitute for the defunct private capital market of earlier times. We saw no reliable signs of any substantial change of these trends in the labor and capital markets.

International trade has fallen in relation to production and income. The underlying causes of this trend are, of course, mainly the great number of impediments to imports that most countries—and, in particular, the bigger countries—have applied in the interest of internal stability and equality. In the Western world—unlike the nations in the Soviet orbit—we rarely think consciously of our economies in terms of long-term developments and trends but fix our attention on the ups and downs from quarter to quarter and year to year; and except for the moments of acute crises, we have been living most of the time in situations where we sincerely hoped that international trade would be freer and move upwards again and we have talked and written much on the assumption that it would.

More recently we have been absorbed by the valiant strivings to restore currency convertibility and to abolish the quantitative and, in particular, the discriminatory trade and payments restrictions that are not part of the several countries' deliberate economic policies but forced upon them by foreign exchange considerations. In our study of these restrictions they stand out as symptoms of the deeper dislocations and frustrations of foreign trade and of the movements of capital and labor caused by the sequence of international crises and the policies of the national welfare states (Chapter VI). From symptoms, however, they have developed into root causes that aggravate the illness, and their expunction is well worth trying.

We have found many difficulties in the way, all arising from deeper and less easily removed elements of international disintegration—among them the dislocations in international trade, the frustration and perversion of the capital market, the failure to agree on international cooperation to stabilize business fluctuations, etc. But we would not consider it improbable that for the industrially advanced countries convertibility of some sort (and with a number of qualifications and exceptions) could be reached within a not too distant future. The main point to retain is, however, that convertibility in this sense is a comparatively minor issue when the problem of international integration is considered. In current discussion there has been an opportunist tendency to exaggerate its importance out of all proportion.

As a case study we analyzed the record of the much-advertized policy towards West-European economic integration (Chapter V). We had to conclude that it had not achieved its goals. The explanation why this policy—undertaken in a region, at a time, and under circumstances which were extraordinarily favorable for its success—nonetheless failed, was found to be in the superficiality of analysis and practical approach. The policy evaded the integration problems on the deeper level of factor movements and never faced the issue of equality between peoples in different nations. Nor was an effective attempt made to establish the basis of international solidarity among the peoples, without which the causes of international disintegration cannot be removed.

The years after the Second World War have seen the emergence of a new phenomenon, international aid, again given mostly by the United States (Chapter IX). It is an interesting innovation, but—except for Marshall aid and other assistance to Western Europe—it has as yet been insignificant and haphazard from a broader economic point of view. The bigger problem of international integration, that of aiding the economic development of the underdeveloped countries, is as yet hardly more than a vision and a challenge.

The problem of the tremendous, and growing, disparities in factor proportions, factor prices and, therefore, living standards between the industrially advanced nations and the underdeveloped ones, which comprise by far the larger part of mankind, was characterized as the main and dominant problem of international integration as this issue faces our generation (Chapter I). In all the chapters up to Chapter IX, which were mainly focused on the relations between the advanced countries, this thought was constantly present in the back of our mind. The existing patterns of labor and capital mobility and international aid were studied also from the viewpoint of whether they could alleviate the plight of the underdeveloped countries. On most points the answers we reached were negative. The rest of the study—more than half the book—was thereafter entirely devoted to the problems of the development of the underdeveloped countries.

In these countries a considerable number of new approaches, the beginning of the breaking down of stale social traditions, and a new realignment of human efforts have been made possible by the war and its aftermath. New independent nations have come into existence and older ones have embraced new aspirations. The backward and economically stagnant populations in Asia, Africa, Latin America, and Southern Europe are seething. In the advanced countries there is increasing awareness of these untold masses of new active participants in the international political concert of nations, seeking their destiny.

We studied the psychological, ideological, and political forces at work in the underdeveloped countries and tried to give due importance to the color question, the nationalistic urge, and the growing feeling of solidarity between the underprivileged nations (Chapter XI). We noticed how the "great awakening" in a real and fundamental sense is nothing less than the rapid and explosive spread over the globe of our Western ideals of liberty and equality. We cannot, therefore, stop it, but are under the inner compulsion to spur it on, whichever way we turn and whatever we do.

We saw how the drive for development—conceived as a political program to apply modern techniques in order to raise levels of living for the masses—is an entirely new thing in history, without any parallel in the industrially advanced, democratic countries' own earlier experience. It also implies a tendency to skip the stage of capital accumulation, and does so while an important element in the situation of underdeveloped countries is that they, unlike the now advanced countries in their time of early industrialization, do not have an international capital market providing them with a cheap and plentiful capital inflow. What is actually happening is that the advanced countries are exporting to the underdeveloped countries the revolutionary idea of the welfare state—which is the final result of generations of stern capital accumulation, economic progress, and national integration under exceptionally favorable circumstances. They are supplying them with some technical advice but not with the requisite capital.

Against this general background we studied the problem of national integration in underdeveloped countries (Chapter XII). We focused our interest on the deeper social changes, necessary to make the integration process possible, and established the urgent need for initial radical reforms of the social structure to break all kinds of rigidities. We saw the paramount danger in many underdeveloped countries, and particularly in the most heavily populated ones, of the present population trends and the pressing need for a deliberate population policy. In the economic field, too, the state has to play a much more decisive role than it ever did in the industrially advanced countries. A serious difficulty arises because the governments and administrations concerned are so much weaker.

The reforms of the social structure in underdeveloped countries and, indeed, their entire social, economic, and political development cannot be patterned on the forms of the developed countries. The underdeveloped countries, if they succeed, will grow into national communities which in many ways will be different from ours, as they have values of their own which should be preserved and developed and which, anyhow, cannot be eradicated without inviting disaster. Certain values, and particularly political democracy, should, however, according to our value premises, be imported together with the new techniques, though again the forms will be different but not necessarily inferior. Success in steering the development in the direction of democracy will depend upon their relative success in economic development.

Our study of the problems of commercial policy of underdeveloped countries showed the bitter failure of all the brave plans drawn up in the closing years of the war and immediately after to alleviate their difficulties in foreign trade by international action to stabilize commodity prices, instigate compensatory capital movements, control industrial cartels, etc. (Chapter XIII). Almost the only recourse therefore left to the underdeveloped countries is self-help and a national policy designed in the national interest.

They will have to stabilize savings on the relatively very high level that corresponds to their development ambitions, and do so under the given conditions of extremely low levels of consumption, little or no capital inflow, and widely fluctuating export proceeds. In their export policies their main interests must be to break the rigidities of their production system, reach a higher diversification of production and export, and, if possible, make fuller use of the opportunities of mutual cooperation. In their import policies they must try to use their foreign exchange as much as possible to buy capital goods. They will have been forced already, for exchange reasons, to interfere radically in their foreign trade; the fact that their economies are underdeveloped and unbalanced provides additional and special reasons for protection. In this respect they are in a very different trading position from that of the advanced countries, and one very different also from that which is, as yet, unequivocally recognized in the advanced countries, either practically in their commercial policies towards the underdeveloped countries or in most of the theoretical literature on their commercial problems.

Our attempt has been to study in broad outline but realistically the problems confronting underdeveloped countries, keeping our eyes wide open for all opportunities and facilities but also facing squarely and analyzing relentlessly the difficulties. Taking together all the inferences drawn from these last three chapters it is impossible to end with any other conclusion than that, short of a number of near-miracles, few underdeveloped countries will succeed in attaining their essential goals. The alternative to reasonable success is political catastrophe.

This is spelled out, since the rational purpose of study and thought must be to find out where we are heading. The present author, however, does not believe in a determinist philosophy of history. He constantly tries to recall that history is man-made and never a blind destiny, determined in advance. Trends do change, the unexpected happens. When the need was greatest, inspiration and leadership have often worked near-miracles in the history of nations.

Our study has been an analysis of international relations in the non-Soviet world. We have not gone into the problem of how the political split between the two parts of the world developed. But I would here add the observation that the study is also relevant to an analysis of this fateful political split. This analysis would have to be based on a thorough understanding of the international relations within the non-Soviet world, as well as of those within the Soviet orbit.

We have, however, taken a summary view of the economic effects in the non-Soviet world of the cold war—these effects being defined as an independent variable—as otherwise our study would have been grossly superficial (Chapter X). These effects are immense, though most of them cannot be assessed with any accuracy; this is so for logical reasons, since the political split and the cold war are such huge historical entities that the hypothetical situation in the world, if they were absent, cannot be ascertained. Generally speaking, the economic effects of the cold war are not very different in character from the effects of the other wars and international crises which have filled these last forty years and forcibly pushed the world in the direction of national economic integration and international disintegration.

We have had reasons to emphasize especially the ideological effects in the underprivileged part of the world of the Soviet system for economic development. It is, indeed, easily understandable why in the non-Soviet world and, particularly, in the United States, interest in the under-developed countries becomes motivated mainly by the fear that these countries may go Communist and that, more particularly, proposals for aiding them and for improving international cooperation as a whole in the non-Soviet world are given this negative motivation. The character of a motivation, even for good deeds, is, however, not without political consequence. Contrary to a popular fallacy, even money is not without a taste and a smell. When dealing with the significant questions of institutional forms for, and political conditions applied to, international aid and cooperation we have seen the paramount importance of this.

The main conclusion that comes out of this study is, however, that *in the present stage of history nations in the non-Soviet world are not prepared in peacetime to accept the degree of international human solidarity which would make possible progress towards international economic integration.* Underneath all the discrete facts and causal relations that have been dealt with in this book and put in some order, this is the hard core of the matter.

The paradox is, of course, that human solidarity within the individual nations has meanwhile been growing rapidly and has now reached an intensity and an effectiveness that could hardly have been foreseen fifty or a hundred years ago. In the highly advanced countries our material progress is founded upon this solidarity; in the less advanced countries the development of national solidarity is the main basis for hope that they, too, will progress. The contradiction in all our policies—and within our national and international institutions and, indeed, in our social sciences, our philosophical thinking, and our political attitudes—has its social determination in this fact that the very growth of national solidarity in practically all its manifestations has implied a shrinking of international solidarity.

THE INTERNATIONAL "CLASS SOCIETY"

While in the nationally highly integrated countries, which are also the rich and progressive ones and where something less than one sixth of mankind lives, class differences have been gradually eradicated, these nations themselves, as nations, are still, more than ever, appearing as an entrenched upper class in world society. To a great extent these elite nations are content to continue living their own national lives, watching their privileges, implicitly convinced of the intrinsic superiority of their ways of life and wanting to have them generally accepted as norms, taking their own interrelations as the important ones and as forming the center of what is recognized as international problems.

Marx's idea that there existed a basis for international solidarity between the poor in all countries was never anything more than a myth. Now it is not even preserved as a myth by the practical men who direct the Labor parties in the several countries. There is no functioning "International Labor Movement"; as I pointed out in Chapter IV, the considerable degree of internationalism which animated the Labor movement and all other popular reform movements in their beginnings generations ago has almost disappeared as these movements have been transformed into important forces in the national political life of the several countries.

The Marxian concept of a "proletariat" never corresponded very closely to reality in most of the countries which are now highly advanced. In any case workers in these countries today do not form a "proletariat" any longer. They enjoy living standards which in many ways are superior to those of the middle classes one or two generations ago. In many of our countries they are well accustomed to support governments of the Labor party and other governments among whose members are many who spring from their midst. In all advanced countries they participate on equal terms in determining the political fate of the national community. Through their political power they have provided social security for themselves, they can save and become small capitalists, they can keep their children in universities and are gradually breaking down the important class monopoly of higher education which earlier existed particularly in Europe. Social mobility is now a rapid and continuous process. In a word, the national community is becoming theirs.

It is, however, not only the high living standards, the ever greater equality of opportunity, and the fuller participation in political responsibility for the national communities that mark off people in the lower income brackets in the advanced countries from the poor masses in the underprivileged world. In relation to these masses they have in their own feelings very definitely become "upper class" themselves. And, even more important, they have acquired vested interests in their nations' privileged position.

In the countries that still have colonies this is true in a very direct sense. In none of these countries—and definitely not in those where the national economy depends heavily on colonial possessions, such as Belgium in relation to the Belgian Congo—have the Labor parties taken a very effective anticolonial stand. Not even in a country like Sweden, which unsentimentally sold for money her last colony more than a century ago, is the colonial issue a living and important one in the Labor movement—in any case not more than it is to other political groups having their moorings in the higher income brackets of the population.

As in the stable upper classes within nations, cohesion between the advanced countries has for many generations become strengthened by ties not only of culture but also of migration and kinship. Between these nations there exists undoubtedly a certain degree of solidarity that the underprivileged nations neither have among themselves nor share with the richer countries. Like the solidarity in any upper class formation in an individual country, it includes also many nations on the fringe. These nations are like the various types of poorer relatives in any healthy specimen of what the sociologists call "the larger family": the prudent struggling young man who has been left with little inheritance, those who are old or sick or have had bad luck, the adventurer, and the prodigal son. In various ways and forms, and with considerable complaints, they are assisted when they get into difficulties. And then there are nations in a more settled middle class position which do not attempt to identify themselves with the really advanced countries but which also feel socially distant from the large group of very poor and underdeveloped ones.

An element of decay in this upper class formation of nations—also often observed in the upper class within a nation—is, however, an increasing internal disintegration. The recent increase in the recourse to aid and assistance as between these nations is to a significant part an effect of this disintegration; it is conscience money—a substitute for a more constructive economic cooperation between them which is failing. We have seen how these advanced nations have not been able to solve in a satisfactory way the problems of freeing and stabilizing their own mutual economic relations.

The major part of the public discussion of international integration is, as a matter of fact, devoted to this intraclass problem, even if in form the interests of the underprivileged nations are included. As we have seen in Chapter IV, this disintegration, even in the partial world of advanced nations, is in many ways the incidental result of the national integration process in the several individual states. A disintegrating upper class is usually not more but less capable of taking a broader view of society, than if it had fewer and smaller internal problems to worry about.

I do not want to press this analogy but I do think that it has an element of relevance. On a fundamental level, the differences between nations have similarities with the differences between social classes in a national community—as they existed before they began to dissolve rapidly, on account of national integration in our modern welfare states.

The larger part of the rest of mankind forms in this sense a lower class of nations—with a number of nations in a middle class position between. As a matter of fact, and considering their actual levels of living, the term "proletariat" would be more appropriate in such an international comparison than it ever was or, anyhow, is now within any of the advanced nations. The "great awakening" in the backward nations is slowly also creating among them the class consciousness without which a social conglomeration is amorphous and unintegrated.

The actual cohesion is, however, as yet extremely weak. The consciousness of unity of interests and destiny has to develop by the breaking down of firmly established traditions. As in the preindustrial, patriarchal national community individuals and families among the poor had their regular primary contacts not so much with each other but with individual upper class families whose clients and dependents they were, so the traditional international relations of backward peoples were bilateral ones with the metropolitan countries.

I do not deny, of course, the strong cultural ties existing among a number of underdeveloped countries. The Latin American nations have in general the same Iberian culture and their allegiance to the Catholic Church is usually strong. Similarly, the Moslem world is very dependent on the Arab tradition. It is the stagnation of culture, however, reflected in the low level of economic development of which it is both cause and effect, which gives full play to the disintegrating forces within these countries and at the same time frustrates their interrelations.

As we have seen, however, cohesion between the underprivileged nations has had its beginning in feelings of solidarity in the most general questions, such as demands for breaking down the remnants of colonialism, for international redistributional measures, better terms of trade, and international price stabilization. The institution of the United Nations has had perhaps its greatest consequence in offering general forums where representatives of the underprivileged nations could meet each other and where attitudes of unity between them could be gradually formed and expressed. As yet their solidarity has not been great enough, and the available technical means for policy planning and execution not accomplished enough for any significant practical cooperation in trade or anything else. But the significant fact is that while the trend of change in the upper class group of nations has been for a long time towards disintegration, frail beginnings of an opposite trend towards greater cohesion are visible in the underprivileged group of nations.

The gradual strengthening of this practical cooperation will in the ordinary way of cumulative social change be both cause and effect of the growth of solidarity in the large lower class of world society. The greatest difficulty to overcome—always a retarding and in some countries perhaps a preventive force—is without doubt the immense social and economic inequalities within these countries, that is, their general lack of national integration.[8]

The great riches of a few in the underprivileged countries should, however, not conceal the main truth that the overwhelmingly great masses of their inhabitants are very poor. It is in this sense that they form a lower class of nations. In our present era, the expression "the international labor movement" can have no real sense except as referring to the beginning of the revolt of this poverty-stricken majority of nations in our world.[9]

THE POLICIES OF THE UNDERDEVELOPED COUNTRIES

The world's hope for a peaceful solution of the political problem raised by the gross inequality of opportunity between nations consists, of course, in the possibility of two great and interrelated changes in the world.

First, that the underprivileged nations succeed in joining forces effectively; as I have repeatedly stressed, it is strongly in the interest of international world democracy that they strengthen their bargaining power.

Second, that, as the present power vacuum is thus filled, a greater equality of opportunity is brought about by peaceful means of international cooperation on the basis of a gradually growing feeling of international solidarity.

If these changes occur, this development on a world scale would be closely parallel to what has actually happened within our own nations during recent generations.

With all the momentous difficulties that the underdeveloped countries have to overcome it must be a source of great inner security to them that their road is so clearly marked and their goal so evident. From the point of view of our value premise of international integration their greatest defect in the concert of nations is quite simply their inability to make their will prevail. Indeed, any real progress towards international integration assumes that they are gradually able to exert a power more in line with the size of their populations. Every year that goes by with the underdeveloped countries still very weak in bargaining power implies a continual imperfection of world democracy and a continual danger of conflicts becoming unmanageable by peaceful means.

If they can secure economic progress and national strength by national integration, this is in the interest of international integration, too. Their strivings for national political and economic independence are at the same time moves towards creating more favorable conditions for international integration. Every increase of bargaining power they can reach by closer cooperation among themselves, within their own region and in the world at large, has the same effect. Even when this cooperation has as its direct aim to protect themselves against exploitation by the advanced countries, the ultimate result, if they are successful, can only be to build a firmer basis for cooperation with the advanced countries too. In all their strivings to improve their economic and political situation they have the same moral certitude as the labor movements in the industrially advanced countries once had when they overcame the impediments of poverty, ignorance, and apathy among the masses: that wherever they succeeded in gaining something for the poor they built a firmer basis for the unity and strength of their nations.

On these principles we cannot hesitate if we have taken to heart the basic ideals of democracy; and the experiences of recent generations of the process of reaching a fuller realization of liberty and equality in the advanced nations bear them out fully. *Only when all these underprivileged nations, with their great multitude of peoples with different facial features, color of skin, religions, folklores, and cultural heritages, have risen to equality of opportunity will the world become integrated.* Faith in this principle is the real content of our value premise.

At that distant time, if it ever arrives, our descendants may even be taking the final steps towards a democratic world government under which all human relations come under the rule and protection of equitable law, decided upon by due democratic process. The now advanced nations would be a tiny minority; numerically they are so even now, but the difference would be that their power in the world would then not be greater than their relative population. The ideals that have animated these nations in their internal progress to equality would, however, have been widely disseminated among other nations that would have by then reached their level. Those in the advanced countries who shudder at such a prospect may be advised to seek consolation by reading how people in the upper classes a few generations ago foresaw barbarianism and the doom of Western culture if votes were given to the poor masses—who, they often thought, had inferior innate moral and intellectual qualities—and by contemplating how wrong these forebodings were.

This is the age-old vision of liberty, equality, and fraternity. The Spanish patriot, statesman, and scholar, Mr. Salvador de Madariaga, a few years before the successful Fascist rebellion in his own country, gave expression to the vision:

It is thus that under our eyes a new society is being formed, a wider Christendom, a *civitas mundi*, less theological than the Christianity of the Middle Ages, less sentimental and abstract than the "Mankind" of our grandfathers. It is not based on the Here-after but on the Here and Now, it does not draw its strength from feelings and opinions but from facts and necessities. For boundary walls it has "nothing but the earth"; for inhabitants, men, races and nations; for powers of moral creativeness, all the cultures; for sources of natural creativeness, places and climates; for guide it has reason, for faith the intuition of an order, that is to say the relatively modest dogma that God is not mad.[10]

The vision is important because it clarifies our value premise. Meanwhile, the important thing in our life from day to day is the direction in which we are moving: whether we are approaching or steadily departing from our ideal.

The role of the underdeveloped countries is clear. They have continuously to push their interests which, almost by definition, are broadly the interests of international integration. The effort from their side is necessary for progress towards equality of opportunity; for, as I have stressed, it would be illusory to expect that the advanced nations would accommodate them merely out of their good will. They must be pressed to it. If they are effectively pressed, however, the underprivileged nations will have many to support them in the advanced countries. For their requests will appeal to ideals which are cherished in these countries, even when they are not lived up to.

THE MORAL DILEMMA IN THE ADVANCED COUNTRIES

In our industrially advanced countries, where levels of living are high, equality of opportunity is substantial, and political democracy is effective, we are looking forward with virtual certainty to continued rapid development on all these fronts. We see no limit to the further perfection of our national communities. One after another our countries are now entering an era where all the social and economic goals that were originally conceived in earlier generations by the political dreamers, planners, and fighters, can be realized and—perhaps even more important—where there is no real struggle about it any longer. As the community is becoming ever more integrated and at the same time rich enough to carry the burdens of social equality, these ideals are becoming accepted by all political parties and all social groups.

In their lifetime the proponents of what is now almost unanimously acclaimed were obnoxious to many—sometimes to most—of their compatriots, but some of them now have statues erected to their memory by grateful nations. And the many more who are forgotten have their indestructible monuments in the national institutions where the values they fought for are being given reality. The century-long struggle for equality of opportunity is coming to an end, because in the advanced nations we almost have it.

As I noted in Chapter III, there is meanwhile disorientation and confusion among those who in our age should represent this essential social momentum in our democracies—the dreamers, the planners, and the fighters, those whose important social function in society is to force a humane direction unto the blind course of Leviathan. If internal discussion in some countries has tended to triviality and in others to hysteria, I believe the explanation is not only the impact of the cold war but also the paucity of real issues which could organize our strivings and give them meaning and farsighted purpose.

What, in the end, are we going to do with our wealth, except to increase it all the time and make it ever more certain that all of us have an equal opportunity to acquire it? I admit that we are not there yet. But to reach it is definitely within our grasp. What then, on the other side of the hills, is our distant goal? What shall we strive for? This is an important issue, for "man doth not live by bread alone."

While the dreamers, planners, and fighters of earlier generations are finally getting almost all they asked for, somehow the "better life" in a moral and spiritual sense, the craving for which was their supreme inspiration, is slow in developing. And there is an uncomfortable and deep uncertainty concerning how we should attain it.

To my mind, there is no doubt that our moral dilemma is related to the fact that the "welfare state," which we have built up, with which we feel deeply identified, which we are not going to give up, and which we are bent upon constantly improving, is nationalistic. Solidarity is rapidly developing but it is increasingly confined within the national boundaries. At the same time, because of revolutionary technological and political changes, nations are inevitably moving towards greater interdependence.

Not merely to save the world, but primarily to save our own souls, there should again be dreamers, planners, and fighters, in the midst of our nations, who would take upon themselves the important social function in democracy of raising our sights—so far ahead that their proponents again form a definite minority in their nations and avoid the unbearable discomfort for reformers of a climate of substantial agreement. This is only possible if they enlarge the scope of their interests to encompass the world scene. They must again become internationalists, as they were when the reform movements started in the wake of the Enlightenment and the French Revolution.

Five years ago the fifteen West-European nations associated with the Council of Europe concluded a Convention for the Protection of Human Rights and Fundamental Freedoms. In Lord Layton's words, "the Convention should be the acid test of democracy; and thus a condition of membership of the club of European democracies."[11] According to Article 63 of the Convention any state may "declare" that it shall extend to its colonial territories; this means that unless such a declaration is made, the Convention does not apply outside the boundary of the metropolitan country. Among the colonial powers in Western Europe, only Britain has made such a declaration. But Britain has not accepted the jurisdiction of the Court of Human Rights, for which provision had been made, nor the possibility of petitions by individuals or organizations; it was these provisions which were supposed to give the "teeth" to this Convention. Belgium and France—and Italy—have not even ratified the Convention. A moment's reflection over this situation is apt to illuminate glaringly our moral dilemma. *Does not the very idea of human rights and fundamental freedoms carry with it the concept of universality?*

A Marxian Parallel

Marx's vision[12] a hundred years ago of the future development of capitalist society, founded upon his determinist philosophy of history, his analysis of the social facts in the early phases of the industrial revolution, and many other ingredients, has, of course, proved to be entirely false, but it is nevertheless highly interesting. It is, as we know, the distinctive attribute of a great scholar that even his mistakes are important.

Marx formed the opinion that the economic inequalities within every nation were bound to grow. Not only would the rich become ever richer, but the poor would become poorer, until it all exploded in a revolution; thereafter the state, being the property and instrument of the upper class, would begin to wither away as unnecessary and the "state of liberty" would reign. During the process of capital accumulation and industrial concentration, on the one side, and the proletarianization of the masses, on the other side, the upper class would consolidate itself and use the entire power of the state to hold down the proletariat. The upper class would remain essentially selfish and the continuation of inexpensive charity would only serve to cover up this fact. In the end the disparity would be so enormous that society would burst. "The knell of capitalist private property sounds. The expropriators are expropriated."

This magnificently dramatic vision of the future was not only founded on a philosophical concept but, as I said, seemed to be built upon a most impressive array of facts. And a lot of things happened exactly as Marx had foreseen them, particularly in the beginning. At one stage of the development in all our countries the police force was used to break up trade unions. In many of them the Church remained for a long time an instrument for preaching contentment, obedience, and discipline to the poor. The army was regularly conceived of, not only as a defense arm in war, but also as a safeguard against the "inner enemy." The upper class was selfish and charity was a joke from the point of view of the ideal of equality. Some industries did consolidate. But other industries did not and various distributive and service occupations increased in a way Marx had not foreseen. The ownership even of the consolidated industries was also dispersed, with consequences that Marx had not taken into consideration. A whole series of other things happened that Marx had not reckoned with or had not seen the full significance of.

The main surprise from the point of view of Marx's prophecy was the gradually developing national solidarity on the basis of which the great changes of capitalist society in the interest of liberty and equality of opportunity could be induced. The ideals of the national state, of the community of destiny and aspirations, and of the intrinsic equality of all the people within its boundaries were stronger than Marx had understood and in the end stronger than the class feelings. Individuals from the upper class went over as fighters in the political struggle for the poor masses and this had an importance for which there was little place in Marx's thinking.

What we have seen in the preceding chapters is, however, that, while national integration has been growing, internationally the world has been disintegrating and international solidarity is at a low point. Disparities in levels of income and living as between nations have been widening and continue to widen. I noted in the first chapter that it is a relevant and immensely important question whether Marx's prophecy, which has been proved wrong for the individual nations, may not turn out to be an accurate forecast in regard to the relations between nations.

The weight of the whole argument of this book is that to prove Marx wrong also in those international relations would require the growth of solidarity among nations on a vast scale. *The concept of the welfare state, to which we are now giving reality in all the advanced nations, would have to be widened and changed into a concept of a "welfare world."* It is probably the only alternative to giving Marx's prophecy its due in the vastly more crucial international sphere, while he has been proved wrong in the national one.

The difficulties in the way of instigating a development in the world, parallel to the development within the nations which made Marx a false prophet, are immense. The concept of mankind is bleak, abstract, and empty of concrete emotions to most people, compared with the concept of the national state. The United States, Sweden, and Great Britain are entities, the reality of which has been experienced for generations as forms for internal struggle, compromise, and cooperation. They have been defended under mutually shared heavy sacrifices against outside dangers. They have a history. And they are functioning, with increasing consequence for all their citizens.

Even at a stage when class cleavages were deeper than now, everybody came together, within a country, on the street, in the church, and in daily work. Geographical migration and to an increasing extent social mobility and the existence of a capital market, on the one hand, and the newspapers and schools, on the other, widened the immediate environment and widened it to the nation. The idea of people's fundamental equality and the ideal of their right to equal opportunity were part of the national creed long before gross inequalities were eradicated. People spoke the same language and shared in the same institutions. All these are significant characteristics of the national state from the very beginning, the absence of which in the larger world implies very much greater difficulties in reaching unity of policy, that is to say, in reaching cooperation.

The most important of the institutions shared was, of course, the national state itself and the most important difficulty in fostering international solidarity is the absence of a functioning world community (Chapter IV). In the national state the police and the army were always under the command of one authority, the government, which gradually became itself the instrument of a functioning democracy, encompassing all the citizens, having equal rights. Only in periods of national decay were there separate armed forces. Before the development of modern military techniques democracy had a basis of firm power in the very nature of infantry: one man, one gun. To an extent something similar was true of the formation of opinions before recent inventions in the field of mass communication and propaganda. The regimentation of minds was less possible.[13]

In the world today we stand, however, in the words of Mr. Adlai E. Stevenson, "shoulder to shoulder—with a hydrogen bomb, ticking in our pocket";[14] I understand that it is now on the cards that technical development will soon make it possible for even small states to find the means of destroying large parts of the world around them. And the perfection and consolidation of the mass communications industry, in the big countries increasingly organized within the framework of the state, influenced by its policy, and recently directly geared to "psychological warfare," is a threat to the liberty of the minds of people that cannot even be contained passively in our pocket but is already at work. As usual, propaganda is most effective in convincing oneself: a nation going all out in using these new unconventional propaganda weapons may easily become, to a degree that makes the thoughtless patriot happy, unflinchingly united, in the belief that it is completely right on every single issue, including all tactical moves by its government—but only at the cost of its growing spiritual isolation from the rest of the world.

It is in this perspective that Lord John Boyd Ord sees what he calls "the White Man's Dilemma":

He can attempt by force to maintain military and economic supremacy, in which case he will be involved in an almost world-wide disastrous war, worse than Korea, the final outcome of which will be the downfall of Western civilisation. On the other hand, he can, as Stringfellow Barr puts it, join the human family and use his present industrial supremacy to develop the resources of the earth to put an end to hunger and poverty with resulting worldwide economic prosperity—in which case he would lose his superior power.[15]

The Western powers are faced with the rising waves of revolt in Asia, Africa, and Latin America against poverty. They can try to resist it by force or keep it off by the offer of technical assistance and trifling loans with political strings attached to them, which will break on the first strain. In that case they will ultimately be destroyed or submerged. On the other hand, either with or without co-operation of the USSR, they could recognise the inevitable and use their overwhelming industrial superiority to create a new world of plenty. In so doing they would gain a new power and prestige by assuming leadership in the march of the human family to the new age of peace and prosperity and the common brotherhood of man, which modern science has made the only alternative to the decline and the fall of the Western civilisation.[16]

. . . This is a hard decision to make. To give up a power goes against the grain, and all the patriotism and pride of race, which has been dinned into him, revolt at the suggestion of the equality of races.[17]

To hope that for the world at large we can remake what we have gradually accomplished in the most advanced national states may seem an utterly utopian dream. The difficulties in the way of its realization have been described in this book. Nevertheless, I for one would not commit myself to the belief that Marx's prediction of cataclysm, which proved wrong for the national states, will prove right in the international field.

The unexpected may happen again. If it happens, the change of attitudes will not come as a sudden dramatic conversion of nations to internationalism but, as I pointed out in Chapter IV, will be rather in the nature of a cumulative process engendered by countless efforts, sustained faithfully over years and decades.

The Role of the United States

A move towards international solidarity would imply readiness to make sacrifices on the part of the industrially advanced countries. The sacrifices would be well worth while in the long run, and they would be small compared with the national income of those countries and even with the normal annual increment. But sacrifices there would be and it is implicit in the very logic of solidarity and international integration that the sacrifices would have to be shared in some equitable manner.

Power over the development would also have to be shared. And there is a close and necessary relation between sacrifices and power that was once expressed in a great principle of the American Revolution that there should be no taxation without representation. Neither can there be any real representation without taxation.

To the discomfort of the American nation and the apprehension of the whole world, an altogether unreasonably large share of the political responsibility for setting the world right, and an equally disproportionate obligation in carrying the financial sacrifices implied, has been thrust upon the United States.

This fact is so blatant that it is obvious to the common man in the United States—to the worker, the farmer, the businessman, the teacher, the preacher, the lawyer, and all the others who form the basis for the collective will in that great democracy. They all feel rightly that "the leadership of the free world"—as the colorful and somewhat simplified American expression runs—is something that is forced upon them by external circumstances, something they did not seek, and something for which their short national history behind the protection of two oceans has hardly prepared them.

Many competent political thinkers in the United States have for a long time clearly seen how fateful have been the consequences of the political vacuum created on the one hand by the sudden decrease after the Second World War of the power of the old European great nations and on the other by the still almost nonexistent bargaining power of the countries in the underdeveloped continents. They have also noted how the old League of Nations, which went on the rocks as the war came near, nonetheless represented, in spite of its major failure to prevent that war, a training school for big and small countries in the art of how to get together and discuss their interrelations: of the two superpowers, which now begin to monopolize the world theater, one—the United States—has not benefited at all from this preparatory schooling and the other, the Soviet Union, was a rather later and irregular participant.

All good Americans are torn between two feelings: on the one hand, that it is a dangerous monstrosity and deeply against their concept of democracy that their will, or anybody else's will, should dominate the policy of a whole group of nations with a total population many times that of the United States; on the other hand, that world events press upon them the necessity of attempting to do exactly that. And they are, of course, perfectly aware that this deeper problem is not in any real sense solved to anybody's satisfaction by a decision to talk about "partnership" instead of "leadership."

In various chapters of this book I have referred to the several elements in the historical process that have led to this dramatic impasse. The most important of them is the economic development itself. Western Europe, ravaged by the war, cut off from its eastern hinterland, and having lost most of its profitable dependencies in the backward regions as well as its investments in the new continents, has shrunk in relative economic importance, while North America has risen as a giant, dominating more and more in production, trade, and capital formation.

The very rapid rise in economic power of the United States during the last fifteen years is to a great extent only a delayed realization of an economic growth which for a whole decade was thwarted by the economic stagnation of the thirties. It is easy to see now that the main defect of the pump-priming policy under the New Deal was that the spending was on altogether too small a scale; the immense needs of the war, as it gradually affected the United States, finally succeeded in bringing into the production line the many millions of unemployed and all the other unused resources, with the result that the economy again developed according to its potentialities. The United States could therefore carry on the war with rising levels of real income and had a much higher productivity when the war ended than before.[18] And contrary to Western Europe there was no destruction by military action.

When the war was over it was therefore natural that the United States should undertake almost singlehanded the responsibility for rendering the financial support that was needed for reconstruction and recovery. This rescue work came to involve much bigger sums and stretch over many more years than was originaly foreseen; it also became almost entirely concentrated on Western Europe.

In the beginning it was to a large part undoubtedly motivated—in the eyes of both the giving nation and the receiving ones—as a postponed sharing in the sacrifices of the common war effort between the United States—which was in the war for a shorter time, had suffered less, and had come out stronger economically—and some of its less fortunate allies. The story of American aid to Western Europe can, however, never be really understood except by taking into account that psychological trait of the American nation which is the tradition of Christian neighborliness and generosity to the needy, the historical roots of which I referred to in Chapter IX.

Against the background of the popular psychological reactions to receiving American aid, which I commented upon in Chapter V, it is easily understandable that the West-European nations—or, rather, those of them that are not as poor and underdeveloped as the southern ones—have honestly wanted to dispense with that aid. Nonetheless, the long period of receiving unilateral aid from the United States has not passed without creating a pattern of thought in Northwest Europe which I consider extremely dangerous for solid and sustained progress towards international integration. To the common man as well as to the average politician in Northwest Europe, the United States is the enormously rich country whose natural role is to take upon itself the financial burden of any international aid in any part of the world that may be required, with only token contributions from other advanced countries.

Now that aid to underdeveloped countries for their economic development is brought up on the agenda, this attitude becomes clearly visible. A main reason why there is no pressure from the other advanced countries radically to internationalize aid and technical assistance to underdeveloped countries—except in the form of relatively minor programs, representing token contributions—is, of course, this feeling that it is natural and right to leave it to the United States to take upon itself to do the main job unilaterally.

Giving aid unilaterally for so many years to other advanced nations has also had its impact upon the Americans' own way of thinking. One reason why this attitude—that it is the United States' natural role to provide most of the international aid that is needed—could exert such a strong hold in all other advanced nations is, naturally, that the same historical experience has conditioned the Americans themselves to feel the same way about it.

As I showed in Chapter IX, in present political conditions unilateral aid on any large scale is bound to have the most serious effects both in the United States and in the receiving underdeveloped countries: at home it can hardly be motivated except as a political device in the cold war; this lowers moral and economic standards in the distribution, direction, and utilization of aid, creates resentments and political splits in the receiving countries, and will in the end only provide valid reasons in the United States for radically cutting down the appropriations. Even more broadly—and apart from these effects—it is an entirely unsound situation for a large part of mankind to become more or less permanently dependent upon receiving charity from one single nation.

Even if that nation were made up of philosophers and saints—which it is not—it could hardly avoid exploiting the situation by pressing its will upon its clients. And even if it did not, the clients would believe that it did, and they would revolt. All our ideals for social interrelations, as they have been formed for many centuries, are against this type of unilateral charity above community control and, therefore, arbitrary in its essence.

It is aid given by a single government I feel apprehensive about; international aid is an even more delicate matter than international lending, discussed in Chapter VIII. The Red Cross, the churches, and the experienced and highly competent American philanthropic foundations have in their constitutions and in the ideals they serve a protection for their moral and political integrity which the state quite simply cannot have, as it is in its very nature an institution for exerting power; and power must demoralize aid.

The world cannot be run as a company town—at least, not if we want it to be a democratic world. None of the virtues of the private corporations, which actually did run towns in our countries a generation or two ago, saved them from causing public resentment; in the end they all had to become integrated under community rules and pay taxes decided upon by the majority of their former clients—who also had to pay taxes.

Resentment—often unreasonable resentment—among the clients is, however, not the only result of such a basically abnormal international relationship; the patron's own moral status becomes affected. Secure behind the two oceans, feeling certain of its basic ideals, experiencing progress and relying firmly upon its rapid continuation, the United States once consistently displayed a quality of great open-mindedness, both to its own shortcomings and to superior values abroad, which was unmatched in any country, small or big, elsewhere in the world. Becoming the patron of the world, the Americans are now in danger of being robbed of this great national quality.

Instead of being open to criticism from outside, the Americans are now in danger of becoming touchy and narrowly nationalistic in their feelings.[19] And the nation is gradually convincing itself—and unfortunately also informing the world—that the United States is superior not only in production but also in everything else: from city management, housing policies, and organization of the labor market, to matters of religion, the definition of academic freedom, the functioning of the democratic process and the general philosophy of life—which is an exaggeration.[20]

Another old trait in Puritan America, self-righteousness, earlier countervailed most of the time by the readiness to learn from criticism, is now taking a stronger hold over the nation. I mention it here as it is, partly at least, an effect of the abnormal relations with all other nations into which the United States has been pushed; at the same time this change must tend, of course, to isolate the nation spiritually and increase the tendencies to resentment abroad that, even without this spur, are bound to result from the abnormal relationship of client and patron.

The inimical effects of unilateral aid given mainly by the United States are in my view so serious that—even giving full consideration to the urgent needs of the underdeveloped countries—I would rather see a short-term decrease in American willingness to give aid than the establishment of the present pattern as a firm one; in the end I expect anyhow that a cutting down of aid will be the result.[21] It might very well be that such a relative withdrawal by the United States would be the most efficient way of placing the necessity of considering a more equitable sharing of burdens before the other advanced countries; this would assume, however, that the American reaction would be directed against the unilateral aid and not against the international schemes under the United Nations.

I am fully aware of what in Chapter IX I called the awkward fact of American bigness and that under any international aid scheme the United States share in the burden would be very large. But it makes all the difference if the other advanced countries also carry their load and if the relatively larger American contribution becomes integrated into an organized international concerted action. The big corporation in an industrial town also contributes the largest share to the municipal finances but does so under general rules, and all other businesses also pay according to their assessed means.

An even more dangerous effect of unilateral aid from the point of view of international integration is, however, that appropriations for aid and technical assistance that are totally insignificant when measured in terms of the world economy become what Professor Jacob Viner has characterized as conscience money, relieving the United States from thinking through the consequences of its basic valuations in the several fields of economic policy. Positive action here would be much more important for the world and even for the underdeveloped countries than any aid and assistance.

What these fields are, I summarize in the next section of this chapter. A general characteristic of these other policy efforts, for which aid and assistance should not be permitted to serve as a substitute, is that, whatever sacrifices—real or imaginary—they would request are common ones. These efforts therefore imply abstention from economic policies that are narrowly nationalistic and so, of course, impediments to concerted international action directed to serving common interests. While unilateral aid is bound in the long run to influence world relations in a way that endangers progress towards international integration, those other policy efforts would all be steps towards such an integration.

In this wider realm there is, indeed, a wide scope for American leadership—and it would be a real leadership, corresponding more closely to our democratic ideals than does the mere picking up of the checks for international charity. The present position is, however, rather that American policy, or the lack of it, often constitutes the chief stumbling block to progress in these policy fields.

TODAY'S PRACTICAL AGENDA

The responsibility for what will happen to the trend of international economic relations—whether its direction will be towards continued disintegration or be changed towards integration—falls mainly upon the industrially advanced countries. For it is part of the present state of international economic disintegration that they have a disproportionately large share of power. It is also these countries that, in a development towards integration, would have to adjust their policies to agree with the pressure from the underdeveloped countries for equality of opportunity. If now in conclusion I proceed to spell out some specific and practical main goals for our efforts to reach a closer international economic integration, these goals are selected as strategic in the sense that it would be of great importance if attitudes in the advanced countries were accordingly changed.

I have expressed the opinion that thorough institutional study should be devoted to the practical problem of building up anew an international capital market that under the radically changed circumstances of today could again make it possible for capital to begin to flow to the countries that need capital import and the industries where capital could be profitably employed (Chapter VIII). A main object would naturally be to assure a substantial capital inflow to underdeveloped countries; but it is recognized that breaking the present trend to capital autarky between the advanced countries is desirable in itself and would generally loosen up international rigidities and create more favorable conditions for the underdeveloped countries to draw effectively on the available capital resources.

There are great diversities on the side of demand as well as of supply and it can be assumed that a re-created effective international capital market would consist of a network of many variegated financial channels; attempts to force the development into a unified structure or system should therefore be resisted. Meanwhile, the International Bank should be given the inducement, and the financial basis, to enlarge its lending operations, particularly for development purposes, to the limits set by its laudable policy of keeping its lending on straight business lines. Even together with the proposed International Finance Corporation—which we now can hope will soon be coming into existence—it will in any case never be able to take care of more than a very small part of the international lending that is rationally called for.

The peoples of the advanced countries should, further, gradually be educated to make the sacrifice of an increasing amount of international aid to underdeveloped countries (Chapter IX). We need particularly to tap more effectively the resources of countries in this group other than the United States. Quite apart from the immediate increase in aid which this would imply, it is probably the only means by which aid to underdeveloped countries can gradually be lifted to any appreciable level as a long-term proposition. A broader participation in international sharing would also help to keep a semblance of political balance in the international aid schemes.

A gradually increasing part of international aid could then be canalized through international agencies. The creation of the proposed Special United Nations Fund for Economic Development would be a first small step in this direction. Aid should be kept separate from credit, and prevented from deteriorating sound business standards in credit affairs; preserving this distinction forms the only basis upon which any volume of increased credit is possible (Chapter VIII).

An internationalization of international aid would be important also in order to tackle more successfully the thorny question of distinguishing between "good" and "bad" backward states. At present it sometimes seems that help tends to go mainly to the undeserving. It is my belief that a stricter adherence to our old-fashioned standards of credit-worthiness—which should be a natural guide in any international undertaking—would go a long way towards correcting the present haphazard and biased distribution of aid. Instead of remaining aloof, advanced countries must be more prepared to come to the aid of those governments that prove themselves willing and capable of tackling with determination their basic problems. It is recognized, of course, that if international aid is swallowed up in the military strategy of the cold war, none of these reforms in the direction of fair standards and good economy is feasible (Chapter IX).

The most hopeful forecast—assuming a much more favorable development than is at present objectively warranted—would have to conclude that in the years immediately ahead foreign credits and aid will only to a small extent fill the real needs of the underdeveloped countries for capital for economic development; if things go less well, foreign credits and aid will continue to be insignificant. Under any assumption, these countries will have to furnish by far the greater part of development capital themselves; they will have to extract it from their citizens by keeping down consumption. In particular, they will have to budget their foreign exchange resources most economically in order to increase their possibilities of importing capital goods for development.

Rather radical interferences in their foreign trade—import restrictions and export subsidies—are inevitable for most underdeveloped countries that want to push ahead their economic development; these countries have also special reasons for protection which developed countries do not have (Chapter XIII). I think we should stop circumventing the plain truth that underdeveloped countries almost by necessity have to regulate their foreign trade and that they have a rational interest in protecting their struggling industries against the competition of the advanced countries, an interest which goes much further than the infant industry argument or any other of the traditional amplifications of the free-trade doctrine. To admit this openly and squarely and to take the consequences in their commercial policy towards the underdeveloped countries—including the abstention from pressing them in bilateral negotiations to open their boundaries to imports which they do not deem that they can afford— is probably the most powerful of the aids to self-aid that advanced countries are at present likely to be prepared to give them.

The appeals to abolish restrictions on international trade and payments have a legitimate address, and that is to the industrially advanced countries. Very much more fundamental changes in these countries' internal and external policies than are usually envisaged or politically feasible within the foreseeable future would be called for to reach substantial results in this direction (Chapters IV and VI). The advanced countries should, in fact, manage their internal affairs and their international relations so as to enable them to take their proper place in a better integrated world economy as creditor countries; and the creditor countries should accept the consequences of their position (Chapters VI and XIII). When creditor countries liberalize their own trade, they raise the level of world trade in general, and at the same time specifically help the underdeveloped countries that are interested in obtaining freer access to markets and maximizing their exports and, consequently, their imports.

A sterner financial policy in those advanced countries that at present are still seeking refuge in the category of underdeveloped countries with exchange difficulties—without having the same good reasons for doing it —would make, of course, a determined move to full convertibility and trade liberalization more possible; the trend to capital autarky as between these countries could then also be broken. Freeing and stabilizing the economic relations between the advanced countries is an international integration goal by itself; it would at the same time have great advantages for underdeveloped countries even if their own currencies could not be convertible and even if, anyhow, they would not be in a position to liberalize their own foreign trade.

Likewise, the underdeveloped countries would reap great advantages from any success the advanced countries would have in perfecting, nationally and internationally, their business stabilization policy. Another service which the advanced countries could render the underdeveloped countries, without any cost to themselves and actually to their own advantage, would be to give their wholehearted cooperation to international efforts to stabilize the prices of staple commodities. The problem is technically complicated but, according to almost unanimous expert opinion, the technical difficulties are not insurmountable.

The new international capital market should be organized so that compensatory capital flows could be induced to counteract the effects of such fluctuations in the export proceeds which in spite of the commodity arrangements would occur. This last mentioned reform, together with the price stabilization measures, would, in fact, provide a much firmer basis for a general policy of counteracting business fluctuations.

Much the same holds true in regard to the problems of international control of industrial cartels. Effective cooperation to solve this problem would be wholesome for the advanced countries themselves and would in particular benefit the underdeveloped ones.

We need to give some thought, too, to increasing the possibilities for individuals, and not simply for money and commodities, to move across the frontiers between our countries. Labor, talent, and knowledge should be allowed to flow more freely. Generally, we should in cooperation find the means to relax the national restrictions which repudiate a fundamental value of Western civilization and cripple us in tackling constructively the formidable international problems before us.

I realize that stressing at the end of my book these concrete and practical issues on today's agenda of our weak international organizations may almost appear an anti-climax to the demonstration I have given of the hugeness of the problems and the need for radical changes in all nations' attitudes to each other. But an international economy, realizing greater equality of opportunity for all peoples in the world will not come about by any single great decision and act. There is no sudden or other way of turning the tide than the laborious one of seeking solutions to concrete and practical issues; if success could be achieved in this direction, a development would have begun which could then gradually gather strength (Chapter IV).

The industrially advanced countries have increasingly during recent years stalled on all these practical matters of international cooperation; my fear is that this may continue and that, at the same time, bitterness will grow in the underdeveloped countries where stagnation will persist and economic development in any case be uneven and too slow. The advanced countries, under the impact of the cold war and the spur of an unbroken sequence of political calamities, have felt compelled to devote an enormous share of their growing wealth to increasing continually their military power of destruction, which under the circumstances is understandable and defensible. But by the logic of tragedy this has also given reason to their economic nationalism and comfort to their conscience when stalling on international cooperation. My fear is that they will continue to find reasons and comforts useful to this end.

To close this book on a tone of fatalism would, however, be contrary to its purpose and its basic nondeterministic philosophy. The future is not a blind destiny but is, instead, under our responsibility. We have the powers to analyze the facts and to establish rationally the practical implications of our ideals. We have the freedom to readjust our policies and, thereby, to deflect and change the trends.

Methodological Note on the Concepts and the Value Premises

THE PLACE OF VALUE PREMISES IN SCIENTIFIC ANALYSIS

"Economic integration" is a value-loaded term. It carries the implication that the attainment of economic integration—in some sense—is desirable.

That a term is value-loaded is, even when used in scientific inquiry, not of itself a ground for objection. It has been a misguided endeavor in social science for a little more than a century to seek to make "objective" our main value-loaded concepts by giving them a "purely scientific" definition, supposedly free from any association with political valuations. To isolate them from such association, new and innocent-looking synonyms were often invented and substituted. On logical grounds, these attempts were doomed to failure. The load of valuations was not there without a purpose and a function, and they soon pierced through the strained "purely scientific" definitions and even crept back into the specially fabricated synonyms.

There is no way of studying social reality other than from the viewpoint of human ideals. A "disinterested social science" has never existed and, for logical reasons, cannot exist. The value connotation of our main concepts represents our interest in a matter, gives direction to our thoughts and significance to our inferences. It poses the questions without which there are no answers.[1]

The recognition that our very concepts are value-loaded implies that they cannot be defined except in terms of political valuations. It is, indeed, on account of scientific stringency that these valuations should be made explicit. They represent value premises for the scientific analysis; contrary to widely held opinions, not only the practical conclusions from a scientific analysis, but this analysis itself depends necessarily on value premises.

A value premise should not be chosen arbitrarily: it must be relevant and significant in relation to the society in which we live. It can, therefore, only be ascertained by an examination of what people actually desire. People's desires are to some extent regularly founded on erroneous beliefs about facts and causal relations. To that extent a corrected value premise—corresponding to what people would desire if their knowledge about the world around them were more perfect—can be construed and has relevance.

By no econometric trick, however, can a value premise be generated by pure reasoning or inferred from facts other than people's actual valuations. Therefore, no discussion of closer international economic integration has any meaning, except within the framework of a set of political valuations which should be made explicit. If a meaning is attached to the concept "integration," without any value premise being stated, there is nonetheless an implied one, usually corresponding to the author's own political preferences or those of his national milieu. Since the premise is concealed, this is not only presumptuous, but actually amounts to a fraud, even though an unconscious one.

The proper method to proceed, instead, would be to seek the foundation for the analysis in an empirical study of people's opinions on the matter under investigation. We should map the field of interests and ideals as they exisit and should confront these volitional forces with each other and with all other facts of the political, social, and economic situation of the world. I believe that the future of practical social science lies in seeking this foundation of a very much modernized political science, making full use of empirical sociology and social psychology.

This was, of course, not possible for the present restricted study of the problem of international economic integration. We have had to be content with what is generally known about what people do desire, based to a large extent on impressions and conjectural inferences. Nevertheless, it is important that the true relations between valuations and research in social science be recognized and that the proper place be reserved in our reasoning for people's political valuations.

A corollary to this general philosophy of the correct method of social science is the open recognition of the fact, stressed in Chapter II, that ordinarily the meaning of value-loaded concepts is indeterminate within a certain field. In fact, people have different and conflicting valuations and, therefore, mean different things when they talk about economic integration as being desirable. It is not a mark of clear thinking that the concept be determined by a definite —and arbitrary—definition; inherent vagueness must be recognized and accounted for.

The unity of a culture consists, however, in the fact that to a relatively large degree there exists a certain community of valuations, which implies that the field of vagueness is limited. This is particularly true of our most general valuations. In this book the concept "economic integration" has been related to the old ideals in Western civilization of liberty and equality and, more specifically, equality of economic opportunity. The trend of development in our advanced countries has been continually towards greater emphasis—and greater national realization—of these ideals. The "awakening" of the backward peoples consists very much in their, too, embracing these Western ideals.

The Classical Theory of the Perfect Market

These ideals were, of course, also basic to the classical economic doctrine. To an economist it would, indeed, be most natural to associate the notion "economic integration" with the theoretical model of the perfect market, governed by the market forces. Such a definition would not necessarily prevent the change of the concept, referred to in Chapter II, to imply the desirability of a dynamic process instead of a static balance.

Viewed from this angle, an economy would be fully integrated when the prices of identical goods and services everywhere tended to become the same and when, in addition, labor of a given kind commanded the same wage, when there was one market for capital with a single rate of interest at comparable levels of risk, and when the rent for the same kind of land had been equalized— in a less than completely atomistic economy: with appropriate amplifications added for noncompeting groups, location of land, etc.

The doctrine of the perfect market represented, as we know, something more than a theoretical tool for economic analysis, namely a valuation of how society ought to operate. From this political angle the significant characteristics of the classical construction refer naturally more to the beneficial effects expected to accrue to the participants in an economy that adhered to the doctrine, and less to the specific policies, or rather absence of policies, by which these effects were supposed to be realized.

The free market economy would, as I have already pointed out, lead to an equalization of the remunerations of the factors of production. In human terms this would take us a long way towards the achievement of the ideal of equality of opportunity, as every kind of productive effort would, without discrimination, be awarded the same pay. And the freedom to move in society without artificial barriers, which for this purpose was assumed in the free market economy, represents by itself an important element of this ideal.

The beneficial effects of the free market economy were furthermore, assumed —and considerable theoretical exertions went into "proving" it scientifically— to include maximizing the total production. In a dynamic setting this would correspond to creating the conditions for rapid economic progress.

Another old Western ideal, closely related to, but not identical with, the demand for equality of opportunity—the equalization of incomes and wealth— was given its due a little more than a century ago by the explicit recognition that the free market economy ought to be perfected by redistributional reforms. The principle of noninterference should, according to the classical doctrine, be adhered to in the sphere of production and exchange, where natural forces worked themselves out to common advantage; but in the sphere of distribution corrections would have to be applied by means of taxation and other interferences with the working of the price mechanism. It was held that otherwise the free market economy would not lead to a desirable social development and this was motivated by the hedonistic law of decreasing marginal utility, according to which a more even distribution would increase "social welfare."

The theory of the free market economy was, therefore, from John Stuart Mill on, always presented with a major reservation underlining the legitimacy of redistributional interferences, and it was believed that they would not change materially the operation of the free market economy in the sphere of production and exchange. This represents an extension of the ideal of "equal opportunity" to incorporate in addition an extra degree of "equalization of realized income and wealth."

Of these three main valuations at the basis of the classical economic doctrine the first one—the demand for equalization of the remunerations of the factors of production—relates directly to the ideals of liberty and equality. During the last hundred years, if anything has changed, it has been towards giving increased emphasis to the demand for equality of opportunity. The two other valuations are partly instrumental to this one. Redistributional reforms are needed in order to give reality to the attempts to establish equality of opportunity. Similarly, a fair degree of economic progress in terms of a rapidly rising level of production is, as we have found, a precondition for all effective attempts to equalize opportunities.

"Economic integration" as an ideal quite clearly cannot be defined by relating the concept to the classical doctrine of a free market economy; we have seen in Capter III that the actual process towards integration within the advanced countries has taken them further and further away from this theoretical model. Nevertheless, as I pointed out in Chapter II, the present study is in line, on a deeper level, with the traditions of political economy, since it is based on those more fundamental valuations, centered on equality of opportunity, upon which the classical doctrine was also founded.

THE CLASSICAL THEORY OF INTERNATIONAL TRADE

The classical theory of international trade was an adjunct to this doctrine of a free market economy. It assumed that all national economies were completely integrated domestically as perfect markets. This was, of course, an unrealistic assumption: only a few countries, and they only in the last two generations, have gradually reached a state that we can meaningfully say approaches national integration; and these higher integrated economies are, as I have pointed out, not of the free market type.

Internationally, the factors of production were assumed to be immobile.[2] This was a strange assumption, as in the nineteenth century and until the First World War there actually occurred, in the partial world which was then actively participating in international intercourse, very substantial movements of labor and capital which considerably contributed to the maintenance of international balance. The assumption has become increasingly realistic, though, during the last decades.

Since factor movements were excluded by hypothesis, complete international equalization of factor prices was not attained even in theory. Such equalization of factor prices as was possible was supposed to come about through the international specialization and division of labor made possible by trade, which was to achieve this purpose by equalizing the prices of goods everywhere in the world, within the limits set by transport costs. The practical conclusion of the theory was therefore the desirability of free trade.

As a matter of fact, international trade is now less free than ever. The national economies are not free market economies and are becoming less so as national integration proceeds. The very effective aid to attaining international balance which, until the First World War—and against the assumption of the classical theory—large-scale factor movements actually gave to trade, has almost disappeared.

As between developed and underdeveloped countries, international trade, as was pointed out in the beginning of Chapter XIII, does not equalize factor prices but rather tends to set up a cumulative process away from equilibrium.[3] The political development has now brought to the forefront the very large, and growing, disparities between these two types of countries, and economic development of the underdeveloped ones has become a recognized main goal of international economic integration.

International economic integration, like national integration, is at bottom a much broader problem than trade and even than economics. It involves problems of social cohesion and practical international solidarity, and the building up of machinery for accomplishing intergovernmental agreements and large-scale political settlements, as a half-way house to the common decisions on economic policy that may be out of reach for our age.

A definition of "international integration" in terms of free international trade is, therefore, as false as one in terms of the perfect market. However, to the extent that the classical doctrine of international trade was founded upon the basic ideals, enumerated in our account of the doctrine of the perfect market, the analysis in this book is, again on a deeper level, in line with the more fundamental intentions of the doctrine.

The rejection of the classical doctrines as appropriate terms for the definition of our value premise, "international integration," does not imply, however, that important elements of theoretical analysis, contained in these doctrines and amplified by the work of generations of economists in the classical line, do not preserve their usefulness as tools in economic research.

Footnotes

CHAPTER I

[1] H. W. Singer, "Economic Progress in Under-Developed Countries," *Social Research,* March 1949, pp. 2 f. "In terms of world income, the situation has probably deteriorated during the last three generations in respect to all three Pigovian criteria: average size, equality of distribution, and stability over time. If we define the 'average' world income as that of the median world citizen, the spectacular improvement which has occurred at one extreme and which has fascinated economists and other observers becomes irrelevant." (*ibid.*)

Professor P. N. Rosenstein-Rodan stressed somewhat earlier the importance of distribution: "But often it is not the absolute amount of wealth and income that counts, but its distribution, and there is no doubt that after a hundred, even a hundred and fifty years of industrial revolutions and great technical progress, the degree of inequality of distribution of income as between different nations is considerably greater today than it was a hundred years or even a hundred and fifty years ago. That is not only a moral, but even more a political and economic problem." ("The International Development of Economically Backward Areas," *International Affairs*, April 1944, p. 158.)

[2] Jacob Viner, "Economic Foundations of International Organizations," *International Economics,* The Free Press, 1951, p. 380.

CHAPTER II

[1] Occasionally the term "the free nations" is used; cf. *Pravda,* November 13, 1954, editorial article "Economic Cooperation and Mutual Assistance among the Free Nations."

[2] I have developed this thought further in *An American Dilemma: The Negro Problem and Modern Democracy*, Harper, 1944, pp. 75 ff. and 1605 ff.

CHAPTER III

[1] Alva and Gunnar Myrdal, *Kris i Befolkningsfrågen*, Bonniers, Stockholm, 1934, p. 202 et seq.; cf. Alva Myrdal, *Nation and Family*, Harper, 1941.

[2] Wilbert E. Moore, *Industrialization and Labor,* Cornell University Press, 1951, p. 16.

[3] See United Nations, Economic Commission for Europe, *Economic Survey of Europe in 1954*, Chapter 7, "The French Economy: Basic Problems of Occupational Structure and Regional Balance," Geneva, 1955.

[4] Cf. my article: "The Trend Towards Economic Planning," *The Manchester School of Economic and Social Studies,* January, 1951.

[5] Calvin B. Hoover, "Institutional and Theoretical Implications of Economic Change," *The American Economic Review,* March, 1954, p. 14.

[6] John K. Galbraith, *American Capitalism: The Concept of Countervailing Power,* Houghton Mifflin, 1952, p. 132.

[7] *Ibid.,* p. 142. "The government has played an important part in this development. Both farmers and workers have sought and received government assistance, either in the form of direct support to their market power or in support to organization which in turn made market power possible. In short the government has subsidized, with its own power, the countervailing power of workers and farmers. . . . This assistance, clearly, explains some part of the self-confidence and well-being which these groups display today" (*ibid.,* p. 152). Galbraith points out that in the United

States the white-collar groups still, on the whole, have not organized themselves for exerting their collective power; this is much less, or not at all, true of the other countries in the industrially advanced group. In Sweden even the Directors-General of the Administration have now a trade union with a salaried representative to negotiate with the state over their wages.

[8] See Appendix.

[9] Dr. Humayan Kabir, *The Welfare State,* Presidential Address at the Twenty-Ninth Session of the Indian Philosophical Congress, Peradeniya, Ceylon, December 18, 1954, p. 12.

Chapter IV

[1] I have developed this argument more fully in "The Trend Towards Economic Planning," *The Manchester School of Economic and Social Studies,* January, 1951.

[2] Raymond F. Mikesell, *Foreign Exchange in the Post-War World,* The Twentieth Century Fund, 1954, p. 523.

[3] United Nations, Economic Commission for Europe, *Growth and Stagnation in the European Economy,* Geneva, 1954, pp. 170 ff.

[4] I am here quoting from an unpublished paper which Professor Svennilson has kindly made available to me; for fuller substantiation I refer to the main work mentioned above.

[5] "Five smaller countries, Italy, Belgium, the Netherlands, Sweden and Switzerland, represent together a market which—measured by their income—is less than one-third of the joint market of Britain, France and Western Germany. *Ceteris paribus,* one would therefore expect the trade between the three bigger countries to be more than twice as large as their exports to the group of five smaller countries. The relative order of magnitude of these two currents of international trade is, however, just the opposite: the latter is twice as big for textiles, two and a half times as big for chemicals, three times as big for machinery, and six times as big for motorcars and other transport equipment" *(ibid.)*.

[6] "The Role of the United States in the World Economy," paper prepared for Columbia University's *Conference on National Policy for Economic Welfare at Home and Abroad,* New York, 1954; to be published.

[7] Cf. Joseph S. Davis, "The Economic Potentialities of the United States," paper prepared for Columbia University's *Conference on National Policy for Economic Welfare at Home and Abroad,* New York, 1954; to be published.

[8] United States, Commission on Foreign Economic Policy, *Report to the President and the Congress,* January, 1954.

[9] Cf. my article "Psychological Impediments to Effective International Co-Operation," *The Journal of Social Issues,* Supplement Series, No. 6, 1952, pp. 12 ff.

[10] *Op. cit.*

[11] In his recent book, *L'Europe sans Rivages* (Presses Universitaires de France, 1954) Professor François Perroux—though working in a conceptual framework, following lines of reasoning, and having his main interest in problems very different from the present author's—arrives at certain general conclusions parallel to those developed in this text: that in the present world the nation-states constitute the main and almost exclusive agencies for policy, that the practical problems, therefore, cannot be to abolish frontiers or create superstates but to reach intergovernmental agreements on the coordination of national policies, and that a primary condition for such an internationalization of national policies is a climate of worldwide economic expansion.

[12] With understandable glee, but at bottom deeply satisfied, as an American citizen, with the basic unity and steadfastness of his nation's internal policy, Mr. Adlai E. Stevenson, the defeated Democratic candidate for the Presidency in the 1952 election, spoke one and a half years later at Harvard University: "Not very long ago there was a lot of 'radical' agitation, so-called in this country. What did the 'radicals' want? They wanted social security, old-age pensions, regulation of utilities and securities, government aid for housing and education, a nine-hour-day and collective bargaining. Those were heresies not long ago, but in 1953 a Republican President raises the welfare state

to Cabinet status and asks for an extension of social security." (*Call to Greatness,* Harper, 1954, p. 102.)

[13] Cf. Gunnar Myrdal, *An American Dilemma,* Harper, 1944, "A Methodological Note on Valuations and Beliefs," pp. 78 ff., pp. 1027 ff.

[14] Cf. my article "Psychological Impediments to Effective International Co-Operation," *The Journal of Social Issues,* Supplement Series, No. 6, 1952, pp. 29 ff.

CHAPTER V

[1] This concentrated note presents only some broad synoptical views on the subject matter. For detailed supporting material of many of the statements made, which may appear to be sweeping without such a verification, I refer to the extensive economic research carried out by the Secretariat of the United Nations' Economic Commission for Europe during the last eight years, the results of which have been presented in its annual Surveys, its Quarterly Bulletins and the several monographs on major European industries and on European trade problems. Special reference should be made to a comprehensive analysis: *Economic Survey of Europe since the War* (Geneva, 1953), of which Chapter 12 bears the title: "Problems of Economic Integration"; to Part III of *Economic Survey of Europe in 1953* (Geneva, 1954), and to: *European Agriculture. A Statement of Problems* (Geneva, 1954). A background analysis of the European economy between the two world wars is now available in a study prepared for the Economic Commission for Europe by Professor Ingvar Svennilson and entitled *Growth and Stagnation in the European Economy* (Geneva, 1954).

[2] I omit another reservation: Inasmuch as the economic union replaces by domestic production some goods previously imported from outside, in which the union has a comparative disadvantage, general international efficiency is reduced. Besides these "automatic" effects, the union may follow protective policies which are just as internationally disintegrating as the similar policies of national states (see Chapter IV). In the present and foreseeable situation of dollar shortage, these effects would probably bring about a better payments situation and would thus not be exclusively disintegrating (see Chapter VI).

More generally, it must be kept in mind, however, that many West-European countries have trading relations with the outside world that are just as important as their trade within the region and in some cases even more so. Britain is, of course, the outstanding example, but it is equally doubtful whether Sweden, Norway, Switzerland, and, looking into the future, Western Germany can derive any advantage from establishing as a permanent policy special ties with other West-European countries at the expense of their overseas trade.

As I already mentioned, I am dealing in this chapter with West-European integration as a technical problem of economics, without regard to any intrinsic value it may possess as a policy tool in the cold war.

[3] See Chapter VIII below.

[4] See Chapter VII below.

[5] Cf. United Nations, Economic Commission for Europe, *Economic Survey of Europe since the War,* Geneva, 1953, pp. 218 ff, and *Economic Survey of Europe in 1953,* Geneva, 1954, pp. 132 ff.

[6] United Nations, Economic Commission for Europe, *Economic Survey of Europe since the War,* Geneva, 1953, p. 145.

CHAPTER VI

[1] United Nations, Economic Commission for Europe, *Economic Survey of Europe in 1954,* Geneva, 1955, pp. 30 ff.

[2] Professor Richard F. Kahn, in an interesting article, "The Convertibility Risk," in *The Financial Times,* September 10, 1954, speaks about "the artificial character of a situation in which there is a widely and strongly held belief that convertibility of sterling is imminent." He adds: "The strength of transferable sterling under the influence of this belief is as misleading as was the strength of sterling before the return to the gold standard in 1925."

3 "I also suspect that the relative smallness of capital flight from Western Europe during the past year or two was much more the result of the eased international political situation than of the influence of policies of monetary restraint or liquidity positions." Arthur J. Bloomfield, Jr., *Speculative and Flight Movements of Capital in Post-War International Finance*, Princeton University Press, 1954, p. 73.

4 Sir Donald McDougall, "A Lecture on the Dollar Problem," *Economica*, August 1954, p. 188.

5 This is Professor Bloomfield's conclusion from his careful study of the problem: "Even if, as a result of a progressive improvement in international payments positions, it should eventually prove possible to free current-account transactions from the restrictive application of exchange (and direct trade) controls and to restore convertibility on current-account over a large part of the world, it is highly probable that a majority of countries would still need or want to maintain some measure of exchange control over private capital movements" (*op. cit.*, p. 86). Bloomfield adds the reflection that "it may legitimately be questioned whether it will indeed be technically feasible to maintain and operate an exchange-control system which applies restrictively to capital movements but permits complete freedom with regard to the making of payments and transfers on current-account, *i.e.* a system which, while involving the licensing of all exchange transactions to make effective the controls of capital movements, permits current-account payments to take place freely" (pp. 86 ff).

6 *Op. cit.*, p. 1.

7 Richard B. Bissel, Jr., "European Recovery and the Problems Ahead," *The American Economic Review*, May 1952, p. 324. Bissel estimates that capital flight from West-European countries in the post war years "must have absorbed a significant fraction of the individual savings that might otherwise have found their way into the European capital markets" (*ibid.*). Bloomfield puts the same thing a little differently: "It is evident . . . that a significant part of the foreign aid of the United States Government has in effect gone to finance hot money movements from the recipient countries to the United States and elsewhere" (*op. cit.*, p. 59).

8 A recent student of the problem, Professor Brinley Thomas, shares Cassel's apprehension: "The barriers against immigration have made a profound difference to the working of the international economy, and this has never been properly recognised in the United States. The Quota Act of 1924 increased the difficulties of the crowded countries of Europe and widened the gap between the standards of living of the Old World and the New. This sharp break with previous policy was bound to cause a continuing state of international instability unless other traditional attitudes were reversed" (*Migration and Economic Growth*, Cambridge University Press, 1954, p. 235). "No interpretation of the lack of balance within the Atlantic economy, which has become so acute since 1945, is satisfactory unless it recognises the extreme difficulty which the economy has found in adjusting itself to the enforced international immobility of labour" (p. 201).

9 Robert Triffin, "International Currency and Reserve Plans," *Banca Nazionale del Lavoro, Quarterly Review*, January-June 1954, p. 21.

10 Triffin is probably aware of the reservation that has to be made to this passage: that much depends on what internal policies are followed by the nations which apply the restrictions. But even if a country follows an expansionist policy at home, aimed at filling to the limit what I have once called "the international space for internal monetary policy," which has been increased by the restrictions, I believe it can be proved that there is an unavoidable residual of depressive effects abroad and that Triffin's statement therefore is correct, though without the reservation these effects may be exaggerated.

11 It should be "endowed with very great financial resources . . . perhaps three or four times as great" (as the International Bank's). It "would be obliged to lend freely when depression was threatening and to cut off lending and to press hard for repayment when employment conditions were buoyant." Different from the Bank, it should "lend at critical times to the most suitable applicants, however poor credit risks they might be, to the extent necessary to get its funds into operation." "International

Finance in the Post-War World," *International Economics*, pp. 334 ff.; cf. *ibid.*, "America's Lending Policy," p. 340, and *International Trade and Economic Development*, Oxford, 1953, p. 92.

[12] United Nations, *National and International Measures for Full Employment*, New York, 1949.

[13] United Nations, *Measures for International Economic Stability*, New York, 1951.

[14] The problem is further discussed in Chapters XI, XII and XIII.

[15] See Chapter VIII.

[16] Roy Harrod, *The Dollar*, Sir George Watson Lectures 1953, Harcourt Brace, 1954, p. 155.

[17] John H. Williams, *Economic Stability in a Changing World: Essays in Economic Theory and Policy*, Oxford University Press, 1953, p. 86.

[18] *International Bulletin of the European Movement*, Paris, March 1954.

[19] *Op. cit.*, pp. 109 ff.

CHAPTER VII

[1] "Indentural labour, i.e. labour under contract of five or ten years, renewable for similar periods, after the abolition of slavery by Britain and the *Code Noir* by France, was responsible for the exodus of considerable numbers of Indian workers to various countries overseas, and this system held the field for long decades until it was abolished in 1921. This was how Indian communities were deposited, generally under duress and under conditions which were perilously near those of slavery, in Mauritius, Fiji, South Africa, the countries of the Caribbean Zone like British Guyana, Trinidad, Jamaica and Surinam, etcetera. In the wake of indentured labour small communities of traders and professional men went out, strengthening economically, culturally and politically these communities of working people. Contemporaneously with this process of indenture, particularly to distant countries, there was a similar process of recruited labour under various types of contract with respect to Ceylon, Malaya and Burma." Lanka Sundaram, "Effects of Emigration on the Economic Situation of the Populations of Selected Asian Countries of Emigration, with Reference to India," Paper for the *World Population Conference*, Rome, 1954. To be published.

[2] In at least some countries, with civil rights securely embodied in unquestioned and unchallengeable legal mores, the issuance of passports became an additional routine function of the local registration authority, such as issuing a birth certificate or driver's licence. The idea of denying a passport was never conceived, because it was assumed and regarded as beyond the realm of discussion that it was none of the state's business to hinder any citizen, or any foreigner for that matter, from leaving the country (unless, of course, he was awaiting trial or it could *prima facie* be established that he was attempting to run away from civil obligations; in such cases a strict and well-defined judicial procedure at the regular courts came into operation). In most countries, however, the issuance of this document became a preserve of the foreign ministries. This seems to have been largely an accident of history, a sort of automatic aftereffect of the war. Had passports been introduced in the free and easy times before the First World War, it is quite possible that the foreign ministries would not have wished to be bothered with such a matter. But as it happened, the basis was laid for the dangerous theory that an individual's going abroad is not his own business but is an administrative and political matter to be considered from the point of view of whether it is "in the national interest."

[3] Cf. Brinley Thomas, *Migration and Economic Growth*, Cambridge University Press, 1954, p. 191.

[4] Of which about two-thirds were from Europe, the rest being mainly from American countries, and especially Canada. The average annual rate of immigration into the United States from Europe since 1946 is between 100,000 and 120,000. In the twenties it was 250,000, dropping in the thirties to 35,000.

Professor Oscar Handlin argues in a recent study that the restrictive official policy of the United States did not fully express the attitudes of the American people. "The peculiarities of the domestic political situation in these years vested control over these matters in the hands of a group of legislators who represented only a minority of the population. An anachronistic committee system and factional divisions in the major parties put a cluster of rural and isolationist Senators and Congressmen into a strategic position from which they effectively frustrated the will of the majority. On such occasions, as the presidential election of 1952, when the issue was openly tested, public sentiment clearly favored a more liberal policy; only the means of implementing that sentiment politically have not yet been found. The actual reception of the newcomers by the American people has reflected the favorable popular sentiment rather than the grudging official policy. The accommodation of the new arrivals in the postwar years showed a popular willingness in the United States to make places for the newcomers in marked contrast to official policy." ("Cultural Adjustment in the United States, 1945-1952," paper prepared for the *World Population Conference*, Rome 1954. To be published. The paper goes on to prove and exemplify this statement.)

⁵ This commonly shared negative attitude to immigration, and the knowledge thereof and of its various causes, is reflected in an equally negative attitude to emigration. The following statement of the Indian position can be taken as fairly typical: "It would . . . appear that in the present context of world affairs, it is just as well that people of India in particular should not venture abroad, if only for the reason that her experience of emigration problems ranging over a century and more had been one doleful saga of exploitation by the Colonial Powers to begin with, and of denial of legitimate rights of emigrants in more recent times." (Lanka Sundaram, *op. cit.*)

⁶ As an illustration of what heavy emigration can do to the age structure, we may quote the following figures of males aged 20–50 years as a percentage of total male population in Italy:

	1881	*1911*
All Italy	40.2	36.6
Calabria	40.1	29.5
Abruzzi	38.8	29.3

(Source: G. Arias, *La Questione Meridionale*, Edit. Nicola Zanichelli, 1919, Vol. I, p. 323, quoted in F. Vöchting, *Die Italienische Südfrage*, Duncker & Humblot, 1951.) Net emigration in the seventies had been 0.36 million, in the tens 1.65 million, respectively 18 per cent and 54 per cent of the natural population increase.

⁷ In the Report of the Parliamentary Commission on Unemployment (Rome, 1953) a calculation is made of the cost to the nation of a level of 460 thousand emigrants a year. It was found that this emigration meant an annual transfer of the order of 650 billion lire to the countries of immigration, corresponding to 6–7 per cent of the Italian national income. The Commission commented that this capital "cannot be made productive in the present situation in Italy . . . but still, it indicates a considerable financial burden for the country of emigration, and a gain for the country of immigration" (Vol. II, tomo 3, p. 245).

⁸ I have much sympathy for the proposals to open the boundaries in thinly populated areas to a large-scale immigration from the severely overpopulated Asian countries, recently voiced again with much emphasis by Professor S. Chandrasekhar in his book, *Hungry People and Empty Lands* (Allen and Unwin, 1954). I am sensitive to the intrinsic immorality of the immigration barriers. And, per se, I am inclined to underwrite Chandrasekhar's statement: "Apart from the moral position of thinly populated and yet prosperous countries in a distressed and overcrowded world, those who oppose international migration as a threat to their high standards of living or to their racial or cultural superiority may be actually losing an opportunity to raise that standard further, and promoting an atmosphere of international distrust and suspicion in which neither the particular 'race' nor culture can progress or succeed unhampered" (p. 18).

Chandrasekhar is careful to stress that his migration scheme can never make more than a minor contribution to the solution of the population problem of the densely populated countries with a high rate of population increase. He assumes international migration to be an element only in a huge world effort towards industrial and economic development of underdeveloped countries; he also assumes a radical and effective world population policy, including a determined drive to spread birth control rapidly in all these countries. If these assumptions are not fulfilled, which I am afraid they will not be during the next period of years, the migration scheme becomes much more questionable.

Chandrasekhar himself evidently despairs about countries like the United States, Australia, and New Zealand ever opening their boundaries for immigration of non-whites. His main hope lies in Africa, Latin America, and the Pacific islands. I am afraid that in most of these areas similar political bars will be upheld. As they are all much poorer and have domestic development problems to solve, which are huge even without having to settle new millions of destitute Asian immigrants—in fact, one of the regular difficulties, as well as opportunities, for economic development even in sparsely settled countries is the existence of surplus labor—they have indeed often better reasons than the richer countries to resist immigration or, at least, to be very selective in regard to the immigrant's skill and possession of capital. In fact, not only the capital needed for settlement but even the costs of transportation and other inci-dentals of migration would, if realistically calculated, add up to sums quite out of proportion to the amounts presently being made available for international efforts of this type.

Basically, my negative attitude to large-scale international migration schemes is, however, determined by three more general considerations: one, that they are utopian and quite out of line with the type of world which is now emerging, where even migration between nations, kindred in culture and on a high level of productivity and income, is almost prohibited; two, that the population problem in the poorer countries is of such a magnitude that it can hardly be much influenced by any imaginable emigration; and, three, that a system of breeding and feeding future emigrants is a costly and irrational means of solving the population question.

It should, however, be added that the denial of emigration opportunities to the poorer countries and, in particular, the color bar, will remain a serious cause of deeply felt resentment in Asia and add its overtone to the growing revolt against worldwide inequality of wealth and opportunity; this problem I deal with in Chapter XI.

[9] The important thing is that economic development must not lag behind. Given sufficient capital, it may well be able to push ahead faster than the rate of natural population increase, and so in sparsely populated areas like Australia may permit, or even require, a regular influx of labor from abroad.

[10] United Nations, Economic Commission for Europe. *Economic Survey since the War*, Geneva, 1953, p. 221.

CHAPTER VIII

[1] South Africa, however, by a systematic enforcement of legalized segregation and discrimination is now attempting this—in modern times and against a majority popula-tion. "As the *apartheid* policy develops the situation it has made is constantly being aggravated and daily becomes less open to settlement by conciliation, persuasion, in-formation or education, daily more explosive and more menacing to internal peace and to foreign relations of the Union of South Africa." (*Report of the United Nations Commission on the Racial Situation in the Union of South Africa*, New York, 1953, p. 118.)

[2] Ragnar Nurkse, "The Problem of International Investment Today in the Light of Nineteenth-Century Experience," *The Economic Journal*, December 1954, pp. 750 *et seq.*

[3] The United Kingdom, France, and Germany each lost $4–5 billion of their prewar investments. The French and German losses were mainly in Europe and the Near East, where the investments had depreciated considerably or became valueless; two thirds of the British losses were due to the liquidation of their United States securities, largely in railroads.

[4] For a fuller discussion of international capital movements before 1914 and in the period between the wars, see, *inter alia*, United Nations Economic Affairs Department,

International Capital Movements during the Inter-War Period, New York, 1949, and Royal Institute of International Affairs, *The Problem of International Investment*, Oxford University Press, 1937.

[5] A recent United Nations study provides a fuller discussion of postwar private capital movements than it is necessary to go into here. (Economic Affairs Department, *The International Flow of Private Capital 1946–1952*, New York, 1954.) If the world supply of private capital has been only half as much as it was then, this would imply that for the other countries (mainly industrial Western Europe) such exports have been on the average only about 20 per cent of the earlier period. It would also imply that the ratio of United States to other private capital exports has shifted from 3:5 to 3:1. This rough calculation is, of course, subject to many qualifications as regards the nature and coverage of the primary statistics of capital movements.

[6] Cf. Ernest Bloch, "United States Foreign Investment and Dollar Shortage," *The Review of Economics and Statistics*, Harvard, May 1953; and United States, Department of Commerce, *Direct Private Foreign Investments of the United States (Census of 1950)*, Washington, D. C., 1953.

[7] Latin America constitutes to some extent an exception to the statement that American private capital has on the whole not assisted the manufacturing industry of underdeveloped countries. The greatest part of that capital in Latin America, however, has been concentrated in the three countries with the largest domestic markets, Argentine, Brazil, and Mexico, and in those countries manufacturing industry has received relatively much more than in the smaller ones. The United Nations study suggests that private capital often needs the attraction of large domestic markets, which most underdeveloped countries are too poor to offer. Cf. also United Nations Department of Economic and Social Affairs, *Foreign Capital in Latin America*, New York, 1955.

[8] See Ernest Bloch, *op. cit.* In four years only $33.6 million was attracted, against a coverage of $200 million, and it is doubtful whether these limited funds would not have been forthcoming in any event. Applications for another $58 million were under consideration at the end of March 1953. (See United States, National Advisory Council on International Monetary and Financial Problems, *Semi-Annual Report to the President and to Congress*, Washington, D. C., July 1953.) The recent Randall Report comments that "to date the program has not greatly stimulated private investment abroad" and gives the figure of $41 million for coverage to new investment.

[9] As far as one can judge from publicly subscribed foreign issues, they have consistently been safe investments such as the Belgian railways, Belgian-guaranteed loans for the Congo, South African investments, and issues of the International Bank; more recently there has even been a large public issue for the United States market. In recent years the annual rate of such foreign capital flotations has risen from $50 million to $100 million. Unofficial estimates of the outflow of private capital suggest that $58 million took the form of private dollar holdings of direct credits and individual investments in 1953, and a further $95 million represented U.S. security buying. (Cf. *International Financial News Survey*, May 13, 1955.)

[10] Some years ago there was a tendency for French private capital to be invested in North Africa for the further reason that it was believed to be a safer place than France in case of war. Also, part of the outflow from Britain was of the capital flight variety (see Bloomfield, *Speculative and Flight Movements of Capital in Post-War International Finance*, Princeton University Press, 1954, pp. 52 ff. *et seq.*).

[11] United Nations, Economic Commission for Europe, *Economic Survey of Europe since the War*, Geneva, 1953, p. 222, footnote 2.

[12] "The residual of 'errors and omissions' in the United States official balance of payments account is doubtless due in part to this inflow. During the years 1946–1952 this residual amounted to $4.3 billion." (United Nations, Economic Affairs Department, *The International Flow of Private Capital 1946–1952, op. cit.*) Arthur J. Bloomfield, in his study cited above in Chapter VI, places less reliance on this relation when measuring the total volume of capital flight to the United States (*op. cit.*, pp. 7 ff.) but does not doubt that it is substantial.

[13] *Economic Stability in a Changing World: Essays in Economic Theory and Policy,* Oxford, 1953, p. 163.

[14] By way of illustration, direct payments to governments by oil companies in 1953 came to more than $160 million in Saudi Arabia, $155 million in Kuwait, and $140 million in Iraq. Persia received $45 million in 1950, and had been offered twice that amount in return for a supplemental agreement. These payments are likely to increase progressively, year by year.

Some petroleum producing countries are putting these payments to much better use than others. In Iraq, for example, 70 per cent of all royalties is earmarked for development schemes; for the time being, however, and until development plans are gotten under way, it is mostly held on account in London. Cf. *The Economist* of February 27, 1954, and United Nations Economic Affairs Department, *Summary of Recent Economic Developments in the Middle East 1952–53,* New York, 1954.

[15] "The interest paid on bonds is far below the yield on direct investments of foreign private capital. Since direct investments constituted less than one-third of total foreign investments in Latin America prior to the First World War, the cost of foreign investment at that time was lower for debtor countries than that typical of recent years, when a high proportion of foreign direct investment has prevailed. . . . It is clear that to maintain a high proportion of private capital would involve a substantial increase in the burden of financial services on the balance of payments." (United Nations, Economic Commission for Latin America, "Preliminary Report of the Secretariat of the United Nations Economic Commission for Latin America," *International Co-Operation in a Latin American Development Policy,* New York, 1954, p. 15.)

[16] *Ibid.* pp. 14 ff. "This contrast between the relatively small share of public resources in foreign investments and the considerable proportion which was previously derived from bond issues needs to be stressed" (p. 15).

[17] *Op. cit.,* p. 37.

[18] Sir Arthur Salter, *Foreign Investment,* Essays in International Finance, No. 12, Princeton University Press, February 1951, p. 55.

[19] The only reference to this problem that I have seen is by Mary Smelker in "Review of Foreign Aid by the United States Government, 1940–51" (*Econometrica,* July 1954). "Considering the diverse character of U.S. grant and loan programs in the last 15 years, it is unfortunate that so many of them have been lumped together under the label of 'foreign aid.' . . . Since there will be a continuing role for U.S. Government capital export for years to come, a more discriminating treatment of loans and credits is called for, one which attempts to evaluate the degree to which specific loan programs were, in fact, aid" (pp. 398 ff.) .

[20] Statement in discussion at Columbia University's *Conference on National Policy for Economic Welfare at Home and Abroad,* New York, 1954; to be published.

[21] Cf. its eighth and ninth annual reports (1952/53 and 1953/54) .

[22] Recently, slightly more direct participation by private investors in new loans from the Bank and in sales from its portfolio has taken place, in most cases without any guarantee by the Bank; see its ninth and tenth annual reports.

[23] The President of the International Bank, Mr. Eugene R. Black, has recently repeated a warning, given in his opening address to the ninth annual meeting of the Board of Governors, against the giving of too much suppliers' credits, "under the pressure of competition, sometimes on inappropriate terms and for the wrong purposes." The specific points he raises in support of his warning are all well taken and worth careful consideration and he is certainly right when he points out that "long-term capital funds represent, in general, the most appropriate method of financing development projects which require heavy capital equipment." (*International Financial News Survey,* October 1, 1954, pp. 113 ff.) Nevertheless, in a situation when so very little long-term capital funds move, I believe that on the whole we have good reasons to welcome the rising trend of medium-term credits being granted in connection with export of equipment, provided that both the importing and the exporting countries acquire the habit of realistically evaluating the risks involved. The Bank's new information service on the nature

and extent of medium-term credit transactions to which governments are a party should certainly contribute towards a correct evaluation of these risks. (Cf. Mr. Black's address to the tenth annual meeting of the Board of Governors, Istanbul, September 1955, reported in *International Financial News Survey*, September 23, 1955.)

[24] Italy, incidentally, is one of the few countries in Europe that has only recently started an export guarantee system.

[25] United Nations, Economic Commission for Europe, *Economic Survey of Europe in 1953*, Geneva, 1954, pp. 203 ff.

[26] Privately circulated memorandum.

CHAPTER IX

[1] The notion that the United States put an end to UNRRA is an oversimplification. Agreement to end UNRRA was reached as early as the August 1945 London meeting, immediately after the Potsdam Conference, and before the cold war had really developed. The cause was a disagreement on the principles of how large the contributions should be and what countries should benefit. (The United Kingdom wanted to transform aid to Italy and Austria from military aid, which burdened her disproportionately, to UNRRA aid, where her contribution would have been less; the Soviet Union insisted on aid for the Ukraine and Byelorussia as a condition for this shift; the Canadians, who had made their contribution to UNRRA in wheat, which was no longer in excess supply, felt that any cash aid they could give should be reserved for the mother country.) In the end, the United States found itself in the position of seeing its share in the cost of UNRRA increased from the already high level of 72 per cent to 77 per cent; yet it had only one vote out of 17 in the determination of the distribution of food and supplies in an organization where the principles of distribution were not very clear. It is not difficult to see that this was an unstable basis for an international organization.

It is quite likely, of course, that the temper of the United States at the end of 1946 was already such that it would not have wished to have UNRRA continue, even if its share in the costs had not been so large; but UNRRA's death notice had been written in August 1945, and the United States was not alone in delivering it.

[2] Not including unspecified amounts of direct military aid for the war in Indo-China.

[3] United States, Department of Commerce, *Foreign Grants and Credits by the United States Government*, December 1953 Quarter (issued April 1954), Washington, D.C.

[4] United Nations, *Measures for the Economic Development of Under-Developed Countries*, New York, 1951, pp. 75 ff.

[5] If we take into account the secondary effects of defense expenditure on private incomes, the total is naturally bigger than the budget appropriations. When, for example, a man is drafted, the difference between his ordinary earnings and his service pay constitutes a loss of income that is analogous to a special tax for defense purposes.

[6] Jacob Viner, "The Role of the United States in the World Economy," paper prepared for Columbia University's Conference on *National Policy for Economic Welfare at Home and Abroad*, New York, 1954; to be published.

[7] Eugene Staley, *The Future of Under-Developed Countries*, Harper, 1954, pp. 362 ff.

[8] Adlai E. Stevenson, *Call to Greatness*, Harper, 1954, p. 92.

[9] *Ibid.*, p. 98.

[10] A. J. P. Taylor, *The Struggle for Mastery in Europe 1848–1918*, Clarendon Press, 1954.

[11] Lord John Boyd Orr, *The White Man's Dilemma*, Allen and Unwin, 1953, pp. 101 ff.

[12] Chester Bowles, *Ambassador's Report*, Harper, 1954. "In India I was often asked: 'Would America be concerned about our poverty if she were not afraid of our going Communist?' My answer was that I believed we would. I fervently hope I am right" (p. 342).

[13] The Randall Commission wished to see the United Nations' Technical Assistance

Program expanded but the United States' share in the cost reduced. "It believes . . . that no country should contribute as much as 60 per cent of the financing of this worldwide cooperation effort." (Commission on Foreign Economic Policy, *Report to the President and the Congress*, 1954, p. 12.)

[14] The Swedish delegate to the Economic and Social Council during three recent years, Dr. Richard Sterner, once openly said it in very simple and straightforward language; he did so in order to persuade the underdeveloped countries to create such conditions at home that the electorates in advanced democratic countries could be convinced that aid would be really effective and worthwhile. Mr. Raymond Scheyven of Belgium, appointed by the United Nations' General Assembly to explore further with governments the possibility of setting up the proposed Special United Nations Fund for Economic Development, made the same point in his recent report: "Before this source of finance [grants from the industrialized countries] can be tapped, the taxpayers must be convinced of the value of the sacrifices asked of them. Their effort must not be compromised by bad political management and the tax they pay must not be a substitute for the taxes that an enormously wealthy ruling class, indifferent to the poverty of its fellow citizens, might be unwilling to pay." (United Nations, General Assembly, Ninth Session, *Official Records*, Supplement No. 19, *Economic Development of Under-Developed Countries*, New York, 1954, p. 8.)

[15] Ragnar Nurkse, *Problems of Capital Formation in Under-Developed Countries*, Blackwell, 1953, p. 61.

CHAPTER X

[1] P. N. Rosenstein-Rodan, "Problems of Industrialisation of Eastern and South-Eastern Europe," *Economic Journal*, 1943, pp. 202-211. I would not want to under-estimate, though, the political difficulties that would have been met in selling such an investment policy to the Western countries, even if there had been no cold war.

[2] For the pertinent facts and the economic analysis of this development, I restrict myself to a general reference to the studies published from time to time by the Secretariat of the United Nations, Economic Commission for Europe in its annual Surveys and Quarterly Bulletins.

[3] Cf. Ingvar Svennilson, *Growth and Stagnation in the European Economy*, United Nations, Economic Commission for Europe, Geneva, 1954.

[4] United Nations, Economic and Social Council, *Official Records*, Eighteenth Session, 801st meeting, July 8, 1954.

[5] A recent joint study by the Secretariats of the Economic Commission for Europe, the Economic Commission for Asia and the Far East, and the Food and Agriculture Organization of the United Nations shows that European exports of capital goods to Asia were limited not by armaments production but by inability of the Asian countries to pay. (*A Study of Trade between Asia and Europe*, Geneva, 1953.) Recent developments have not changed this situation. Cf. United Nations, Economic Commission for Europe, *Economic Survey of Europe in 1954* (Geneva, 1955) and United Nations, Economic Commission for Asia and the Far East, *Economic Survey of Asia and the Far East* (Bangkok, 1955).

[6] A typical example of this way of reasoning is: "By the middle of 1953, the United States' gross national product had reached an annual rate of $370 billion, about 20 per cent higher in real terms than the level three years earlier. The dominant factor in this increase was rearmament." (Organization for European Economic Co-Operation, *Economic Conditions in Canada and the United States*, Paris, 1954, p. 13.)

[7] From the general point of view of price fluctuations and the allocation of resources for rearmament, America's favorable position must not be forgotten. Postwar experience has shown how very much easier, and with very much less disastrous effects on employment and incomes, the American economy has been able to absorb even violent shocks. It is, of course, in part the old story of starting from a position with bigger margins. Capitalism in America under present conditions has for this and other reasons shown itself to be a more flexible economic system than in other countries.

8 John J. McCloy, *A New Background for Banking,* American Bankers' Association, New York, October 19, 1954, p. 10.

9 The European countries suffered from higher import prices, especially for raw materials. As suppliers, the countries of Asia and Latin America were threatened by inflation, as a result of higher export revenue, the more so since raw materials contribute so greatly to their total exports. They were even less well equipped to deal with the problem, by taxation and controls and the like, than were the more regulated and experienced European countries.

On the other hand, these countries enjoyed for a short time extraordinary export incomes, and some of them utilized a large part of them productively or made provision for the lean years to come.

10 George F. Kennan, *Realities of American Foreign Policy,* Princeton University Press, 1954, p. 118.

11 *New York Herald Tribune,* European Edition, November 18, 1954.

12 I think that virtually all students of the Soviet economy would accept this as an objective statement of fact. It is not endangered by the recognition that the huge percentage increases claimed in earlier years reposed on extremely shaky statistical foundations (notably the upward bias in the old Soviet index of industrial production resulting from an admixture of "1926–27 prices" and of current, inflated prices for new items of production).

It falls outside the scope of this book to give further elaboration to the statement made in the text, to draw the inferences which are possible concerning the further development of agriculture and consumers goods industries (which have till now been lagging behind), or to amplify the statement so that it covers other Eastern European countries in the Soviet orbit. For these matters, as well as for substantiation of the main assertion in the text, I refer to the critical analyses of the economic development of the Soviet Union and the other Eastern European countries contained in the four recent annual Surveys, and in some articles of the Quarterly Bulletins published by the Secretariat of the United Nations' Economic Commission for Europe.

13 As regards China, an article, "Economic Development in Mainland China 1949–53," published on the responsibility of the Secretariat of the United Nations' Economic Commission for Asia and the Far East, appeared in the November 1953 issue of its *Economic Bulletin for Asia and the Far East,* Bangkok, 1954. See also, United Nations, Economic Commission for Asia and the Far East, *Economic Survey of Asia and the Far East* (Bangkok, 1955), Introduction and Section on mainland China.

14 This is, of course, a question where thick layers of propaganda from both sides have to be dug through to get to the bottom of the matter, and even writings with scientific pretensions—again on both sides—not to speak of official and government-sponsored literature, are under the influence of propaganda. All judgment is therefore for the time being difficult and remains uncertain.

There are, in addition, ingredients of a temporary nature only, that have also to be cleaned out in a rational analysis. In the early years after the war several of the Eastern European nations in the Soviet orbit were looked upon as former enemies and many of them paid heavy reparations. In the Soviet Union itself there was a strong conviction that it was really the Soviet Union that had won the war and had done so at terrific sacrifices for the Soviet peoples. The manifestly higher standard of living in those countries neighboring on the West, who had been on the other side in the great struggle, seemed undeserved. These feelings were very strong in regard to Eastern Germany, but they existed also in relation to other East-European nations. Such feelings might be criticized as partly founded upon wrong beliefs or it might be held that they are in themselves unfair valuations. The point here is that they do not necessarily correspond to lasting attitudes. The defection of Yugoslavia and the serious disturbances in Eastern Germany, Czechoslovakia, and Hungary have not passed unnoticed in Moscow; people in the West are sometimes inclined to cling to an overoptimistic—or, let us rather say, overpessimistic—assumption that the government of the Soviet Union never learns from experience.

There is still another element that should be left out of *this* consideration as extraneous, namely the effects of the system itself, implying the suppression of civil rights and liberties and many other hardships inflicted upon the peoples. This most serious problem is, however, not germane to the present discussion of exploitation by the Soviet Union of its allies. It serves, though, as a powerful counterweight to the positive attractions of the Soviet system. For reasons which have already been indicated, this counterweight is likely to be much less effective in the vast underdeveloped areas of the world than in European countries.

[15] United Nations, Economic Commission for Europe, *Economic Survey of Europe in 1954*, Chapter V, "Foreign Trade of Eastern Europe and the Soviet Union," Geneva, 1955.

[16] *Ibid.*, p. 125. The statement in the text is further developed in the following way: "This approach, if not pushed to the extreme, can offer very great advantages in that it does not allow economic development to be blocked, as frequently happens in other countries, by too static and limited a view of comparative costs. It recognizes that real costs are less than apparent costs, if employment is thereby given to labour which would otherwise be idle, and it proceeds on the implicit assumption that any existing cost disadvantages will be more or less eliminated in future as a balanced industrial structure is built up together with adequate supplies of skilled labour, transportation and power facilities, and other external economies" (p. 126). A footnote adds: "More precisely stated, the assumption is that, after a country achieves a given level of economic development, its scale of costs for producing various kinds of primary commodities and manufactured goods will not be so different from the corresponding scales of costs in other countries that it could have obtained a better total return by concentrating on foodstuffs or textiles, for instance, and exporting these goods in payment for imports or other commodities. For a fuller statement of the necessity for a dynamic view of cost conditions in regions or countries undergoing economic development, see Chapter 6 of this *Survey* and Chapters 14 and 15 of the *Economic Survey of Europe in 1953*."

The introduction of these dynamic elements into the calculation of comparative costs does not per se assume a Soviet system of economic development; in Chapter XIII, on the commercial policy of underdeveloped countries, I discuss this in the setting of the development process of an underdeveloped country that does not apply the Soviet system. But the point in the text is that it is a natural element in planning under the Soviet system and that, indeed, under the Soviet system the natural tendency, at least in the beginning, is for it to become exaggerated in the direction of nationalistic autarky.

CHAPTER XI

[1] United Nations, Economic Affairs Department, *National and per capita Incomes, Seventy Countries. 1949*, New York, 1950. The relative positions of some countries (e.g. Germany, Austria, and Japan) have changed, but broadly speaking the comparisons remain valid.

[2] At the rich end of the scale, high food prices—quite out of line with exchange rates—tend to overstate levels of income in countries like the United States and Switzerland.

[3] United Nations, Social Affairs Department, *Preliminary Report on the World Social Situation*, New York, 1952.

[4] Source: Food and Agriculture Organization, *The State of Food and Agriculture 1954*, Rome, 1954. I quote from the foreword: ". . . in 1953 heavy surpluses of certain commodities accumulated in some countries, though there was little improvement in the diet of millions of inadequately fed people over large areas of the world."

[5] Put in economic terminology the problem can be expressed in this way: supply in agriculture is highly elastic in North America, which is rich, but highly inelastic in most of the world outside, which is poor. The problems with which recent FAO conferences have been struggling—still only on the discussion level—are: how to integrate into one market two areas with such different supply elasticities, and who is to pay for a redistribution of surplus produce to the benefit of the underconsumer.

Part of the problem, but only part of it, is whether it is consistent and possible to integrate in this way one commodity market, while leaving others unintegrated.

[6] In the United States alone, it was 150 per cent; even if we make the less favorable comparison with 1937, the increase was still 100 per cent.

[7] The international measurement of production in common units gives rise to various practical and theoretical problems. The figures quoted, which are estimated on the basis of the 1937 weights used until recently by the United Nations Statistical Office for its world index of industrial production, do not pretend to any great accuracy; they serve only as an illustration of unquestionable and well-known trends.

[8] Felipe Pazos, "Economic Development and Financial Stability," *Staff Papers*, International Monetary Fund, October 1953, p. 229.

[9] W. W. Rostow, *The Process of Economic Growth*, Clarendon Press, Oxford, 1953, p. 226.

[10] Gunnar Myrdal, *An American Dilemma. The Negro Problem and Modern Democracy*, Harper, 1944.

[11] United States National Commission for UNESCO, Fourth National Conference, "Race Relations in World Perspective," Background Discussion Paper for Group B. 4, *America's Stake in International Co-Operation*, 1953 (mimeographed), p. 10.

[12] This solidarity operates on the political plane. As already observed in Chapter I and as will be further shown in Chapters XIII and XIV, it has not, as yet, led to any appreciable practical cooperation in the economic field.

[13] Adlai E. Stevenson, *Call to Greatness*, Harper, 1954, p. 1.

[14] Cited from Philip C. Jessup, "The Two Chinas and U. S. Recognition," *The Reporter*, July 6, 1954, p. 22.

[15] H. W. Singer, "Obstacles to Economic Development," *Social Research*, Spring 1953, p. 20.

[16] *Ibid.*, p. 27.

[17] *Ibid.*, p. 30.

[18] This is, of course, understood by the intellectual leaders in the underdeveloped countries. The Indian Prime Minister, Pandit Nehru, giving a press conference at the ending of the recent meeting in Jakarta of the Prime Ministers of the five Colombo Pact countries, pointed out that aid from abroad "is not much good" for Asian countries if they are unable to develop their own resources. "Self-help and self-reliance is the thing, and austerity is at present the prerequisite for future prosperity." (*New York Herald Tribune*, International Edition, December 31, 1954.)

A large number of financial experts recently assembled for an ECAFE Working Party had this to say on the general point: "The experts felt . . . that to reduce the magnitude of deficit financing governments should take all possible measures to obtain from taxation the necessary funds for development expenditure. Asian nations must rely mainly on their own resources to produce the large funds required for essential economic development, the experts emphasised. External aid might greatly assist Asian economic development but the first need was for an increase in domestic savings, even if for the sake of savings consumption might have to be kept down. The Working Party expressed the opinion that to attain higher living standards Asian nations must be willing to accept present sacrifices and, if need be, a still further lowering of living standards before they will be able to reap future benefits." (United Nations' Information Centre, Geneva, *Press Release*, No. ECAFE/213, November 1954.)

[19] W. Arthur Lewis, "Economic Development with Unlimited Supplies of Labour," *The Manchester School of Economic and Social Studies*, May 1954, p. 155.

[20] "At that time, mid- or late 18th century, many of the developed countries of today were already advanced economically—by contemporary standards; had already experienced fairly sustained growth over the earlier centuries, and enjoyed political independence in doing so; and were the direct participants and beneficiaries of the extension of knowledge and changes in attitudes that constituted the three revolutions mentioned (*i.e.* the intellectual, political, and geographical revolutions which occurred between the 13th and 16th centuries). In contrast, most underdeveloped countries of today are inheritors of much older civilisations which, however economically superior

ın the distant past, include strongly entrenched elements that constitute serious obstacles to the adoption of the modern industrial system. They face the problems of development after decades, if not centuries, of political subjection which, granted some beneficial effects, left a heritage against which the newly established independent regions must struggle. Thus, they must approach the task of utilizing the available potential of economic knowledge not from the position of near leadership and at the end of a cumulative process of preceding growth and learning carried on under conditions of political independence; but from the position of laggards by a long distance and after a period in which internal organisation was distorted either by political subjection or by co-existence with the aggressive leaders of the economic civilisation of the West." (Simon Kuznets, "Under-Developed Countries and the Pre-Industrial Phase in the Advanced Countries: An Attempt at Comparison," paper for the *World Population Conference*, Rome, 1954, to be published.)

[21] See Kuznets, *op. cit.* "One must conclude that the pre-industrial level of per capita income) in the developed countries was several times that of most under-developed countries today."

[22] Lord John Boyd Orr, *The White Man's Dilemma*, Allen and Unwin, 1953, p. 101.

CHAPTER XII

[1] H. L. Keenleyside, "Administrative Problems of the Technical Assistance Administration," *The Canadian Journal of Economic and Political Science*, August 1952, p. 346.

[2] Eugene Staley, *The Future of Under-Developed Countries*, Harper, 1954, p. 210.

[3] Jacob Viner, "America's Aims and the Progress of Under-Developed Countries," *The Progress of Under-Developed Areas*, edited by Bert F. Hoselitz, University of Chicago Press, 1952, p. 199.

[4] Tarlok Singh, *Poverty and Social Change*, Longman, Green & Co., 1945, p. 194.

[5] United Nations, *Measures for the Economic Development of Under-Developed Countries*, New York, May 1951, pp. 13 ff.

[6] Tarlok Singh, *op. cit.*, p. 193.

[7] See T. B. Lim, "Redistribution of Income in Under-Developed Territories," *Income Re-distribution and Social Policy*, edited by Alan T. Peacock, Jonathan Cape, 1954, pp. 278 ff.

[8] *Ibid.*, pp. 282 ff.

[9] United Nations, Department of Economic Affairs, *Land Reform: Defects in Agrarian Structure as Obstacles to Economic Development*, New York, 1951, p. 89.

[10] J. K. Galbraith, "Conditions for Economic Change in Under-Developed Countries," *Journal of Farm Economics*, November 1951, pp. 695 ff.

[11] United Nations, *op. cit.*, p. 21.

[12] *Ibid.*

[13] J. K. Galbraith, *op. cit.*, pp. 694 ff.

[14] Eugene Staley, *op. cit.*, pp. 210 ff.

[15] United Nations, *op. cit.*, p. 39.

[16] I am aware that my opinion is not shared by all who have studied the problem, for instance the United Nations experts who wrote the report *Measures for the Economic Development of Under-Developed Countries* (*op. cit.*, p. 52).

[17] Jacob Viner, *International Trade and Economic Development*, Clarendon Press, Oxford, 1953, p. 117.

[18] "Over-crowding of farm lands occurs not only in the regions where the density of population is high but also in under-developed countries which have a relatively low ratio of population to total land area. In Latin America, although vast regions of the interior remain almost uninhabited, the density of agricultural population in the cultivated areas is generally high. This is true particularly in Central America. . . . Africa, which also ranks as one of the most sparsely settled continents, has a higher rate of agricultural population to arable land than Latin America.

". . . The mere existence of unoccupied land does not mean that there is no problem in making room for an increasing agricultural population. Much of the land which is not being cultivated is unsuitable for farming, and much of that which is technically usable is poor, remote, or inaccessible. To bring it under cultivation often requires large capital investments, and sometimes also a kind of technical knowledge and aptitude which the people of the region lack." (United Nations, Social Affairs Department, "Population Growth and the Standard of Living in Under-Developed Countries," paper prepared for the *World Population Conference*, Rome, 1954, to be published.)

[19] Frank W. Notestein, "Summary of the Demographic Background of Problems of Under-Developed Areas," *The Milbank Memorial Fund Quarterly*, July 1948, p. 253.

[20] Cf. Simon Kuznets, "Under-Developed Countries and the Pre-Industrial Phase in the Advanced Countries: An Attempt at Comparison," paper prepared for the *World Population Conference*, Rome, 1954, to be published.

[21] United Nations, Economic Commission for Europe, *Economic Survey of Europe in 1954*, Chapter 7, "The French Economy: Basic Problems of Occupational Standards and Regional Balance," Geneva, 1955.

[22] H. W. Singer, "Population and Economic Development," paper prepared for the *World Population Conference*, Rome, 1954, to be published.

[23] Mr. Samuel W. Anderson, the Assistant Secretary for International Affairs, United States Department of Commerce, has recently considered this problem for two representative countries, India and Brazil. His general conclusion is: ". . . that the population growth in prospect in the underdeveloped countries sets up such a strong current against which the forces of development, especially that of capital formation, must swim as to call into question the realism of the projected development itself."

His analysis of India's problem is based upon the First Five Year Plan and he assumes an unchanged rate of population increase. Even on that conservative assumption he demonstrates that the fulfilment of the plan assumes that consumption will remain at the current level for some considerable time; to this he adds the comment: "The big question in my mind is whether or not a country situated as is India with such urgent need for higher nutrition and some relief from the grinding poverty of the masses can possibly stand another period of 15 or 20 years without any improvement in the average standard of living of the people." He therefore doubts the feasibility of the capital formation which is foreseen in the plans.

His analysis of the development problem of Brazil—a country with a higher rate of population increase, and larger incomes and savings—leads to a similar conclusion: "Here again, in the judgment of this writer, there is a great doubt as to whether the social ferment and the intense desire of the people for a larger share in the comforts of the modern world will permit the holding down of consumption in order to generate capital at the rate projected."

Apart from catastrophe, or massive capital aid from the advanced countries, for which he does not see the political possibilities, or a return of high death rates, which he considers unthinkable in the modern world, he sees only one way: the stabilization of the populations of the underdeveloped areas. ("Population Growth and Capital Requirements in Under-Developed Countries," paper prepared for the *World Population Conference*, Rome, 1954, to be published.)

[24] Frank W. Notestein, *op. cit.* p. 252.

[25] S. Chandrasekhar, "Population Growth, Socio-Economic Development and Living Standards," *International Labour Review*, June 1954, p. 537. Exception should probably be made for Catholic Latin America. Chandrasekhar develops his point further: "Any scheme for a network of birth control clinics as a part of national health services, must take into consideration the aids and obstacles peculiar to these countries. The mere mention of birth control for these under-developed areas conjures up all kinds of difficulties—religious, cultural and social. The truth is, however, that countries such as India, Japan, Ceylon, and Malaya are more advanced than many countries in the West as far as the public and government reception of this idea is concerned. The alleged religious opposition to the idea, be it from Hinduism, Islam or Buddhism, is simply not there. The Hindu attitude towards the question is one of tolerance, for Hindu scriptural texts have always made the distinction between two ways of life—the ideal and the permissible. The "ideal way" is for a score of saints; the "permissible

way" is for the millions of ordinary people. It was recently announced in Egypt that the higher Muslim divines had given their approval to birth control, since no contrary injunction can be found in the Koran. Japan has taken to birth control on a large scale, and the Government has even gone to the extent of legalising abortion, which is outside the pale of planned parenthood. More important is the attitude of the mothers, for after all it is they who should decide in the final analysis what they want. Recently several surveys on the question were made in urban and rural areas in India. About 60 to 70 percent of the Indian mothers and fathers approached clearly expressed themselves in favour of birth control. The real opposition is not even from the indigenous Catholics in these areas (for they know only too well how difficult it is to bring up a family of six children on, say, 100 rupees a month) but from the Western Catholic missionaries." (*Ibid.,* pp. 537 ff.)

[26] H. W. Singer, "Economic Progress in Under-Developed Countries," *Social Research,* March 1949, pp. 4 ff.

[27] Singer rightly stresses the fact that the absence of a technology that is at the same time modern—in the sense of incorporating the latest contributions of scientific knowledge—and in harmony with the factor endowment of underdeveloped countries must be classed as one of the major obstacles to economic development. ("Obstacles to Economic Development," *Social Research,* March 1953.)

"First, the initial expense of any investment is very high, and thus the scanty resources of underdeveloped countries are insufficient for a balanced type of development, which is the only kind that is reasonably productive.

"Second, the elaborate and highly expensive capital goods in which modern technology is incorporated are too difficult to produce in underdeveloped countries, and therefore have to be imported. This puts pressure on those countries' foreign exchange, and it makes equipment expensive to them, through the added cost requirements associated with dispatch, transport, and installation.

"Third, the labor-saving faculty of modern technology is largely wasted in underdeveloped countries, because alternative employment opportunities are lacking—and are indeed prevented by the very expense of the technological investment. This factor greatly reduces the social productivity of new investment in such countries.

"Fourth, the effective life of the expensive equipment in which modern technology is incorporated is often much shorter in underdeveloped countries than in those that are industrialized. For this there are various reasons, such as that operation is less careful, that there are lower standards of maintenance and care in use, that repair facilities are inaccessible." (*Ibid.,* pp 26 ff.)

Cf. also Singer's article "Problems of Industrialisation of Under-Developed Countries," *International Social Science Bulletin,* Vol. VI, No. 2, 1954, pp. 220 ff.

[28] United Nations, *op. cit.,* p. 30. The same thought runs through Professor Morris E. Opler's book, *Social Aspects of Technical Assistance in Operation,* UNESCO, Paris, 1954, which summarizes the findings of the UNESCO Conference in 1953 of social scientists and experts on the social aspects of technical assistance in the economic development of underdeveloped countries: "Actually, the elements of way of life are so inter-dependent that an important shift seldom, if ever, has occurred in a country, without significant changes in outlook and in social relations." (p. 37.)

[29] W. W. Rostow, *The Process of Economic Growth,* Clarendon Press, Oxford, 1953, p. 257.

[30] Norman S. Buchanan, "Deliberate Industrialisation for Higher Incomes," *The Economic Journal,* December 1946, p. 552.

[31] John H. Williams, *Economic Stability in a Changing World,* Oxford University Press, 1953, p. 38 *et seq.*

[32] Jacob Viner, "America's Aims and the Progress of Under-Developed Countries," *op. cit.,* p. 199.

[33] W. W. Rostow, *op. cit.,* pp 257 ff.

[34] Eugene Staley, *op. cit.,* p. 239.

[35] United Nations, Economic Commission for Asia and the Far East, *Economic Survey of Asia and the Far East, 1953.* Bangkok, 1954, p. 24.

[36] H. W. Singer, "Obstacles to Economic Development," *op. cit.*, pp. 21 ff.

[37] Pandit Nehru, Speech of 18 February, 1953, in the House of the People, *Indian Press Release*, IN 5-53.

[38] Tarlok Singh, *op. cit.*, p. 37.

[39] See United Nations, Economic Commission for Europe, *Economic Survey for Europe in 1953*, Geneva, 1953, pp. 182 ff.

[40] See United Nations, Social Affairs Department, *Selected List of Books, Pamphlets and Periodicals in English on Community Organization and Development*, New York, 1953, and *Report on the Mission on Community Organization and Development in South- and South-east Asia*, New York, 1953.

[41] Cf. Alva Myrdal, "A Scientific Approach to International Welfare," *America's Role in International Welfare*, edited by Arthur Altmeyer, Alva Myrdal and Dean Rusk, Columbia University Press, 1955.

[42] This new technique will often include a certain degree of mechanization, even in countries with a surplus agricultural population. First, mechanization often makes it possible to raise yields and reduce harvest losses very considerably, and to open up new land that could not otherwise have come under the plough, even in countries with population pressure. Secondly, in areas where yields are so low that draught animals eat a large share of the harvest, the possibility of using the output for yield animals instead may be a strong argument for mechanization, in spite of the existence of surplus labor and the lack of new land to open up.

[43] Ragnar Nurkse, *Problems of Capital Formation in Under-Developed Countries*, Blackwell, 1953.

[44] Cf. Gunnar Myrdal, "The Trend Towards Economic Planning," *The Manchester School of Economic and Social Studies*, January 1951, pp. 34 ff.

[45] Humayan Kabir, *The Welfare State*, Presidential Address, Twenty-Ninth Session of the Indian Philosophical Congress, Peradeniya.

[46] Norman S. Buchanan, *op. cit.* p. 552.

[47] United Nations, Social Affairs Department, "Population Growth and the Standard of Living in Under-Developed Countries," paper prepared for the *World Population Conference*, Rome, 1954, to be published.

[48] Ragnar Nurkse, *op. cit.*, pp. 94 ff. As example of imperfections in the latter respect, Nurkse cites "America's post-war aid to the Philippines (which in six years absorbed $760 million, apart from a roughly equal sum of U. S. Government payments on current account)."

[49] Herbert S. Frankel, *The Economic Impact on Under-Developed Societies*, Blackwell, 1953, pp. 99 ff. "In all the multitudinous aspects of their daily life the peoples of the under-developed world require to perfect new attitudes and aptitudes: be they in maintaining the fertility of the land, or in educating their children; or be they in hygiene, nutrition, and general habits of consumption and production. . . . Similarly . . . incorruptibility in administration . . . will not result from mere commands and exhortations. All such changes are slow, and cannot be greatly influenced by the rapid injection of capital from abroad. In fact, of course, the belief in the miracles to be brought by 'capital investment' per se is an illusion. In particular, it overlooks the fact that the essence of capital itself is that it wears out rapidly unless continuously renewed, repaired or maintained." Cf., for a systematic treatment of the problem, "Economic Motivations and Stimulations in Under-Developed Countries," General Report on the Round Table Organized by the International Research Office on the Social Implications of Technological Change, UNESCO, Paris, March 1954, *International Social Science Bulletin*, October 1954.

[50] United Nations, *Measures for the Economic Development of Under-Developed Countries, op. cit., pp.* 86 ff.

[51] Cf. Alva Myrdal, "A Scientific Approach to International Welfare," *op. cit.*

[52] Jonathan Bingham, *Shirt-Sleeve Diplomacy: Point-4 in Action*, John Day, 1954, p. 198.

Chapter XIII

[1] United Nations, Economic Commission for Latin America, *The Economic Development of Latin America and its Principal Problems,* by Raúl Prebisch, New York, 1950.

[2] *Ibid.,* p. 7.

[3] *Ibid.,* p. 2.

[4] *Ibid., p. 7.* Cf. Wadia, P. A., and Merchant, K. T., *Our Economic Problem,* New Book Company, 1943. "We would urge . . . the imperative need of working out the assumptions and theories suited to under-developed countries. Western economic theories and models are not applicable in their entirety to these countries, and planning on Western lines would accentuate rather than solve the problem (p. V).

[5] Jacob Viner, *International Trade and Economic Development,* Clarendon Press, Oxford, 1953, p. 7.

[6] The main features of production and consumption regulations under the Soviet system for economic development of underdeveloped countries have been referred to in Chapter X. In the commercial field these internal regulations are complemented by a complete state monopoly of foreign trade and, in addition, by a curtain controlling foreign influences on consumption patterns and other economic norms that might disturb national planning. Incidentally, the other important historical example of an underdeveloped country that, under strict government control in the early stages, advanced its industrialization at a very rapid pace, was Japan, which also applied the policy of an isolating curtain.

[7] I have given the reasons for this position in my book *The Political Element in the Development of Economic Theory,* Routledge & Kegan Paul, 1953, pp. 129 ff., particularly pp. 134 ff.

[8] I have developed this point further in three lectures given in Cairo in October 1955 under the auspices of the National Bank of Egypt, to be published under the title: *Development and Under-Developed. A Note on the Mechanism of National and International Inequality.*

[9] Folke Hilgert, "Uses and Limitations of International Trade in Overcoming Inequalities in World Distribution of Population and Resources," paper prepared for the *World Population Conference,* Rome, 1954, to be published. Cf. Wadia, P. A., and Merchant, K. T., *op. cit.* "This so-called free trade has always been a one-sided affair which has resulted in an inequitable division of labour, condemning the economically backward countries to a perpetual 'hewers of wood and drawers of water' status" (p. 44).

[10] United Nations, Economic Commission for Latin America, *op. cit.,* pp. 1 ff.

[11] J. K. Galbraith, "Conditions for Economic Change in Under-Developed Countries," *op. cit.,* p. 690.

[12] Stacy May, "The Outlook for Industrial Raw Materials Demand in 1980 and its Relation to Economic Development," paper prepared for the *World Population Conference,* Rome, 1954, to be published.

[13] France and Italy have, unlike the European countries mentioned in the text, been struggling under worsening terms of trade—undoubtedly a contributory cause, as well as partially an effect, of their relative economic stagnation.

See the forthcoming book by C. P. Kindleberger, *Europe's Terms of Trade,* a draft of which the author has kindly made available to me.

[14] United Nations, Economic Affairs Department, *Relative Prices of Exports and Imports of Under-Developed Countries,* New York, 1949, p. 7.

[15] *Ibid.,* p. 126.

[16] United Nations, Economic Commission for Latin America, *op. cit.* pp. 10 and 14.

[17] W. A. Lewis, "Economic Development with Unlimited Supplies of Labour," *The Manchester School of Economic and Social Studies,* 1954, pp. 183 ff.

[18] United Nations, Economic Affairs Department, *Relative Prices of Exports and Imports of Under-Developed Countries, op. cit.,* p. 17.

[19] United Nations, Economic Commission for Latin America, *Economic Survey for Latin America 1951-52,* New York, 1953, pp. 1 ff.

[20] United Nations, Economic Commission for Latin America, *op. cit.,* pp. 9 ff.

[21] H. W. Singer, "Economic Progress in Under-Developed Countries," *Social Research,* March 1949, pp. 3 ff.

[22] United Nations, General Assembly Resolution 623 (VII), adopted on December 21, 1952. *Official Records,* Seventh Session, Supplement 20. Italics are mine.

The resolution also deals with the need for international price stabilization in the short run and for national economic planning in the underdeveloped countries. I have abstracted what it had to say about relative prices.

[23] I have developed this thought in *Realities and Illusions in Regard to Inter-Governmental Organizations,* L. T. Hobhouse Memorial Trust Lecture No. 24, Oxford University Press, 1955.

[24] United Nations, *Commodity Trade and Economic Development,* New York, 1954, p. 3.

[25] *Ibid.,* pp. 3 ff.

[26] United Nations, Economic Affairs Department, *Instability in Export Markets for Under-Developed Countries,* New York, 1952.

[27] "Investigation of the trade of two important under-developed countries in 1948 (chosen as a representative year before the Korean hostilities) discloses that 55 percent of the imports of one and 70 percent of the imports of the other were plainly essential consumer goods; between 10 percent and 20 percent were apparently non-essential, or of doubtful classification; while capital goods accounted for 35 percent and 12 percent, respectively. We think that these figures may be taken as fairly typical. If we suppose that in an under-developed country 60 percent of export proceeds are required to finance essential imports of consumer goods, then a 20 percent fall in those proceeds (other prices remaining constant) will halve the amount available for other imports, including capital goods. The instability of the balance of trade of some of the poorer countries thus means that in the absence of large foreign exchange reserves, they are in no position to plan a continuing development program involving imports." (United Nations, *Commodity Trade and Economic Development, op. cit.,* p. 11.)

[28] United Nations, *Commodity Trade and Economic Development, op. cit.,* p. 16.

[29] United Nations, *Measures for International Economic Stability,* New York, 1954, p. 13.

[30] Ragnar Nurkse, *Problems of Capital Formation in Under-Developed Countries,* Blackwell, 1953, p. 117.

[31] *Ibid.,* p. 101.

[32] The building up of a variety of institutions, serving the purpose of promoting individual savings, and organizing them and making them fruitful to the saver and to the community, should be given a high priority in every development plan. To be effective, the institutions have to be adapted to different individual needs and possibilities and must fit into the community patterns; they must aim at encouraging planned and "goal-directed" saving. Even if, at least in the beginning, the financial results would not constitute more than a trickle of new capital disposal, the effects in rationalizing attitudes and mobilizing ambitions might be crucially important.

[33] United Nations, *Measures for International Economic Stability, op. cit.,* p. 18.

[34] United Nations, *Commodity Trade and Economic Development, op. cit.,* p. 19.

[35] *Ibid.,* p. 18.

[36] *Ibid.,* p. 17.

[37] One of the United Nations expert groups argued—and in principle they were, of course, right—that even "expanding the rate of development in under-developed countries, in times of recession, through foreign lending . . . would obviously help both lending and borrowing countries." ,United Nations, *Measures for International Economic Stability, op. cit.,* p. 27.) As the experts pointed out, however, using the development needs of underdeveloped countries as a huge counter-cyclical stock of reserve orders for the advanced countries' industries meets with various practical difficulties, as do all public works programs. They therefore concluded that "as a rule the most useful and practicable general objective is . . . a steady rate of economic development" (*Ibid.,* p. 28). If this should assume anything in the neighborhood of a capital inflow large enough to provide full compensation for adverse changes in real export proceeds, it would, however, as I have pointed out in the text, involve disposal

of capital sums far above anything that can reasonably be expected to be made available. What we are really discussing corresponds to what the physicians call minor remedial means, but the argumentation of the economists refers most often to a radical cure, which is quite out of question. But, naturally, the conclusions hold *a fortiori*.

38 "A fundamental principle of all schemes should be that, save in exceptional cases, they do not attempt to make the average price over a period of years higher or lower than it would otherwise have been. Their objective should be merely to reduce fluctuations around the long-term trend" (United Nations, *Measures for International Economic Stability, op. cit.*, p. 21). "What should be stabilised are short-term fluctuations around long-run price movements—be they up, down or continuing on an even level" (United Nations, *Commodity Trade and Economic Development, op. cit.*, p. 25.).

39 Even in recent literature pronouncements are often made by writers, faithful to the ideals of those times, which remind us of what at the end of the war was believed to be not only desirable but possible. Professor W. W. Rostow, for instance, writes as follows: "It seems inevitable that the world trading area will have to establish a common view of future demand requirements in certain directions, generate the capital necessary to produce supplies on an adequate scale, and make guarantees covering substantial time periods concerning the income to be derived from the furnishing of such marginal supplies. The idea of buffer stocks, to maintain a smooth flow and a stable price level for such commodities, is by no means new. It must be placed, however, in the framework of a longer-run calculation of requirements and longer-run guarantees of income." (*The Process of Economic Growth*, Clarendon Press, Oxford, 1953, pp. 253 ff)

40 League of Nations, *Economic Stability in the Post-War World*, Geneva, 1945.

41 The idea of establishing a World Food Reserve within the framework of the United Nations was again brought up at the ninth session of the General Assembly of the United Nations; a resolution, requesting the Food and Agriculture Organization to study the possibilities of establishing such a reserve to relieve emergency situations and to counteract excessive price fluctuations and draw up a full report, was adopted by the General Assembly on December 14, 1954 by a vote of 46 to 0 with one abstention —the abstaining government was, however, the United States, which has the food surpluses.

42 United States, The President's Materials Policy Commission, *Resources for Freedom*, Washington, D. C., 1952.

43 United States, Commission on Foreign Economic Policy, *Report to the President and the Congress*, Washington, D. C., January 1954.

44 The United States declined to be represented on the Commission except by an observer. The United States has also disassociated itself from the recent attempts to make GATT a medium for reaching commodity agreements; neither is the Soviet Union a member of GATT. Attempts to reach concrete results without the participation of these two dominant countries seem doomed to failure: for the time being these attempts serve mainly as a motivation for not tackling the problems seriously in ECOSOC and the General Assembly.

45 See the forthcoming book by C. P. Kindleberger, *Europe's Terms of Trade*.

46 The Economic Commission for Europe has, through its several technical committees, sponsored intensive studies on the conditions for future supply and demand of forest products, certain steel products, coal, electric energy, oil, etc. If these studies have till now usually been more directed to serve the needs of the advanced countries, it is because, until recently, the underdeveloped countries in Europe have not been too eager to press their interests, which nobody can effectively do for them. The situation changed somewhat after the Secretariat's study on the development problems of Southern Europe (contained in *Economic Survey for Europe in 1953*, Geneva, 1954). In the worldwide organizations, however, and in the regional Commission for Asia and the Far East and that for Latin America, many of the expert or secretariat studies made have been called for on the initiative of the underdeveloped countries.

47 United Nations, Economic Commission for Europe, *Economic Survey of Europe*

since the War, Geneva, 1953, pp. 182 ff. and *Economic Survey of Europe in 1954*, Geneva, 1955, pp. 4 ff.

[48] United Nations, Economic Commission for Latin America, "Preliminary Report of the Secretariat of the United Nations Economic Commission for Latin America," *International Co-Operation in a Latin American Development Policy*, New York, 1954, p. 72.

[49] *Ibid.*, p. 73.

[50] *Ibid.*, p. 72.

[51] *Ibid.*, p. 74.

[52] See the interesting statements on this problem by Professor Klaus Knor, when questioned by Senator Malone before a Senate Committee on his participation in the United Nations' group of experts who wrote the report on commodity trade and economic development (United States Senate, Special Sub-Committee on Minerals, Materials and Fuels Economics of the Committee on Interior and Insular Affairs, Part 5, *Commodity Trade Agreements under United Nations' Auspices*, Washington, D.C., May 26, 1954, pp. 95 ff., especially pp. 99, 101, 102.)

[53] United Nations, Economic Commission for Europe, *The Price of Oil in Western Europe* (mimeographed but on sale), Geneva, 1955.

[54] Ragnar Nurkse, *op. cit.*, pp. 101, 22. Nurkse's point is hypothetical; he explicitly stresses that the argument should not be taken as a forecast.

[55] *Ibid.*, pp. 104 ff.

[56] It is interesting in this connection to study the monetary policy of the Soviet Union. Generally it is the most orthodox and conservative monetary policy in the world. When the government decides to give consumers a share in the benefits of rising productivity, it follows David Ricardo's and David Davison's prescription that it should be done by means of lower prices and not higher earnings. Nevertheless, though it could easily be avoided, prices are regularly fixed slightly lower than the equilibrium level, so that the shops are cleared rapidly and a pressure on producers kept up. This is done deliberately and is supposed to make for efficiency.

[57] V. K. R. V. Rao, "Investment, Income and the Multiplier in an Under-Developed Economy," *The Indian Economic Review*, February 1952, p. 66.

[58] *Ibid.*, p. 64.

[59] If I have any criticism against Nurkse's very clear analysis, it is that he conducts it on such a static basis that he largely misses the importance for the savings problem of efforts to raise production and the supply of consumption goods.

[60] *Op. cit.*, p. 67.

[61] *Ibid.*, pp. 140 ff .

[62] United Nations, Economic Commission for Europe, *Economic Survey of Europe Since the War, op. cit.*, p. 179.

[63] United Nations, Economic Commission for Europe, *Economic Survey of Europe in 1953, op. cit.*, p. 179.

[64] Cf. United Nations, Economic Commission for Europe, *Economic Survey of Europe since the War, op. cit.*, p. 220 and *Economic Survey of Europe in 1953, op. cit.*, p. 178.

[65] This is recognized and stressed in the United Nations, Economic Commission for Latin America, "Preliminary Report of the Secretariat of the United Nations Economic Commission for Latin America," *International Co-Operation in a Latin American Development Policy, op. cit.*, pp. 64 ff.

Cf. also Felipe Pazos, "Economic Development and Financial Stability," *Staff Papers*, International Monetary Fund, October 1953: "What really happens is a change in the composition of imports, consumption goods from light industry being replaced in part by capital goods and in part by more valuable consumption goods whose importation is made possible by the higher income level. This means that tariff increases in such countries would not necessarily restrict international trade, or export unemployment, or hurt highly developed countries, although they would harm some individual industries, compensation therefor being effected through an increase in purchases made from other industries in the same countries" (p. 248).

In the text I have qualified the statement by a reservation: "on the whole." Naturally, development and commercial policies following out the recommendations in the text would considerably change economic conditions in both underdeveloped and developed countries, and a comparison with the situation *ex ante* becomes difficult. Developed countries would have to readjust their exports and their production to the changed import demands from underdeveloped countries; some of them might end up by having a smaller total volume of exports, others might increase their exports; all would have to bear the burden of adjustment. The tendency towards increased self-sufficiency among underdeveloped countries would per se tend to decrease their total volume of imports; but insofar as they are successful in initiating an economic development, this would instead tend to increase their import demands.

[66] United Nations, Economic Commission for Latin America, *International Co-Operation in a Latin American Development Policy, op. cit.,* pp. 69 ff.

[67] George F. Kennan, *Realities of American Foreign Policy,* Princeton University Press, 1954, pp. 107 ff.

[68] Jacob Viner, "America's Aims and the Progress of Under-Developed Countries," *The Progress of Under-Developed Areas,* University of Chicago Press, 1952, pp. 185 and 196.

[69] *Press Release,* GATT/185, Geneva, 11 November 1954.

[70] The last mentioned reason for protection has every possibility of becoming all-embracing: "Given the demands of modern warfare this argument can be extended to industries covering the greater part of our economy. Indeed, few items in the tariff could not, by a little sophistry, be justified on the grounds of national defense." (E. J. Mishan, "Can the United States Contribute Further toward International Solvency?" *The Review of Economics and Statistics,* November 1954, p. 431.)

[71] United Nations, Economic Commission for Europe, *Economic Survey of Europe in 1954, op. cit.,* Chapter VII, "The French Economy: Basic Problems of Occupational Structure and Regional Balance."

CHAPTER XIV

[1] Gunnar Myrdal, *An American Dilemma,* Harper, 1944, pp. 1023 ff.

[2] Ignorance is seldom random; see Gunnar Myrdal, *op. cit.,* "The Convenience of Ignorance," pp. 40 ff. *et seq.*

[3] Gunnar Myrdal, "The Relation Between Social Theory and Social Policy," *The British Journal of Sociology,* September 1953, pp. 211 ff.

[4] I will personally never forget my experiences during a visit to Washington in the late fall of 1943. Once I gave a lecture to a random American audience of civil servants, university professors, and other people interested in public affairs, sponsored by highly placed public figures from both political parties; the lecture was about Scandinavia and the war. In my lecture I was not devoting much interest to the Soviet Union; the views on conditions in the Soviet Union which could perhaps have been inferred from my lecture were the views most Swedes had and have and, in the main, the same as I hold today after considerably more study and experience. Even while I was speaking I felt uncomfortably that the audience was critical and unfriendly to an extent I was not accustomed to in America. After the lecture there was an outburst of what I regarded as rather naïve questions implying that I had been unappreciative of the Soviet Union, by not talking more about that country and not taking up a number of things. Didn't I know that there was religious freedom in the Soviet Union? Why hadn't I mentioned that the Soviet Union had the most democratic constitution in the world? Wasn't it worth while pointing out that "in a deeper sense" the trade unions in the Soviet Union were more democratic than the A. F. of L. and the CIO? Why had I not understood the significance of the fact that, after the end of the war, the United States and the Soviet Union were going to collaborate in settling all world problems, including those in the Scandinavian corner which I had talked about? I had apparently not understood that the United States relied upon the Soviet Union to exert a great influence on the problems I had been discussing.

At another occasion about the same time I participated in a meeting of distinguished experts on foreign affairs from the administration and the universities. Among many other things that were new and strange to me, I was then informed that American thinking was developing on the lines that only the Great Powers should be allowed to have any military defense forces, while small countries like my own would be disarmed in the interest of world peace. I recall that the former Swedish Minister to Washington, Mr. Waldemar Boström, who was with me on that occasion, took very firmly the same position as I did, which perhaps it is unnecessary now to elaborate.

A Swede is apt to remember also one practical effect of this turn of mind—the emphatic refusal of the United States to do anything to influence their great ally to give Finland easier peace terms; Britain took the same line. It was left to the Swedes alone, as the Finns' only friend in court, to do their best to get a reasonable peace settlement with the Soviet Union—and particularly to strive for a scaling down of the war indemnities—and to help them economically during a most difficult period. Immediately after the end of the war in Europe, however, the Finns could not merit any credits or other considerations from the United States—now, because they were paying war indemnities to the Soviet Union.

[5] Gunnar Myrdal, *Warnung vor Friedensoptimismus,* Europa Verlag, Zurich, 1945, p. 39. (Translation from the Swedish original, published in January 1944.)

[6] Gunnar Myrdal, "The Relation Between Social Theory and Social Policy," *op. cit.,* pp. 235 ff.

[7] William E. Rappard, *The Quest for Peace Yesterday and Today,* The David Davies Memorial Institute of International Studies, London, 1954, p. 11.

[8] It is in the southern, not the northern, part of the American hemisphere that it may happen that one is invited to eat on gold plates. It is in the Far East that the upright young American from Middletown—accustomed to get up early in the morning to prepare breakfast for his wife and often even in the middle of the night to change diapers for the crying baby—has to learn how to be attended on by servants, and many servants, when he is appointed to a junior diplomatic post there. It is in the South, not in the richer North-West, Europe that the congressman, who is out junketing to study for himself how the American taxpayer's money is spent, may taste subtle upper class pleasures which he has only read about in novels.

The very big difference in income and wealth in the underdeveloped countries tends to accentuate class differences, the more since so much goes for ostentatious consumption and since wealth tends to be measured in terms of command over labor for personal attendance.

[9] The traditional song of the Labor movement, "The International," is, of course, grossly inappropriate in all advanced countries and has always been a literary exaggeration. Even in the Soviet Union, where it was first used as the state anthem—stolen from the Labor movement, according to the Social-Democrats—it has been for many years left in oblivion. But in many underprivileged countries this appeal would still have a basis of factual validity, word for word.

[10] League of Nations: Letter of Salvador de Madariaga to Paul Valéry, contained in *A League of Minds—An International Series of Open Letters,* Geneva, 1933.

[11] Lord Layton, "Europe's Convention on Human Rights," *European-Atlantic Review,* Spring 1955, pp. 6 ff.

[12] To a social scientist Karl Marx is one of the classics. He has greatly influenced the scientific study of history. As I have had the occasion to show in another connection, American sociology has been deeply imbued, though mostly indirectly and sometimes unconsciously, with Marxian thinking. In economics Marx has in particular influenced business cycle theory.

I am stressing these trite facts in passing since one of the elements in the ideological impact of the cold war has been to make "Marxism" in a rather uncertain meaning of the term an object of intense dislike. Universities have been intimidated to explain that they give a place to this old classic's theories in their curricula only in order to strengthen and harden the students for the fight against Communism.

This is, of course, a little worse than nonsense; and the fact that I cannot pretend to be much of a Marxian scholar and that also for various reasons in my work over the years I happen to be less in debt, even indirectly, to Marx than the majority of my fellow social scientists, cannot prevent me from reacting against this creeping anti-intellectualism by stressing here Marx's great importance in the development of all our social sciences and, consequently, his well merited place in the history of Western thinking.

[13] Gunnar Myrdal, *The Political Element in the Development of Economic Theory*, Routledge and Kegan Paul, 1953, pp. 204 ff.

[14] Adlai E. Stevenson, *Call to Greatness*, Harper, 1954, p. 17.

[15] Lord John Boyd Orr, *The White Man's Dilemma*, Allen and Unwin, 1953, pp. 99 ff.

[16] *Ibid.*, p. 102.

[17] *Ibid.*, p. 100.

[18] Economists generally, including the present author, feared towards the end of the war that in the normal course of business development the United States was likely to experience a serious business depression after the very accentuated war boom. We were mistaken. The United States has instead—with some minor intermittent recessions —enjoyed a remarkably steady progress and showed a resilience to change which in the beginning of the period cannot be explained in terms of the effects of high expenditure for armaments. This, and certain experiences in Western Europe in recent years that do not fit any better our concepts of business fluctuations, have convinced me that we need a radical overhaul of the entire theoretical framework within which we analyze short-term economic movements, including the whole complicated system of analysis which for the sake of brevity I might be permitted to call "post-Keynesian." I believe a critical analysis could very usefully start by asking why and how we went wrong.

We might in this connection recall that, as Gustav Cassel predicted quite early (*Theoretische Sozialökonomie*, Wintersche Verlagsbuchhandlung, 1918, p. VII) the First World War in its time also changed the institutional conditions so fundamentally that earlier business cycle theory became largely obsolete. Among changes brought about by—or during—the Second World War are the entirely changed role of governments in economic life, the changed economic philosophies steering the policies of governments and various public organs in their reactions to business fluctuations, possibly also a changed pattern of reactions on the part of business—though we do not know as yet very much about this factor—and, in particular, a different system of functional relations between actual changes and expectations.

[19] America as the country of many contradictions harbored plenty of nationalistic narrowmindedness even at the time of its greatest openness to outside criticism. It was during the New Deal period that an economist, writing a comprehensive report on the problem of social security for the government, was instructed to quote as little as possible from foreign sources.

[20] At a press conference in London a few years ago, one of the most broadminded and progressive members of the United States Senate, disturbed by the tendencies to monopoly in Britain, proposed that by subsidy from the United States Government three professorships in monopoly theory should be created at the universities of Oxford and Cambridge and at the London School of Economics to teach the English about the dangers of monopoly in business. The good intention of the suggestion should not be doubted. Several scholars at these three seats of learning have made particularly prominent contributions to monopoly theory. It is, perhaps, in no way remarkable that the American senator was not aware of this. Remarkable and illustrative of the new mode of American thinking is, however, first, that he assumed that this was not the case and, second, that he did not feel any hesitation in thinking that aid given by the American Government could properly be used for the purpose of changing the opinion of the British people through implementing their national institutions.

[21] I always felt that the late Senator Robert A. Taft, with whose views on various matters I often was in disagreement, was well aware on a deeper level of his political thinking of the important points I have developed in this section.

APPENDIX

[1] Cf. Gunnar Myrdal, *An American Dilemma*, Harper, 1944, pp. 1063 ff. For a fuller treatment of the value problem, see the methodological appendices to the book mentioned, the article "The Relation between Social Theory and Social Policy," *The*

British Journal of Sociology, September 1953, pp. 238 ff., and *The Political Element in the Development of Economic Theory*, Routledge and Kegan Paul, 1953, particularly the preface to the English edition.

[2] From the point of view of their basic valuations as those were sometimes expressed in general terms, it may perhaps be thought that in the back of their minds the classical authors had a theoretical model of a worldwide perfect market; the theory of international trade would then represent an approximation to greater realism. At the same time they were undoubtedly, however, good nationalists and citizens of a country conscious of the advantages of being ahead of the rest of the world. ". . . it must be realised that this consumption which was regarded as the end of economic activity was the consumption of a limited community, the members of the nation-state. To the extent to which they repudiated former maxims of economic warfare and assumed mutual advantage in international exchange, it is true that the outlook of the Classical Economists seems, and indeed is, more spacious and pacific than that of their antagonists. But there is little evidence that they often went beyond the test of national advantage as a criterion of policy, still less that they were prepared to contemplate the dissolution of national bonds. If you examine the ground on which they recommended free trade, you will find that it is always in terms of a more productive use of *national* resources. . . . I find no trace anywhere in their writings of the vague cosmopolitanism with which they are often credited by continental writers. I do not claim this as a virtue—or as a deficiency; the question of the extent to which, at the stage of history, it was incumbent on political thinkers to transcend the ideas and the criteria of the nation-state is a matter of great difficulty. All that I contend is that we get our picture wrong if we suppose that the English Classical Economists would have recommended, because it was good for the world at large, a measure which they thought would be harmful to their own community. It was the consumption of the national economy which they regarded as the end of economic activity." (Lionel Robbins, *The Theory of Economic Policy*, Macmillan, 1952, pp. 9 ff.)

Marshall was entirely in line with classical tradition when he wrote: ". . . the notion of national trade has been bound up with the notion of solidarity between the various members of a nation." He observes in this connection that "it is becoming clear that this (Great Britain) and every other Western country can now afford to make increased sacrifices of material wealth for the purpose of raising the quality of life throughout their whole population. A time may come when such matters will be treated as of cosmopolitan rather than national obligation; but that time is not in sight." (Alfred Marshall, *Industry and Trade*, Macmillan, 1919, pp. 4 ff.)

[3] I have developed this thought in *Development and Under-development. A Note on the Mechanism of National and International Inequality*; lectures given in Cairo under the auspices of the National Bank of Egypt, to be published.

List of Literature Referred To in This Book

ANDERSON, SAMUEL W., *Population Growth and Capital Requirements in Under-developed Countries,* paper prepared for the *World Population Conference,* Rome, 1954, to be published.

ARIAS, G., *La Questione Meridionale,* Edit. Niccola Zanichelli, Bologna, 1919.

BINGHAM, JONATHAN, *Shirt-Sleeve Diplomacy: Point-4 in Action,* John Day Co., New York, 1954.

BISSEL, RICHARD B. JR., "European Recovery and the Problems Ahead," *The American Economic Review,* May 1952.

BLACK, EUGENE R., "Opening Address to the Annual Meeting of the Board of Governors of the International Bank for Reconstruction and Development," *International Financial News Survey,* Washington, D. C., October 1, 1954,

———, "Opening Address to the Annual Meeting of the Board of Governors of the International Bank for Reconstruction and Development," *International Financial News Survey,* September 23, 1955.

BOYD ORR, LORD JOHN, *The White Man's Dilemma,* Allen and Unwin, London, 1953.

BLOCH, ERNEST, "United States Foreign Investment and Dollar Shortage," *The Review of Economics and Statistics,* Harvard, May 1953.

BLOOMFIELD, ARTHUR J. JR., *Speculative and Flight Movements of Capital in Post-War International Finance,* Princeton University Press, Princeton, 1954.

BOWLES, CHESTER, *Ambassador's Report,* Harper, New York, 1954.

BUCHANAN, NORMAN S., "Deliberate Industrialisation for Higher Incomes," *The Economic Journal,* December 1946.

CASSEL, GUSTAV, *Theoretische Sozialökonomie,* Wintersche Verlagsbuchhandlung, Leipzig, 1918.

CHANDRASEKHAR, S., *Hungry People and Empty Lands,* Allen and Unwin, London, 1954.

———, "Population Growth, Socio-Economic Development and Living Standards," *International Labour Review,* June 1954.

COLUMBIA UNIVERSITY, *Conference on National Policy for Economic Welfare at Home and Abroad,* New York, 1954; to be published. For papers referred to, see: DAVIS, JOSEPH S., and VINER, JACOB.

DAVIS, JOSEPH S., "The Economic Potentialities of the United States," paper prepared for Columbia University's *Conference on National Policy for Economic Welfare at Home and Abroad,* New York, 1954; to be published.

Economist, The, February 27, 1954.

EUROPEAN MOVEMENT, *International Bulletin of the European Movement,* March 1954, Paris.

FRANKEL, S. HERBERT, *The Economic Impact on Under-Developed Societies,* Blackwell, Oxford, 1953.

GALBRAITH, J. K., "Conditions for Economic Change in Under-Developed Countries," *Journal of Farm Economics,* November 1951.

——, *American Capitalism. The Concept of Countervailing Power,* Houghton Mifflin, Boston, 1952.

HANDLIN, OSCAR, "Cultural Adjustment in the United States, 1945-1952," paper prepared for the *World Population Conference,* Rome, 1954, to be published.

HARROD, ROY, *The Dollar,* Sir George Watson Lectures, 1953, Harcourt Brace, New York, 1954.

HILGERT, FOLKE, "Uses and Limitations of International Trade in Overcoming Inequalities in World Distribution of Population Resources," paper prepared for the *World Population Conference,* Rome, 1954, to be published.

HOOVER, CALVIN B., "Institutional and Theoretical Implications of Economic Change," *The American Economic Review,* March 1954.

INTERNATIONAL BANK FOR RECONSTRUCTION AND DEVELOPMENT, *Eighth Annual Report 1952/53; Ninth Annual Report 1953/54,* Washington, D. C.

INTERNATIONAL MONETARY FUND, *International Financial News Survey,* May 13, 1955.

ITALY, Parliamentary Commission on Unemployment, *Report,* Rome, 1953.

JESSUP, PHILIP C., "The Two Chinas and United States Recognition," *The Reporter,* July 6, 1954.

KABIR, HUMAYAN, *The Welfare State,* Presidential Address at the Twenty-Ninth Session of the Indian Philosophical Congress, Peradeniya, Ceylon, December 18, 1954.

KAHN, RICHARD F., "The Convertibility Risk," *The Financial Times,* September 10, 1954.

KEENLEYSIDE, H. L., "Administrative Problems of the Technical Assistance Administration," *The Canadian Journal of Economic and Political Science,* August 1952.

KENNAN, GEORGE F., *Realities of American Foreign Policy,* Princeton University Press, Princeton, 1954.

KINDLEBERGER, C. P., *Europe's Terms of Trade,* to be published.

KNORR, KLAUS, see UNITED STATES (THE SENATE).

KUZNETS, SIMON, "Under-Developed Countries and the Pre-Industrial Phase in the Advanced Countries": paper prepared for the *World Population Conference,* Rome, 1954, to be published.

LAYTON, LORD, "Europe's Convention on Human Rights," *European-Atlantic Review,* Paris, Spring 1955.

LEAGUE OF NATIONS, Letter of Salvador de Madariaga to Paul Valéry in *A League of Minds: An International Series of Open Letters,* Geneva, 1933.

——, *Economic Stability in the Post-War World,* Geneva, 1945.

LEWIS, W. ARTHUR, "Economic Development with Unlimited Supplies of Labour," *The Manchester School of Economic and Social Studies,* May 1954.

LIM, T. B., "Redistribution of Income in Under-Developed Territories," *Income Redistribution and Social Policy,* edited by Alan T. Peacock, Jonathan Cape, London, 1954.

MADARIAGA, SALVADOR DE, Letter to Paul Valéry. *See* LEAGUE OF NATIONS.

MARSHALL, ALFRED, *Industry and Trade*, Macmillan, London, 1919.

MAY, STACY, "The Outlook for Industrial Raw Materials Demand in 1980 and its Relation to Economic Development," paper prepared for the *World Population Conference*, Rome, 1954, to be published.

McCLOY, JOHN J., *A New Background for Banking*, American Bankers' Association, New York, October 19, 1954.

McDOUGALL, SIR DONALD, "A Lecture on the Dollar Problem," *Economica*, August 1954.

MERCHANT, K. T., see WADIA, P. A.

MIKESELL, RAYMOND F., *Foreign Exchange in the Post-War World*, The Twentieth Century Fund, New York, 1954.

MISHAN, E. J., "Can the United States Contribute Further Toward International Solvency?" *The Review of Economics and Statistics*, November 1954.

MOORE, WILBERT E., *Industrialization and Labor*, Cornell University Press, Ithaca and New York, 1951.

MYRDAL, ALVA, *Nation and Family*, Harper, New York, 1941.

——, "A Scientific Approach to International Welfare," Lecture at Columbia University, March 25, 1953, in the Florina Lasker Lecture Series, *America's Role in International Social Welfare*, by Alva Myrdal, Arthur J. Altmeyer, and Dean Rusk, Columbia University Press, New York, 1955.

MYRDAL, ALVA and GUNNAR, *Kris i Befolkningsfrågan*, Bonniers, Stockholm, 1934.

MYRDAL, GUNNAR, *An American Dilemma: The Negro Problem and Modern Democracy*, Harper, New York, 1944.

——, *Warnung vor Friedensoptimismus*, Europa Verlag, Zurich, 1945.

——, "The Trend Towards Economic Planning," *The Manchester School of Economic and Social Studies*, January 1951.

——, "Psychological Impediments to Effective International Co-Operation," *The Journal of Social Issues*, Supplement Series, No. 6, 1952.

——, "The Relation Between Social Theory and Social Policy," Conference of the British Sociological Association, 1953, *The British Journal of Sociology*, September 1953.

——, *The Political Element in the Development of Economic Theory*, Routledge and Kegan Paul, London, 1953.

——, *Realities and Illusions in Regard to Inter-Governmental Organisation*, L. T. Hobhouse Memorial Trust Lecture, No. 24, Oxford University Press, London, 1955.

——, *Development and Under-Development. A Note on the Mechanism of National and International Inequality*, Lectures given in Cairo in October 1955 under the auspices of the National Bank of Egypt. To be published.

NOTESTEIN, FRANK W., "Summary of the Demographic Background of Problems of Under-Developed Areas," *The Milbank Memorial Fund Quarterly*, July 1948.

NURKSE, RAGNAR, *Problems of Capital Formation in Under-Developed Countries*, Blackwell, Oxford, 1953.

——, "The Problem of International Investment Today in the Light of Nineteenth Century Experience," *The Economic Journal*, December 1954.

OPLER, MORRIS E., *Social Aspects of Technical Assistance in Operation*, UNESCO, Paris, 1954.

ORGANISATION FOR EUROPEAN ECONOMIC CO-OPERATION (OEEC), *Economic Conditions in Canada and the United States*, Paris, 1954.

PAZOS, FELIPE, "Economic Development and Financial Stability," *Staff Papers*, International Monetary Fund, October 1953.

PEACOCK, ALAN T., editor, *Income Redistribution and Social Policy*, Jonathan Cape, London, 1954.

PERROUX, FRANÇOIS, *L'Europe sans Rivages*, Presses Universitaires de France, Paris, 1954.

PREBISCH, RAÚL, *The Economic Development of Latin America and Its Principal Problems*, see UNITED NATIONS, ECONOMIC COMMISSION FOR LATIN AMERICA.

RANDALL REPORT, see UNITED STATES.

RAO, V. K. R. V., "Investment, Income and the Multiplier in an Under-Developed Economy," *The Indian Economic Review*, February 1952.

RAPPARD, WILLIAM E., *The Quest for Peace Yesterday and Today*, The David Davies Memorial Institute of International Studies, London, 1954.

ROBBINS, LIONEL, *The Theory of Economic Policy*, Macmillan, London, 1952.

ROSENSTEIN-RODAN, P. N., "Problems of Industrialisation of Eastern and South-Eastern Europe," *Economic Journal*, 1943.

——, "The International Development of Economically Backward Areas," *International Affairs*, April 1944.

ROSTOW, W. W., *The Process of Economic Growth*, Clarendon Press, Oxford, 1953.

ROYAL INSTITUTE OF INTERNATIONAL AFFAIRS, *The Problem of International Investment*, Oxford University Press, Oxford, 1937.

SALTER, SIR ARTHUR, "Foreign Investment," *Essays in International Finance, No. 12*, Princeton University Press, February 1951.

SINGER, H. W., "Economic Progress in Under-Developed Countries," *Social Research*, March 1949.

——, "Obstacles to Economic Development," *Social Research*, Spring 1953.

——, "Problems of Industrialisation of Under-Developed Countries," *International Social Science Bulletin*, Vol. VI, No. 2, 1954.

——, "Population and Economic Development," paper prepared for the *World Population Conference*, Rome, 1954, to be published.

SINGH, TARLOK, *Poverty and Social Change*, Longman, Green & Co., London, 1945.

SMELKER, MARY, "Revue of Foreign Aid by the United States Government, 1940-51," *Econometrica*, July 1954.

STALEY, EUGENE, *The Future of Under-Developed Countries*, Harper, New York, 1954.

STEVENSON, ADLAI E., *Call to Greatness*, Harper, New York, 1954.

SUNDARAM, LANKA, "Effects of Emigration on the Economic Situation of the Populations of Selected Asian Countries of Emigration, with Reference to India," paper prepared for the *World Population Conference*, Rome, 1954, to be published.

SVENNILSON, INGVAR, *Growth and Stagnation in the European Economy,* see UNITED NATIONS, ECONOMIC COMMISSION FOR EUROPE.

TAYLOR, A. J. P., *The Struggle for Mastery in Europe 1848-1918,* Oxford University Press, Oxford, 1954.

THOMAS, BRINLEY, *Migration and Economic Growth,* The University Press, Cambridge, 1954.

TRIFFIN, ROBERT, "International Currency and Reserve Plans," *Banca Nazionale del Lavoro, Quarterly Review,* January-June 1954.

UNITED NATIONS, DEPARTMENT OF ECONOMICS AND SOCIAL AFFAIRS, Foreign Capital in Latin America, New York, 1955.

———, Economic Affairs Department:

Land Reform: Defects in Agrarian Structure as Obstacles to Economic Development, New York, 1951.

Instability in Export Markets of Under-Developed Countries, New York, 1952.

International Capital Movements During the Inter-War Period, New York, 1949.

International Flow of Private Capital 1946-1952, The, New York, 1954.

Relative Prices of Exports and Imports of Under-Developed Countries, New York, 1949.

Summary of Recent Economic Developments in the Middle-East, 1952-53, New York, 1954.

———, ECONOMIC COMMISSION FOR ASIA AND THE FAR EAST (ECAFE):

Economic Bulletin for Asia and the Far East, Vol. IV, No. 3, Bangkok, November 1953.

Economic Survey of Asia and the Far East, 1953, Bangkok, 1954.

Economic Survey of Asia and the Far East, 1954, Bangkok, 1955.

(Together with the Economic Commission for Europe and the Food and Agriculture Organization): *A Study of Trade Between Asia and Europe,* Geneva, November 1953.

———, ECONOMIC COMMISSION FOR EUROPE (ECE):

Economic Survey of Europe Since the War, Geneva, 1953.

Economic Survey of Europe in 1953, Geneva, 1954.

Economic Survey of Europe in 1954, Geneva, 1955.

European Agriculture. A Statement of Problems, Geneva, 1954.

Growth and Stagnation in the European Economy, by Ingvar Svennilson, Geneva, 1954.

A Study of Trade between Asia and Europe (See ECAFE).

———, ECONOMIC COMMISSION FOR LATIN AMERICA (ECLA):

Economic Development of Latin America and its Principal Problems, The, by Raúl Prebisch, New York, 1950.

Economic Survey of Latin America 1951-52, New York, 1953.

"Preliminary Report of the Secretariat of the United Nations Economic Commission for Latin America," *International Co-Operation in a Latin American Development Policy,* New York, 1954.

———, ECONOMIC AND SOCIAL COUNCIL:

Eighteenth Session, *Official Records,* 801st Meeting, July 8, 1954.

———, EDUCATIONAL, SCIENTIFIC AND CULTURAL ORGANIZATION (UNESCO):

Round Table Organized by the International Research Office on the Social Implications of Technological Change. General Report: "Economic Motivations and Stimulations in Under-Developed Countries," March 1954, *International Social Science Bulletin* No. 3, 1954.

————, Experts' Reports:
Commodity Trade and Economic Development, New York, 1954.
Measures for the Economic Development of Under-Developed Countries, New York, May 1951.
Measures for International Economic Stability, New York, 1951.
National and International Measures for Full Employment, New York, 1949.
Report of the Mission on Community Organization and Development in South and Southeast Asia, New York, December 1953.

————, Food and Agriculture Organization:
The State of Food and Agriculture 1954, Rome, 1954.

————, General Assembly:
Report of the United Nations Commission on the Racial Situation in the Union of South Africa, New York, 1953. (General Assembly, *Official Records*, Eighth Session, Supplement No. 16.)
Resolution 623 (VII), of December 21, 1952 (Seventh Session, *Official Records*, Supplement 20.)
Economic Development of Under-Developed Countries, Ninth Session, *Official Records*, Supplement No. 19, New York, 1954.

————, Social Affairs Department:
"Population Growth and the Standard of Living in Under-Developed Countries," Paper prepared for the *World Population Conference*, Rome, 1954. To be published.
Preliminary Report on the World Social Situation, New York, September 1952.
Selected List of Books, Pamphlets and Periodicals in English on Community Organization and Development, New York, March 1953.

United States Commission of Foreign Economic Policy: *Report to the President and the Congress*, Washington, D. C., January 1954 (Randall Report).

————, Department of Commerce: *Direct Private Foreign Investments of the United States (Census of 1950)*, Washington, D. C., 1953.
Foreign Grants and Credits by the United States Government, December 1953 Quarter (issued in April 1954).

————, National Advisory Council on International Monetary and Financial Problems: *Semi-Annual Report to the President and to Congress*, Washington, July 1953.

————, National Commission for UNESCO, Fourth National Conference, 1953: *America's Stake in International Co-Operation*, "Race Relations in World Perspective" (mimeographed).

————, President's Materials Policy Commission: *Resources for Freedom*, Washington, D. C., 1952.

————, Senate: 83d Congress, Hearing before the Special Sub-Committee on Minerals, Materials and Fuels Economics of the Committee on Interior and Insular Affairs, Part 5: *Commodity Trade Agreements under United Nations Auspices*, Washington, D. C., May 26, 1954.

VINER, JACOB, *International Economics,* The Free Press, Glencoe, Ill., 1951.

————, "America's Aims and the Progress of Under-Developed Countries," *The Progress of Under-Developed Areas,* edited by Bert F. Hoselitz, University of Chicago Press, Chicago, Ill., 1952.

————, *International Trade and Economic Development,* The Clarendon Press, Oxford, 1953.

————, "The Role of the United States in the World Economy," paper prepared for Columbia University's *Conference on National Policy for Economic Welfare at Home and Abroad,* New York, 1954; to be published.

WADIA, P. A., and K. T. MERCHANT, *Our Economic Problem,* New Book Company, Bombay, 1943.

WILLIAMS, JOHN H., *Economic Stability in a Changing World. Essays in Economic Theory and Policy,* Oxford University Press, New York, 1953.

WORLD POPULATION CONFERENCE, ROME, 1954. For papers cited, see: ANDERSON, SAMUEL W.; HILGERT, FOLKE; KUZNETS, SIMON; MAY, STACY; SINGER, H. W.; SUNDAROM, LANKA; and UNITED NATIONS, Social Affairs Department.

Index